# Health in the Marketplace

# HEALTH IN THE MARKETPLACE

## Professionalism, Therapeutic Desires, and Medical Commodification in Late-Victorian London

Takahiro Ueyama

The Society for the Promotion of Science and Scholarship
Palo Alto, California

The Society for the Promotion of Science and Scholarship, Inc.
Palo Alto, California

©2010 The Society for the Promotion of Science and Scholarship

The Society for the Promotion of Science and Scholarship is a nonprofit corporation established for the purposes of scholarly publishing, to benefit both academics and the general public. It has special interests in European and British studies.

Printed in the United States of America

Library of Congress Cataloguing-in-Publication Data

Ueyama, Takahiro.
   Health in the marketplace : professionalism, therapeutic desires, and medical commodification in late-Victorian London / Takahiro Ueyama.
      p. cm.
   Includes index.
   ISBN 0-930664-29-9 (alk. paper)
   1. Medicine--Marketing--England--London--History--19th century. 2. Medical instruments and apparatus--England--London--History--19th century. 3. Patent medicines--England--London--History--19th century. 4. Commercial products--England--London--History--19th century. I. Title.
   R487.U39 2010
   610.28'4--dc22

                                                      2010014443

To my parents and Kumiko

# Contents

*Forty pages of illustrations follow page 226.*

# List of Illustrations

# Acknowledgments

This book has distinctly benefited from the support of many people and institutions. The debts I owe—both intellectual and personal—are correspondingly diverse, to the point that I fear I may unintentionally omit some deserving individuals or institutions.

My deepest thanks go to my two chief mentors at Stanford: Peter Stansky, an extraordinary teacher who has always given me intellectual and moral support, and Timothy Lenoir, who first opened my eyes to the field of the history of science and technology and sparked the idea of this project. I am also indebted to Paul Seaver for his generous guidance, and to Paul Robinson for his constructive criticism and suggestions.

For their financial support of this project in its various stages, I would like to thank the Fulbright Program, the Toyota Foundation, the Abe Fellowship Program, the Department of History at Stanford University, and the Japan Society for the Promotion of Science for both a Grant-in-Aid for Scientific Research and (more recently) a Grant-in-Aid for Publication of Scientific Research Results.

My special thanks go to Takenori Inoki, my teacher at Osaka University, who first encouraged me to pursue historical studies, to Hiroshi Yamanaka with whom I have had many stimulating conversations on the history of science, to Akihito Suzuki who taught me the pleasure of poking around in archives, and to Derede Arthur without whose critical and refining skills this project could not have been completed. Indeed, my debts to friends in academia are too numerous for all to be mentioned here, but I continue to appreciate the many formative discussions I had with other graduate students in the History program at Stanford—my friends Amir Alexander, Joshua Feinstein, Andrew Harris, Christophe Lécuyer, Patricia Mazon, Michael Saler, Jennifer Stine, and Joseph Ward.

Beyond Stanford, I received generous advice and assistance from the Wellcome Institute for the History of Medicine, in London, through which I greatly benefited from the discussions with the following distinguished historians: Bill Bynum, J. S. Jacyna, Christopher Lawrence, Iwan Rhys Morus, M. Neve, John Pickstone, Roy Porter, John Senior, and Akihito Suzuki. Not only did they help me make my way through the bewildering labyrinth of research, but they also all read early drafts of this work and gave me constructive criticism. I am also grateful to Sally Bragg, a secretary at the Institute, for her great kindness in rendering my life more comfortable there, on a practical basis.

During my research in London I discovered how pleasurable—although challenging—it is to search archives for historical evidence. Indeed, I am indebted to many archivists—not only at the Wellcome Institute but also at the Bodleian Library at Oxford University, the British Library, the Patent Office, St. Bartholomew's Hospital, the Royal College of Physicians, London Hospital, the Public Record Office, the Institution of Electrical Engineers, the British Medical Association, the Westminster City Archives, and the Guildhall Library Archives. Sadly, I cannot list here all the individuals who helped me in these places, but my special thanks go to Julie Anne Lambert at the John Johnson Collection at the Bodleian Library, and Lenore Symons at the Archives Department of the Institution of Electrical Engineers. I would also like to thank all who provided me with illustrations or else permitted me to reproduce them.

At a later stage, Seth Koven made substantial comments on the manuscript, and I am indebted to him for such help in shaping it into a book. I also remain very grateful for the valuable comments I received from audiences when I spoke at the following institutions (listed in order of my talks): the Wellcome Institute, Stanford University, the Institute for Research in Humanities at Kyoto University, the North American Conference on British Studies, the University of California at Berkeley, Keio University, Osaka University, and the University of Manchester.

A short section of my study has already been published in *Medical History* and thanks are due to Caroline Tonson-Rye for her meticulous editorial assistance. Kenneth Romeo and Roderick Wilkinson also provided excellent editorial support in the rest of the work at a later stage, and both Norris Pope of Stanford University Press and Janet Gardiner of SPOSS graciously undertook the complicated production of this book.

Finally, and above all, I want to dedicate this book to my parents and Kumiko, as a way of thanking them for their unwavering encouragement throughout the time that this work was in progress.

# Health in the Marketplace

# Introduction

Multinationals, like the poor, seem to have always been with us, and it is sometimes easy to forget that their global preeminence often derives from humble and even surprising origins. For example, GlaxoSmith-Kline, the second largest pharmaceutical company in the world, was established in 2001 by the merging of two pharmaceutical companies— SmithKline Beecham and Glaxo Wellcome. The former was itself the result of the 1989 merger between the Beecham Group and SmithKline Beckman, which in turn had derived from a drugstore in Philadelphia. One of the latter's progenitors, Burroughs Wellcome, was founded in London in 1880 by two American pharmacists, Henry Wellcome and Silas Burroughs. Another one, Glaxo, had originated from a New Zealand baby food manufacturer and when it opened its new units in London in 1935 it absorbed the long-standing pharmaceutical manufacturer Allen & Hanburys Limited. Though lost amidst the successive corporate mergers, Beechams, Wellcome, and Allen & Hanburys are all remembered for the role they played in the emergence of giant multinational drug makers.

Although these druggist entrepreneurs successfully upgraded their businesses within the last decades of the nineteenth century to form larger and more scientific pharmaceutical organizations, they began their businesses as, respectively, a mere patent medicine vendor, a pill manu-facturer, and a Quaker pharmacist. The history of Beechams can be traced to one Thomas Beecham, a popular vendor of patent nostrums and peddler of herbal remedies. Often proclaiming himself "Dr. Bee-cham" in his advertisements despite the absence of any recognized medical degree, he began to transform his business into a larger and more lucrative enterprise as early as the mid-nineteenth century. In 1859, Beecham opened the company's first factory in St. Helens, Lancashire to expand his production line of pills. The advertising catchphrase he began to use in the local press, "Worth a Guinea a Box," soon became a popular symbol for those seeking self-medication *à bon marché*. His son, Joseph Beecham, who was knighted in 1911 and became a baronet in 1914, turned his father's successful drug company into a veritable pharmaceu-tical empire almost solely on the strength of his innovative advertising strategies.[1] Following a parallel trajectory, Allen & Hanburys originated from a mercantile business owned by the notable Quaker William Allen with the assistance of his second wife's kin, the Hanbury family. A suc-cessful producer of cod liver oil, Allen & Hanburys founded its own factory in the East End in 1878. Moreover, even in these early days of the history of drug companies, a certain multinational flavor was pre-sent: American contributions to the development of the British pharma-ceutical industry were initiated by two young immigrants, Henry Well-come and Silas Burroughs, who brought with them a new system of what they called pharmaceutical preparations. With this new system, the two entrepreneurs emphasized accurately measured preparations as a feature of their business and sold easily administered forms of medicine, such as coated pills, capsules, cachets, and tablets under the trademark name "Tabloid." Since previously in the United Kingdom most of the medicines were sold as powders or bottled liquids, Burroughs Wellcome Company successfully expanded the market for their drugs not only to doctors but also to drugstore chains.[2]

---

[1] For the business history of the Beecham Company, see H. G. Lazell, *From Pills to Penicillin: The Beecham Story* (London: Heinemann, 1975); Anne Francis, *A Guinea a Box: A Biography* (London: Robert Hale Limited, 1968).
[2] F. B. Smith, *The People's Health 1830–1910* (London: Weidenfeld and Nicolson, 1990), 343–345.

What accounts for the phenomenal success of these pharmaceutical businesses? Clearly clever advertising and some technological innovations such as the "Tabloids" played a role, but the remarkable receptivity they encountered for their products can best be explained by a changing ethos in the medical marketplace—an ethos these medical entrepreneurs at once tapped into and helped give material form. These dealers in mass-produced patent medicines were able to expand their indigenous market in response to the rapidly growing public demand for various kinds of health commodities. Although attaching importance to scientific pharmaceutical research in their laboratories, Allen & Hanburys and Burroughs Wellcome & Company generated enormous profits simply from dealing with medicated cod liver oils and malt wines.

Realizing the profits that might be made, these earliest embodiments of pharmaceutical manufacturers began to play an extremely capitalistic game—one which perhaps inevitably produced tensions between them and medical professionals. By 1880, the British Medical Association began an exposé campaign against the proprietary medicine traders, calling them at one point "quack pill-vendors" dealing in dangerous "secret remedies." At the same time, medical doctors disparaged Joseph Beecham for, in one example, selling his infamous abortifacients. It was not, to be sure, the kind of history that a pharmaceutical giant such as GSK would want to have well-known today. And yet this history, far from being arcane or obsolete, can tell us much today about the sometimes converging, sometimes diverging, interests of medical entrepreneurs and medical professionals.

What makes the history of late-nineteenth-century British medical practices particularly worth exploring is that we can observe in this period, much as in our own, the rapidly growing healthcare and therapeutic market. The market was rife with brand-name medical preparations such as Dr. Scott's Little Liver Pills, Campbell's Cherry Cough Cure, Clark's Blood Mixture, Midow Welch's Pills, Roche's Herbal Embrocation, Dr. Armstrong's Influenza Mixture, Wellcome's Tabloid, Dr. J. Collins Brown's Chlorodyne, Roper's Royal Bath Plasters, Dr. Coffin's Medico-Botanic Dispensary, Smedley's Chilly Paste, and so on. These drugs as well as other types of medical commodities were ardently demanded not only by middle-class consumers but also by working-class families who wanted to buy cheaper medicaments. It was Jesse Boot, the first Baron

Trent, who, capitalizing on such a boom, entered the drug retail business in Nottingham in 1874 by using a revolutionary business method. Benefiting from economies of scale, he purchased bulk proprietary articles from patent medicine suppliers and, by focusing on products with high turnover and low-profit margins, sold them at far lower prices than other retailers could afford. With his innovative price-cutting strategy and the catchphrase "Health for a Shilling," Boot's company was soon transformed into a national retail chain selling the company's own patent medicines.[3] But Boot's aggressive capitalism caused a tumult within the medical profession. As Chapter One demonstrates, the debate and struggle that emerged between medical doctors, pharmaceutical men, and manufacturers to dominate the expanding therapeutic market shed new light on the changing relationship between the commercialization of medicine and medical professionalization.

The medical market of this period abounded with both the patent medicines and "secret remedies" of the pharmaceutical manufacturers as well as with a plethora of technological devices similarly designed to reverse illnesses and produce health: electrotherapeutic chains, electric belts, corsets, and other medico-electric appliances like Pulvermacher's electric chains, Harness's Electrophatic belts, Magnetic Curative Appliances, Macaura's Blood Circulator, Dr. Scott's Electric Hair Brush, Boyd's Medico-Electrical Vitalizer, and so on. In addition, Victorian entrepreneurs were willing to enter the medical business by establishing new types of for-profit hospitals, nursing homes, infirmaries, and medical spas. Some of these establishments called themselves "medical institutes" and claimed to provide medication for a reasonable price to a wider range of customers. Many regular doctors, in turn, became involved with entrepreneurs' businesses by providing "medical certificates" for their products and services, and over time some cooperated even further with these entrepreneurs as they accommodated themselves to the latter's high-risk, high-return ventures.

Such developments reveal that Victorian conceptions of health were

---

[3] For the history of the Boots Company, Stanley Chapman, *Jesse Boot of Boots the Chemists: A Study in Business History* (London: Hodder and Stoughton, 1974); Christopher Weir, *Jesse Boot of Nottingham* (Nottingham: The Boots Company, PLC, 1994).

changing as a result of being driven by, or pandered to, by legions of these medical entrepreneurs. It is out of this setting that numerous kinds of "quackish" remedies flourished in a new modernized and "scientific" form. Together with various types of alternative medicines like home-opathy, herbalism, and massage therapy, quackish entrepreneurs exploited public concerns about the healthy body. While Georgian-period nostrum quacks only sold each medicament once in each place during their journeys, late-nineteenth century businessmen help create prodigious trading opportunities in the field of medicine. The Victorian purveyors of medical commodities, however, were by no means the same blatant frauds the quack mongers of the eighteenth century had been. Rather, it was precisely because these businessmen themselves aspired to scientific status that the problem for professionals occurred on the shady borders between regular and irregular practitioners. Since many other medical commodities on the market echoed the language of the health culture promoted by medical doctors, the commodification of health services created rather than blurred the demarcation between doctors and others involved in medicine. As a matter of fact, the specter of quacks, though wearing more capitalistic, technical, and scientific garb, never completely faded away. Wondering "why, in this educated period, they [quacks] are as numerous, or more so, as in the dark ages, and can still undoubtedly produce large numbers of genuine cures," Alfred Shofield argued in 1903 that "the public, curiously enough, set a far higher value on a 'cure' than the trained professional man."[4] Thus, even by the turn of the twentieth century, quacks had not been eliminated, and the struggle for market profits between professional doctors and quackish entrepreneurs had not been resolved.

The medical commodities of the period bloomed because the health culture in which they were rooted became terra firma in the public imagination; doctors could no longer remain indifferent to silver-tongued presentations by entrepreneurs of commercial medicine and the charm of profits promised. In spite of the control of health care exercised by medical professionals, therefore, the collaboration between medical professionals and medical marketers became more entangled

---

[4] Alfred T. Shofield, *Nerves in Disorder: A Plea for Rational Treatment* (New York and London: Funk & Wagnalls, 1903), 112–113.

and more extensive than in any previous age. Thus, the seemingly well-established professional viewpoints of medical practitioners in Victorian Britain can largely be seen as the response of elite doctors to the threat posed by the ongoing industrialization and commercialization of society.[5]

To understand this phenomenon of "medicine in the marketplace," this book intends neither to narrate a history of business heroes working against a tide of modern giant pharmaceuticals nor to describe medical professionalism's triumph over quackery. Rather, this book offers a different story—one that was populated by long-forgotten entrepreneurs and charlatans as well as by both principled and sometimes not-so-principled medical professionals. It explores both the struggles and the often very provisional, tension-fraught bonds that were forged between manufacturers of medical commodities, technicians and engineers, and professional physicians.

Thus this book investigates how in the late nineteenth and early twentieth centuries capitalism created a new commercialized medical culture and shook the preexisting professional eithos regarding medicine and healthcare. By "capitalism" I mean an economic and social system in which a person's behaviors and decisions about the allocation of resources are driven by market forces and profit incentives. This book shows how the potency of market capitalism interacted with certain kinds of cultural forms to create controversy among medical professionals, capitalists, and the public about what the boundaries and practices of the medical and health-related domain ought to be. Focusing on the intricate influence of market forces on this medical domain, this study places medicine in the context of various facets of commodity culture and medical commercialization, and it articulates the ways in which market capitalism permeated the apparently well-established professional purity of medical practice.

But this infection of medical purity by, as it were, the toxic foreign agent of capitalism is precisely the malady that professionalized medi-

---

[5] Although a fine piece of work on medical orthodoxy and the medical fringe, William Bynum's and Roy Porter's edited volume oddly ends its investigation in 1850. See W. F. Bynum and R. Porter, eds., *Medical Fringe and Medical Orthodoxy, 1750–1850* (London: Croom Helm, 1987).

cine has been most at pains to conceal—and the medical establishment has proclaimed, on the contrary, the long association of medical science and medical practices with the public interest. Because the essential role of medicine has long been considered the preservation of human life and the improvement of people's health, it has often been stated that medicine should first and foremost put the public benefit as its highest priority. And indeed, until the latter half of the twentieth century there was strong condemnation of a business-oriented approach to medical services and treatments, and sharp lines of demarcation were drawn between the practice of traditionally trained medical professionals and those of the businessmen whose interest in the medical field was more commercial. In supposedly stark contrast with entrepreneurs in the field of medical commodities, the medical profession's interaction with the market was mediated by the state or by professional associations through the standardization of patient fees, constraints on how medical professionals advertised their practices, avoidance of viewing clients as customers, and the legitimization of new medical technologies by professional authorities. In the name of public health, competition among physicians or hospitals was limited and the services provided by them were regulated by the government or by public organizations. In fact, the enactment of the 1946 National Health Service Act[6] was supposed to proclaim medicine a heroic exception that had escaped the intrusion of capitalistic logic of laissez-faire competition, profit-maximization, and so on.[7]

---

[6] On the National Health Service, see the following studies: Charles Webster, *The National Health Service: A Political History*, (Oxford: Oxford University Press, 1988); Charles Webster, "The National Health Service, the First 40 years: Conference held by the Society for the Social History of Medicine," Institute of Historical Research, Senate House, London, April 1988, *Social History of Medicine*, 1 (1988): 256–261; and Daniel Fox, *The National Health Service and the Second World War: The Elaboration of Consensus* (Manchester: Manchester University Press, 1986).

[7] On how American medicine has dealt with the public interest ideal, see Rosemary Rogers, *American Medicine and the Public Interest: A History of Specialization*, 2nd ed. (Berkeley, Los Angeles, and London: University of California Press, 1998); Judith Walzer Leavitt and Ronald L. Numbers, eds., *Sickness and Health in America: Reading in the History of Medicine and Public Health* (Madison: University

Yet at the same time, medical commodities have always been produced within a commercial context, as have been medical services. For
as long as medical doctors and hospitals have operated within a capitalistic system, they have had to face strong commercial pressures, and their
responses to these pressures have been complex and diverse—hardly a
monolithic submission to a public-benefit ideology, as has been commonly supposed by other historians. It is less known, however, that in
the later Victorian era—well over one hundred years ago—these various
responses existed as strongly, and elicited counter-responses as complicated and contradictory, as any responses or counter-responses of today.
A study of these tensions and the shifting conflicts and alliances between medical professionals, technologists, and businessmen in the past
can perhaps teach us much about their vexed relations in the present.
To this end, this book explores the various late-nineteenth-century medico-social phenomena of medicine's first full encounter with capitalism.
And it provides a narrative that accounts for the way in which socio-
economic and professional interests both conflicted and overlapped
among medical doctors, medical instrument engineers, quack physicians,
manufacturers of patent medicines, and consumers of health-related
services and goods. It is a narrative with, I believe, profound implications for how we understand the nature of the relationship between
medical professionals, technology, and the commercial sector today.

### Medicine and Health Care in the Contemporary Market

In one capacity, then, this is a history book—but one that uncovers
in history the manifestations of market forces where it has long been
assumed none existed. This is also a history that traces in the exalted
profession of medicine an old and intimate connection with the cash
nexus that even today practitioners are loath to admit, even when evidence of such intimacy seems present nearly every day in the news. Insofar as it reveals the long-standing, clandestine existence of a "medical-
industrial complex"[8] that threatens the ideal of public health, the story

---

of Wisconsin Press, 1978).

[8] A. S. Relman, "The New Medical-Industrial Complex," *New England Journal of Medicine*, 303 (1980): 963–970.

in this book mirrors and illuminates major concerns and issues in contemporary medicine and health care in America (and other countries of the developed world). Tellingly significant about this investigation of medicine in *fin-de-siècle* Britain is the hitherto-unrecognized fact that—not just in America and not just in the last few decades—medicine and money have been intimate partners indeed.

All too often, recent alterations in the practice and financing of American medicine have been heralded as both more innovative and more threatening to "traditional medical practice" than is actually the case. For example, in the closing chapter of his voluminous work on the formation of American medical profession, "The Coming of the Corporation," Paul Starr describes the rise of corporate-style health care in the 1970s and 1980s that, he insists, began to jeopardize the sovereignty and autonomy of physicians. Certainly much that Starr observes is true: the government policy to increase the number of doctors in the 1970s and 1980s resulted in a drastic surplus of physicians that created an economic collision between private doctors and hospitals over patients, and as a result, a number of for-profit hospital chains like Hospital Corporation of America, Humana, and Kaiser Foundation Hospitals were established. Merging the old-style nursing homes and proprietary hospitals, these corporations began to exert strong bargaining power in negotiations over rewards with staff physicians. As Starr notes, "Pressure for efficient, business-like management of health care has also contributed to the collapse of barriers that traditionally prevented corporate control of health services."[9]

Today this trend of corporate medicine, far from waning, continues to gather steam: investor-owned businesses have grown into major industry components. These businesses include nursing homes, home-care services, diagnostic laboratories, and emergency services, and they have begun to take over a great deal of the health care system. Since the Reagan-era encouragement of market-oriented policies and privatized health care, Americans have witnessed both the transformation of public health into an enormous capitalistic market and the increasing domination of the traditional doctor-patient relationship by a cost-oriented cor-

---

[9] Paul Starr, *The Social Transformation of American Medicine: The Rise of a Sovereign Profession and the Making of a Vast Industry* (New York: Basic Books, 1982), 428.

porate control of medical practice.[10] Health scholars note that both the lack of an effective health security system and its substitution by managed care or by HMO models lets the initiative of hospital management be handed over from the medical profession to insurance companies.[11] But the many studies of this "transformation" fall short if they fail to adequately consider its historical antecedents, and if they imagine medical practitioners have ever been immune from or operated outside the forces of the marketplace. Responding adequately to the current market domination of American medicine requires that we first understand the failed responses to its antecedent forms in the nineteenth century.

Modern pharmaceutical companies are another player in this capitalistic game. Since the heyday of the bio-ventures of the 1980s, an enormous amount of corporate capital has been dispersed as research funds to the cutting edge of bio-medicine.[12] Academic researchers seemingly cannot dispense with financial ties to drug companies—so much so that it is often alleged that the industry has converted academic research into company subsidiaries. In the 1990s the leading medical journals such as the *New England Journal of Medicine* started to warn the public against the

---

[10] On market-oriented health care, see Regina Herzlinger, *Market Driven Health Care: Who Wins, Who Loses in the Transformation of America's Largest Service Industry* (Reading, Massachusetts: Perseus Books, 1997); Ronald M. Andersen, Thomas H. Rise, and Gerald F. Kominski, *Changing the US Health Care System: Key Issues in Health Services Policy and Management,* (San Francisco: Jossey-Bass, 2001; and Regina R. Herzlinger, ed., *Consumer-Driven Health Care: Implications for Providers, Payers, and Policy Makers* (San Francisco: Jossey-Bass, 2004).

[11] For the history of the American hospital system, see Charles Rosenberg, *The Care of the Stranger: The Rise of America's Hospital System* (New York: Basic Books, 1987); and Rosemary Stevens, *In Sickness and in Wealth: American Hospitals in the Twentieth Century,* (New York: Basic Books, 1981).

[12] For the relationship between university and industry in the field of biomedicine, see, for example, Martin Kenny, *Bio-Technology: The University-Industrial Complex* (New Haven and London: Yale University Press, 1986); Henry Etzkowitz and Loef Leydesdorff, eds., *Universities and the Global Knowledge Economy: A Triple Helix of University-Industry-Government Relations* (London and New York: Continuum, 2001). The best book discussing the invasion of a capitalistic approach to academia in general is by Sheila Slaughter and Larry L. Leslie, *Academic Capitalism: Politics, Policies and the Entrepreneurial University,* (Baltimore: The Johns Hopkins University Press, 1997).

potential bias or conflict of interest among many authors of scientific studies bought or paid for by private companies.[13] Moreover, what has eroded the professional credentials of medicine is not limited to therapeutics and drugs. The food industry, the most influential business fundamentally related to our individual well-being, has for some years now been altering the politics of regulation regarding the efficacy and safety of both nutraceuticals and dietary food. In America, as Marion Nestle eloquently describes, as a result of campaign funding and corporate donations, the very government that is supposed to protect the public interest ends up instead protecting the interests of the food and drug industries.[14]

Certainly on one level, the present capitalistic turn of medicine reflects people's commercially influenced desires and attitudes toward health care. The influence of television commercials selling drugs, medications, medical equipment, and health-related supplies with doctors' recommendations and scientific certifications is ubiquitous, and doctors themselves advertise on television the medicines and appliances they have invented—while through the same medium hospitals promote their facilities' amenities to better attract customers. Medical products advertised and traded in the market today go far beyond what was once understood as "treatment"—they include aesthetic dentistry, corrective

---

[13] Many scientists and sociologists recently have explored the problems and ethical issues regarding the university/industry relationship and the resulting conflicts of interest and debates over the intellectual property of academic research. The following articles are just a few of the thousands of pieces of literature on this subject: D. Blumenthal, N. Causino, E, G. Campbell, and K. S. Louis, "Relationships between Academic Institutions and Industry in the Life Sciences—An Industry Survey," *New England Journal of Medicine*, 334 (1996): 368–374; D. Blumenthal, "Academic-Industry Relationships in the Life Sciences," *Health Policy Report*, 348 (2003): 2452–2456; D. Blumenthal, N. Causino, and E. G. Campbell, "Academic-Industry Relationships in Genetics: A Field Apart," *Nature Genetics*, 16 (1997):104–108; D. Blumenthal, E. G. Campbell, and J. S. Weissman, "The Social Missions of Academic Health Centers," *New England Journal of Medicine*, 337 (1997): 1550–1553; Sheldon Krimsky and L. S. Rosenberg, "Financial Interest and Its Disclosure in Scientific Publications," *Journal of the American Medical Association*, 280 (1998): 225–227.
[14] Marion Nestle, *Food Politics: How the Food Industry Influences Nutrition and Health* (Berkeley: University of California Press, 2002).

body-casts, laser eye-surgery, elixir medications, anti-aging drugs, dietary supplements, and all manner of other remedies and fixes. The health-related market has expanded too far for it to be considered as simply having to do with "medicine," in the traditional meaning of that term. Current reports claim that almost forty percent of American citizens use alternative forms of treatment such as aroma-therapy, herbal medicine, massage, acupuncture, Qigong, and Zen meditation.[15] People want to buy these medical products and techniques to acquire a longer, fuller, and more rejuvenated life. In general, medicine has become not simply a means of restoring health but also a way of increasing the richness and satisfactions of life. Therefore, it may matter little whether or not people's desires are realized through scientific methods.

In the meantime, scientific and traditional medicine is forced to respond to the public's ever-growing desire to buy a healthy body. In the medical treatment market, each year new medical technologies, unimagined even a few decades ago, are being introduced: cell therapy, regeneration medicine, organ transplant, gene therapy, genetic diagnosis, and the like. There is no doubt that all of these advanced and expensive medical innovations have been made possible through, and accelerated by, the commercialization of medicine and the growth of medical capitalism. While it is true that the relentless pursuit of profits has driven innovations and technological advancements to the benefit of health care, it is also true that both doctors and patients do not unconditionally favor technology-oriented treatments—and as we shall see in this book, the same response was true for the Victorians.

The problems of current medicine summarized above have been explored by many scholars from various perspectives. Those studies, however, fail to answer one very important question: namely, how and why did these problems emerge and evolve? Although investigations in this book reveal the historical reality of *fin-de-siècle* Britain, they also serve to

---

[15] For alternative medicine in the United States, see the following books: Mary Ruggie, *Marginal to Mainstream: Alternative Medicine in America* (Cambridge: Cambridge University Press, 2004); James C. Whorton, *Nature Cures: The History of Alternative Medicine in America* (Oxford: Oxford University Press, 2002); and Robert D. Johnston, ed., *The Politics of Healing: Histories of Alternative Medicine in Twentieth-Century North America* (London: Routledge, 2004).

document the origins of what we observe today in the United States, where medical capitalism manifests itself most ubiquitously: they show that the Victorians—like ourselves—debated the decline of medical professionalism; they, too, grappled with ambiguities about drug effectiveness and regulation; they, too, worried about the uncertain boundaries between science and quackery, orthodox and alternative medicines; and they, too, were concerned about the power game between the medical profession, capitalists, and drug manufacturers. This book suggests that such unease is inevitable when profit-driven commercialism and market capitalism intrude into the medical domain.

### *Medicine in the Early Era of Commodification*

This book focuses on the 1880s and 1890s, and on London cases, for the most part, but—as I have already suggested—the phenomena it describes continue to make their impact felt today. The 1880s and 1890s were watershed years, as the documents and data archived in the Patent Office demonstrate. In 1855—the first year in which the number of medical commodities patented was first recorded—60 patents were issued, *inter alia* for electrical devices and appliances, disinfectants, and dentistry equipment. The number of patents issued each year over the next 30 years fluctuated between 41 and 98, until 1884 when it spiked upward to 167, more than doubling the previous year's figure and marking the beginning of a rapid rise in the annual number of medical patents issued, to 308 in 1908. As Fig. 1-1 shows, and as is argued throughout this book, there was a thoroughgoing structural change in the demand for, and supply of, medical commodities in the mid-1880s. Evidence of this dramatic transformation is further supported by a surge at this same time in medical advertising ephemera and handbills, which are now archived in the John Johnson Collection at Oxford.

Indeed, we can trace many of the roots of today's consumerist hopes for the role of medicine to *fin-de-siècle* Britain, where the last decades of the nineteenth century witnessed the development of a new level of industrialization, and as Hobsbawm has shown, the beginnings of mass production and mass consumption.[16] Commodity fetishism, anticipated

---

[16] E. J. Hobsbawm, *Industry and Empire* (London: Penguin Books, 1968).

by the Great Exhibition of 1851, dazzled Victorian society with the
wondrous new things market capitalism could provide and the hope it
proffered that in time such marvels would penetrate all levels of society.[17] As one advertising agency put it, "In food, dress, drink, smoking,
etc., the poor want what the rich have as a matter of course, and the best
is done to obtain it."[18] Indeed, by the waning years of the century commodity culture had indeed spread noticeably to all classes of society: as
an advertising agency put it in 1885, "What were once luxuries are now
necessaries."[19] Middle-class people sought new products and spent
more money on self-indulgence: pianos, fine furniture, gramophones,
watches, jewelry, electric devices and fancy soaps all entered the domain
of everyday lives.[20] Victorian London became a place where the ongoing
development of the city, promoting the prosperity of the middle class,
began to create flamboyant, sparkling, and often seductive spaces of
consumption.[21]

---

[17] See Asa Briggs, *Victorian Things* (London: Penguin Books, 1988).

[18] *Smith's Advertising Agency, Successful Advertising: Its Secrets Explained* (London:
Smith's Advertising Agency, 1885), 2.

[19] Regarding the advertisements of this period and their impact on women's
purchasing power, see Lori Anne Loeb, *Consuming Angels: Advertising and Victorian Women* (Oxford: Oxford University Press, 1994). See also Erika Rappaport,
*Shopping for Pleasure: Women in the Making of London's East End* (Princeton: Princeton University Press, 2000).

[20] Fraser W. Hamish, *The Coming of the Mass Market, 1850–1914* (London: Archon Books, 1981).

[21] Recently many historians have refocused on commodity culture by analyzing
advertisements as cultural artifacts. One voluminous book edited by John
Brewer and Roy Porter explored various facets of goods and consumption, and
Jackson Lears has written a massive history of advertising, exploring in particular how commercial life expanded and the notion of abundance emerged in
nineteenth-century America. See John Brewer and Roy Porter, eds., *Consumption
and the World of Goods* (London and New York: Routledge, 1994), and Jackson
Lears, *Fables of Abundance: A Cultural History of Advertising in America* (New York:
Basic Books, Harper Collins, 1994). See also Rosalind Williams, *Dream Works:
Mass Consumption in Late Nineteenth Century France* (Berkeley: University of California Press, 1982). In addition, Simon J. Bronner, ed., *Consuming Visions: Accumulation and Display of Goods in America, 1880–1920* (New York: Norton and
Company, 1989) is notable for its consideration of consumer behavior during

Much like consumers today, *fin-de-siècle* Londoners lived in a mass culture of commodified abundance and spectacular consumption. New urban public spaces such as cafés, theatres, department stores, music halls, arcades, and boulevards were being developed, and the consumption they encouraged was not simply the purchasing of commodities, but the adoption of an entire nexus of behaviors, attitudes, and beliefs. In other words, the creation of these public spaces enabled a process by which consumers projected themselves into the social identities and connotations enshrined in the commodities associated with these public spaces. For consumers, buying and enjoying goods became a capitalistic form of self-definition. In this highly developed consumer society, every social nexus that had traditionally remained non-commodified—including those surrounding political ideology, education, religious beliefs, and even scientific and medical procedures—became literally and figuratively commodified. Urban consumers were positioning themselves to choose what they wanted from among "the leviathans of trade and industry," and medical goods proved to be no exception.[22] Consumers relied on quite a diverse assortment of objects to represent and fulfill their desires—*inter alia*, medical gadgets such as the electric belt, the horse-action saddle, ozone paper, the Turkish bath, the dumb-bell, the tricycle, the patent masticator, thermal socks, and pimple squeezers. Also included were patent medicines such as blood purifiers, nervous tonics, and cod liver oil, all marketed as medical commodities useful for a healthy life. Advertisements for these commodities appeared throughout newspapers and magazines circulating most particularly in London. In turn, middle-class Londoners' strong desires and requirements for an idealized life in the city—a healthier, stronger, richer, and fuller life—created a demand for these remedies. And, in turn, an increasing interest in progressive evolutionism and a fear of nervous degeneration instigated the desire for a decidedly healthier life.[23] As Chapter Two will

---

the 1880s and 1890s. Another important book is by Chandra Mukerji, *From Graven Images: Patterns of Modern Materialism* (New York: Columbia University Press, 1983), in which she elegantly uses the trade in prints for her own historical analysis.

[22] William Stead, Jr., *The Art of Advertising: Its Theory and Practice Fully Described* (London: T. B. Browne, Ltd., 1899), 13.

[23] The Victorians' obsession with—and fear about—nervous degeneration and

show, however, such interests and fears were hardly *sui generis*: ubiquitous advertisement of these commodities, relying not only on bombastic
pictorial images of a healthy body and mind but also on dazzling commercial language, at once both produced and exploited a widely held
aspiration to acquire robust health, a vigorous body, perfect health, vital
energy, and supreme strength.

Turning from the demand-side of medical care to its suppliers, we
find in the late Victorian era an early popularity of the application of
new technologies to medical practice. As early as 1896, William Roent-
gen had brought into the hospital ward his newly invented X-ray body-
imaging machine. From the 1880s, bacteriology had become accepted,
and auxiliary examinations and clinical pathology advanced equally
steadily in a number of hospitals. In particular, as Chapter Three describes, many British doctors were keen to apply new electrical technologies and instruments to medical practice, and they went so far as to
collaborate with other professional groups such as electrical engineers,
who were interested in their technology's application to the socially
beneficial and commercially promising field of medicine. To make use
of these new medical technologies, hospitals and clinics needed to equip
themselves with costly machines, instruments, and institutional developments—all of these innovations were required to meet the growing
consumer demand for these kinds of newly technologized medical services.

By the late nineteenth century, a new form of collaboration between
medical practice and capitalistic activities was emerging, amidst a rising
material culture in which the body was seen as secular property and
health as a purchasable commodity. It was also a response both to the
democratization and urbanization of society, and to the technologization
of medical practice. Could doctors be completely indifferent to the latter? Did the broader public's concern for leading an energetic and

---

debility may have created a cultural environment that fostered the burgeoning
growth of health-related commodities. See Janet Oppenheim, *Shattered Nerves:
Doctors, Patients, and Depression in Victorian England* (Oxford: Oxford University
Press, 1991). In addition, one of the important studies discussing the Victorian
obsession with the healthy body and mind is by Bruce Haley, *The Healthy Body
and Victorian Culture* (Cambridge, Massachusetts: Harvard University Press,
1978).

healthy life have no influence on British medicine and medical practices? It can be argued that that these new pressures eroded the entire body of traditional medicine and medical professionalism.

However, many historians have urged that in the face of these challenges, elite professionals attempted to regulate doctors' behavior according to a nineteenth-century gentlemanly standard. According to this view, the rise of professionalism via bureaucratic or state control in the Victorian era is said to have gradually displaced market forces,[24] and the professionalization of medicine in turn served to strengthen control and to rescue the profession from the unseemly hustle of the medical marketplace.[25] This often-articulated Whiggish view of nineteenth-century medicine has met with support from such sociological accounts of Victorian professionalization as Harold Perkin's theory that industrial entrepreneurialism, which experienced its heyday during the mid-Victorian era, was gradually replaced by a professionalism attempting to rationally control market-driven anomalies through the calculating nature of the bureaucratic state's *modus operandi.*[26]

This account is also sustained by the traditional view of this period, as classically depicted by A. V. Dicey and politically supported by Fabian historians such as the Webbs, Toynbee, and others: on the basis of their personal experience and principles, they argued that the transition from individualism and *laissez-faire* capitalism to collectivism and centralized administrative growth helped create the welfare state.[27] These scholars viewed the mid-Victorian period as the high tide of collectivist politics and state intervention in monitoring and caring for the health of vulnerable citizens; the Apothecaries Act of 1815 and the Medical Act of 1858 were prime examples of state regulation. Such historians went on to ex-

---

[24] Magali Larson, *The Rise of Professionalism: A Sociological Analysis* (Berkeley: University of California Press, 1977).

[25] On occupational diversity in the eighteenth century, see Margaret Pelling, "Occupational Diversity: Barber-Surgeons and the Trades of Norwich, 1550–1640," *Bulletin of the History of Medicine,* 56 (1982): 484–511.

[26] Harold Perkin, *The Origins of Modern English Society, 1780–1880* (London: Routledge & Kegan Paul, 1968); *The Rise of Professional Society: England since 1880* (London: Routledge & Kegan Paul, 1989).

[27] Albert Venn Dicey, *Lectures on the Relation between Law and Public Opinion in England during the Nineteenth Century* (London: Macmillan, 1905).

plain that the government delegated monitoring authority to elite organizations within the medical profession—such as the General Medical
Council and the Medical Register—that established standard and legitimate practices for medical services and suppressed any aggressive intrusions by market forces.

More recent historians, however, have emphasized the development
of an affluent private sector, and insist that late-Victorian society was
less monolithic—less collective and organic—than Dicey and others had
argued.[28] José Harris, for example, writes:

> Dicey's account ignored the rapid penetration of market relation-
> ships in the later nineteenth century into many spheres previously
> occupied by the older-style organism: the displacement of friendly
> societies by industrial assurance companies, the eclipse of sub-
> scriptions by fees in hospitals, medicine, and private education,
> and the advance of commercialized leisure and spectator sports
> were a few cases in point.[29]

Harris' understanding that market forces in fact had a strong influence on medical circles is compelling, and my research for this present
book fully bears out her conclusions. She goes on to observe that
"There were many aspects of modern urban and industrial life pressing
individuals into an apparently more uniform and communal mould; but
the very same pressures also generated the opposite process—
proliferation of an infinite variety of tastes, styles, functions, habits, and
beliefs, and an accentuated emphasis on private life and personal relationships." It is important to detect that behind the very "public" domain and its documentation lie hidden the "private lives" of patients and
customers of medicine, and that there also emerged people's real demand for medical services. As long as we continue to look only at the

---

[28] While Derek Fraser insists that both state interventionism and *laissez-faire*
ideology originated from the same philosophical roots—Benthamite individualism—many scholars have taken it for granted that collectivist politics have long
dominated British welfare society. Derek Fraser, *The Evolution of the British Welfare State: A History of Social Policy Since the Industrial Revolution*, 2nd ed. (London:
Macmillan, 1984), 99–123.

[29] José Harris, *Private Lives, Public Spirit: Britain 1870–1914* (London: Penguin
Books, 1993), 12.

"public" sphere, at historical factors that are related only to state regulation, we lose the real pulse of a society.

In the later Victorian period, responding to high consumer demand for more refined care than was available in charitable hospitals, entrepreneurs began to establish a number of commercial—private—medical institutions. For example, the pay hospital movement, led by Henry Burdett, was sustained primarily by the middle classes who "could afford to make some payment" for the superior care they received.[30] In the 1870s, a Matlock businessman, John Smedley, made a considerable fortune from the 172-bed Hydropathic Institution he built.[31] Along much the same lines, herbal medicine grew more commercial in the 1870s as an increasingly popular area of self-help, distinct from the practice of professional medicine in the mid-Victorian era: the Medical Botanical Institute, for instance, was opened on Southampton Street in Camberwell by the medical herbalist D. Stokes, and it became a profitable medical institution.[32] Moreover, the fashionable spas of the eighteenth century and the faith in water cures were given a new lease of life by venture capital: privately-owned institutions—such as the spa at Malvern run by John Gully—attracted thousands of patients, including notable public figures such as Charles Darwin.[33] Private nursing-homes proliferated, too: by 1900 in London alone, there were more than 50, most of them run by non-medical proprietors and provided as an alternative to pay wards in the hospitals.[34] As Michael Worboys has shown, the private sanatoria for consumption and cancer that were founded by business-minded practitioners largely outnumbered public ones until 1907.[35]

---

[30] Brian Able-Smith, *The Hospitals, 1800–1948: A Study in Social Administration in England and Wales* (London: Heinemann, 1964), Chapter 9.

[31] Kelvin Rees, "Water as a Commodity: Hydropathy in Matlock," in Roger Cooter, ed., *Studies in the History of Alternative Medicine* (Basingstoke: Macmillan, 1988).

[32] The Medical Botanical Institute's supply of "Herb Healing" was, however, censored by the Royal College of Physicians: RCP, MSS., 2412/95.

[33] Janet Browne, "Spas and Sensibilities: Darwin at Malvern," in Roy Porter, ed., *The Medical History of Waters and Spas*, Medical History Supplement no. 10 (London: Wellcome Institute for the History of Medicine, 1990).

[34] *Matthews' Manual of Nursing Homes & Hydros of the British Isles and Guide to Spas and Health Resorts* (London: Alex. Matthews, 1915).

[35] Michael Worboys, "The Sanatorium Treatment for Consumption in Britain,

Were popular expectations of medicine and health care transformed by modern consumer society? In the socio-economic climate of nineteenth-century London—whose society was becoming ever more commercialized—what enabled medical commodities to flourish so strongly, and what element of that climate so captured the minds of consumers? Were members of the purchasing public simply duped by dazzling advertisements—simply lured into taking massive doses of marketed medicines? If they were inclined more toward the habitual use of various medicinal goods, what forces persuaded them that it was in their own best interest to do so? In short, what did the ongoing commodification and commercialization of medicine influence, and how did these developments interact with the traditional professional medical establishment?

Answering these questions is not easy: it requires us to explore not only the extensive public records of the professional medical establishment and the institutes of scientific learning, but—more importantly— also to look at very private spheres. But information from these— information embedded in the behaviors, reactions, and demands of doctors, patients, entrepreneurs, and consumers—unfortunately is as difficult to access as it is indispensable for understanding the complexities of a society becoming more professionalized. Consequently, this book's charting of market forces' invasion of the field of medicine and medical professionalism is a story containing frequent exceptions and contradictions. Essentially, a historical mosaic needs to be constructed from the patchwork of newspapers, private documents, minutes, advertisements, and patent documents—some well-known and some very obscure.[36] By

---

1890–1914" in John Pickstone, ed., *Medical Innovations in Historical Perspectives* (New York: St. Martins Press, 1992).

[36] Some of the documents I used to uncover private spheres are witnesses' testimony, minutes of meetings, police examination records, newspaper columns, and applications to the patent office. I also explored the language of proprietary medical advertisements in the magnificent John Johnson Collection at the Bodleian Library in Oxford, which holds over 400 manufacturers' advertising ephemera, handbills, and newspaper cuttings. In many ways, these are the equivalent of the eighteenth-century metropolitan quack handbills that Roy Porter has examined in *Health for Sale: Quackery in England, 1660–1850* (Manchester: Manchester University Press, 1989). My examination was supplemented

introducing them into the traditional historical narrative of the period, a more complex picture emerges.

The narrative of this book not only spotlights the influence of commercialization on the field of medicine but it also depicts the conflict of interests between doctors' professional ethics of service and a commercial ethos that helped trigger the public's desire to acquire good health. Chapter One starts with a reconsideration of the long patent medicine controversy—that is, the medical doctors' campaign against proprietary medicine dealers, or quacks, in their view—in the context of the ongoing penetration by market mechanisms into the medical and pharmaceutical domains. In presenting the debates and pecuniary struggles between doctors, chemists, and proprietary manufacturers, this chapter throws new light on a hitherto neglected aspect of medical professionalism. Chapter Two turns its attention to the cultural and socio-psychological environment that enabled an unprecedented boom of patent medicines in the later nineteenth century—a period in which a motley assortment of medicinal manufacturers extensively advertised blood purifiers, nerve tonics, and pills and wafers for indigestion, dyspepsia, and biliousness. The public bought these products not primarily because they found themselves to be sick, but more because these products were sold as therapeutic commodities inducing a fantasy of achieving a well-balanced and healthy bodily constitution, vitality, and the like.

The medical commodities traded in the Victorian market were not limited to drug preparations. Chapters Three and Four focus on electrical devices and gadgets extensively sold for nervous ailments and loss of energy: electrical chains, electric belts, hats, magnetic curative appliances, and many other types of electric machines and instruments related to electricity and electrotherapeutics. These chapters highlight forgotten quackish entrepreneurs and company-style electric capitalists who created irksome disciplinary problems for the established medical profession. What distinguished these products from patent medicines was the intermediary role that electrical engineers played between doctors and devices. People swallowed pills because they wanted to increase physical

---

with investigation and analysis of the patent medicine advertisements that appeared in *Health, The Christian Age, The Graphic, The Illustrated London News,* and other serial publications.

health, whereas wearing electro-therapeutic devices reflected Victorians' technologically oriented sensibilities of the body electric. Chapter Three discusses the theoretical background out of which electro-therapeutics emerged—the relation between nervous force and electricity, Victorian sense and sensibility of the body electric, and the British acceptance of medical electricity—and examines the strategies through which electrical engineers, newly emerging professionals, exploited the advancement of electric applications to the body. Chapter Four investigates a historical drama in which newly established electro-therapeutic institutes led to disciplinary debates with the Censors' Board of the Royal College of Physicians in London regarding the unprofessional conduct of medical doctors employed in profit-making activities in those institutes. In sum, these two chapters discuss how strengthening the nexus of medical en- trepreneurship and commercialization was keenly pursued by profes- sional engineers and electrotherapy charlatans alike as they sought to market their medico-electric services and appliances.

Chapter Five supplements the arguments of the previous chapters by providing a case-study on massage, a therapy newly imported and re- garded as captivatingly exotic. Like electrotherapy, it involved manual dexterity, and in the 1880s the "massage establishments" that mush- roomed in London created sex-scandals and incurred a wrathful cam- paign of opposition from the British Medical Association.

The terminology, case examples, and debates studied in this book all present a clear picture of capitalism's incursion into the world of science and knowledge. Nineteenth-century British society's overt embrace of medical professionalization no doubt enabled doctors to retain their strong grip on medical services, even as elite doctors faced the develop- ing expectation that science, too, must become the object of market ac- tivities and thus become commercialized. By understanding medical per- sonnel and consumers of medicine as equal participants in a highly commercialized society, this study reveals that uniformity was neither the sole nor the principal characteristic of the nineteenth-century British medical profession. Surrounded by pressures from the public's health culture and the concomitant commodification of medicine, all players in the medical field—from doctors to entrepreneurs and from inventors of medical instruments to quackish capitalists—were engaged in a tug-of- war over the profits to be made. The chapters of this book reexamine the relationship between the two faces of medicine: its traditional manifestation as a body of scientific and professional knowledge, and its newer manifestation as a collection of commercial and entrepreneurial endeavors. In so doing, this study treats popular medical treatments seriously, in order to reconsider the relationship between the meritocratic power of professionalism and the *laissez-faire* forces of medical markets and entrepreneurship. The attempt here to untangle the highly intertwined relationships between professional authority and medical capitalism in the late nineteenth century surely also sheds light on what we see and experience today. In our modern society medicine and medical care need capitalist ventures to promote innovation and ensure optimal allocation of medical resources, even though the excesses of unregulated market capitalism can reveal the dark side of those same market forces. By exploring in some detail the historical dramas that initially accompanied capitalism's intrusion into the medical field, this book seeks to deepen our understanding of both the disadvantages and the efficacious power of the commingling of market forces and medicine.

CHAPTER 1

## *Profession and Market: The BMA's Campaign Against Patent Medicine Reconsidered*

The size of the proprietary medicine trade at the end of the nineteenth century was unprecedented. It was said that the market had as many as ten thousand vendors who together sustained at least nineteen thousand employees. These so-called patent medicine businesses dramatically sur-passed the older quack nostrums in terms of both the form and the scale of their financial operations. Their heavy capitalization was the most striking characteristic of these corporate-style traders. A. J. White, Ltd. started business with a huge capital investment of £1,000,000 in 1897 and soon was earning an annual profit of £900,000 by selling its famous "Mother Siegel's Syrup." Coleman & Company, the proprietor of the blood- enriching wine "Wincarnis," employed four to five hundred people and had an impressive capital of £250,000. Stephen Smith & Company, the proprietors of "Hall's Wine," had working capital of £175,000, and Daisy, Ltd. in Leeds, the makers of "Daisy Powders," had a sum of £15,000. The owners of these businesses made huge fortunes, some of which they passed on, as in the case of the £1,111,000 legacy left by George Taylor Fulford, the proprietor of "Dr. William's Pink Pills for Pale People."[1]

---

[1] *Parliamentary Papers (1914) IX: Select Committee on Patent Medicines*, published as *Report from the Select Committee on Patent Medicines, together with Proceedings of the Committee, Minutes of Evidence, and Appendices*, Ordered by the House of Commons,

Indeed, proprietary medicine was beginning to appropriate ever larger shares of the growing consumption of medical products. The sales income from patent medicines rose from £600,000 in 1860 to £3 million in 1891 and to £5 million by 1914.[2] Considering that the population in England and Wales nearly doubled during this same period, this abrupt and disproportionate demand for proprietary medicine signaled a new environment in which consumers of medicine began to consider their health in a way quite different from before.

Another notable feature of these proprietary traders was their advertising strategies, following to some extent mid-century quack pill-vendors such as James Morison and Thomas Holloway, also the founders of Royal Holloway College.[3] As early as in 1836, Holloway established himself as a foreign and commercial agent in London. What made his business so special was his genius for recognizing the potential of advertising. His expenditure on advertising pills rose steadily from £5,000 a year in 1842 to over £50,000 by the time of his death in 1883. An enormous amount of this money was spent on inserting advertisements for patent medicines in newspapers and periodicals and on pushing promotional pamphlets, diaries, and almanacs under people's front doors. Similarly, the comparatively small-time proprietors of "Daisy Powders" spent £3,000 a year during this period, and the much larger Coleman & Company had an advertising annual budget of £50,000 that enabled it to employ thirty to forty people in its own advertising bureau.[4] Indeed, the total annual expenditure of these companies on advertising was estimated to have run up to £2,000,000 in Britain alone.[5] This seems at odds for an era that many historians have equated with the triumph of professionalism and the supposed concomitant reluctance of professionals to become in-

---

1914 (London: Wyman and Sons, Ltd., 1914), xiii-xiv. E. S. Turner, *The Shocking History of Advertising* (London: Michael Joseph, 1953).

[2] S. W. F. Holloway, *The Royal Pharmaceutical Society of Great Britain 1841–1991: A Political and Social History* (London: The Pharmaceutical Press, 1991), 308.

[3] As for James Morrison's pill business, see W. H. Helfand, "James Morrison and his Pills," *Transactions of the British Society of the History of Pharmacy*, 1 (1974): 101–135.

[4] *Report from the Select Committee on Patent Medicines*, 501.

[5] Ibid., x.

volved in such profit-seeking activities.[6]

Like Thomas Holloway, Thomas Beecham was another famous patent medicine dealer who used the influence of the media by investing a considerable amount of money to advertise his laxative pills under the now well-know slogan "worth a guinea a box" in newspapers and other advertising outlets. His son, Joseph Beecham, went on to build a business empire through his innovative advertising strategies, which included buying advertising space on billboards and railway fences. It was said that the younger Beecham spent as much as £100,000 on advertising in 1912. It soon became impossible to travel in either Britain or the United States without seeing Beecham's advertisements along both roads and railways. Beecham's advertising method was very audacious: the advertisement often contained his own picture, a strong reliable face with side whiskers, with a bold claim such as "THE WORLD'S FAMILY MEDICINE. A family Medicine is a necessity. The human body is an intricate piece of machinery which is easily put out of order." He even exploited church-goers' use of hymn books by circulating them at low prices to working-class families before Christmas, perhaps in the vain hope that congregations might instead sing the advertised words of celebration for Beecham's pills: "Hark! The herald angels sing, Beecham's pills are just the thing. Peace on earth and mercy mild. Two for man and one for child."[7]

Such blatant capitalizing of medical products did not, of course, go unchallenged by medicine's more consciously professional ranks. Beginning in the 1880s, for instance, the British Medical Association (henceforth BMA), the central institution for maintaining doctors' medical au-

---

[6] Sociological studies of the professionalization of medicine roughly parallel Harold Perkin's account of the development of modern English society as establishing a professional ideal. See Harold Perkin, *The Origins of Modern English Society, 1780–1880* (London: Routledge & Kegan Paul, 1968), and *The Rise of Professional Society: England since 1880* (London: Routledge & Kegan Paul, 1989). See also Magali Larson, *The Rise of Professionalism: A Sociological Analysis* (Berkeley: University of California Press, 1977). For the medical profession, see Noel Parry and José Parry, *The Rise of the Medical Profession: A Study of Collective Social Mobility* (London: Croom Helm, 1976).

[7] "Sir Joseph Beecham Found Dead in Home—By the Sale of His Pills He Had Become the Third Richest Man in England," *The New York Times*, October 24, 1919.

thority, began a militant campaign against what it described as the "palpable quacks and vendors of either dangerous or insidious wares."[8] The doctors repeatedly claimed that patent medicine was just "a misnomer," and its purveyors nothing but quack mongers. The medical elite stigmatized such products as "secret remedies"[9] and scoffed that "to call a secret nostrum a patent medicine is like calling a jay a peacock."[10] In their campaign, the association initially relied on the power of professional regulation.

The main prosecuting body for this effort was the BMA's Parliamentary Bills Committee. Chairing the Committee from 1872 to 1897, Ernest Hart was the editor of the BMA's official organ, the *British Medical Journal* (*BMJ*). The initial tactic of Hart and the BMA in the war against manufacturers of proprietary medicine was to disclose details of ingredients of famous proprietary products and their production costs. By emphasizing the cheap and tawdry nature of marketed medicines, doctors intended to educate consumers about a drug's worthlessness and induce them to return to professional medical diagnosis and treatment. Furthermore, the BMA's exposé revealed that some products sold in the market contained poisonous and addictive narcotics such as opium, potent doses of alcohol, and even morphine, which they discovered in Beecham's Pills. The BMA argued that medicines containing these drugs were likely to cause serious injury to habitual pill takers.[11]

The revelations first appearing in serial format in the *British Medical Journal* were later compiled and published in 1909 as *Secret Remedies: What They Cost and What They Contain*. The book's sales success led the BMA to publish a sequel entitled *More Secret Remedies* in 1912.[12] Although the

---

[8] "The Press, the Quacks, and the Public," *British Medical Journal*, 2 (January 27, 1894): 208.

[9] "The Sale of Proprietary Medicines Containing Poisons," *British Medical Journal*, 1 (May 5, 1894): 745–746.

[10] "A Silent Revolution," *British Medical Journal*, 2 (November 5, 1892): 1018–1019.

[11] *British Medical Journal*, 2 (September 13, 1890): 639; 2 (December 26, 1891): 1356–1360; 1 (May 7, 1892): 978–979 and 995–996; 1 (April 21, 1894): 870; 2 (September 10, 1892): 602; 2 (October 1, 1892): 756; 2 (December 3, 1892): 252; and 1 (April 29, 1893): 911–912.

[12] *Secret Remedies: What They Cost and What They Contain* (London: British Medical

doctors' concerns about patent medicine outlined briefly here have drawn the attention of some historians, the latter's examination has relied almost exclusively on materials taken from this professional association's perspective.[13] To understand this controversy only through materials such as the articles published in the *BMJ*, *Secret Remedies*, or *More Secret Remedies*, however, is to focus on only half of the story. Studies that do this have not only failed to investigate the intra-professional struggle between medical doctors and pharmaceutical men, but they have also strangely neglected even to examine this interesting debate, which was amply recorded in the *BMJ*'s report—an account that makes it hard to jump to the conclusion that all trade owners were little more than swindlers. In fact, many of them attempted to fight back against the medical profession, first by forming a Proprietary Article Section at the London Chamber of Commerce, which was at the time chaired by none other than Sir Joseph Beecham, and then by issuing circulars and pamphlets published by the Chamber.

In essence, traditional historiography has assumed that the BMA's campaign was nothing less than a further step towards greater medical professionalization, with doctors trying to use state or government regulation to strengthen their professional grip on the medical market. Reexamining this campaign, however, reveals that it was not without more mixed meanings. The ideological machinery used to justify proprietary medicine is particularly interesting. In this tug-of-war, both sides relied heavily on an ideology of public interest, with doctors denouncing secret remedies as "grave public offences." Patent medicine marketers countered these attacks by championing market mechanisms which they argued would eventually advance the public benefit. Consumers' desires to buy health in the form of the "therapeutic commodity," such vendors insisted, would be achieved only through full market capitalism. And the doctors themselves were scarcely immune to market relations: the pecuniary interests of many

---

Association, 1909); *More Secret Remedies: What They Cost and What They Contain* (London: British Medical Association, 1912).

[13] F. C. Trig, "The Influence of Victorian 'Patent Medicines' on the Development of Early Twentieth-Century Medical Practice," University of Sheffield, Ph.D. dissertation, 1982; Peter W. J. Bartrip, *A Mirror of Medicine: A History of the BMJ, 1840–1990* (Oxford: Clarendon Press, 1990), 189–202; and W. H. Fraser, *The Coming of the Mass Market, 1850–1914* (London: Macmillan, 1981).

of these professionals, though veiled behind their oft-argued ideology of public interest and public protection, was a crucial factor behind doctors' efforts to drive proprietary medicine men out of the market.

By looking at a number of patent medicine controversies in light of this cultural and economic setting, it is possible to reconsider the different implications of the medical doctors' anti-quack campaign against proprietary medicine. Therefore, this chapter reconstructs the debates and pecuniary struggles between doctors, chemists, and proprietary manufacturers in order to throw new light on the hitherto neglected relationship between professional ideology and medical capitalism.

## *Professionalism or Commercialism?*

Other journals and newspapers were reluctant to join the *BMJ*'s campaign against proprietary medicine dealers for fear of losing the revenue earned from patent medicines' advertisements. The press was long silent after Ernest Hart in the *BMJ* harshly accused "a large proportion of the newspaper press of this country with sacrificing their duty, the honour of their calling, and the public interest to the inducement of palpable quacks and vendors of either dangerous or insidious wares."[14] Hart next turned to pressing the Pharmaceutical Society to police patent medicine manufacturers,[15] and he aggressively used the Pharmacy Act of 1868, which prohibited unqualified persons from selling any medicinal preparation containing poisons. The Act stated that, "from and after the 31st day of December 1868, it shall be unlawful for any person to sell or keep open shop for retailing, dispensing or compounding poisons, or to assume or use the title chemist and druggist, or chemist, or druggist, or pharmacist, or dispensing chemist in any part of Great Britain, unless

---

[14] "The Press, the Quacks, and the Public," *British Medical Journal*, 1 (January 27, 1894): 208. See also "Press Notices and Quack Remedies," *British Medical Journal*, 2 (July 15, 1893): 135; "Quack Advertisements and the British Press," *British Medical Journal*, 2 (July 22, 1894): 191; "Poisoning by Misadventure: Opinions of the Press," *British Medical Journal*, 1 (January 27, 1894): 208.
[15] See Virginia Berridge and Griffith Edwards, *Opium and the People: Opiate Use in Nineteenth-Century England* (London: Allen Lane and St. Martin's Press, 1981). David Taylor, *The Consumer Movement, Health, and the Pharmaceutical Industry* (London: Office of Health Economics, 1983).

such person shall . . . be registered under this Act." With this, the Pharmaceutical Society had become the only professional association vested with prosecuting powers, a privileged status it made every effort to defend, and that Hart and the BMA were determined to see exercised.

However, in spite of Hart's repeated requests to "exercise the power specially conferred upon that body for the protection of the public," the Pharmaceutical Society remained unwilling to publicly confront and prosecute the manufacturers and traders of proprietary medicines.[16] Seemingly irritated by these pharmaceutical men's shilly-shallying attitude, the *BMJ* several times criticized "the inaction of the Pharmaceutical Society" by noting that "it will be the duty of the Council of the Pharmaceutical Society to enforce that restriction vigorously" and that "the Pharmaceutical Society had for a long series of years been supine in the matter."[17] Finally, replying to Hart's grilling inquiry on September 13, 1892, Michael Carteighe, then president of the Society, answered, "I see it stated in certain journals connected with Pharmacy, that the Council is thought to be indisposed to take action," and guaranteed in his letter to "carry out the provisions of that Act until the illegal sale by unregistered persons of proprietary preparations containing poison is discontinued."[18] As the *BMJ* wrote triumphantly, Hart's continuous appeals to the Public Prosecutor, his reports on the chemical analyses of these products to the Treasury solicitor, and the *BMJ*'s own articles and essays

> Put such pressure on the Council of the Pharmaceutical Society as induced them to undertake seriously on their part the duty to fulfil, in this matter which they had for many years wholly neglected to fulfil, in the fear, we believe, that the trade, their constituents, might disapprove from selfish reasons.[19]

---

[16] *British Medical Journal*, 2 (December 26, 1891): 1360.

[17] *British Medical Journal*, 2 (November 7, 1891): 1009; 1 (May 7, 1892): 979; 1 (February 18, 1893): 367.

[18] "Letter from Ernest Hart, 'The Sale of Poisonous Proprietary Preparations,'" the Pharmaceutical Society, *Minutes of Council* (archive of the Pharmaceutical Society), 10: 194–195, and reply from the President. Also see the correspondence between Ernest Hart and M. Carteighe, President of the Pharmaceutical Society, the Pharmaceutical Society, *Minutes of Council*, 10: 194–195 and 195–196.

[19] "Secret Medicine Containing Poison," *British Medical Journal*, 2 (September 10,

This observation by the *BMJ* was not off the mark. The Pharmaceutical Society had not taken action, partly because patent medicine was exempted from Section 16 of the Act, but more because not a few members of the Society were in fact associated with the trade:[20] many druggists and chemists of the Society, associated as they were with proprietary medicine companies, were not happy about medical doctors' interference in their domain of the pharmacy.

Finally, with Hart's repeated demands that the Pharmaceutical Society "put in force the long dormant and neglected powers which the law gives them,"[21] the Society at last "set seriously to work to carry out its statutory duty" in February 1893.[22] However, Hart's victory was far from complete. The Queen's Bench in October 1893 returned a verdict exonerating Key's Linseed and determining that the company was exempted under certain clauses of the Pharmacy Act. According to the court judgment, "A medicinal preparation, containing poison, can be sold without regard to the provisions of that [Pharmacy] Act if the preparation be the subject of a patent."[23] This verdict was so unexpected and influential that the BMA had to change its tactics in order extend its supervision over patent medicine proprietors.

Following this legal defeat, the BMA began to appeal to the public in its war against the manufacturers of proprietary medicine. From 1904 onward, the *BMJ*, under the leadership of Hart's successor Dawson Wil-

----

1892): 602–603.

[20] For the reluctance of the Pharmaceutical Society to act against the makers of patent medicines, see "Parliamentary Bills Committee," *British Medical Journal*, 2 (November 7, 1891): 1009; "Secret Remedies and the Pharmacy Act," *British Medical Journal*, 2 (December 26, 1891): 1359-1360; "The Irregular Sale of Poisons," *British Medical Journal*, 1 (May 7, 1892): 978-979; "Secret Medicines Containing Poison," *British Medical Journal*, 2 (September 9, 1892): 602–603; and "Sale of Secret Remedies Containing Poison: Unpublished Penalties," *British Medical Journal*, 2 (December 3, 1892): 1252.

[21] "Secret Medicines Containing Poison," *British Medical Journal*, 2 (September 9, 1892): 603; "Silent Revolution," *British Medical Journal*, 2 (November 4, 1893): 1019.

[22] "The Patent Medicine Abuse," *British Medical Journal*, 1 (February 18, 1893): 367.

[23] "Patent Medicine and the Sale of Poisons," *The British Medical Journal*, 2 (October 28, 1893): 958–959.

liams, began publishing detailed lists of ingredients in, and the production costs of, famous proprietary products.[24] The BMA assumed the public would be astonished, awakened, and enlightened once they could compare these drugs' market value to their real value in terms of the cost and safety of their ingredients. With the permission of the *BMJ* and the Finance Committee of the BMA in 1908, these revelations were published in 1909 as *Secret Remedies: What They Cost and What They Contain*.[25] Considering the major newspapers' refusal to advertise the book, it was a *succès fou*: 62,000 copies were sold. As noted above, these sales made it possible to publish a further volume, *More Secret Remedies*, in 1912.[26] It may well have been the success of these books that sparked the government's decision to inspect proprietary medicines, beginning with an appointment of a Select Committee in 1912.[27] During the sessions of Parliament, forty-two witnesses—including doctors, newspaper owners, and proprietors of patent medicines—were called. In 1914, full discussions of more than 14,000 responses to questions were published under the title of *Report from the Select Committee on Patent Medicines*.[28]

Why was the body of professional pharmacists and chemists so re-

---

[24] The first article was "The Composition of Certain Secret Remedies," which carried the analyses of several "cures" for epilepsy. *British Medical Journal*, 2 (December 10, 1904): 1585–1586. Examples of this series appears, for instance, in the following volumes of the same journal: 2 (December 10, 1904): 1599–1600; 2 (July 7, 1906): 27–28; 2 (December 8, 1906): 1645–1647; 2 (January 26, 1907): 213–214; 2 (July 6, 1907): 24–25; 2 (August 31, 1907): 530–532; and 2 (December 7, 1907): 1653–1658.

[25] British Medical Association, MS, MCSC, XVII, Minutes of Council, January 27, 1909, 70–71. *Secret Remedies: What They Cost and What They Contain* (London: British Medical Association, 1909).

[26] The *Daily Express*, the *Graphic*, the *News of the World*, the *Daily Chronicle*, and the *Star* refused to publish advertisements for *Secret Remedies*. See *Report from the Select Committee on Patent Medicines*, x-xi. *More Secret Remedies: What They Cost and What They Contain* (London: The British Medical Association, 1912).

[27] In April 1912, a select committee of inquiry into the patent medicine business was formed in the House of Commons.

[28] *Parliamentary Papers (1914) IX: Select Committee on Patent Medicines*, published as *Report from the Select Committee on Patent Medicines, together with Proceedings of the Committee, Minutes of Evidence, and Appendices*, Ordered by the House of Commons, 1914 (London: Wyman and Sons, Ltd., 1914).

luctant to take action? What intra-professional tension among a wide range of pharmacists prevented professional regulations from being implemented? What did these professional men think about the patent medicine manufacturers and their retailers? Faced with an expanding drug market, these pharmaceutical men oscillated between identifying with their profession and engaging in the commercial trade in pharmaceutical products. Yet although professional chemists first fought bitterly with proprietary medicine men, by the early 1900s they ended up in a surprising economic collaboration. The process by which they came to ally with one another is quite interesting.

In the 1880s and 1890s, professional pharmaceutical companies had two sources of income: from the sale of prescriptions by elite pharmacists and from the sale of advertised proprietary medicines in the small shops of rank-and-file chemists. Therefore, the proliferation of patent medicines and the accompanying blatant commercialism of the mass market eroded the market share of these private chemists and conflicted with the interests of professional pharmacists.[29] By the turn of the century, proprietary medicines were starting to be sold extensively in groceries and general stores. Department stores, such as Spiers & Pond's and Harrods, had also adopted a strategy of selling patent medicines at reduced prices. And most damagingly, the drug store chains represented by Jesse Boot's in the Midlands, Parks and Lewis & Burrough's in London, Day's and Timothy White's in the South, and Taylor's and Inman's in the North, were contributing to a downward spiral in retail prices.

The most serious threat to small retail chemists came from Jesse Boot, who inherited a herbalist store in Nottingham from his father, John Boot, changed it to a chemist shop, and later developed the business into a nationwide retail network. His business strategy was innovative: he targeted working-class families seeking medications and medicinal goods at an affordable price. As economic historians have shown, the 1870s were a period of recession in which prices fell—which tended to benefit employed members of the working classes. Moreover, during the 1870s and

---

[29] As for the process by which the manufacturers first came into conflict and later collaborated with professional chemists, I owe my understanding to S. W. F. Holloway, *The Royal Pharmaceutical Society of Great Britain, 1841–1991* (London: The Pharmaceutical Press, 1991). See, in particular, 307.

1880s, the rapid development of the railways, the introduction of steamships, and the opening of the Suez Canal made it possible to import larger shipments of grains and refrigerated meat from America, Australia, and South Africa—which in turn led to a downward pressure on retail prices, particularly for imported and raw materials. As a result, the living standards of the working class improved: its members were able to spend more money on products other than their daily necessities; they were able to improve and broaden their diet; and they were also able to consume larger amounts of drugs and medical goods.

Boot's business of "low margin and high turnover" was eagerly welcomed by the working class. Retail chemists usually sold drugs at a twenty-five percent profit margin, which they considered a fair profit, while on the other hand, Boot boasted as low as five percent margins in his dispensaries. Soon, Boot became a central target of opposition from retail chemists, who resented the new-style competition. Condemning the owners of drug store chains such as Boots, Days, and Taylors as "cutters," in the 1890s they expressed their outrage in trade journals such as the *Chemist and Druggist*. Notably, William Samuel Glyn-Jones, a professional chemist and owner of the dispensing business Glyn & Company on London's East India Dock Road, found the retail chains' price-cutting policies on proprietary medicines to be the cause of his own loss of sales, so he decided to tackle the problem by trying to unify the efforts of retail chemists.[30] He launched a monthly circular, the *Anti-Cutting Record*, and in its first issue he wrote: "The time has arrived when something must be done if the rank-and-file of the retail drug trade are not to be completely wiped out." He sent 5,000 copies of the pamphlet to private retail chemists throughout Britain, and at his initiative in January 1896, the Proprietary Articles Trade Association (henceforth PATA) was formed to maintain the prices of retail medicines.[31] (Fig. 1-1.)

What Glyn-Jones intended to achieve was so-called resale price main-

---

[30] "Sir W. F. Glyn-Jones, His Life and Work," *Pharmaceutical Journal and Transactions*, 65 (1927): 285–287.

[31] W. F. Glyn-Jones, "The Anti-Cutting Record," *Pharmaceutical Journal and Transactions*, 55 (1895): 404; "The Proprietary Articles Trades' Association," *Pharmaceutical Journal and Transactions*, 56 (1896): supplement, xxxix; "The Proprietary Articles Trades' Association," *Pharmaceutical Journal and Transactions*, 57 (1896): 17; and "An Anti-Cutting Crusade," *Chemist and Druggist*, 47 (1895): 700.

tenance. He argued that "the public did not expect chemists to work for nothing, but they would certainly go where they could get things cheapest. That was the only reason of their forsaking the chemist for the stores. But if the prices were all fixed, there would be no inducement to go to the stores or such places."[32] Protecting the proper prices, Glyn-Jones stated, "was not only a question of ensuring a better profit on proprietary articles, but, what was more important to them, to rob the cutter and stores of the advantage which followed their sale of these goods to the public."[33] To that end, he planned to announce an official list of "legitimate" retailers who joined the PATA and protected proper prices by demarcating "illegitimate" ones, mostly large-scale retailing firms, who were selling patent medicines at unfairly low prices. In response to Glyn-Jones' invitation to join his campaign, a dozen patent medicine proprietors allowed their company names to be listed. Among them was the owner of the popular drug "Dr. Scott's Little Liver Pills," who, at a PATA meeting in 1896, expressed his gratitude that "the increased sale of their pills proved that they were right in their belief. . . . Formerly they had the greatest difficulty in getting [retailers] to exhibit showcards or distribute handbills, or in any way assist the sale of their pills. Now, however they were having applications for handbills, etc., from hundreds of retailers in all parts of the country."[34]

As price-cutting was the most effective method for companies to attract customers and increase their market share, Glyn-Jones' campaign inevitably provoked harsh protests from retail companies such as Boots. It was Jesse Boot who fiercely protested against the PATA by sending strongly worded letters to the *Chemist and Druggist*, noting "As you may have noticed the strongly antagonistic position to this Association [PATA], . . . from our manufacturers' point of view there is much to be said in favour of keeping the trade free and open as against any system of restriction. . . . This movement [by PATA] is simply organized . . . in order to regain the trade out of the hands of the grocers and the progressive firms and bring it back to themselves at full prices."[35] Boot's counterblast

---

[32] *Chemist and Druggist*, 50 (1897): 803.

[33] *Chemist and Druggist*, 48 (1896): 748.

[34] "Statement at PATA meeting," *Chemist and Druggist*, 49 (1896): 487.

[35] *Chemist and Druggist*, 49 (1896): 523.

was forceful, and he used advertising as a bludgeon. To all stocked products of Dr. Scott's Pills he attached warning labels:

> Important Notice. —— Every buyer of Dr. Scott's Pills from BOOTS should know why the price has been raised, READ ROUND THE BOX. The makers of these Pills having joined a RING to force up prices, they will not allow them to be sold under 1s. per box, otherwise BOOTS, the Cash Chemists, would gladly sell at less. This being so, BOOTS strongly urge the public not to give 1s. for them.[36]

For large-scale retailers represented by Boots, a price-cutting policy was not a self-centered moneymaking strategy. Rather, they believed it ought to be praised and defended for its benefit to the public. The fixed retail prices that the PATA aimed to achieve were "a nice little plot hatched for the benefit of the retailer and the wholesale middleman" to the disadvantage of general consumers.[37] Therefore Boot decided to attach warning announcements to all proprietary articles that he sold and continued to declare that competition in the market was the only way to benefit consumers.

Hitherto, the Pharmaceutical Society, representing professional pharmacists, had done nothing about this battle between price-cutters and small private chemists and appeared to have adopted a wait-and-see strategy. Even within the Pharmaceutical Society, the pecuniary potential from the developing health market caused a split among the membership between the conflicting priorities of professionalization and commercialization. In 1890 the president, Michael Carteighe, long concerned about the professional status of pharmacists, insisted that "the time is, no doubt, coming when we shall have to choose between being traders with no conditions or pharmacists with all the advantages of that calling."[38] He made every effort to ostracize members who were associated with co-operatives and attempted to strike their names from the register for their allegedly unprofessional conduct. Such actions, however, evoked resistance from members who grumbled about the Society's inaction in protecting the pharmacists' trade. In the meantime, the large-scale capitali-

---

[36] *Anti-Cutting Record*, August–September, November, 1896.
[37] Ibid.
[38] *Pharmaceutical Journal and Transactions*, March 20, 1890, 800.

zation of patent medicine was indeed intimidating to self-employed small chemists' shops. Faced with the substantial obstacles of doctors dispensing medicines and consumers using patent medicines to self-medicate, some chemists opted to become employed in retail chain companies. Meanwhile, others sought to gain a professional monopoly over the market and began to press the council of the Pharmaceutical Society to regulate manufacturers.

On March 29, 1890, David Storrar, the chairman of the Society's Edinburgh section, challenged the Society's council at a meeting. "The professional and trade elements are as antagonistic as ever," he insisted, "and it may almost be admitted that the growth of professionalism with all its advantages has this disadvantage, that it has destroyed to some extent our capacity for successful trading."[39] According to him, the Pharmaceutical Society had been formed in 1841 first and foremost for "the protection of those who carry on the business of chemists and druggists. . . . The more scientific and ambitious members of the craft," he went on to say, "have moulded the policy of the Society and have kept the professional more than the trade element of its work in view."[40] In contrast, he noted, unregistered chemists were forming pure trade associations, such as the United Society of Chemists and Druggists or the Proprietary Articles Trade Association, which (in his view) were focused on moneymaking. Storrar's complaints were evidently justified; droves of professional chemists were leaving the Society for more remunerative compensation for their services. By 1900, the Society included as registered members only 4,000 out of 14,000 of all chemists in Britain, "the practical result of all this being that registered men get all the kicks while unregistered men pocket the half-pence." Objecting to Pharmaceutical Society President Carteighe's suggestion that the Society would soon need to declare its allegiance to professionalism, Storrar claimed that it was time to "widen our entrance to the Society" and "do our very utmost to induce those outside to join us."[41] Only the grand unification of professional chemists and ordinary retailers, he believed, would enable the So-

---

[39] David Storrar, "The Future of Pharmacy as a Trade and as a Profession," *Pharmaceutical Journal and Transactions*, March 29, 1890, 798–801.
[40] Ibid., 798–799.
[41] Ibid., 800.

ciety to press the government to grant them the authority to regulate the pharmaceuticals market and prohibit unqualified persons from dispensing medicines. "In this democratic age," Storrar wrote, "when anything which savours of privilege is objected to, the word 'protection' has an ugly sound, and yet if the claim for protection is a just one it should be made."[42]

Even before Storrar, state protection of the pharmaceuticals market was a special concern for many members of the Pharmaceutical Society.[43] On February 2, 1889, Campbell Stark, for example, asked "What chance is there in the future of obtaining a monopoly of the practice of our art, and how is that monopoly to be obtained?"[44] His suggestion was simple: pharmacists should be rewarded with the same economic protection that the state awarded other professions, such as the professional monopolies enjoyed by doctors and lawyers. In any event, Storrar's article, pinpointing most chemists' anxiety, soon raised a debate within the Society over its members' professional and commercial affiliations. In a subsequent meeting in Edinburgh, some wanted to make "every member, or even a majority of them connected with the Society . . . go forward unitedly and get what is wanted and bring a state of things which would infinitely better their position." At the same, others lamented that, because "many members and associates had turned their back on the Society," it was losing the political power it had once possessed.[45]

Storrar's argument could not be ignored since he was a central member of the Society and had touched on an anxiety shared by many members. Against these protests, the council of the Society argued that "Free Trade has become an accepted fact" and showed little interest in protectionist

---

[42] Ibid., 801.

[43] To understand the extent to which members of the Pharmaceutical Society were anxious about trade interests, see the correspondence from members to the council. See, for example, William Warren, "Chemists' Trade Interest," *Pharmaceutical Journal and Transactions*, April 19, 1890, 867; Warren, "Chemists' Trade Interest," *Pharmaceutical Journal and Transactions*, April 26, 1890, 886–887; and H. A. Thomas, "Chemists' Trade Interest," *Pharmaceutical Journal and Transactions*, May 8, 1890, 905–906.

[44] Campbell Stark, "Trade Protection: Its Present Relation to Pharmacy," *Pharmaceutical Journal and Transactions*, February 2, 1889, 618–623.

[45] "An Evening Meeting in Edinburgh," *Pharmaceutical Journal and Transactions*, April 26, 1890, 879–882.

legislation. On the contrary, in 1890 a proponent of price regulation wrote that he believed that "protection of the trade interests of chemists is to be sought for rather as the result of individual action and concerted co-operation among chemists themselves, than from any legislative measures."[46] Later that summer, another member declared that "the idea that the profession and the trade of pharmacy are distinct and incompatible is incorrect, for they are closely interwoven, and the most successful man from a professional point of view will probably draw the largest returns from his business."[47]

Trapped by a belief in pure professionalism, the council spared no pains to eliminate the unseemly trappings of the cash nexus from its professional boundaries. "Even with a reduction of the number belonging to the Society," the council declared, it would be a worthy sacrifice, "to secure greater unity of action within a more limited range for the advantage of pharmacy and its followers."[48] Thus, Carteighe, the Society's president, in the following annual general meeting centered his condemnation on commercial members, and in his presidential address he insisted that "this Society has dealt generously by the trade from its foundation; I say that it proposes to deal generously by the trade now; but the trade must take the trouble to understand our constitution, and must not expect us to say we will guarantee a man an increase of £100 a year in his profits if he will come into the Society."[49] After Carteighe's address the audience was apparently enraged, and one professionalist diehard shouted, "It is pharmacy! pharmacy! pharmacy! not trade! trade! trade! They are incompatibles; they will never mix. An explosion will result by and by if you try to mix them."[50] Against this flag waving by professionalists, dissenters such as Spink and Guyer, both proprietary medicine men, insisted, "unless something [is] done, and at no distant period, you

---

[46] "Chemists' Trade Interest," *Pharmaceutical Journal and Transactions*, April 12, 1890, 838–839.

[47] "Trade Interest," *Pharmaceutical Journal and Transactions*, June 14, 1890, 1027–1028.

[48] "Trade and Profession," *Pharmaceutical Journal and Transactions*, April 26, 1890, 877–878.

[49] Michael Carteighe, "Forty-Ninth Annual General Meeting," *Pharmaceutical Journal and Transactions*, 1891, 957–975.

[50] Ibid., 967.

will have to read the obituary notice of the Pharmaceutical Society."[51] Criticizing the council's excessive inclination for educational and academic requirements, they bemoaned the loss of the Society's *raison d'être* as an interested association and as an advocate for commercial traders. The growth in pecuniary opportunities revealed by an expanding health market highlighted very real economic motives and created conflicts of interest and identity within the professional pharmacy group.

However, by 1899, when Glyn-Jones was elected to the council of the Pharmaceutical Society, it seems that the mindset of pharmacists and chemists had changed: they no longer believed pure professionalism could withstand the forces of market capitalism. As a sign of this change, the Society had begun to seek ways for even rank-and-file member chemists to survive this new level of competition: in 1898, it planned to introduce an amendment to the Companies Acts prohibiting retail companies from selling medicines unless a qualified chemist was involved with the business. This amendment included the statement, "It shall be unlawful for any number of persons to form a company or corporation under the Limited Liabilities Act to engage in any business or profession which as individuals it would be unlawful for them to engage in."[52] In explaining this new law, Glyn-Jones criticized chain stores, noting that although they ran hundreds of stores, these drug retailers "employ not a single qualified man." This new legislation must have created a serious crisis for the retailers; consequently, they gradually explored ways of improving ties with professional pharmacists. Proprietary medicine manufacturers such as Elliman's, Ltd., Allen & Hanbury's, and Burroughs' Wellcome, fearing the damage that price-cutting activities would have on the public image of their brands, were gradually persuaded by Glyn-Jones' demands and consented to maintain basic retail prices. For their part, retail companies such as Boots began to realize that, in order to ensure the future success of their businesses, they needed to recruit competent and qualified professional chemists to staff their retail stores. Jesse Boot's joint-stock company, Boots Cash Chemist, for example, employed 434 qualified chemists in its 329 branches.[53] On the other hand, many quali-

---

[51] Ibid., 963.

[52] *Chemist and Druggist*, 53 (1898): 88-89.

[53] *Chemist and Druggist*, 61 (1902): 679; 63 (1903): 786.

fied chemists, having given up the idea of running their own small shops, preferred to work (whether or not as managers) at corporate-styled proprietary companies.

By 1900, a period of rapprochement between manufacturers and pharmacists began with retail price maintenance being accepted by most medical manufacturers. Multiple retail companies quietly stopped struggling with the PATA and Glyn-Jones, some of them even joining the Association, and agreed to adhere to fixed prices for medicines. By 1912, when Glyn-Jones became a member in the government's Select Committee on Patent Medicine, the period of opposition between manufacturers and professional chemists had ended. Glyn-Jones was even reported to have rendered enormous assistance to the retail companies in the hearings before the committee.[54] Furthermore, the fact that professional chemists tended to supply chemicals and extracts to these companies suggests the extent of the by-then closer collaboration between professional chemists and these proprietary companies.[55]

*Pecuniary Clashes: Doctors vs. Pharmaceutical Men*

Despite widely stated claims to the contrary, most proprietary medicine companies, with the exception of the truly bogus vendors of cures for cancer, syphilis, or consumption, were far from being the quack mongers that doctors alleged, and frequently sold health boosters and family medicines for minor ailments. Although from different educational and occupational backgrounds, both professional chemists and proprietary medicine men shared similar economic concerns, particularly an interest in protecting the pharmaceuticals trade and preventing medical doctors' entry into the health-related market. In the late nineteenth century, professional tension between medical men and pharmaceutical groups—in relation to doctors' dispensing of medicines, on the one hand, and chemists' prescribing of them, on the other—brought issues of professional boundaries to the fore. Pharmacists insisted that many

---

[54] J. A. Kenninham, "Memorial Tribute to Glyn-Jones," *Pharmaceutical Journal and Transactions*, 65 (1927): 292.

[55] *Report from the Select Committee on Patent Medicines*, 420. See also in this report John Charles Umney's reply to the questions by Henry Norman, the chair of the committee.

doctors were often far from professional. In 1864, the *Chemist and Druggist* warned that "many medicines are dispensed by doctors' wives, errand boys and other useful servants."[56] In the meeting of the Leeds Chemists' Association, Mr. Edward Thompson, a member, stated that although a doctor was "denouncing neighbouring druggists for depriving him of patients . . . he himself was keeping an open shop, poaching upon the domain of the druggists, and throwing down those external distinctions by means of which the public might judge between the surgeon and the druggist."[57] Indeed, up to eighty percent of medicines at that time were said to be dispensed in doctors' surgeries by unqualified assistants.[58] For that reason, professional chemists and the proprietary medicine manufacturers felt a growing antagonism toward medical doctors.

As a result, the House of Commons' Select Committee on Patent Medicine, in which medical doctors attempted to uncover the vices of patent medicines, also became an arena in which pharmaceutical men officially opposed what they held to be the unprofessional practices of doctors. In other words, the long patent medicine controversy, which extended from 1894 to 1914, was an economic battle over who—doctors or chemists—would dominate the burgeoning health industry market.

That the patent medicine controversy was not merely a campaign by medical doctors to enhance their own professional standing becomes clear when one realizes that the campaign ended up being furiously opposed by professional chemists. Far from being a simple issue of professional regulation, the essence of the patent medicine controversy manifested itself in a variety of changing social and pecuniary relations between doctors, chemists, and proprietary medicine manufacturers. While it was in doctors' interests to protect their dominance within the health market by preventing the dispensing of medications without their consultation, chemists and proprietary men found it in their interest to present a common front against the doctors' attempts to limit their activities.

---

[56] "Doctors and Chemists," *Chemist and Druggist*, 1 (1864): 77.
[57] "Mr. Edward Thompson on the Position of the Chemist and Druggist," *Chemist and Druggist*, 1 (1864): 11–12.
[58] S. W. F. Holloway, *The Royal Pharmaceutical Society of Great Britain, 1841–1991* (London: The Pharmaceutical Press, 1991), 84.

In 1909, under pressure from the BMA, the Privy Council requested that the Local Government Board distribute a questionnaire to all medical doctors of England and Wales on whether or not unqualified medications—including patent medicines—were detrimental to the health of their patients. The replies received from 1,600 doctors were published as a Local Government Blue Book.[59] In summary, this blue book advised that first, the composition of all advertised remedies should be stated; second, their prescription and analysis should be determined by government analysis at the vendors' expense; and third, the sale of infants' foods should be regulated. Furthermore, it strongly recommended preventing chemists from prescribing any medications, even for simple and trifling ailments. Of course, its attempt at prohibition—revealing the medical profession's ulterior intention to compel all persons to consult a doctor—provided further impetus to both pharmacists and manufacturers to shelter their trade's interests. Reacting to popular complaints that doctors were magnifying simple ailments into portentous proportions in order to charge larger bills, on December 3, 1910 the *Chemist and Druggist* carried an article stating that "the only logical outcome of this part of the Report would be the total prohibition of the sale of medicines not actually prescribed by medical men."[60] Fearful that state legislation would allow doctors to monopolize the health market, the Proprietary Articles Section of the London Chamber of Commerce (henceforth PAS), which had been formed on behalf of patent medicine business two years before, became a political bridgehead for both patent medicine men and pharmaceutical groups.[61]

[59] "The Practice of Medicine and Surgery by Unqualified Persons in the United Kingdom," Local Government Blue Book, Cd. 5422 (London: Wyman & Sons, 1909).

[60] "Chemists, Herbalists, Bonesetters, Itinerant Quacks," *Chemist and Druggist*, 77 (1910): 47.

[61] The archives of the Owners of the Proprietary Articles Section of the London Chamber of Commerce are held in the Guildhall Library, London. See Council Minutes, 1911–1914, MS 16,456, vol. 5: 42, 51, 94, 106, 131, 222, 287, and 348. The concerns of manufacturers were expressed in several articles published in *The Chamber of Commerce Journal*. See, for instance, "Patent Medicines," *The Chamber of Commerce Journal*, March 1911, 77; "The Sale of Patent Medicines," *The Chamber of Commerce Journal*, December 1911, 375; "The Sale of Patent Medi-

The PAS mainly consisted of the owners of more than four hundred firms and companies manufacturing patent medicines and foods, such as H. Davenport (J. H. Davenport, Ltd.), Joseph Beecham (Beecham Company), E. Pickering (F. Newbery & Son, Ltd.), C. R. Wylde (Thomas Keating), C. Ratcliffe (W. J. White, Ltd.).[62] It is important to note, however, that the ideology and membership of the PAS were closely associated with professional pharmacists, of whom many were members of the Pharmaceutical Society. For example, Hood, the originator of Hood's Sarsaparilla, was a qualified chemist who had served as an apprenticeship to Dr. Samuel Kidder. The first chairman of the PAS, John Charles Umney, was simultaneously a managing director of Wright, Layman, and Umney, Ltd., sellers of Marza Wine, and a senior member of the Pharmaceutical Society. He had won bronze and silver medals in practical chemistry, and for carrying out the Sale of Food and Drugs Act, had worked as a member of the Committee of Reference in Pharmacy for British Pharmacopœia, and the Joint Committee of the Society of Public Analysts and the Pharmaceutical Society.[63] (Fig. 1-2.)

In 1910 a professional chemist, Frederick Phillips, F.C.P. and F.C.S, teamed up with proprietary medicine men to publish *A Sequel to "Secret*

cines," *Chamber of Commerce Journal*, June 1912, 167; "Select Committee on Patent Medicines," *The Chamber of Commerce Journal*, June 1912, 177; and "Report of Select Committee on Patent Medicine," *The Chamber of Commerce Journal*, October 1914, 349–350.

[62] According to the description of London Chamber of Commerce, in the PAS "there are in all about 300 manufacturers of patent and proprietary medicines and foods, most, if not all, of whom are advertisers, many of them large advertisers, and in most cases firms of long standing, many having been in business over half-a-century, and the articles they own and manufacture are well known, approved of, and sold all over the world." Guildhall Library, MS 16, 718, London Chamber of Commerce, Owners of Proprietary Articles Section, Special Committee, 1 (April 5 and July 3, 1912), 15, 18, and attachments on pages 39, 119, 120.

[63] John Charles Umney was the first Chairman of the Owners of Proprietary Articles Section in the London Chamber of Commerce and was succeeded by Joseph Beecham on June 17, 1912. Umney had an influential career: he was one of the most influential professional chemists of the day, a member of the Pharmaceutical Society, and then president of the British Pharmaceutical Conference.

*Remedies"*, a strenuous rebuttal of the BMA's *Secret Remedies*.[64] In this treatise, Phillips compared self-medication of minor ailments to small repairs at home and denounced what he termed the medical profession's self-interested protectionism, by stating that "Every man has the right to select his own method of medication, and there would, probably, be a certain amount of resentment on the part of the public to any great interference [by the government]."[65] He also wrote that "the obvious intention of the book [*Secret Remedies*] is to prevent entirely the sale of any proprietary article, and to close absolutely the door against any medical advice or treatment being given, save that prescribed by their [doctors'] own august selves."[66] Compiling in this book official comments from leading patent medicine companies such as Beechams, Stedman, Veno, Figuroids, and Hood, Phillips showed that most of these patent medicines' originators were medical doctors or qualified chemists and that the ingredients analyzed by *Secret Remedies* were incorrect in numerous cases. He observed that "just as there are honest, and unscrupulous doctors (many being struck off the rolls periodically), so there may be good, and worthless secret remedies, and one has to discriminate in the employment of either."[67]

Furthermore, addressing the issue of "the dispensing doctor who frequently leaves the mixing of his medicine in the unqualified hands of his wife or housekeeper," Philips argued that "the Association [BMA], before spitefully and wrongfully attacking others, should see that its own members have a clean slate." He claimed that "The Club doctor, with his barrel of stock medicine, will probably have treated many diverse ailments with his nostrum. . . . I have no doubt that, generally, those mixtures were as good as any for the patients; but what one objects to is the pretension, that the physician carefully prepares separate and distinct prescriptions, for the varied conditions of different patients, coupled with the suggestion that proprietary medicines are 'cure-alls.'"[68] It is true that British

---

[64] George Frederick Phillips, *A Sequel to "Secret Remedies"* (London: Sixpence Net, 1910).

[65] Ibid., 56.

[66] Ibid., 52.

[67] Ibid., 9.

[68] Ibid., 53.

medical doctors, even in the early twentieth century, were habitually prescribing or giving their patronage to certain proprietary remedies. Not surprisingly, Phillips harshly criticized doctors' imposture, insisting that "A pair of bandits armed with knives could hardly slash into one another more than fully qualified medicos of to-day attack those who do not agree with them. There seems to be one point on which medical men and patent medicine vendors do agree, and that is the uncertainty of 'expert' opinion."[69]

The tactics of the PAS in its war against doctors to spotlight the "purely class interest of the medical profession" must have been somewhat successful, at least in the realm of journalism.[70] Replying to the PAS's circular, "Private and Confidential," which had been directed to the owners of newspapers and journals, the *Daily Press, John Bull*, and the *Daily Dispatch* joined the counterattack against the medical profession in articles with provocative titles such as "Agitation that Imperils a Huge Industry, Chamber of Commerce Protest." On May 18, 1912, for instance, an article in *John Bull* acidly noted, "The doctors themselves utilised the same formulae as that on which these medicines are compounded, but charge four or five time as much for them."[71] About two weeks earlier, the *Daily Dispatch* had explained the situation as follows:

> The value to the public of patent medicines is so well established and so clearly recognised (say the proprietors and vendors of these articles) that any attempts to impose restrictions in regard to the sale of these effective, cheap, and easily procurable remedies would be certain to arouse wide-spread and bitter resentment. Patent

---

[69] Ibid., 55.

[70] "Private and Confidential," dated March 18, 1911, was circulated by the London Chamber of Commerce to owners of many newspapers. This copy of the document, signed by Thomas J. Barratt, the Chairman of the London Chamber of Commerce, is held in the Archives of the Wellcome Institute of the History of Medicine, SA/BMA/C.429.

[71] Extracts of articles related to the London Chamber of Commerce's agitation against doctors are held in the Archives of the Wellcome Institute. See SA/BMA/C.429/9 for a May 4, 1912 article in *The Newspaper Owners*; SA/BMA/C.429/10 for a April 27, 1912 article in the *Daily Press*; SA/BMA/C.429/11 for a May 18, 1912 article in *John Bull*; and SA/BMA/C.429/14 for a May 7, 1912 article in the *Daily Dispatch*.

medicines, it is argued, save doctors' bills, and so long as these remedies are wholesome and efficacious it is doubtful whether the public desire very much to know just what they are composed of. . . . The great majority of people know their ailments. They know when they have a cold, or a headache, or a bilious attack, and they know which proprietary remedy will give them relief.[72]

In the following year, the PAS published a booklet entitled "The Agitation against Patent and Proprietary Medicines and Foods." Highlighting doctors' pecuniary interests, the pamphlet asked, "Is everyone to be forced to go to a doctor when afflicted with some little ailment?"[73] The secret of the formulas and the trade mark titles underwritten by them, the book emphasized, was the only protection for the proprietary medicine business and should be protected by the Trade Marks Act of 1875. Disclosing the formulas of all advertised remedies as doctors were demanding, the booklet reminded its readers, would mean the ruin of every proprietary medicine business, because once the formula for a famous proprietary medicine was published, its title or trade name would become *publici juris.* Thus the famous Beecham's Pills, for example, could be cloned by rival manufacturers and marketed at a lower cost; examples would be "Smith's Beecham's Pills" or "Jones's Beecham's Pills," "Beecham's Pills, made by W. Jones, according to the actual formula published by Beecham himself on every box of his pills." By printing "Smith" or "Jones" in very small letters and the title "Beecham's Pills" in large bold letters, imitators could thus act as parasites on the capital invested by Beecham in the development and manufacture of its products.[74] Demanding the disclosure of the formulas of all proprietary remedies, the booklet insisted, would be a draconian measure, and the equivalent of throwing the baby out with the bathwater. The relatively few noxious nostrums and their vicious advertisements then in circulation instead could be dealt with

---

[72] "Patent Medicines: Agitation that Imperils a Huge Industry," *The Daily Dispatch*, May 7, 1912.

[73] *The Agitation Against Patent and Proprietary Medicines and Food, the 'Owners of Proprietary Articles Section' of The London Chamber of Commerce,* published in Oxford Court, Cannon Street, London, 1912. This is held in the Archives of the Guildhall Library, MS 16,688, 8, no. 14.

[74] Ibid., 7, no. 10–12.

through existing laws, such as the Sale of Food and Drugs Acts of 1875 and the Indecent Advertisements Act of 1889. Moreover, the PAS claimed, the public's interest in this matter was exclusively in medical results; they had little interest in ingredients. "If it is advisable for people to know what ingredients they are taking," the booklet asked, "why should not a physician write his prescription in English instead of Latin? Why should it be compulsory in the one case if not in the other?"[75] It stressed that in 1911, among 419 deaths caused by narcotics such as morphine and strychnine and 486 deaths caused by carbolic acid and oxalic acid, not a single one was due to a proprietary medicine. Indeed, it continued, the poisons not infrequently prescribed by the medical profession rarely appeared in proprietary drugs because of the restrictions of the Poisons and Pharmacy Act. "Fatalities resulting from the mistakes of doctors, many reported and many not," it concluded, "are by no means infrequent."[76] Thus, the witnesses and debates between doctors and proprietary men in the Select Committee in the House of Commons reveal vividly the medico-social environment of the period, in which doctors entered in the competitive health market.

One liability that doctors faced was that at the turn of the century, their knowledge about *materia medica* was so limited that they were to some extent dependent upon the manufacturers of patent medicines. As John Lawson, manager of Daisy, Ltd., and the proprietor of the famous "Daisy" cure for headache and neuralgia, stated before the Select Committee, many companies sent representatives to doctors to explain the therapeutic effects of a particular drug and to get them to prescribe their proprietary medicines.[77] When Dr. Alfred Cox, then BMA's newly appointed medical secretary, appeared as a witness to confirm that doctors never prescribed secret remedies, insisting "that is a very long and honourable tradition in the profession . . . not to order a remedy unless you know what is in it," his words were soon contradicted by another witness, the consulting and analytical chemist Ernest Parry. As a Fellow of the Chemical Society and a Member of the Society of Public Analysts, Parry testified that doctors often ordered proprietary remedies that were "secret

---

[75] Ibid., 12, no. 20.
[76] Ibid., 13, no. 22.
[77] Ibid., 583, no. 11001–11008.

remedies" and whose composition they did not in fact know.[78] Like Lawson, Parry explained that doctors often gained their information about patent medicines from manufacturers' salesmen. The debate between Parry and Cox showed the acrimony between the two professions about the legitimacy of each other's practices. Cox began by asking the chemist:

Do I understand that in your opinion the travelers[sic] for the manufacturers of proprietary medicines to a large extent educate the doctor in chemical knowledge?" —— [Parry responded] I do not think they educate him very much in chemical knowledge, but I think he depends for his therapeutics to some extent on them.

You surprise me rather, because former witnesses have suggested that doctors are peculiarly lacking in sufficient chemical knowledge? —— Of course, the time placed at a medical man's disposal for chemistry, pharmacy, and therapeutics during his curriculum is very short.

It is going much further, if I might venture to say, and to suggest that doctors are lacking in therapeutic knowledge? —— Yes.

Would you think they were more lacking in therapeutic knowledge than in chemical knowledge? —— I would not like to say lacking, but their training is such that the time devoted to pharmacy.

What I do not quite understand is this, whether you want to suggest that a particular mode or combination of well-known remedies is what the travelers[sic] are able to teach the doctors about, or whether you go so far as to suggest that the actual constitutes themselves are not, so far as their therapeutic value is concerned, sufficiently known to the doctors? —— I think that there are a very large number of new combinations of these drugs made by the private firms from their own knowledge, and they then present these to the medical profession, telling them, "This combination is exceedingly successful, will you try it?"[79]

Similarly, another chemist observed, "the person who popularises one of these things under a fancy name is a person who spends a great deal of

[78] Ibid., 596, no. 11245; 597, no. 11255–11258; and 124, no. 2055.
[79] *Report from the Select Committee on Patent Medicines,* 630, no. 11845–11851.

money in bringing it to the notice of the medical profession and so forth in order really to educate them."[80] Moreover, as another witness disclosed, doctors were commonly shareholders in the proprietary medicine companies—a finding that led the committee to ask what was proper medical etiquette in prescribing and dispensing medicine.[81]

As the hearings before the committee progressed, it became clear that there was furious competition between doctors and chemists in pursuit of a lucrative health market. In his questions to Cox, the chemist Glyn-Jones, then a member of the Committee and the president of the PATA, reminded him that the medical profession's skirts were far from clean: the *British Medical Journal (BMJ)* itself had recently carried advertisements for bogus medicines such as Bromidia and Angier's Emulsion.[82] Jabbing Cox further with the fact that the doctor himself had said to the London Chamber of Commerce that the medical profession's agitation was "for reasons purely selfish," Glyn-Jones attempted to highlight the doctors' money-grubbing interests behind their self-righteous agitation. To queries about what doctors found to be fraudulent in the case of Beecham's Pills, Cox answered, "We are performing a public duty in pointing out that he [the public] could get the same things very much more cheaply."[83] Glyn-Jones then asked the doctor:

> Let me take another instance; take the case of a doctor who is treating a chronic case; the doctor does not always see the patient when they come for "repeats" of their medicine? —— [Cox responded] No.
>
> They come and say, "I want a bottle of my medicine," and the dispenser dispenses it and gives it to them? —— Yes.
>
> The doctor himself has rendered no service in regard to that? —— No.
>
> But there is a charge made for that medicine? —— Yes, I think that is customary, certainly.

---

[80] Charles Umney, ibid., 450, no. 7886.

[81] Ibid., 428, no. 7486.

[82] Ibid., 138, no. 2329.

[83] Ibid., 141, no. 2411.

That is generally 1s. 6d or 2s.? —— I suppose it varies.

Supposing the patient took his medicine away and analysed it, and found it only cost a penny, you do not suggest that he would have an action for fraud against the doctor? ——I do not.

So that really there is no difference so far as the cost of the thing is concerned, between the doctor and the chemist, or anyone else, where the doctor actually charges for the medicine supplied? —— Quite so.[84]

Since the overcharging by doctors was in many ways analogous to that of the traders, Alfred Cox was finally forced to admit that "there is a good deal to be said for all the dispensing being taken out of the hands of the doctors, and all the prescriptions being taken out of the hands of the chemists."[85]

Witnesses' repeated denunciations of trade unionism within the medical establishment must have touched doctors' raw nerves. To deny their own pecuniary advantage from suppressing patent medicines, some doctors went so far as to suggest the possibility that doctors in fact benefited from the ineffectiveness of such medicines. Indeed, Dr. Chapple attempted to lead doctors to state that the delay of treatment caused by taking proprietary medicines at an early stage of a disease would cause a patient's condition to deteriorate, thereby increasing the doctor's work and eventually creating greater revenue for the doctor.[86] For example, Chapple asked Dr. Cushny, Professor of Pharmacology at University College, the following question, after suggesting that a delay in initial treatment would indeed prolong a doctor's involvement:

Therefore they [doctors] derive a profit [from quack remedies]? —— Yes. I did not quite like the idea of the medical profession deriving a profit from it, and I did not understand exactly what you are aiming at.

Would it be true to say that it is in the financial interest of the medical profession that this traffic in patent medicines should go

[84] Ibid., 142, no. 2419–2425.
[85] Ibid., 143, no. 2429.
[86] Ibid., 107, no. 1691–1698.

on? —— I really could not determine exactly whether the medical men lose more or gain more by this traffic. It would be very difficult to say, and I should not like to make a definite statement.

Is it not the case that it is a popular notion that the agitation by the medical profession against secret remedies is due to the fact that they look upon quackery as competition which lessens their profits? —— Yes.[87]

In asking these questions, Chapple wanted to show that doctors were acting for the public benefit in opposing patent medicines because their suppression would remove a source of doctors' "indirect profit."

The questioning in November and December of 1912 of John Charles Umney, the first chairman of the Proprietary Articles Section, brought the debate and antagonism between doctors and chemists to its climax. Throughout his testimony, Umney stressed that doctors' agitation against proprietary medicine benefited not the public but only the doctors themselves. "Supposing it were possible tomorrow to abolish all existing proprietary medicines," Chapple asked, "who would suffer most?" Umney answered, "I would rather say, who would benefit most? The medical profession would benefit most." Chapple again asked, "I am coming to that. Who would suffer most?" Umney immediately replied, "The public, of course." Astonished by his answer, Chapple several times tried to get Umney to admit that, in such a situation, people would go to a dispensing chemist such as Umney rather than a doctor:

I suggest that if you could abolish all the advertised remedies to-day for disease, in 99 out of every 100 cases those who consume those remedies would not go to doctors, but would go to pharmacists? —— [Umney replied] I do not agree with you at all. I do not think they would go to the pharmacists. If I had thought they would all go to the pharmacists I would not have appeared here, because my trade is almost entirely with the pharmacists.[88]

Do you not think it is the case that the profession of pharmacist really suffers from the prevalence in the proprietary article industry

---

[87] Ibid., 343, no. 5773–5777.
[88] Ibid., 431, no. 7528–7534.

of advertising? Is not there a legitimate inference from these replies
that the profession of pharmacy in this country suffers from the
proprietary articles business —— The profession of pharmacy
suffers in this country mostly from the medical profession doing
their own dispensing.[89]

After publishing the exposé *Secret Remedies*, medical doctors wanted to
demonstrate the fraudulent nature of patent medicine vendors in tandem
with professional pharmacists in the official arena of parliamentary
committees. What came to light, however, was that the pharmacists regarded doctors as more harmful than proprietary manufacturers to their
pecuniary and professional interests. These parliamentary committees
indeed reveal that doctors and pharmacists were struggling with each
other in the early twentieth century—a clash that shows how medical
capitalism had intruded into the field of medicine.

### *Charles Umney and the Market Mechanism of Medicine*

Pecuniary clashes, however, did not entirely account for the confron-
tation between doctors and pharmacists. The record of the parliamentary
debates between them also highlighted the fundamental difference in
their views of health and the means by which people should acquire it.
This difference is very interesting and important for fully understanding
the patent medicine controversy and its significance at the turn of the
twentieth century—an issue not previously explored by historians. The
two sets of arguments were strikingly different, but more importantly,
doctors believed that health should be treated as the domain of professional medical services, whereas pharmacists, as typified by Umney and
his testimony before the Select Committee, viewed consumers' obses-
sions with health as arising out of the culture of commodification.
Consumption entails commodification, the process by which services
were to be replaced by goods, and this is likely what doctors saw as most
objectionable about the proliferation of patent medicines. Doctors, of
course, wanted their services to be predominant in every sector of the
health industry. By contrast, pharmacists, emphasizing the right to
self-medicate, argued that the commodification of health advanced safe

---

[89] Ibid., 428, no. 7477; 448, no. 7852; and 450, no. 7890.

medication, at least for minor ailments. Answering Chapple's question regarding the safety of patent medicine, Umney insisted that "The proprietary man has spent a large sum in making a reputation, and he is going to maintain that reputation by seeing that everything is as perfect as it can be."[90] Umney thus centered his condemnation of doctors' negligence on the fact that patent medicine and people's use of it to treat minor ailments were phenomena operating largely according to economic principles and market mechanisms.

In his statement as a representative of the PAS to the London Chamber of Commerce, Umney first of all stressed that patent medicine should be seen in the same light as any other ordinary commodity. By arguing that "the vendors of proprietary medicines should be, and are, like the vendors of other articles of commerce," Umney objected to doctors' claims that advertisements and labels of patent medicine should be controlled with special regulation.[91] He argued that the "large powers vested in the Director of Public Prosecutions, in the police, in the Board of Trade, in the Board of Customs and Excise, and in the Pharmaceutical Society" could eliminate the most egregious cases of bogus medicine sales, such as (first) those of "abortifacients and anti-conception remedies and remedies purporting to affect sexual virility;" (second) "remedies advertised or held out as specially applicable to ailments peculiar to women;" or, (third) "remedies claiming to cure the diseases of cancer, consumption, rupture (other than by mechanical appliances), locomotor ataxy, Bright's disease, diabetes, and syphilis." Umney also emphasized that "The members of this section [of PAS] desire to dissociate themselves entirely from this class of business."[92] According to Umney, bona-fide patent medicine businesses dealt mainly with minor ailments and health-maintaining elixirs for everyday self-medication. And Umney was right. What were advertised most in the market, as will be explored at length in the next chapter, were not medicines for diseases, which needed professional diagnosis or treatment, but ones for "little health"—such as indigestion, nervousness, and sleeplessness—as well as health-boosters to be used to gain energy or robust health. These results were what the era's health-

---

[90] Ibid., 432, no. 7544.
[91] Ibid., 372, no. 6275.
[92] Ibid., 373, no. 6275.

obsessed consumers demanded. They were free to choose what they wanted amidst a blizzard of commodities, the more so since they could change from one medical commodity to another in the pursuit of the most suitable product for them.

Umney's recognition of patent medicines as marketable commodities led him to condemn doctors for their misleading presentation in *Secret Remedies* and their attempt to evaluate a medicine's value solely by the cost of its ingredients. From the economic point of view, Umney said, "the estimation of the [medicine's] costs in that book is absolutely ridiculous . . . [and] the allegations are absurd as omitting, even if they were true, which is not the case, the principal item of cost in any article put on the market."[93] In any market system, Umney noted, consumers would expect to pay not simply for the chemical and raw components, but for the capital invested in developing the final products. The doctors' exposé did not convey "any reference to labour, to packing, or to marketing in any shape or form. One might as well say that the value of a motor-car was the value of the steel in it."[94]

Here Umney clearly expressed his notion that a proprietary medical item was a mass-produced commodity, belonging therefore to a category entirely different from medical services. In producing commodities, he argued, a different accounting calculation should be applied than the one used for providing services. Whereas services could be demanded and supplied according to individual requests, commodities, which were uniformly produced on a massive scale, became less expensive through their economy of scale. Low cost, he insisted, was a significant benefit that only market mechanisms could realize. Umney suggested that "the price of a present proprietary article" was less than the one a dispensing chemist could charge for the same article.[95]

In addition to the lower cost of mass-produced proprietary medicines, Umney also stressed their "uniformity" of production to further show that "the public greatly benefited by the production of proprietary articles." During the Select Committee proceedings, Chapple asked whether "the profession of pharmacy in this country would be willing to do away

---

[93] Ibid., 435, no. 7627.
[94] Ibid., 370, no. 6247 and 6248; 422, no. 7627.
[95] Ibid., 432, no.7546.

with proprietary articles, and could, and would supply to the public all that proprietary articles now supply, and find them cheaper and better articles, and that in their hands it would be safer than in the hands of the advertisers?" To Chapple's question, Umney replied, "I do not agree with you at all. I say that a proprietary medicine made on a big scale by a man who has a big stake is far more likely to be uniform than is a particular medicine made up by various people all over the country."[96] Umney urged that uniformly constituted medicines, distributed through the market system to local districts where people had little access to consulting doctors, contributed broadly to the public benefit.

Thus, in rebutting Chapple's suggestion that the safety and benefit of the public would be better off if individual pharmacists were to dispense to each patient, Umney argued:

> The money the man has spent in popularising a patent medicine is a reason why he is going to be very careful of his own reputation, and for that reason he is going to produce the best of everything, which might not be the case in the case of prescriptions dispensed in different parts of the country, with drugs in different conditions of staleness.[97]

Running throughout Umney's arguments, it is clear, is an assumption that the value and use of medicines should be dependent upon market forces. Reflecting people's prudence and tastes, the market, he asserted, would destroy sub-standard and non-beneficial medicines and promote the most effective ones. In order to gain significant commercial success, the commodity must be of distinct medical value. The chairman in one session asked Umney, "You say you are not aware that any proprietary medicine has at any time had more than a transient[sic] commercial success, unless possessed of distinct medicinal value?" Umney replied, "Yes. That is my opinion; I know of no proprietary medicine which has been a commercial success which has no valuable properties. The public are not going to be fooled very long."[98] A dyed-in-the-wool free-marketer, Umney simply objected to any interference with market mechanisms.

---

[96] Ibid., 448, no. 7852.

[97] Ibid., 432, no. 7545.

[98] Ibid., 374, nos. 6295 and 6296.

Only through long-term competition, he believed, could the best products and optimal economic results be achieved. The availability of numerous alternative medicines, advertised as having the same medical value, would lead to healthy competition and ensure rational and fair business practices, which would ultimately advance public benefit and safety.

## Conclusion

In conclusion, it is incorrect to consider that the doctors' exposé campaign against proprietary medicines in *Secret Remedies* was primarily motivated by their professional moral code and ideals. Behind the scenes and arguments of the patent medicine brouhaha, there lay both the doctors' strong antipathy toward the market-driven entrepreneurship of early pharmaceutical developments, and the growth of medical capitalism. The broader context of the patent medicine controversy was the triangular battle over the cash nexus between the medical profession, professional pharmacists, and proprietary medicine manufacturers.

A number of historians have argued that the emergence of patent medicine and the controversy surrounding it both illustrate the extent to which the doctors' professional domain came to extend to all aspects of medical care, and also demonstrate the doctors' growing professional uniformity. But this interpretation is problematic, as the next chapter shows in its exploration of the cultural and economic implications of the uproar caused by the unforeseen boom of the patent medicine business. One indicator of this boom was that late-Victorian society witnessed a superabundance of medical commodities including mechanical machines, gadgets, and appliances. Another indicator was the prevalence of a health culture in which people regarded health as purchasable through what can be called "therapeutic commodities" that caught up consumers in a fantasy of achieving a more healthy body and a more vigorous and energetic life. Such commodification of health went hand-in-hand with the mid-nineteenth century rise of entrepreneurialism in British society. In promoting and profiting from this new therapeutic ethos, the health industry as a whole became more capitalistic, a trend that medical doctors could not ignore. Looking at the consumer angle and at the traditional medical establishment's connections with high commerce, however, enables us to find that professionalization was not, in fact, the sole or primary guiding ethos for many traditionally trained doctors.

The investigations in Chapter Two show that the traditional account of medicine's professionalization, although still useful as a sociological analysis of the medical elite, fails to explore fully the patent medicine controversy. Examined within a broader social context, this controversy was a long one, extending from 1884 to 1914, and it was a signal event in the growing economic struggle between doctors, pharmacists, and proprietary manufacturers: in varying degrees they were all in pursuit of the profits to be gained from the expanding health market—and very competitively, too, behind the façade of their oft-articulated professional ideals. At a minimum, the sociological story of medical professionalization needs to be reconsidered: in the context of the burgeoning commodity culture and the increased commercialization and democratization of society, professional men need to be considered as full participants in the broader economic, cultural, and industrial developments of the era. Looking at increasing commercialization and the emergence of professionalization together, therefore, will enable us to understand that late-Victorian medical practitioners were less under the sway of the medical profession's traditional ethos than has been previously thought—in fact, their attitudes and practices were permeated by market forces, laissez-faire ideologies, and the growth of medical capitalism.

# CHAPTER 2

# Purchasing Health: Medical Consumerism and the Commodity Culture, 1884–1914

Just as in the past, modern-day consumers of medicine and medical services also struggle with a number of anxieties. Are the drugs really beneficial? Who guarantees the effectiveness of medicines, and how is this done? Where is the boundary between legitimate and illegitimate medicine? And although we seek medicine and medical services at a reasonable price, we also fear market forces, and laissez-faire competition might encourage quacks and other medically dubious enterprises. Indeed, these issues date back a long time.

As is the case today, the nature of late-nineteenth-century medicine raised doctors' anxiety about protecting their professional dignity and moral code from the unrelenting capitalization and commercialization of society. Acting as watchdogs over the conduct of members of their profession, traditionalist doctors strongly opposed the entry of market forces into medical practice and often censured their peers who were deemed to be associating too closely with commercial medicine. Permitting market mechanisms to encroach upon medicine, they felt, endangered it as a profession.

The case of patent medicine suggests the extent to which "modern" consumerism had invaded the realm of medicine. This is especially evident in the fact that doctors, finding the power of their professional authority or the extent of state regulation limited, felt that they had to alert consumers directly through publications that sought to alarm. Behind the ongoing professionalism in the public sphere of medicine, it is also true that people began to grow more wary of established medicine and started to regard their health exclusively as their own private concern. As this chapter argues, this shift also suggests of people's changing mentality within the privatized realm of the burgeoning medical commodities market. In focusing on the rise of people's increasingly "modern" expectations concerning medicine, as well as in exploring the convoluted imbrications between public medicine and private health, this chapter casts much new light on established views of Victorian medicine. Moreover, by examining advertisements of patent medicines, this chapter also spotlights the ways in which late Victorians were consumers of medicine and other health-related goods in a cultural and psychological milieu similar to that of today.

Focusing on the patent medicine controversy, the first question to be asked is, where do the public and private spheres manifest themselves and at what points do they overlap? The campaign by the British Medical Association (BMA) and Ernest Hart against the proprietary medicine trade was sometimes denounced as supporting a kind of "medical trade-unionism," which would protect doctors' pecuniary dominance over all areas of medical service.[1] Against this charge, medical doctors argued that only the professional expertise of medical men could save the public, "inasmuch as no class of men [other than the medical profession] have a better opportunity of forming a correct opinion as to the injurious results of the present unrestricted sale of these preparations."[2] Medical doctors also insisted they were protecting a naïve public from the evils of manipulative advertising. The 1914 *Report from the Select Committee on Patent Medicines* summarized the view of medical professionals as follows:

> For all practical purposes, the British law is powerless to prevent any person from procuring any drug, or making any mixture, whether potent or without any therapeutic activity whatever (so long as it does not contain a scheduled poison), advertising it in any decent terms as a cure for any disease or ailment, recommending it by bogus and selling it under any name he chooses, on the payment

---

[1] "Patent Medicine," *British Medical Journal,* 1 (March 29, 1884): 627.
[2] Ibid.

of a small stamp duty, for any price he can persuade *a credulous public*
to pay.[3]

As this remark suggests, the medical profession adhered to an old-
fashioned image of gullible consumers misled by flamboyant advertisers.

However, it is worth asking, were Victorian consumers of patent
medicines really foolish victims of capitalistic traders? Were those customers suffering from serious diseases? Were they really desperate in their
dash to look for remedies? Were they so pitiful and gullible that the elusive
language of advertisements could easily deceive them into buying inef-
fective drug products? What activities did advertising propaganda include
and what roles did this play in selling patent medicine? And, what were the
strategies that patent medicine businessmen took to persuade consumers,
what form did their ads take, and why did they choose these methods? I
believe we should free ourselves from the assumption that consumers of
commercially available drugs and remedies were so passive as to naïvely
believe the catchphrases used in advertisements. In fact, to fully understand the patent medicine controversy, it is important to reexamine the
role of these consumers as active participants in a highly developed consumer society, and to see them as mature and modern consumers of
medicine and medical care.

The second half of the nineteenth century witnessed not only the
development of a new level of industrialism, as Hobsbawm has shown,
but also the early signs of mass production and mass consumption.[4]
Commodity fetishism, such as at the Great Exhibition in 1851, dazzled
Victorian society with the wondrous new things provided by market capitalism, and hope was proffered that, in time, such marvels would penetrate all levels of society;[5] as one advertising agency put it, "In food, dress,
drink, smoking, etc., the poor want what the rich have as a matter of
course, and the best is done to obtain it."[6] In fact, by the waning years of

---

[3] Italics added. *Report from the Select Committee on Patent Medicines, together with Proceedings of the Committee, Minutes of Evidence, and Appendices, Ordered by the House of
Commons, to be Printed* (London: Wyman and Sons, Ltd., 4 August 1914), ix.

[4] E. J. Hobsbawm, *Industry and Empire* (London: Penguin Books, 1968).

[5] See, for instance, Asa Briggs, *Victorian Things* (London: Penguin Books, 1988).

[6] *Smith's Advertising Agency, Successful Advertising: Its Secrets Explained* (London:
Smith's Advertising Agency, 1885), 62.

the century commodity culture had indeed spread noticeably to all classes of society. "What were once luxuries are now necessaries," an advertising agency wrote in 1885.[7] As many historians have argued, it was the middle-class family who became the focus of most advertisers' efforts. The steady progression of earnings, together with a sense of ease that came with a more mature form of industrialization, surrounded the middle class with material acquirements, bodily comforts, and a wider range of entertainments. The middle-class began to seek new products and spend more money on self-indulgent items, such as scented soaps, finer furniture, pianos, gramophones, watches, jewelry, and electric devices, all of which entered the domain of people's everyday lives.[8] Victorian London, in particular, was becoming more intensely developed, promoting the prosperity of the middle class, and flamboyant, sparkling, and often seductive areas of consumption were being created: not unlike consumers today, *fin-de-siècle* Londoners lived in a world of commodified abundance and a mass culture of spectacular consumption. New urbanized public spaces such as arcades, cafés, theatres, department stores, music halls, and boulevards were emerging and becoming common elements of city life.

*Consumerism, Advertising, and Modern Hedonism*

The literature on the history of consumption and commodity culture is massive. However, determining when Britain became a modern consumer society has never been a matter of agreement.[9] Since the pioneering book *The Birth of a Consumer Society* by McKendrick, Brewer, and Plumb, many studies have focused on the eighteenth century or else on the mid-Victorian period as the heyday of the consumer movement—in which "men pursue 'luxuries' where they had previously bought 'decen-

---

[7] Ibid., 2.

[8] Fraser W. Hamish, *The Coming of the Mass Market, 1850–1914* (London: Archon Books, 1981).

[9] For example, J. Thirsk has argued that the early Industrial Revolution was propelled by the seventeenth-century manufacturing industry, which produced luxurious consumer goods for an emergent middle class. See, for instance, *Economic Policy and Projects: The Development of a Consumer Society in Early Modern England* (Oxford: Clarendon Press, 1978).

cies,' and 'decencies' where they had previously bought only 'necessities.'"[10] But recent historians have also shifted their analysis from the eighteenth century to the nineteenth century and afterward. It was during these later periods when the much expanded commodity market increased a consumer's liberty to choose from among various attractive alternatives; it was a time when an abundance of images and information about different commodities began to foster the consumer's imagination; it was a era in which a democratic consumer ideology, underpinned by personal autonomy, emerged to assert the right of equal access for all to those commodities.[11]

The life-styles, patterns, and peculiarities of consuming agents have also been a controversial subject among scholars. As consumption connotes material luxury and prodigality, which historically belonged to aristocratic extravagance, the emergence of large-scale consumption in society was often associated with an entrepreneurial desire to emulate higher classes and to ascend to the topmost levels of a rapidly industrializing society. As a result, scholars working on this subject have frequently attributed modern consumerism to the full-fledged rise of the

---

[10] N. McKendrick, J. Brewer, and J. H. Plumb, *The Birth of a Consumer Society: The Commercialisation of Eighteenth-Century England* (London: Hutchinson, 1982). By arguing that the Industrial Revolution was made feasible only by a vigorous desire to consume the products of industry, this trio of historians successfully rehabilitated a pre-existing emphasis on the supply-side economy advanced by socio-economic historians. They suggest that in addition to the Industrial Revolution, another revolution occurred in England: consumer desire for marketable goods. The key factor the three historians regard as explaining the rise of the consumer society was the desire for social emulation. "In imitation of the rich," McKendrick writes, "the middle ranks spent more frenziedly than ever before, and in imitation of them the rest of society joined in as best they might." Hence consumer demand, according to McKendrick, was fueled most by people's desire to climb the ladder of class strata and social competition.

[11] For a discussion on the chronology of the rise of consumerism, see Peter N. Sterns, "Stages of Consumerism: Recent Work on the Issues of Periodization," *Journal of Modern History*, 69 (1997). Recently many historians have refocused on commodity culture by analyzing advertisements as cultural artifacts. On various facets of goods and consumption, see, in particular the voluminous work, John Brewer and Roy Porter, eds., *Consumption and the World of Goods* (London: Routledge, 1994).

middle class.[12] The psychology of consumerism is explained as a mimicry of near-nobles or—at least—one's immediately higher social stratum, as well as businessmen's inventiveness in providing eye-catching products for an industrializing society. In a Veblenesque interpretation, if consumption were motivated by a desire to "display" one's wealth or "pecuniary strength," male dominance in commercial activities should have been sustained.[13] Meanwhile, some historians have reversed this male-domination scenario to argue that, enchanted by aristocratic behaviors of consumption, women-as-consumers emasculated men by having them indulge in a lifestyle of luxury and prodigality.

However, scholars have argued recently that in the increasingly modern consumer society of the nineteenth century, women were no longer

---

[12] McKendrick et al. have emphasized the rise of the middle class. Colin Jones, moreover, argues that during the French Revolution, the middle class played an important role in the growth of consumption: see Jones, "The Great Chain of Buying: Medical Advertisement, the Bourgeois Public Sphere, and the Origins of the French Revolution," *American Historical Review*, 101 (1996): 13–40. For nineteenth-century consumption, see also Rosalind Williams, *Dream Works: Mass Consumption in Late Nineteenth Century France* (Berkeley: University of California Press, 1982). Also, Simon J. Bronner, ed., *Consuming Visions: Accumulation and Display of Goods in America, 1880–1920* (New York: Norton & Company, 1989) suggests a consideration of consumer behavior during the period covered by this book. Another important work is by Chandra Mukerji, *From Graven Images: Patterns of Modern Materialism* (New York: Columbia University Press, 1983). Mukerji elegantly uses the trade in prints as the basis of her own historical analysis.

[13] In his 1919 study, *The Theory of the Leisure Class*, Thorstein Veblen argues that the central motive for consumption is not simply to satisfy needs but rather to "display" one's wealth or "pecuniary strength." Thorstein Veblen, *The Theory of the Leisure Class: An Economic Study of Institutions* (London: George Allen and Unwin, 1957), 31. Consumption, according to Veblen, is also motivated by such interpersonal reciprocity as what he calls the "bandwagon" and the "snob" effect, wherein consumers' behaviors influence one another in such a way that some people desire to buy goods because everyone else buys them (bandwagon) or choose not to buy for the same reason (snobbery). See Harvey Leibenstein, "Bandwagon, Snob, and Veblen Effects in the Theory of Consumers' Demand," in Edwin Mansfield, ed., *Microeconomics: Selected Readings* (New York: Norton, 1982), 12–30. Thus, arguing that human motivation is based in competition, envy, and vanity, Veblen suggests that people strive for scarce commodities to emulate higher social status.

seen as credulous tender females who were overwhelmed by luxurious and sensuous commodities produced and provided by male entrepreneurs.[14] In her *Consuming Angels: Advertising and Victorian Women*, for example, Lori Ann Loeb describes "empowered women" who as consumers were independently and aggressively pursuing their own luxury and their own entertainment. Even though the women in advertisements never lost the femininity of the ideal Victorian family woman, Loeb argues, they often expressed masculine tastes and engaged in many male occupations and pastimes. "The victim may not be as victimized as she appears," in the private sphere, claims Loeb. "As society moved from an ethic of production to an ethic of consumption, the role of women as household purchasers acquired new social significance . . . [as] . . . the focus of family life."[15] In addition, Loeb's consuming women bought goods in pursuit of pleasure and satisfaction through their acquired material objects, and wielded the power of imagination or "self-illusory hedonism" (an expression borrowed from Collin Campbell's *The Romantic Ethic and the Spirit of Modern Consumerism*).[16] Influenced by Harold Perkin, however, Loeb oddly insists that what sustained this consumerism was "the triumph of the entrepreneurial ideal" in the male-dominated middle class culture, which by the late Victorian era had achieved "political democratization" and turned its attention to "material democratization."[17] She argues that the puritan ethic of self-help, temperance and competition, together with the victory of state protectionism, generated an egalitarian concept of equal accessibility to greater amounts of new commodities, but she does

---

[14] Regarding the advertisements of this period and their impact on women's purchasing power, see Lori Anne Loeb, *Consuming Angels: Advertising and Victorian Women* (New York and Oxford: Oxford University Press, 1994). Much can also be learned from reading an excellent review essay by Mary Louise Roberts, "Gender, Consumption, and Commodity Culture," *American Historical Review*, 103 (1998): 817–844. See also Erika Rappaport, *Shopping for Pleasure: Women in the Making of London's East End* (Princeton: Princeton University Press, 2000). Another important work is Victoria de Grazia, ed., with Ellen Furlough., *The Sex of Things: Gender and Consumption in Historical Perspective* (Berkeley: University of California Press, 1996).

[15] Loeb, *Consuming Angels*, 19.

[16] Ibid., 33.

[17] Ibid., 162.

not offer a compelling argument as to why women did not become the primary purchasers of commercial goods in this highly entrepreneurial scene.

In contrast, Jackson Lears, in his seminal work, *Fables of Abundance: A Cultural History of Advertising in America*, portrays the age of modern consumerism as one in which the Old World's conception of luxurious abundance, often associated with "women-as-fecund-earth" and feminine fertility, was passing away.[18] Denying the widely-used concept of Veblen's "conspicuous consumption," Lears writes that "of course fashionable and luxury artifacts constituted an imprimatur of upward mobility, but they had many more complex meanings as well."[19] Lears argues quite convincingly that in the late nineteenth century, which witnessed an un-paralleled explosion of mass production and mass consumption in America, there emerged a new style of consumerism that featured the "disembodiment of female icons of abundance."[20] Buying luxury com-modities had long been seen as perilous and they were regarded as an exotic allure that tempted one to live a prodigal life. Modern consumerism, however, represented the victory of the rationalized factory system with its managerial efficiency of a mass production and corporate culture. The advertisements in this new age, therefore, signaled not so much indul-gence and "effeminate luxury," as masculine materialism and the "abun-dant" availability of plentiful commodities; advertisements reflected the images of factories rather than the goddess of land-fertility as they had in previous eras. Even when women appeared in these advertisements, Lears explains, they played a passive role as the "beneficiaries of the largesse generated by the male genius of mass production."[21]

In this chapter, I agree with the arguments of Loeb, Lears, and others that British consumer society emerged fully fledged during the nineteenth century. However, my explorations of the advertisements of patent medicine and health-related commodities lead me to disagree with Loeb's assertion that feminine images were the primary icon and attraction used

---

[18] T. J. Jackson Lears, *Fables of Abundance: A Cultural History of Advertising in America* (New York: Basic Books, Harper Collins, 1994).
[19] Ibid., 61.
[20] Ibid., 109.
[21] Ibid., 120.

to promote them. Rather, the pictures and language of patent medicine that appeared in ephemera, circulars, and magazines were full of expressions stressing the masculinity of both men's and women's bodies by focusing on "vitality," "vigor," "strength," and so on. By contrast, there were very few advertisements that emphasized femininity in developing or maintaining good health—there is very little evidence to support Loeb's argument that women-as-consumers dominated advertising messages. In fact, the woman appears most often in patent medicine advertisements not as a pill-swallowing "angel" but a person wearing an appliance or gadget, such as an electric belt and corset, which symbolized the direct infusion of invigorating "nervous energy" and "nervous vitality" into the body. This absence of emphasis on femininity, I think, suggests that the consumer culture of this period was indeed very masculine with male doctors and engineers using electricity to revitalize enervated female bodies. I believe that if there were a Victorian illness which best conveys the gendered image of bodily health, it would be the woman's "deficiency of nervousness and energy" and the need for electrotherapy. In the next chapter, I will discuss this Victorian view of the body electric.

Therefore I agree with Lears' observation that advertising language did not emphasize femininity, but I disagree with his portrait of commodity-purchasers of either gender as very passive creatures who projected themselves before the male-dominated commercialism and managerialism of the factory system. Moreover, in construing this period as marking the triumph of corporate bureaucracy, Lears underestimates the agency of consumers and fails to understand how canny consumers took the initiative in enjoying their role and in choosing what they really wanted to acquire. In order to fully reevaluate the behaviors and mindsets of consumers of medicine in the urbanized commercial setting, I have used Colin Campbell's insightful model of consumers based upon "modern hedonism," a model which unfortunately is greatly oversimplified by Ann Loeb.

Campbell starts by simply questioning whether "modern consumption" is such a puppet-like and other-directed pattern of behavior and asks who is really pulling the strings during consumption. In his words, historians of consumption base their assumption on "traditional" hedonism, completely neglecting the very different motivation underlying "modern" hedonism. He notes that traditional hedonists wanted to obtain materials to satisfy their demand for pleasure, to reduce discomfort, and to seek more "decent" and more "luxurious" goods; thus their mentality was totally subject to external stimuli acting on each hedonist's "sensation." By contrast, "modern hedonism presents all individuals with the possibility of being their own despot, exercising total control over the stimuli they experience, and hence the pleasure they receive."[22] Modern hedonists or consumers are not deluded by mere sensory stimulation, Campbell insists; they hold "autonomous self-illusory or imaginative" power over the possible pleasures attainable through consumption. Thus consumption is seen as a rather private, covert, and inconspicuous activity, while at the same time consumers "employ their imaginative and creative powers to construct mental images which they consume for the intrinsic pleasure they provide."[23] As in the experience of window-shopping, consumers with a still vague image of what they desire look for material, projecting their imagination or "day-dreaming or fantasizing" trials against reality. This "testing" of their imagination, in reality, creates a "feedback" process of disillusion- and illusion-making in their minds, which itself becomes an essential pleasure for consumers. "The modern hedonist," Campbell argues, "is continually withdrawing from reality as fast as he encounters it, ever-casting his day-dreams forward in time, attaching them to objects of desire, and then subsequently 'unhooking' them from these objects as and when they are attained and experienced."[24] Campbell's argument is the most thought-provoking reconsideration among the histories of consumerism and provides clues for understanding late-nineteenth-century consumers of patent medicines. The consumers, whose existence we can infer from the advertising languages in this period, were very different from the easily cajoled and inert ones supposedly typical of the eighteenth century.

In discussing the eighteenth-century origin of the rapid increase in demand for consumer goods, McKendrick relies on the rise of advertisements and rampant salesmanship. Eighteenth-century evidence, he

---

[22] Colin Campbell, *The Romantic Ethic and the Spirit of Modern Consumerism* (Oxford: Blackwell, 1987), 76.
[23] Ibid., 77.
[24] Ibid., 86–87.

notes, demonstrated for the first time that "consumers were being bullied and cajoled into buying by insistent siren voices of advertisement."[25] He argues that with eager advertising and inspired sales skill, "profit-seeking men of business" successfully manipulated consumer demand. Similarly, in exploring the spread of quack nostrum mongers during the Georgian period, Porter describes the consumers of these dubious remedies as manipulated victims. According to him, quacks wielded great word-power in utilizing fierce "sales-talks," "buzz-words of natural philosophy," "exotic tags," and the "mysteries of names."[26] Their tactics of "mingling hard and soft sells, excitement and amusement, bathos, pathos, titillation" all dazzled patients to good account. Thus, "the quack's clientele may be compared to a demagogue's auditors, a preacher's congregation, or to theatre-goers."[27] In short, Porter also sees the consumer as the dupe of merchants' manipulations.[28]

If nineteenth-century purchasers of patent medicine, however, were modern consumers, as Campbell persuasively argues, and if patent medicine marketers targeted such mature consumers, the strategies and approaches taken by the advertisers of these products must have also been modern. In the early 1800s, however, there were very few daily newspapers in London, and each one ran only one or two advertisements, which in turn were not printed for free because of restrictions ranging from censorship to stamp taxes and paper duties. Even well into the mid-nineteenth century, advertisements were printed in black-and-white and had no pictorial illustrations: it is perhaps better to regard these advertisements as printed announcements or information about certain goods and products that were presented with simple repetition, basic

---

[25] McKendrick et al., *The Birth of a Consumer Society*, 148.

[26] Roy Porter, *Health For Sale: Quackery in England, 1660–1850* (Manchester: Manchester University Press, 1989), 94, 102, and 109.

[27] Ibid., 94.

[28] But it seems clear that the promotion of proprietary medicines, whether in the eighteenth or nineteenth century, did not accord with the Veblenesque theory of social emulation. It is not compelling to assume that people bought new drugs in order to emulate other social strata or imitate a higher class of people. It is probably for this reason that McKendrick does not dwell on the case of James Graham, the sex therapist who is the main character of Porter's quack story. McKendrick does, however, briefly mention Graham's skill in advertising.

headlines, and small emblems. Even though there were a few advertising agencies, these were little more than intermediaries between mercantile clients and the press, because their work was mainly that of placing announcements with newspaper or magazine publishers. The merchant himself, or his clerks, generally prepared the advertising with little thought given to catchphrases and similar hallmarks of modern advertising.

From the mid-1880s, however, the old-style advertisements using a few lines of "copy" in narrow columns were being replaced by bombastic pictorial advertising with attractive displays or illustrations, used in part—of course—to overcome consumers' skepticism, indifference, prejudice, and tendency to procrastinate.[29] That advertisements ceased to depend on simply misguided sensationalism for their effect is principally shown by the rapid emergence and activities of professional advertising agencies. From the 1870s onward, new advertising men with expert knowledge of the media began to recruit educated people, thus starting the formation of a respectable profession.[30] According to Diana and Geoffrey Hindley, the development of these agencies was a part of the Americanization of English society. Traditionally, British businessmen regarded advertising as rather undignified and a waste of money, but a new style of marketing—a scientific and managerial approach to advertising and promoting product sales through a blaze of publicity—came from the United States, where full-service agencies, such as N. W. Ayer in Philadelphia, began large-scale advertisement on a national basis. British agencies were eager to learn new techniques from the American advertising industry, and in so doing they were hoping to establish their own professional identities as advertisers.

Many large agencies whose offices were in central London—such as Smith's Manual Advertising Agency and T. B. Browne, Ltd.—began to pursue their businesses in a modern way, and they typically contained a number of specialized departments. They used technically advanced pictorial illustrations and photographs created by numerous artists in their design departments; they produced serial pamphlets or handbills, and

---

[29] In *The Illustrated London News*, for example, the first printing of pictorial advertisements was in 1888.

[30] Diana Hindley and Geoffrey Hindley, *Advertising in Victorian England, 1837–1901* (London: Wayland Publishers, 1972).

they employed psychologists as consultants, to make their catch sentences more persuasive. The *Graphic* and the *Illustrated London News* were representative of these publications, both having copious advertising that used innovative drawing and painting. But even smaller publications began to include multiple illustrated advertisements. According to the list where Smith's Agency advertised, there were about seventeen weekly and bi-weekly papers published in London. Established in 1891, *Science Shifting*, for example, was a chatty journal about science inventions, discovery, and health, and it sold 32,000 copies per day. *Mechanical World*, which provided practical information to users of machinery and electricity, was established in 1876 and had a circulation of 22,000. Another such paper was the *English Mechanic*, which was established in 1895 and sold 20,000 copies per week.[31] Like Moody's Printing, to name a famous example, these advertising agencies often bought bulk page space from the media at discount prices and resold the divided space to clients at the standard rate. They even issued their own pamphlets, published full scale annual handbooks, and distributed regular circulars.

Initially, pictorial illustrations were mainly run in inexpensive papers and journals whose readers were mostly of the working class. Illustrated advertisements were slower to make their way into publications directed at the middle-class because of the long-standing impression that such advertisements consisted of fraudulent statements and information to promote products of poor quality. The editors of middle-class publications feared that such graphic descriptions would disturb their respectable tone. But by the 1880s even the most respectable publications had begun to include some form of elegantly captioned illustrations. "Pictorial advertising is the most popular form of advertisement," William Stead at the T. B. Browne advertising agency wrote in *The Art of Advertising.* "A picture appeals to all classes of the community, whether educated or uneducated.

---

[31] *Smith's Advertising Agency, Successful Advertising: Its Secrets Explained* (London: Smith's Advertising Agency, 21st ed., 1885), 295. Publications listed are *The Capitalists* (est. 1885); *Commercial Intelligence* (1898); *Electrical Engineer* (1883); *Electricity and Electrical Engineering* (est. 1890); *Family Doctor* (1895); *The Hospital* (1886); *Insurance Post and Remembrancer* (1879); *Insurance Record* (1863); *Insurance World and Monetary Record* (1879); *London Commercial Records* (1876); *Medical Press and Circular* (1825); *Newspaper Owner & Modern Printer* (1898); *Polytechnic Magazine* (1879); and *Vegetarian* (1888).

Anyone can understand a picture."[32] Meanwhile, a professional standard of advertising was gradually established and accepted in late-Victorian society. Respectable publications came to admit that pictorial advertisements, even though exaggerated, conveyed indispensable information about products, a commercial message to the public, and the possibility of gaining benefit or happiness by using the commodities. In a sense, advertisements gradually changed from being mere descriptions of goods for sale to providing the fantasy and entertainment associated with the commodities themselves.

Furthermore, advertising agencies' tactics of "attractive display or illustration, especially the latter, if apt and *à propos*, by gratifying the eye and pleasing the mind," were not intended merely to manipulate consumers' minds; on the contrary, they were to cultivate their hedonistic desires.[33] New advertisements were said to have the most effect, "not by what they say, but what they imply or leave to be inferred. Advertisements of this nature skillfully drawn often lead a reader to view the article advertised in a more favourable light than that in which even the advertiser himself could portray it in actual words." As Smith's Advertising commented, "The mind of the reader has unconsciously assimilated the things implied over and beyond the things said and as the power of imagination is great, the result conduces to the advertiser's interest."[34] Consumer desire, agencies clearly understood, was not a pre-existing emotion to be exposed, but rather was constructed in the exchange between consumers' imaginations and the realities they encountered. Therefore, it was along the interstices between fantasy and reality where agencies sought to locate their advertising in order to inculcate favorable impressions of the commodities they marketed.

Advertising agencies were fully aware of, and often stressed their profession's development into, "a new method of a Democratic age."[35] "The Advertising Agent" William Stead wrote, "gauges the taste of the public he has to address, and then chooses his means in accordance with

---

[32] William Stead, Jr., *The Art of Advertising: Its Theory and Practice Fully Described* (London: T. B. Browne, Ltd., 1899), 97.
[33] *Smith's Advertising Agency*, 67.
[34] Ibid., 68.
[35] Stead, *The Art of Advertising*, 12.

what he knows will be the best way to interest it." Reflecting the steady change in public attitudes from political democracy to material democracy, Stead here emphasized that advertising also needed to be a consumer-oriented business. "The Advertising Agent is the nerve-centre of modern industry," he went on to say. "He is the first to feel every influence which affects industry, whether for good or ill. He keeps, as it were, his finger upon the commercial pulse of the world, counts his beats, and adjusts the method and quantity of advertising accordingly."[36] To that end, professional knowledge, marketing research into the public's psychology, and long experience were definitely required. Phillip Smith, another big agency, emphatically warned advertisers not to return to the outmoded excessive approach, writing that, "The day of successful claptrap and vulgarity, still more the day of exaggeration and deceptive misrepresentation, is quickly passing away."[37] "The truth should look like truth," Smith went on to say, "An advertisement should look to be so genuine that there is no need to make any special claim of genuineness . . . the whole truth, and nothing but the truth; and that is frankness."[38] Advertising agencies frequently recommended to advertisers that protecting clients should be "one of the great essentials of security . . . that you should endeavour to give as much as you possibly can to your customers."[39]

Such admonitions from advertising agencies must have stemmed from the suspicious and vigilant attitude of the modern consumer. One instance of such consumer skepticism involved the Carbolic Smoke Ball Company, which had sold antiseptic medication as an "inhalation cure for coughs, colds, hay fever, deafness, catarrh, neuralgia etc."[40] The company published an advertisement in the *Pall Mall Gazette* promising to pay £100 to any person who had caught influenza after having used a smoke ball three times daily for at least a fortnight and announcing that £1,000 had been deposited with the Alliance Bank to meet emergencies. With a sound

---

[36] Ibid., 42.

[37] Phillip Smith, *Successful Advertising: Its Secret Explained* (London: Smith's Advertising Agency, 24th ed., 1909), 19.

[38] Ibid., 45.

[39] Ibid., 11.

[40] The John Johnson Collection (hereafter JJC), Bodleian Library, Oxford University, Patent Medicine Box 5: Well-known patent medicines.

instinct that "either I shall not get the influenza, or I shall get the £1,000," one Mrs. Carlill bought and used the balls and yet fell ill with influenza within a week. When faced with the company's repeated refusal to pay her the promised compensation, she and her husband brought the matter to court, which proceeded to debate whether the words used in advertisements had the binding power of an official contract. On July 5, 1892, Justice Hawkins himself determined that an advertisement was valid as a contract even without an official stamp; he brought a verdict for the plaintiff to recover £1,000.[41]

On the same day, *The Times'* leading article found in this case "not a little edification," and declared itself impressed by the emergence of "some people who will perform very onerous conditions if the end propose is adequate, but whose determination to get their rights is equal to their constancy in the performance of the imposed duty."[42] The message of Mrs. Carlill's case and *The Times'* article certainly suggests that modern advertisements were read critically by discerning modern consumers. Consumers had little resemblance to the credulous and undemurring "sheep" once manipulated by intriguing jingles, such as those of the eighteenth-century quack pill vendors. That Londoners in this period constituted a modernized consumer society is important to recognize: they were canny shoppers; they tended to procrastinate in buying; and they enjoyed window shopping. That is, they were at once skeptical and critical, if nevertheless attracted to and influenced by advertising.

What fueled the commodity culture of late-Victorian England was doubtless the force of advertising activities whose primary sponsors, it is important to note, were proprietary medicine marketers. By the end of the nineteenth century, patent medicine advertisements, forming at least twenty to thirty percent of all advertisements, both led and sustained commodity culture. In the 1880s and 1890s, Britain experienced acute industrialization and a transformation of society: people wanted more than just an adequate level of daily life. They wanted to become caught up in advertising's chimerical images of ideals, prosperity, and achievement. Imaginary possession of a healthy body was a common desire, not only for the middle class but also for working-class people. It was during these

---

[41] *The Times*, June 20, July 5, July 6, and December 8, 1892.
[42] *The Times*, July 5, 1892, 3.

years that innumerable patent medicines flooded the market. And that market was enormous. Before the late-nineteenth century, health and the means by which it was maintained had been considered less amenable to material exchange and relatively unrelated to the burgeoning commodity culture. Thereafter, however, there were many people who regarded health as something one could purchase—something akin to the comfort they could get by buying other goods. Patent medicines and other kinds of therapeutic commodities were like other marketable goods: they captured consumers' hedonistic imaginations and ultimately transformed the human body into a field of commercial capitalism.[43] It was through this commodification of health that patent medicines were produced, promoted, and came to be desired by consumers in late-nineteenth-century Britain.

*Therapeutic Fantasies and Therapeutic Commodities*

Indeed, patent medicine's customers were devoted actors in a highly modernized form of consumption and were far more alert to their own interests than the medical profession, their would-be defenders, believed. Doctors' prevailing professional views on the risk of advertised medications appear to have been limited strictly to their effectiveness (or not) in curing particular diseases. But as the form and language of patent medicine advertisements indicate, consumers began to regard patent medicines first and foremost as commodities, rather than only as remedial medications.

In the British Medical Association's exposés—*Secret Remedies* and *More Secret Remedies*—quack medicines were classified according to the particular kinds of diseases that they were advertised as being able to treat: examples were Cough Medicines, Catarrh and Cold Cures, and Kidney Medicines. My research, however, suggests that by contrast, purely medicinal preparations were frequently not advertised. In the John Johnson Collection, for example, Cancer Remedies and Consumption Cures con-

---

[43] Thomas Richards' book explores many varieties of advertising, much of it related to the British Empire and to patent medicines: see his *The Commodity Culture of Victorian England: Advertising and Spectacle, 1851–1914* (London: Verso, 1990).

stituted merely 1.7 percent of all the advertisements.[44] In fact, as we have seen in the previous chapter, many patent medicine vendors stressed the bona-fide nature of their business by insisting that they were not involved in fraudulent advertising for remedies for cancer, consumption, syphilis, or for medicines for abortions; all such advertising, they declared, should be punished by public prosecution.[45]

What indeed did people expect when they bought patent medicines? What was the main public role played by these health-inducing preparations? As far as the listed medicinal virtues in the advertisements are concerned, these medicaments were demanded as enhancements for everyday life. Sagacious consumers of patent medicines very likely understood the implicit message in the advertisements. In 1900, Andrew Wilson, a popularizer of health culture, observed that "this is a pill-swallowing age and a potion-loving generation."[46] Not because they were actually sick did members of the public buy patent medicines, but because drugs and health-drinks were sold as therapeutic commodities. Advertisements' creation of therapeutic fantasies or illusions was bound to entail manipulation. However, in modern society, as Wolfgang Haug argues in his *Critique of Commodity Aesthetics*, "manipulation could only be effective if it 'somehow' latched on to the 'objective interests' of those being manipulated."[47] "Now what is necessary," Haug goes on to say, "cannot be distinguished from what is unnecessary but which one can no longer do without."[48] Modern consumers' hedonism thus led them to perceive commodities not only for their practical use in the reality of everyday life, but for the social and cultural fantasies that they projected.

---

[44] Although I have not yet made a statistical survey of the advertisements appearing in the *Illustrated London News*, the *Graphic*, and *Health*, I have examined the advertisements dating from 1870 to 1910 and found that none before the mid-1880s employed highly extravagant illustrations.

[45] *Report from the Select Committee on Patent Medicines*, 366–455. In the following chapter I discuss this point in detail.

[46] Andrew Wilson, *Brain and Body: The Nervous System in Social Life* (London: James Bowden, 1900), 12.

[47] Wolfgang Fritz Haug, *A Critique of Commodity Aesthetics: Appearance, Sexuality and Advertising in Capitalist Society*, trans. by Robert Book (Minneapolis: University of Minnesota Press, 1986), 6.

[48] Ibid., 53.

In the case of patent medicine, the mixture of the public's therapeutic fantasies and real needs manifested themselves at various levels in the advertising language of the time.

What these manufacturers targeted were people with physical or psychic loss of energy, nervous prostration, loss of appetite, irritability, nausea, palpitation, weakness, and so on. Voguish terms like "nervous," "lost energy," and "impure blood" in the advertisements aroused consumer demand by associating products with imaginary states of well-being, and by fueling desires for a more animated life apparently required by a rapidly industrializing society that seemed to demand more energy than urban-dwellers' constitutions were able to supply. "It is not a question of absolute illness," Wilson wrote, "but rather one of 'little health.' We are not exactly ill, and we are not precisely well." He went on to highlight why the public needed these new types of medicines:

> Our brain-cells to-day are doing ten times the work of those which belonged to our forefathers, and as a result they rebel the sooner, and the more frequently against the strain to which they are subjected. The busy man or woman to-day is essentially a 'neurotic' subject. I do not mean to imply that we are invalids, or even that we are incapacitated from duty, but we are certainly as a race more subject to nervous ills than were our parents, and the life of to-day has nothing at all in common with the slow, peaceful existence led by our grandparents.[49]

Medical commodities were increasingly offered not simply to satisfy people's wants and needs, but—as commodities—as cultural artifacts to be promoted through mass advertising.

Advertisements often alluded to conditions such as nervousness, biliousness, and feeble circulation in depicting gendered images of bodily (ill) health. For example, many of the advertisements for patented tonic drinks depicted gloomy and depressed-looking Victorian ladies likely to faint at any moment and suffering (so the advertisements claimed) from dizzy spells when they stood up. Of particular interest for the gendering of nervous ailments is that women were frequently depicted in adver-

---

[49] Andrew Wilson, *Brain and Body: The Nervous System in Social Life* (London: James Bowden, 1900), 10–11.

tisements for medical gadgets and appliances in a manner intended to represent middle-class women's suffering from wracked nerves, weakness, and depression—all symptoms thought to be curable with electrical treatment. While patented pills were swallowed in the therapeutic desire of acquiring a healthy body, electrical appliances (which will be fully discussed in the next chapters) were used as a result of a growing Victorian sensibility concerning "the body electric" and particularly the strong fear of women losing their nervous energy.

For this loss of nervous energy, many kinds of tablets and powders claimed to contain the "constituents of the Gastric or digestive juice."[50] In other words, patent medicine vendors were not exactly dealing in *materia medica* but rather promoting health enhancers as part of a clearly remunerative business. For example, Guy's Tonic, one of the more widely advertised pick-me-ups, proclaimed "Good Appetite—Good Health!" With this tonic, the advertisements promised, "the digestive functions of the Stomach are so invigorated, their powers are so much amplified, and healthy peptones of good are formed, [which] penetrate through the walls of the Stomach and travel by their own routes to the Blood."[51] Lactopeptine, which claimed to provide "much additional gastric juice," was recommended to readers for the "Common-sense Management of the Stomach."[52] The three ingredients of Lactopeptine were advertised as ptyalin for dissolving starchy matters, pepsin for dissolving fleshy matters, and pancreatine for dissolving fatty matters. "It is really absurd nowadays to let INDIGESTION terrorise you and shut you out from the good things of the table. Instead of surrendering to it, fight it, fight it with Lactopeptine."[53]

It is hard to classify these preparations as pure medicine. Pepsalia was advertised as a cure for indigestion, and called itself "not a medicine, but a Table Condiment. A pleasant, appetising, and agreeable substitute for Table Salt."[54] Hood's Sarsaparilla, which it was said was extracted from Sarsaparilla Root, was advertised in a similar fashion.

---

[50] *Illustrated London News*, November 5, 1898, 988.

[51] *Illustrated London News*, February 5, 1898, 197.

[52] *Illustrated London News*, September 14, 1901, 401.

[53] *Illustrated London News*, February 16, 1901, 249.

[54] *Graphic*, January 9, 1892, 55.

AFTER DINNER
To prevent that feeling of fullness and
distress, aid digestion and assimilation
of food, cure headache and biliousness
TAKE HOOD'S PILLS[55]

These sound like nothing more than medicine-like "pick-me-ups" that must be habitually taken as daily therapeutic supplements in order to feel better. For disorders such as indigestion, for example, consumers were free to choose from numerous preparations whose advertising slogans all promised the same effects and that were similarly marketed: Cooper's Tonic & Pills; Beecham's Pills, Bile Beans for Biliousness; and Page Woodcock's Pills.

"Nerve tonics" were a favorite item in patent medicine manufacturers' inventories—these entrepreneurs were aware that nervous ailments such as neurasthenia and nervous prostration were societally created diseases for which doctors had failed to supply a remedy. Physicians generally recommended that patients suffering from nervous disorders distance themselves from their work; Silas Weir Mitchell's famous "rest cure" (discussed in Chapter Five) is a case in point. To mitigate stress from modern urban living, neurologists and doctors in the late nineteenth century tended to prescribe Mitchell's rest cure, and they recommended that patients stay in bed on a fatty diet for several weeks in order to increase their body's supply of "fat and blood."[56] But such advice from medical professionals did not accord with the dominant entrepreneurial ideology of the era, the therapeutic ethos of promoting an overflowing of energetic health. Indeed, it is often perceived that patent medicines highlighted the worthlessness of doctors' advice, by making use of Victorian self-help ideology: indeed as a Dr. Birley proclaimed in his advertisement, "It is painfully evident that something more is urgently wanted— something more simple and decided in its action."[57] J. C. Eno's

---

[55] "Hood's Sarsaparilla (blood purifier)" in JJC, Patent Medicine Box, Miscellaneous Patent medicines.

[56] Regarding Weir Mitchell, George Beard, and theories held by other doctors, see Chapter Five below.

[57] "Dr. Birley's Syrup of Free Phosphorus, the Great Brain and Nerve Food," in JJC, Patent Medicine Box 1.

advertisement puffed that "Eno always advises every man to be his own doctor, and shows how the general health may be kept good, and life prolonged, by attention to a few simple rules of a diet, exercise, cleanliness, &c."[58] According to these patent medicine manufacturers, doctors cured illnesses but failed to provide a state of general health for their patients. Thus there was a large and untapped market for the nutraceutical industry.

Many doctors viewed blood-disorders as a critical cause of nervous fatigue. The promise of "a perfect blood builder and nerve restorer" could attract sufferers from nervous debility to Dr. William's Pink Pills.[59] The analeptic effect of coca leafs discovered in South America led to the introduction of various medicinal coca wines to the market, such as Hall's Coca Wine, which was hyped as an "'The Elixir of Life,' prescribed for MENTAL AND PHYSICAL FATIGUE" (Fig. 2-1).[60] Marza Wine, similarly, was claimed to produce "RICH RED BLOOD." "WHY TAKE MEDICINE?" the advertisements asked, "Drink WINE. It is the finest tonic! It is peculiarly Palatable!! It is rich in Iron, Coca, Phosphorus, and Pepsin!!! It is a Happy Combination!!!!"[61] For weakly men and women, another "powerful nerve stimulant," Armbrecht Coca Wine, could "relieve the dullness and drowsiness of nervous debility."[62] Again, it was patent medicine manufacturers who first noticed that appealing to the desire to promote self-healing could indeed be a most lucrative business.

More commonly, sellers of patent medicine sought scientific validation in their advertising and in this way they contributed to consumers' therapeutic day-dreaming. For consumers, reading these patent medicine advertisements was like reading a medical encyclopedia: a one-page advertisement included detailed descriptions of the disease's symptoms, and a multi-page pamphlet might contain a full-blown survey of seemingly scientific or up-to-date medical knowledge. Disease etiology also received

---

[58] J. C. Eno, Groat Market, Newcastle-On-Tyne, Extract from Eno's popular family medicine book, *The Stomach and Its Trials*, JJC, Patent Medicine Box 9, Mother Siegel's Syrup, JJC. Also see its advertisement "No Doctor," *Health*, July 8, 1892.

[59] Dr. William's Pink Pills for Pale People, JJC, Patent Medicine Box 4.

[60] Hall's Coca Wine, in JJC, Patent Medicine Box 2.

[61] Marza Wine, in JJC, Patent Medicine Box 3.

[62] *Illustrated London News*, October 28, 1899, 636.

extensive theoretical explanations. Moreover, the medical information in each advertisement was couched in sufficiently scientific terminology as to influence consumers' imaginations and enable them to choose from numerous rival drugs. For example, the seven-page advertisement for Dr. Birley's Phosphorus, sold as "Brain and Nerve Food," was illustrated with the latest mapping of the brain and pictures of microscopic sensory and motor nerve cells to suggest the routes by which this chemical food would circulate through the brain.[63] Leo's Microbe Pills, as another example, circulated ephemera that used pictures of various microbes to show "the origin of disease" and cited statements from the "indisputable evidence of the scientific men of the nineteenth century." The advertisement for Figuroids, an anti-fat pill promoted as a "Scientific Obesity Cure," included illustrations of blood vessels and cells and guaranteed to squeeze the "Adipose" out of "Fat Cells," which would thereby transform fat cells into normal cell formations.[64] Evidently it was no longer enough simply to run a sensationalist advertising campaign and attract attention to an ailment through shocking pictures—manufacturers of patent medicine sought to convey knowledge through dazzling tactics that would both entice consumers and expand their imagination. This is yet another example of how in the late-Victorian period advanced scientific and medical knowledge itself was becoming a profitable commodity. Thus, what was sold in the market was not just a therapeutic commodity. Something intangible was added to the product: information, knowledge, suggestions, and a number of novel concepts were becoming sources of profit for medical capitalists.

Yet health knowledge that was only apparently scientific also appealed to consumers who prided themselves upon their rationality. For example, the marketability of so-called blood purifiers remained long dependent on popular beliefs cultivated by mid-Victorian quacks such as James Morison, the youngest son of Alexander Morison and a dyed-in-the-wool irregular who called himself "Hygeist." The younger Morison owned the "British College of Health," and used it to conduct a harsh campaign against professionally trained doctors by issuing the *Hygeian Journal* as well

---

[63] "Dr. Birley's Syrup of Free Phosphorus, the Great Brain and Nerve Food," in JJC, Patent Medicine Box 1.
[64] Figuroid, Scientific Obesity Cure in JJC, Patent Medicine Box 2.

as many other books and almanacs touting his vegetable pills. He marketed his Universal Vegetable pills as "purgatives" and claimed they were a panacea that worked by cleansing the entire human body. In his "Morisonian System of Health & Vegetable Universal Medicine," he claimed that the cause of all diseases lies in the blood, alleging that "the vital principle is contained in the blood" and "all diseases arise from the impurity of the blood, or in other words, from acrimonious humours lodged in the body."[65] In the 1850s and 1860s, Morison and his College argued against the vaccination project initiated by the government, denouncing it in numerous pamphlets as the "barbarous, disgusting, irrational practice of intruding bestial, diseased humours into the vital stream of life."[66] Morison and his followers lobbied influential notables, such as the Earl of Derby, to stop the Compulsory Vaccination Act by describing it as a "medical imposture" by doctors and arguing that it was poisoning the public.[67] His strategy of bombarding the public with his hygienic philosophy, combined with his attacks on orthodox medical knowledge, was very successful and contributed handsomely to the profitability of his business.

---

[65]A number of Morison's advertising flyers and pamphlets are held in the John Johnson Collection (JJC), Well Known Patent Medicines Box 6. See, for example, "British College of Health: The Hygeian System of JAMES MORISON, the Hygeist, showing the fallacy of the Organic Theory of Doctors." Morison's hygienic well-known tenets were as follows: "1. The vital principle is in the blood. 2. Everything in the body is derived from the blood. 3. All constituents are radically the same. 4. All diseases arise from impurity of the blood, or in other words, from acrimonious humors lodged in the body. 5. Pain and disease have the same origin, and may therefore be considered synonymous. 6. From the intimate connection with subsisting between mind and body, the health of the one must conduce to the serenity of the other. 7. Proper purgation by vegetables is the only effectual mode of eradicating disease. 8. The discovery of a VEGETABLE COMPOUND, capable of being digested, and mixing with the blood, so as to impart to it the energy requisite for ridding the body of all impurities, was a desideratum."

[66] "The Morisonian Monument Erected in Front of the British College of Health, New Road, London, The 31st of March, 1856," in JJC, Patent Medicine Box 6.

[67] His brother, John Morison of the British College of Health published several open letters to the Earl of Derby. See "Vaccine Poison," in JJC, Patent Medicine Box 6.

In the popular imagination, Morison's ideas never died out. Although colored by new knowledge of physiology and lacking Morison's pseudo-scientific assertions, twenty years later his focus on the significance of impure blood continued to be present in the catchphrases of advertisements for various blood purifiers—one of the most extensively advertised kinds of patent medicines. Indigestion, loss of energy, nausea after meals, liver disorders, and rheumatism were all trumpeted as serious ailments that blood purifiers could remedy. "For the Blood is the Life, Keep the Blood Pure & the Health of the System will Follow," claimed Clarke's Blood Mixture, a brand manufactured from 1872 to 1909.[68] Similarly, Boyd's Celebrated Blood Purifier was "warranted to cleanse the BLOOD from all impurities."[69] Fraser's Sulphur Tablets—of which a million free samples were distributed as a result of advertising—could "permeate the blood with an aerial anti-septic force, in which germs, microbes, and corrupt diseases atoms cannot live."[70] Swift's Specific Vegetarian Purifier boasted of offering the "only vegetable blood purifier on the market."[71] Symptoms of impure blood would appear as skin ailments such as "boils, pimples, blotches, sores, eruptions, rashes, tetter," for which Bile Beans for Biliousness promised to be the most efficacious.[72] Blood purifiers, in short, were sold as "Strength Restorers." Health thus meant more than just being free of disease: it was the abundant state of vigor signified in "The Fountain of Health," where Vogeler's Curative Compound was illustratively marketed as "the Queen of Medicines."[73]

As Roy Porter has suggested, mid-Victorian quacks such as Morison emerged out of the flowering of earlier methods of unorthodox healing: homeopathy, mesmerism, phrenology, hydropathy, medical botany, and the like. In marked contrast, however, few patent medicines in the late nineteenth century emerged as challenges to the tenets of professional medicine.[74] For most advertisements of patent medicines, a scientific

---

[68] Clarke's Blood Mixture, *Health: a Popular Home Journal and Family Medical Guide*, June 19, 1909. iv.

[69] Boyd's Celebrated Blood Purifier, JJC, Patent Medicine Box 1.

[70] Fraser's Sulphur Tablets, JJC, Patent Medicine Box 5.

[71] Swift's Specific Vegetarian Purifier, *The Graphic*, Feb. 4, 1888, 127.

[72] Bile Beans for Biliousness, JJC, Patent Medicine Box 5.

[73] Vogeler's Curative Compound, *Illustrated London News*, Feb. 25, 1896, 35.

[74] Porter, *Health for Sale*, 228–235.

mien and pretence of knowledge of physiology were indispensable, and some even went so far as to sneer at doctors' insufficient knowledge of *materia medica.*[75] Some advertisements exploited the Samuel Smiles' self-help tradition by highlighting doctors' incompetence and their expensive consultancy fees. Mother Siegel's Syrup, for example, carried a one-page story advertisement explaining how one woman consulted doctor after doctor, but none could treat her indigestion and loss of appetite. "The doctors may not understand this," the ad assured its readers, "but Mother Siegel did, and her medicine cures it."[76] However, as I will discuss later, the confrontations between doctors and patent medicine proprietors were based less on issues of scientific validity than on disagreements over how far the public's health concerns should be resolved through market mechanisms.

In sum, by considering the controversy surrounding patent medicine only as a step toward professionalized regulation of medicine, one loses sight of an important element of late Victorian commercial culture: patent medicine's extraordinary growth was, in essence, a culture which can be defined in Raymond Williams' terms as a "structure of feeling" or "a particular sense of life, a particular community of experience hardly needing expression."[77] It is thus important to explore patent medicine as a representation of people's collective psyche. In so doing, we are able to understand more clearly why patent medicine flourished as it did, and why professional doctors responded to it in such a serious and vehement way. In the following pages, I will reconsider patent medicines, their advertising language, and the debates they caused, principally in light of the burgeoning health culture of the late-Victorian public.

*Health Culture, Nutrition, Foods, and Manufacturers*

Dwelling as they did upon various signs of illness and providing detailed information on many diseases in their advertisements, manufacturers of patent medicine did not seek strategies of dealing with the truly diseased as much as engagement with the minds and imagination of

---

[75] *Report from the Select Committee on Patent Medicines*, 603. Witness after witness called from patent medicine manufacturers in the Parliamentary Committee testified to the shortage of doctors' knowledge in *materia medica.*

[76] "Were These Doctors Ignorant?," *Health*, July 8, 1892, iv.

[77] Raymond Williams, *The Long Revolution* (London: Chatto & Windus, 1961).

consumers worried about their health. This is perhaps not surprising, given that the market potential for people concerned about their health far exceeded the market potential for people already in bad health. Patent medicines thus often emphasized "the preventative arts of Medicine."[78] For example, Lamplough's Pyretic Saline, using the slogan "Prevention is better than Cure" was sold for "Heartburn, Lassitude, or Low Spirits."[79] Although doctors ridiculed such compounds as "Cure Alls,"[80] the ills depicted in these advertisements were mostly matters of poor health such as indigestion, sleeplessness, nervousness, languor, melancholia, headache, and dizziness. By curing them, manufacturers insisted, patent medicines were also efficacious in preventing more serious diseases. In short, behind the rapidly expanding market for patent medicines lay consumers' growing obsession with the therapeutic maintenance of a healthy body—an obsession that was forming what can be called a "health culture."

Patent medicine advertisements highlighted their products' efficacy as therapeutic, preventative regimens. Norton's Camomile Pills, another famous blood purifier, explained that

> [E]very person in his lifetime consumes a quantity of noxious matter, which if taken at one meal would be fatal: it is those small quantities of noxious matter, which are introduced into our food, either by accident or willful adulteration, which we find so often upset the stomach, and not unfrequently lay the foundation of illness, and perhaps final ruination to health. To preserve the constitution, it should be our constant care, if possible, to counteract the effect of these small quantities of unwholesome matter.[81]

This manufacturer clearly understood that to sell consumers the hope of being healthy, it was necessary to provide an apparently scientific explanation of how its pills were good as therapeutic preventative regimens.

---

[78] Norton's Camomile Pills, in JJC, April 1889, Well Known Patent Medicines Box 6.

[79] Lamplough's Pyretic Saline, "From Infancy to Age," *Health*, November 14, 1884.

[80] *Secret Remedies: What They Cost and What They Contain* (London: British Medical Association, 1909), 270–271.

[81] The pamphlet of Norton's Camomile Pills, in JJC, Well Known Patent Medicines Box 6, 3.

For earlier promoters of preventative or sanitary medicine such as Benjamin Ward Richardson, the quest for public health was partly motivated by an imperialist or nationalist desire to arrest the ongoing process of British racial degeneration, as his motto cautioned: "National health is national wealth."[82] Twenty years later, however, this health culture entered the domain of the individual family, and so the late nineteenth century witnessed a proliferation of popular books on preserving health. Some publishers produced book series for different health problems, such as *Aids to Long Life, How to Use our Eyes and How to Preserve Them, The Hygiene of the Skin: A Treatise on Hygiene and Public Health, How to Live Long,* and *Sound Bodies for Our Boys and Girls.*[83] Members of the medical profession in turn published "Health Maxims" that contained thousands of medical aphorisms.[84] *The Modern Family Doctor,* a popular encyclopedia of medicine, stated that "the duty of every man is to preserve his health, not to attempt to combat diseases. The layman cannot substitute, but he may anticipate, the work of a doctor, by healthy living, and by taking precautionary measures."[85]

The activities of Dr. Andrew Wilson illustrate the spread of ideas of sanitation and public health among members of the general public from the 1880s onward. In 1883, he started his own periodical, *Health: A Weekly Journal of Sanitary Science,* which was "intended to be a thoroughly popular Journal, which may be read by all classes with pleasure and profit."[86] In the opening address of *Health,* Wilson wrote that "the last ten years have

---

[82] Benjamin Ward Richardson, *Health and Life* (London: Daldy, Isbester, 1878), 11, 13, and 40.

[83] Chatto & Windus published *Aids to Long Life: A Medical, Dietical, and General Guide in Middle and Old Age* by N. E. Davies; *How to Use our Eyes and How to Preserve Them* by John Bowning; and *The Hygiene of the Skin* by J. L. Milton. Sampson and Low, Marson, Searle and Rivington published *A Treatise on Hygiene and Public Health* by Dr. A. H. Buck; *How to Live Long* by W. W. Hall; and *Sound Bodies for Our Boys and Girls* by W. Blaikie.

[84] See W. W. Hall, MD, *Health Maxims, Physical, Mental, and Moral* (New York: Hurd and Houghton, 1875).

[85] *The Modern Family Doctor: A Guide to Perfect Health* (London: T. C. & E. Jack, 1914), x.

[86] "To Our Readers," in *Health: A Weekly Journal of Sanitary Science,* April 13, 1883, 1.

witnessed a literally marvelous revolution in the attitude of the public towards Health-questions."[87] The preservation of health and the prevention of disease, which had traditionally been taught from above by government officers or medical authorities, had now become the active concern of individuals. Wilson observed:

> The people are slowly but surely awakening to a knowledge of the fact that man's health, fortunes, and misfortunes are largely of his own making. Knowledge of the laws of life, of the structure and functions of our bodies, and of the causes of disease, is the information which is now demanded by young and old, by rich and poor alike.[88]

Established to "serve as a much-needed link of connection between the purely professional journals and the lay public,"[89] *Health* carried original medical articles, weekly jottings from leading medical journals, and family guides to the sanitary sciences, all couched in entertaining terms to "interest and amuse as well as to instruct" the public.[90] Diffusing knowledge about the health sciences among people "in language which a child may understand" was indeed the journal's central policy. Throughout his writings, Wilson attached importance to the idea of self-help in preventative medicine. In contrast to Richardson's motto, Wilson's notion that "the progress of health is, after all, an individual rather than a national question" epitomizes his belief in popularizing health culture.[91]

According to Wilson, the human body has a natural healing power of its own: "As in the body political, so in the body natural, there is a 'balance of power.' . . . When the pendulum of action has swung to the side of disease, there is a tendency to bring its motion back to a state of equilibrium."[92] For Wilson and his colleagues, often all that medicine can do is to

---

[87] Ibid.
[88] Ibid.
[89] *Health*, May 11, 1883, vii.
[90] "Editorial Address," in *Health*, April 11, 1884, 1.
[91] Andrew Wilson, *A Manual of Health Science, Adapted for use in schools and colleges and suited to the requirements of students preparing for the examinations in hygiene of the science and art department, etc.*, 2nd ed. (London: Longmans, Green and Co., 1890), 7.
[92] Andrew Wilson, *Health for People* (London: Sampson Low, Marston, Searle, & Rivington, 1886), 101.

help nature operate the therapeutic power inherent in the human body—rather than combat disease. No believer in mysterious natural powers, Wilson attempted to explain the body's processes by reworking evolutionary concepts. In the struggle for existence and for adapting to its surroundings, he believed, the body had developed biologically favored organs or body parts and accumulated "an overplus of power" within them. The healing power of nature, Wilson argued, is nothing less than this "excess or overplus of vital strength and energy, which has been collected and intensified in the best of the race, and in the best of our organs."[93] Nature's swinging back to a state of equilibrium is thus akin to a "certain deposit-receipt at the bank of bodily power." Overly drawn deposits, on the other hand, cause disease, strain, and injury. According to Wilson, "the healthy body, in truth, is a soil which is perpetually rejecting the disease-matter which it inhales into its lungs, ingests with its food."[94] Thus, each individual's careful and incessant effort to keep the balance of nature's power is instrumental in maintaining health.

Patent medicine advertisements frequently relied on such popularized notions of health culture. According to advertising for Guy's Tonic, for example, the causes of decreases in nature's surplus deposits are to be found in the "perversions or extremes of the natural forces by which we are surrounded."[95] By noting that "the Body should be freed from an undue accumulation and retention of gaseous and fermenting waste of a semi-poisonous nature," it insisted that Guy's Tonic helps the body utilize nature's own process of maintaining health.[96]

In short, health culture nurtured an understanding that the most effective method of enhancing one's health was not through taking medicine, but through building preventative knowledge as an effort to keep at bay the forces of disease. Throughout his writings, Wilson always argued that people must be knowledgeable about pure foods, pure air, pure water supply, healthy homes, well-fitting clothing, and cleanliness of the body, and he emphasized food as the linchpin of a preventative health regimen. Comparing the body with a continuously-burning fire, Wilson wrote that

---

[93] Ibid., 107.

[94] Ibid., 108.

[95] Ibid., 107.

[96] Guy's Tonic Treatment, in JJC, Patent Medicine Box 2.

"in the body, a kind of chemical burning is always going."[97] Just as a fire would die out without a constant supply of fuel, the body would become diseased without fresh and "nitrogenous" foods.

Such ideas about preventative medicine being made possible by the use of medical commodities became popular and helped create a shared health culture by the 1880s; this was demonstrated by the public's enthusiastic attention paid to the International Health Exhibition that opened on June 18, 1884.[98] Illustrating all the elements assumed to contribute to a healthy life, the Exhibition provided a "Sanitary Show" of health commodities for the public.[99] In booth after booth of its "Health Section," numerous foods, clothes, a newly patented drainage system, and hygienic types of dwellings were vividly displayed to the public. In addition, various kinds of amusements were provided, in order to make the Exhibition as popular an event as possible: daily performances by military bands amused "visitors whose desire to be entertained" was "greater than their interest in sanitary and hygiene questions."[100] But the Exhibition's primary purpose was didactic. In a speech given on its opening day, the Prince of Wales noted that "for scientific and educational purposes the public at large may derive even greater benefit from it than they can get by merely coming here to enjoy the Exhibition as a place of recreation."[101] The Exhibition's Educational Section highlighted recently invented teaching appliances, arts, and handicrafts. As "the public themselves should consider, much more than they do, the utility and the means of maintaining their own health," the Exhibition purported to be a pedagogical environment in which all the social classes within London could gather and be immersed in the new health culture.[102]

---

[97] Andrew Wilson, *How to Keep Well* (London: W. & R. Chambers, 1906), 102.

[98] Many newspapers and periodicals welcomed this Exhibition and carried articles on its purpose and its illustrations. See, for example, the articles in *The Illustrated London News*, 1884.

[99] For spectacular scenes from the proliferating exhibitions of the nineteenth century, see Richard D. Altick, *Shows of London* (Cambridge, Mass.: Harvard University Press, 1978).

[100] "The International Health Exhibition," in *Health*, May 9, 1884, iv.

[101] *The Health Exhibition Literature*, 24–25.

[102] *The Health Exhibition Literature*, vol. 8, printed and published for the Executive Council of the International Health Exhibition, and for the Council of the

By its very nature, however, the Exhibition was doomed to be primarily a spectacular display of objects.[103] Even though it was intended to
demonstrate a semiotic concept of health, such an intention could be
realized only by displaying commodities regarded as vital ingredients for
living a healthy life. For the more than three thousand exhibitors, the
Exhibition became a golden opportunity to advertise their manufactured
objects as the means of promoting the ideal and the reality of health. In
short, capitalistic interests inevitably permeated the Exhibition's organization and display.

All along the "great central avenue" of the Exhibition lay the Food
Section. Representing nutritious foods from all parts of the world,
specimens ranged from unprocessed vegetables and fruits (displayed as
paper and clay facsimiles), to a number of newly manufactured foods
such as "compressed food," "regimen bread," liquid nutrition, and other
artificial substances, which were all said to have various medicinal virtues
(Fig. 2-2). Perhaps not surprisingly, there arose a concern that in this main
gallery "the commercial interest was mainly predominant."[104] Ernest
Hart, a member of the Executive Council of the Exhibition, was bewil-
dered by his anticipated roles both as promoter of the Exhibition and as
vigorous prosecutor of patent medicines. In a lecture before the Society
of the Exhibition, Hart expressed his deep anxiety that consumers' high
demand for cheap and simplified foods had promoted the "introduction
of articles called 'substitutes'" by manufacturers. Fearing that the Health
Exhibition might boost food adulteration, Hart could only persuade
himself that the Exhibition's International Jury "has, we trust, done
something towards putting a stop to a trade which, while it enriches the

---

Society of Arts (London: William Clowes and Sons, Ltd., 1884), 4.

[103] Thomas Richards, starting his narrative with the Great Exhibition of 1851,
has explored the ways in which the burgeoning commodity culture and advertisements could be seen as an emergence of theatrical spectacle in bourgeois
society: *The Commodity Culture of Victorian England: Advertising and Spectacle, 1851–
1914* (London: Verso, 1991).

[104] Ernest Hart, *The International Health Exhibition: Its Influence and Possible Sequels, A
Paper read before the Society of Arts*, November 26, 1884 (London: Smith, Elder and
Co., 1885), 11. See also his report on the Exhibition, "Abstract of a Lecture on
the International Health Exhibition of 1884: Its Influence and Possible Sequels,"
*British Medical Journal*, 2 (December 6, 1884): 1115–1122.

unscrupulous trade, places the honest manufacturer in an awkward position."[105]

With "a considerable number of tests and analyses" the jurors awarded selected exhibitors 200 diplomas of honor, 270 gold medals, 580 silver medals, 670 bronze medals, and 100 special letters of thanks.[106] But such awards were not entirely impartial. In selecting the jurors, the "most scrupulous care" had been taken "to meet the view of the Exhibitors themselves." Although the Executive Council actually awarded the jury positions, the exhibitors themselves were requested to list their preferences as to the "three gentlemen to be recommended as Jurors." To select the final jurors from the list, the Commission "endeavoured to give full weight to the opinions expressed by Exhibitors" in order that "awards will be satisfactory alike to the Exhibitors and public."[107] Despite Hart's concerns, manufacturers consequently had a strong hand in the awards process, and their participation in the Exhibition turned out to be a boon in terms of advertising.

Patent foods sold as having medicinal effects jostled each other in the displays along that central avenue of the Exhibition. For example, an American manufacturer, Murdock Liquid Food Company, displayed "a raw extract of beef, mutton, and fruits, condensed manifold," which was used in American hospitals for men and women with chronic illnesses.[108] Mellins, which was most frequently advertised as an artificial food for infants and invalids, claimed to have a "high degree of alkalinity, in order to neutralise the acidity of cow's milk and that of the cereals." Its inventor, G. Mellin, also displayed his Lacto-Glycose, "a substitute for the natural food of very young children."[109] Many other substitutes were also exhibited, such as Crawford's "amylaceous food," Mottershead's "peptonised food," and Benger's "liquor pancreaticus." There was also Dr. Druitt's remedy for nervous exhaustion, as well as Loeflund's "Pure

---

[105] Ibid., 12.

[106] Ibid., 14.

[107] "The International Health Exhibition," *Health*, May 9, 1884, iv.

[108] "The International Health Exhibition Supplement," Second Notice, *Health*, May 16, 1884, iv.

[109] "The International Health Exhibition Supplement," Third Notice, *Health*, May 23, 1884, iii. This series went to fourth and fifth notices: May 30, 1884, iii–vi; and June 6, 1884, iii–vi.

Hordeum" and Barf & Wire's "Krechyle," which were respectively displayed as medicinal beef and malt extracts.[110]

Roughly speaking, in fact, half of the patent medicines colorfully advertised on the market called themselves patent foods, nutritious substitutes, medicinal drinks, and meat or vegetable extracts. Cod liver oil was a frequently advertised natural regimen. From the early 1870s, Dr. de Jongh's Light-Brown Cod Liver Oil was put on the market for "prostration and emaciation, where the vital forces are reduced, and where life appears to be even at its lowest ebb."[111] Similarly, Allen & Hanbury first became world famous for its successful sale of BYNIN, the mixed combination of malt extract and cod liver oil. The company also sold as "A Specific for NEURALGIA" or "TONGA," a medicinal fluid extracted from the "Barkes, Roots, and Leaves of several plants."[112] Cod liver oil was often sold as an emulsion. "Scott's Emulsion," one advertisement proclaimed, "is a NET GAIN. . . . In thousands of cases, ordinary food, even if digested, is not enough to meet the demands upon it [the body]. The vital spark burns low in consequence, and there is constant danger."[113]

Though Mellins was no doubt a brand of artificial food, many other nourishments which were "already cooked requiring neither boiling nor straining" were also on the market.[114] Artificial food became a mainstay for Allen & Hanbury's business. "No Better Foods Exist," the company boasted, than "a nourishment peculiarly adapted to the digestive organs of Infants and Young."[115] Dr. Ridge's Patent Cooked Food and Benger's Food, displayed at the Exhibition, were other brands helping infants and other persons suffering from digestive trouble.[116] The medicinal virtues

---

[110] Ibid., *Health*, May 23, iv–v.

[111] Dr. de Jongh's Light-Brown Cod Liver Oil, *Illustrated London News*, December 21, 1884, August 30, 1884, and in JJC, Well Known Patent Medicine Box 6.

[112] Allen & Hanbury's advertisement of "Bynin" and "Tonga," in JJC, Patent Medicine Box 1.

[113] Scott's Emulsion, *Graphic*, January 1, 1898, 26.

[114] Mellins' Foods were extensively advertised in many journals. See, for example, *Health*, March 29, 1889 and March 10, 1893.

[115] Allen & Hanbury's Infants Food, *Illustrated London News*, January 13, 1894, 64.

[116] "Ridge's Food is Enjoyed by All the Young Masters," *Health*, February 10,

of such daily foods and drinks, often supported by doctors' recommendations and certificates, became fanciful strategies for many manufacturers. For example, cocoa manufacturers never failed to miss a chance to publicize their product's medicinal qualities. The earliest advertisements of Van Houten Cocoa and Cadbury's Cocoa always accentuated the nitrogenous, body-building—thus highly therapeutic—virtues. Van Houten, it was claimed, would "smooth the nerves and is alike strengthening. . . . Its nourishing qualities enable the blood to build up, during sleep."[117]

Another interesting instance of the public's concern and demand for nutritious food was Hovis, the nationally marketed brand of enriched brown bread. Launched in the 1880s as Smith's Old Patent Germ Bread at a time when white bread was already popular, Hovis was sold as patented bread, as the "Only Food that will Prevent or Cure Indigestion" because it returned wheat germ to white flour. From the 1890s, numerous advertisements for Hovis in popular newspapers and magazines boasted of the bread's therapeutic effect of curing indigestion and developing good bones, body tissue, and muscles. These advertisements illustrated how a scaled balance of nutrition guaranteed the benefits of its brown bread: "1-1/2 lbs. HOVIS is more digestible and nourishing than 1 lb. of WHITE BREAD and 1/2 lb. of BEEF STEAK."[118] Hovis also asserted that for the "formation of sound teeth, strong bones, vigorous constitution," Triticumina Bread was worth buying.[119] Some years later, in 1911, the *Daily Mail* began to run a campaign to make brown bread the "standard bread," insisting that white bread was a serious underlying cause of the deterioration of the nation's public health. The press employed the study of the Cambridge biochemist Frederick Gowland Hopkins, who was doing experiments on the existence of what were later labeled "vitamins." The *Daily Mail's* campaign highlighted the importance of nutrients by returning to the traditional way of making bread. Although people in the baking trade spearheaded a boycott of the *Daily Mail* for its bread campaign, British consumers continued to see Hovis bread as a nutritious

---

1893; Benger's Food, *Graphic*, April 7, 1906.

[117] Van Houten Cocoa, *Graphic*, March, 29, 1902, 439; Cadbury's Cocoa, for example, *Health*, February 15, 1889.

[118] "Hovis, at One Third the Cost," *Health*, June 16, 1893, 2.

[119] "Triticumina Bread: Entire Wheatmeal Malt Bread," *Health*, January 13, 1893.

product.[120]

Various kinds of medicinal extracts such as Coleman's Liebig's Extract
of Meat and Malt Wine occupied a considerable market share of patent
medicine. The Maltine Company sold Carnrick's Beef Peptonids, "Concentrated Powdered Extract of Beef, Partially Digested and Combined
with an Equal Portion of Gluten."[121] Lion Brand Essence of Beef was
another extract for "invalids & Persons of Weak Digestion."[122] Gordon's
Extract, sold as a pure vegetable essence and "the great panacea," could
"Cure Disordered Liver and Chronic Indigestion," and "Cure those
Discharged from Hospitals as Incurable."[123]

Today these various substitutes, extracts, and drinks would be catego-
rized as food products, but in the late nineteenth and early twentieth
centuries manufacturers instead stressed the medicinal virtues of their
panoply of products. As a result, many of these products drew condemnation from elite doctors. Nonetheless, despite—or possibly because
of—such opposition from professional doctors, patent foods and medicines continued to flourish. By exploiting people's obsession with health,
these manufacturers of patent medicines used advertising language that
easily caught consumers' attention and encouraged them to imagine alternatives to professional medical treatment. The newly emerging health
culture, partly cultivated by medical doctors such as the popularizer Andrew Wilson, opened a Pandora's box, as doctors' medical services were
increasingly replaced by medical commodities. And, *fin-de-siècle* capital
never overlooked the profit that could be gained through the commodification of this health culture.

### A Robust Body, Perfect Health, and "Physical Culture"

While throughout history being healthy and nurturing one's physical
well-being have no doubt been central preoccupations for many people,

---

[120] For the *Daily Mail's* campaign for brown bread as standard bread, see Mark
Weatherall, "Bread and Newspapers: The Making of 'A Revolution in the Science
of Food,'" in Harmke Kamminga and Andrew Cunningham, eds., *The Science and
Culture of Nutrition, 1840–1940* (Amsterdam: Rodopi, 1995).
[121] Carnrick's Beef Peptonids, *Health*, April 13, 1883.
[122] Lion Brand Essence Beef, *Health*, July 17, 1885.
[123] Gordon's Extract, *Health*, August 28, 1885.

the motivations for this concern, and the forms in which this concern is manifested, have varied greatly. In pre-modern England, the quest for health had manifested itself within communal, religious, or ethical boundaries. Maintaining a healthy body was a means to a more practical end: mere survival, in a period in which life was often precarious, had been necessary for the subsistence of the family and social and spiritual communities. Sustaining a healthy life, to put it simply, had become integrated into what it meant to be a good Christian. As Roy Porter has described, this godly motivation for being of good health could—and was—taken to extremes, and was exploited by charlatans, such as the notable eighteenth-century quack James Graham, who played the role of a "vaudeville Messiah" with his "Temple of Health" that seemed to have attracted many of its patients for its sex-therapy.[124]

By the end of the nineteenth century, however, people gradually began to seek vigorous health as a means of fulfilling individual, discretionary desires. This change in the perception of what constituted good health was the result of new desires rooted in modern consumers' understanding of the body as a secular object. As the emergence of a mass market contributed to the leveling of a class hierarchy through impersonal material exchange, an individualized health ethos helped generate a proliferation of therapeutic medical commodities. For the late nineteenth-century public, being healthy meant not only acquiring a properly functioning body but also seeking to release untapped reservoirs of abundant and exuberant energy and gaining access to a richer, fuller life.[125] Many people regarded physical strength as the most vigorous—and therefore the most desirable— manifestation of good health.

With so many people being deeply concerned about their health, medical commodities companies became socially acceptable—as we shall see—and they flourished in the same niche that many of the patent

---

[124] Porter, *Health for Sale*, 161–163.

[125] Lears argues that consumers' desires for self-realization promoted the proliferation of consumption culture in the United States. See his "From Salvation to Self-Realization: Advertising and the Therapeutic Roots of the Consumer Culture," in T. J. Jackson Lears and Richard Wightman Fox, eds., *The Culture of Consumption: Critical Essays in American History, 1880–1980* (New York: Pantheon Books, 1983). See also Lears, *Fables of Abundance: A Cultural History of Advertising in America* (New York: Basic Books, 1994).

medicines proprietors strove to occupy through their advertisements. The
medical commodities businesses used the same advertising techniques, too,
in simultaneously producing and exploiting strong aspirations for vigorous
health; they used the same key terms as did the advertisements for patent
medicines—"perfect health," "robust body," "vital energy," "supreme
strength," "bodily vigor," "robust masculinity," "long life," and the like.

In the cross-class pursuit of bourgeois consumption, an openly competitive society enabled people to seek increasingly hedonistic satisfaction.[126] Epitomizing the superfluity of desire, flawless health became a
sign of ultimate achievement. Many books gave instructions on how to
gain perfection in life, first and foremost in the form of health: *Perfect
Health for Women and Children; The Modern Family Doctor, A Guide to Perfect
Health; The Secret of Perfect Health; The Key to Perfect Health and the Successful
Application of Psycho-Therapeutics*, and so on.[127] Perfect enjoyment of life
was also associated with physical beauty, which in turn was associated
specifically with health: "perfect health is the foundation of all culture of
physical beauty," wrote one of these authors. "We cannot add or take
away one inch form our stature, but the well-knit, supple frame of perfect
health does a great deal to atone for excess or surplus."[128] Advertising
language no doubt reflected this perfectionist psychology. For example,
Hood's sarsaparilla always promised "perfect health restored."[129] Other
advertisements went so far as to dispense psychological advice along with

---

[126] Lori A. Loeb rejects Veblen's view of consumption as a result of social
emulation and, along with Perkin and McKendrick, emphasizes the private,
autonomous and inconspicuous aspect of consumption. She sees the key to
consumer demand in a bourgeois culture as the seeking of egalitarian equal
opportunity. *Consuming Angels: Advertising and Victorian Women* (Oxford: Oxford
University Press, 1994).

[127] Elizabeth Sloan Chester, *Perfect Health for Women and Children* (London:
Methuen & Company, 1912); anonymous, *The Modern Family Doctor: A Guide to
Perfect Health* (London: T. C. & E. Jack, 1914); Walter S. Moon, *The Secret of Perfect
Health: Disease Rendered Preventible and Removable by Washing its Germs out of the Body*
(London: Offices of Sanitary Engineering, 1890); and Arthur Hallum, *The Key to
Perfect Health and the Successful Application of Psycho-Therapeutics: A Practical Guide to
both Operator and Patient* (London: St. Clements Press, 1912).

[128] *The Modern Family Doctor*, 262.

[129] Hood's Sarsaparilla, in JJC, Well Known Patent Medicines, Outsized Material.

a recipe for health: an advertisement of J. C. Eno, a brand of fruit salt supposedly salutary for health, preached that "Perfect Happiness lies First of All in Perfect Health, and does not Grieve for the things which we Have Not, but Rejoices for Those Which We Have."[130]

Moreover, products sold for brain or nervous health were often considered as a great means of acquiring perfect health. There was Bromo-Phosph, sold as "Brain Food" and reputed to restore the energy and vital force of the entire body; adverts claimed that "it prevents Decay of Nerve Force, adds zest and pleasure to life by invigorating the whole frame."[131] The promise of robust health called the public's attention to how medicine could help people to achieve a fully prosperous and pleasant life: "Robust Health," an advertisement for Bile Beans vaunted, "is the thing necessary to complete enjoyment of life," while another famous liver pill, Beecham's, was always asserted "TO BUILD ROBUST HEALTH."[132]

Advertisements also often emphasized virile masculinity as a symbol of a happy, healthy life. Many of the patent medicine advertisements focused on nervousness, debility, and weakness, all three of which were seen as hallmarks of women's commonly unhealthy state of being. Recovering strength and vitality was often emphasized as being important for both men and women. In the modern urban environment, masculinity was not simply a gendered attribute; rather, it became associated with a unisex achievement of good health. Typical indeed were the words "vigor," "vitality," "valorizing," "strong," and "vigorous health":

HOOD'S SARSAPARILLA
which makes rich, healthy
blood and thus gives strength
and elasticity to the muscles,
vigor to the brain, and health
and vitality to every part of
the body. Hood's Sarsaparilla
MAKES THE WEAK STRONG

---

[130] Eno's Fruit Salt, *Graphic*, April 2, 1900, 73.

[131] Bromo-Phosph or Brain Food, in JJC, Patent Medicine Box 1.

[132] Bile Beans and Beecham's Pills, both in JJC, Well Known Patent Medicines, Box 5.

Similarly, Guy's Tonic, promised to restore "Muscular Vitality" and was said to give its user "that Vigour and alertness that are signs of returning Health." Its advertisement depicted two men, respectively toasting and thanking the product for the vivacity and strength it had given them (Fig. 2-3).

What cultural meanings underlay these advertising words? In other words, when the public consumed these commodities, what imaginary landscape was associated with what products? The inextricable mesh of images these words conveyed to consumers can best be understood by looking at Britain's burgeoning "physical culture" and its identification of muscular vitality with general health.

Small wonder, then, that this was the period in which gymnastics, body-building, and all kinds of sports activities were introduced as health-related disciplines. For late Victorians, being healthy signified a vitality-acquiring process, and for that purpose, various kinds of physical exercises were recommended as having medicinal virtues. Archibald Maclaren, founder of the Oxford gymnasium and an apostle of physical education for school boys and school girls, defined health as "that amount of vital capacity, which shall enable each man in his place to pursue his calling and work on in his working life."[133] Gymnastic exercises and training, Maclaren wrote, aimed to achieve "the strengthening, the developing of his body, muscle and joint, organ and limb; [to] make him a man, and as a man give him power over himself."[134] As Bruce Haley has elegantly described in *The Healthy Body and Victorian Culture*, the years between the 1850s and 1880s saw the rise of a new mood in which various sports became a national mania. All well-known modern sports including football, hockey, croquet, lawn tennis, badminton, bicycling, boxing, wrestling, gymnastics, golf, and exercising with dumb-bells (an activity that had once been the object of ridicule by gentlemen) were developed into respectable educational disciplines in that period. It is significant that they were accepted and celebrated as a part of physical education which would provide healthy and vigorous life for young men.[135]

---

[133] Archbold Maclaren, *A System of Physical Education, Theoretical and Practical* (Oxford: Clarendon Press, 1885), 24.

[134] Ibid., 91.

[135] Bruce Haley, "Growing Up Healthy: Images of Boyhood," in *The Healthy Body*

The development of a physical culture was first recognized by those upper-middle-class enthusiasts who saw a pedagogical role for sports in the fashioning of the true manly gentleman.[136] By the end of the century, however, physical culture expanded to become a predominant concern for a wide range of Victorians who worshipped physical vigor and robust muscularity, sought out exercise, and bought or began seeking to use various exercise machines. Even as tricycling was in demand as a bourgeois substitute for aristocratic sports, horse-riding's shaking-the-liver movements were believed to help squeeze waste out of that organ.[137] For similar purposes, Vigor & Company extensively marketed such machines as the Vigor's Home Rower, a perfect chest and muscle developer, and Vigor's Horse-Action Saddle, a perfect substitute for a live horse (Fig. 2-4). The advertisement for this machine claims that "It invigorates the system by bringing all the Vital Organs into Inspiriting Action. It is a complete cure for Obesity, Hysteria, and Gout." Interestingly, the man depicted in the advertisement was a bearded, aristocratic-looking gentleman. The machine was clearly intended to attract even men from the lower-middle class who wanted to mimic the exercise habits of gentlemen—a circumstance revealed by the beard of the man in the illustration.[138]

The way in which urban dwellers in the Victorian age believed in the importance of physical culture and exercise habits was quite similar to our own thinking. Dr. Allinson, a popular health writer, in 1892 wrote in his *Medical Essays*, for instance:

As a rule, English people eat too much food and take too little exercise. Let us follow the daily routine of many town-dwellers. They get up in the morning, swallow a hurried meal, and go off to business by 'bus, tram, or train; write all the morning until dinner time, take this meal leisurely, read the paper, and then return to their

*and Victorian Culture* (Cambridge: Cambridge University Press, 1978).

[136] Bruce Haley, "Anarchy and Physical Culture," in *The Healthy Body and Victorian Culture*.

[137] "The Tricycle and its Relations to Health," *Health*, June 20, 1884, 162–164.

[138] "Vigor's Home Rower: A Perfect Chest and Muscle Developer," *Illustrated London News*, February 1, 1896, 152; "Horse Exercise at Home, Vigor's Horse-Action Saddle," *Illustrated London News*, March 16, 1895, 336; "Live Your Life Healthy," *Graphic*, January 11, 1896, 55.

offices, where they sit writing until 4, 5, or 6 pm. Then they ride home, get their evening meal, and in many instances never stir out again, but read the latest novel, the evening paper, or study, or else practise on the violin, piano, etc. They retire to bed at 11 or 12, and think they have done wisely.[139]

He strongly urged urbanites to do daily exercises on a regular basis, including three-hour walks or a tricycle regimen designed to increase blood circulation throughout the body.

Physical culture was not only popularized but institutionalized. Emphasized as a tool of military discipline in France and Germany, the gymnasium was introduced into late-Victorian England as a means of providing health-enhancing exercises, and private gymnastics institutions soon became the clearest symbol of this physical culture. For example, on fashionable Regent Street, the London Polytechnic Institute directed as of 1881 by Quintin Hogg—an Eton graduate and later Chairman of the East India Company—had previously focused on providing education for working-class youths. However, it quickly became a well-known social club with well-designed exercise machines, a swimming pool, and other exercise facilities that were offered to the lower-middle-class public. By 1882, its membership exceeded 3,000.[140] Hogg had earlier realized the importance of athletic exercise combined with a Christian education and an education that was both technical and practical: in 1865 he had opened a boarding school on York Street, for the philanthropic purpose of helping homeless and destitute boys on the lowest rung of the social ladder.[141]

---

[139] Thomas Allinson, *Medical Essays, Reprinted from the Weekly Times and Echo*, 2 volumes (London: Renshaw, 1892), 24.

[140] The records of the London Polytechnic Institute are held at the University of Westminster Archives. See, for example, *The Polytechnic: (The Pioneer Institute for Technical Education), Its Genesis and Present Status* (London: The Polytechnic, 309 Regent Street, 1892). See also F. A. McKenzie, "The Regent Street Polytechnic: England's Largest Educational Institute," *Windsor Magazine*, 8 (October 1898).

[141] See Gerard Van de Linde, "Mr. Quintin Hogg and the London Polytechnic," *The Clerks' Journal*, October 1, 1888, 3–4; Sarah A. Tooley, "The Polytechnic Movement: An Interview with Mr. Quintin Hogg," *The Young Man: A Monthly Journal and Review*, 101 (May 1895): 145–150. Both journals are held at the University of Westminster Archives.

Under the aegis of trained gymnasts, Hogg's Polytechnic Institute offered many classes using dumb-bells and bar-bells, rowing exercises, parallel bars, flying rings, high jumping, vaulting-horses, and trapezes.[142] The Institute, appealing to people's quest for physical development and muscular health, often advertised its gymnastic facilities in health-related journals as tools for curing back pain, rheumatism and stomach troubles. Whereas physical sports had once been solely the domain of the well-to-do, Hogg's Institute offered a more democratic vision of health: the gymnasium and other facilities at the Institution were open to any member of the public who bought tickets at three shillings per annum in addition to the regular subscription (Fig. 2-5).

Another health regimen, body-building, emerged within this physical culture and eventually took hold in late-Victorian society. The best-selling health manual of body building, William Blaikie's *How to Get Strong and How to Stay So*, appeared in numerous editions from its first publication in 1880. It acquired a wide range of readers in both the United States and Britain, a testament to the transatlantic cultural environment in which health was preceived as an epiphenomenon of muscular vigor.[143]

"Never, since the world began," Blaikie wrote, "was the art of body-building so well understood as it is now. Your lacks; your weakness; your probable length of life, can be gauged with a certainty well-nigh unerring."[144] Observing that frequent complaints of the blockage of physical vitality were closely connected with mental strain, fretfulness, anxiety, and depression, Blaikie stressed throughout the book the usefulness of body-building or "vigorous muscular exercise for all parts of the body" in order to rescue people from both physical and mental "running down." Capitalizing on the extent to which sedentary occupations—for instance, teaching, office work, practicing law, publishing, and performing medical duties—had increased rapidly from the 1880s onward, he argued that a vigorous mind required a vigorous body. Moreover,

---

[142] Wilson's journal, *Health*, carried an introductory article on Hogg's gymnastic facility. See "Gymnastics at the London Polytechnic," *Health*, November 14, 1884, 106–108.

[143] William Blaikie, *How to Get Strong and How to Stay So* (London: Sampson Low, Marston & Company, 1899).

[144] Ibid., 466.

he emphasized that these most learned professions needed greater physical endurance: "to win lasting distinction in sedentary, in-door occupations, which task the brain and the nervous system, extraordinary toughness of body must accompany extraordinary mental powers. . . . The sound body is at the bottom of all."[145] Blaikie's championing of people exercising to gain "an unusual store of vitality," "the stout bodily frame," and "bodily stamina" eventually carried the day, with exercise coming to embody the entrepreneurial ideal in Victorian England.[146]

Best illustrating this ideal was a body-builder's success story and his commercial entry into the medical domain. Although now faded from memory, a few generations ago Eugen Sandow represented the quintessence of the strongman. Born in 1867 in Königsberg, East Prussia, with the name Friedlich Wilhelm Müller, Sandow toured widely throughout Europe as a circus performer and model for art studios and anatomy classrooms before contributing directly to England's physical culture from the late 1890s onward as the billboard figure for a well-developed muscular body.[147] Sandow's physical appearance, and his activities as the muscular apostle for the health businesss, were doubtless important in helping transform Britain's physical culture from being a backroom hobby to occupying the forefront of the British social scene. A down-at-heel body-builder until 1889, during the 1890s Sandow won enthusiastic acclamations as the strongest man in the world through his innovative and

---

[145] Ibid., 62.

[146] Ibid., 466, 467, and 470.

[147] For the life and activities of Eugen Sandow, see the books and publications produced by himself and his Institute of Physical Culture: *Body-Building, or Man in the Making: How to Become Healthy & Strong*, 1905; *The Construction and Reconstruction of the Human Body: A Manual of the Therapeutics of Exercise, With a Foreword by Sir A. Conan Doyle.*, 1907; *Life is Movement: the Physical Reconstruction and Regeneration of the People*, 1919; *The Power of Evidence, Being a Series of Reports of Patients Treated by the Sandow Method*, 1919; *Sandow's Curative Chart, 1910; Strength and How To Obtain It*, 1897. Information on Sandow's colorful life is scattered, limited and unreliable. One good biography is Charles T. Trevor, *Sandow the Magnificent: His Life as Adventure, Amazing Feats of Strength, and Exploits as a Strong Man* (London: The Mitre Press, 1946). The most extensive study of Sandow's life is David L. Chapman, *Sandow the Magnificent: Eugen Sandow and the Beginnings of Body-Building* (Urbana and Chicago: University of Illinois Press, 1994).

well-performed muscle-strength shows at music halls and theaters throughout Britain.[148] On the stage he lifted not only heavy bar-bells, dumb-bells, and even a horse, but also famously supported a grand piano with eight players on his chest in the wrestler's bridge-like position. During a successful tour in the United States, Sandow attracted large audiences with showy performances such as fighting with a lion in a cage. Crowds adored him, and he was treated like an early movie star and, in fact, in 1894 starred in a short film shot by Edison Studios with the company's new Kinetoscopy technology.[149]

Sandow's reputation as a reborn Hercules soon spread to nearly every quarter of the British Isles. Yet his gentlemanly looks and behavior—as well as his distinguished talent as a propagandist and marketing genius—also enabled him to go beyond being just another body-building showman. Given his enthusiastic audiences, he recognized the broader public's desire to become stronger, healthier, and more physically perfect. Initially, in 1887, he opened his first school, the Institute of Physical Culture, on St. James' Street in London, where he trained instructors of body-building and provided a fashionable therapeutic retreat. Subsequently he published a considerable number of books, pamphlets, and advertising brochures, and in 1889 he even established his own periodical, *Sandow's Magazine of Physical Culture*. His most widely disseminated book, *Strength and How to Obtain It*, went through several editions, and its sales were said to have exceeded 200,000 copies.[150] He successfully earned admirers among all classes, including such celebrities as the famous author Conan Doyle and the pianist Ignace Paderewski, and in 1911 he was even

---

[148] Sandow appeared on the British social scene in 1889, when he defeated the athlete-showman duo known as Sampson and Cyclops. These two showmen had attracted large audiences to the Royal Aquarium in Westminster for their strongman performances, during which they lifted dumb-bells and broke chains around their chests—favorite attractions among Londoners of the day. To make their show appear credible, Sampson had announced a prize of £100 to anyone who could duplicate the feats performed by his pupil Cyclops, and £500 to the person who could surpass those feats. Sandow successfully challenged Sampson and Cyclops and earned the enthusiastic support of London's music-hall goers.

[149] Chapman, 76–78.

[150] Eugen Sandow, *Body-Building, or Man in the Making: How to Become Healthy and Strong* (London: Gale & Polden, 1905), 34.

appointed as an adviser on Physical Culture to King George V.

In short, Sandow was a phenomenon. Most striking, however, was his outstanding talent as a businessman. Soon after founding his first school Sandow realized that the business of weight training could be extended beyond being an amusement for working-class men to embracing up-per-middle-class professionals who began to seek out weight training as a viable means of achieving maximum health.[151] Sandow therefore estab-lished his institutions in the heart of London (in Piccadilly Circus and other central places), and made each a sort of clubhouse with a luxurious environment full of ornamentation, in order to make his muscle-building business attractive to both gentlemen and ladies. Emphasizing exercise's ability to reduce obesity, to slim double chins and round hips, to plump up skinny arms, and to rehabilitate facial muscles, Sandow also attempted to woo women clients to an establishment intended strictly for ladies at 115A, Ebury Street.[152] Even more audaciously, he also began to invent and sell medico-physical appliances, patenting them and extensively mar-keting them: "Sandow's Own Combined Developer," the "Symmetrion" for women, the "Spring-Grip Dumb-bell," and so on.[153] His health business went on to sell "Sandow's Embrocation," a liniment for athletes, and "Sandow's Health and Strength Cocoa."

Sandow brought physical culture to the center of public attention by emphasizing that his physical training was useful as a new and physio-logical medicine. In his treatise *The Construction and Reconstruction of the Human Body*, for example, he explained how the exercise of mus-cles—promoting the circulation of the blood and enhancing a more energetic metabolism—produced genuine therapeutic effects and gave followers of his methods "perfect health." Using medical terminology

---

[151] He wrote, "The eternal complaint of some men that they cannot find time in the morning to exercise before starting for business, and that they are too tired when they return home induced me to set up a school in the heart of the City." *Body-Building, or Man in the Making*, 41.

[152] Eugen Sandow, *Strength and How to Obtain It*, 32.

[153] "Sandow's Own Combined Developer" was a combined machine of a rubber exerciser, chest-expander, light dumb-bells, and weightlifting apparatus. His "Symmetrion" was a band exerciser intended to achieve a symmetric form. The "Spring-Grip Dumb-Bell" was a device designed to be adjustable to users' strength by the addition or subtraction of springs.

with equal emphases on utility and efficiency, Sandow explained how exercise benefited the body:

> Exercise of the muscles therefore leads, as we have seen, to a greater flow of blood to the muscular tissue, to a greater waste of its tissue, and to a more rapid elimination of carbonic acid, and a more complete, if not a greater, elimination of waste nitrogenous products which go to the formation of urea. It also leads to a more perfect nutrition of the muscular fibres, which not only repair their waste but increase in size, and this extra nutrition involves a more perfect utilisation of the food stuffs introduced into the body.[154]

Year after year, Sandow's attempts to combine his physical culture with the semblance of medical knowledge became more conspicuous. He began to call his system "scientific curative physical culture," even as his treatise *The Power of Evidence* boldly advocated "the Sandow method of curing illness without medicine" and prescribed exercise treatments for each of twenty physical disorders, including liver trouble, rheumatism, insomnia, infections of the heart, anæmia, and skin disorders.[155] For twenty-four physical ailments, his Institute even compiled a series of health brochures called the *Complete Health Library*, which explained "how the reader may cure himself or herself or a child by means of simple scientific exercise entirely at home."[156] According to a four-page advertisement in *The Daily Mail*, his Institute offered these booklets free to the readers of the newspaper.[157] Like the proprietors of many other contemporary commercial medical institutions, Sandow also sought the collaboration of medical professionals by employing doctors in his Curative Institutes to carry out physical examinations or by obtaining more than a hundred testimonials from eminent physicians on Harley Street, the center of a prestigious area in which the number of doctors, hospitals, and clinics increased in the late nineteenth century.

---

[154] Eugen Sandow, *The Construction and Reconstruction of the Human Body*, 86.

[155] Eugen Sandow, *The Power of Evidence: The Sandow Method of Curing Illness Without Medicine* (London: Sandow Curative Institute, Ltd., 1919).

[156] See the four-page advertisement in "The Sandow Curative Physical Culture," Special Supplement to *The Daily Mail*, April 26, 1909, held in the JJC, Outsized Material Box.

[157] Ibid., loc. cit.

Testimonials about Sandow's medical contributions were far from
scarce and came from physicians and eminent public figures alike. For
instance, W. T. Stead, editor of the *Pall Mall Gazette*, wrote, "Other people
found hospitals for diseases. . . . Sandow has founded a hospital for health.
It is not alone an establishment for curing illness; it is an institution for
maintaining, preserving and improving health."[158] Despite his obvious
commercial interests, Sandow avoided prosecution by notable watchdogs
of bogus health businesses. Henry Labouchère of *Truth*, for example,
sent investigators to Sandow's Institute, but concluded with praise: "I am
convinced that physical culture—in the right hands—is a powerful—a
very powerful—weapon ready to the hands of those who have set out to
fight the good fight against disease."[159]

Here, a view developed that muscular vigor signaled a life of health.
Indeed, a glance at many patented commodities sold as having medical
virtues reveals that many attempted to capitalize on these popular aspirations for muscular vitality and accompanying health. Bovril, a famous
medical meat extract that sold as a "strengthening & invigorating bever-
age," displayed in its advertisement a muscular man fighting with a roaring
lion. It manufacturers also proclaimed "Cold, Chills, influenza and epidemic diseases attack the weak—Bovril makes people strong" (Fig.
2-6).[160] The early advertisement for Hovis brown bread showed a picture
of a strongman whose muscles consisted of stacked-up Hovis loaves and
boasted that eating Hovis led to the formation of "good Bone, Brain
Flesh, and Muscle. Hovis Builds Up Strong Men" (Fig. 2-7).[161] Another
advertisement depicted a muscular arm built by an artificial food which
"supplies the Organic Phosphates, Albuminoids, and other constituents
necessary for the full development of the bones and muscles of young
Infants and growing Children" (Fig. 2-8).[162] These illustrations also called
upon Greek and Roman imagery to emphasize the masculinity of the
naked body, signaling what people perhaps most craved and consumed in
the highly industrialized urban milieu of London. Interestingly, in the very

---

[158] *The Power of Evidence*, 13.
[159] Ibid., 14.
[160] Bovril, *Illustrated London News*, March 17, 1894, 339.
[161] Hovis, *Graphic*, January 29, 1898, 155.
[162] Frame Food Diet, *Illustrated London News*, November 26, 1898, 807.

extensive John Johnson Collection, there are no advertisements of these muscle boosters that picture muscular women. In the strategies behind these advertisements, the language of Victorian sensibility clearly differentiated between muscular men and nervous or neurotic women.

All in all, the language of patent medicine advertisements often exploited an imaginary landscape of ideal health that was evoked through vivid pictorial images and punctuated with words such as "energy," "vitality," "masculinity," and "strength." In these ways, the diffusion of physical culture undoubtedly produced a good commercial environment for the many stamina-forming drugs on the market.

### Medical Professionalism and Commodity Culture

What this chapter has shown are the cultural and psychological settings related to commodity, health, and well-being. A deep-rooted cultural obsession with being healthy and strong led to an increasing desire to consume medical commodities as a part of one's daily therapeutic regimen. With this growing demand, late-nineteenth-century entrepreneurs envisioned the opening up of prodigious business opportunities in the field of medicine. But as many historians have argued, this was also a period in which collectivist politics dominated, in which a chorus of professions attained triumphant social stature, and in which the state interfered and inspected on behalf of a supposedly powerless public.[163] How did members of the authoritative medical profession react to this rising commodity culture? Did they succeed in oppressing it? As a matter of fact, the ubiquitous medical commodities of the period, blooming on the terra firma of a growing health culture, spread so widely and rooted so deeply in the public imagination that doctors could not long remain indifferent to alluring displays of commercial medicine and the suggestion of profits these conveyed. In spite of attempts at professional control, collaboration between medical professionals and medical marketers became more entangled and pervasive than ever before. Many regular

---

[163] As I have discussed in the Introduction of this book, it is very important to look at and explore private lives and personal activities even in the age of overwhelming state regulation, in order to see the historical reality. See José Harris, *Private Lives, Public Spirit: Britain 1870–1914* (London: Penguin Books, 1993).

doctors, in cooperation with capitalists, accommodated themselves to high-return ventures, in the interests of pecuniary gain.

For many medical practitioners, capital gain was indeed irresistible. This desire for personal profit proliferated despite the risk of professional denunciation from elite doctors insistent on keeping up at least the façade of dignity and solidarity in the medical profession. As a result, in the late nineteenth century, disciplinary bodies such as the General Medical Council, which policed the professional behaviors of rank and file practitioners under the Medical Act of 1858, summoned and censored a large number of doctors for their ethical and professional misconduct.[164] Similarly, the Censors Board of the Royal College of Physicians (henceforth RCP) was swamped with proceedings against its members who were associated with trade or medical companies.

Not the inevitability of prosecution, but the unabashed proliferation of alleged violations, makes it difficult indeed to assert that by the century's end professionalism had achieved a monolithic dominance. In fact, commercial and capitalist interests kept a vigilant watch on the medical market, and these interests were ready to exploit any discrepancy in doctors' views on commercialism. Doctors' collaboration with businessmen in this period is clearly shown in the proliferation of advertisements for medical appliances, drinks, foods, and other commodities that were fully supported by doctors' testimonials or certificates, a practice that habitually incurred the censorship of the RCP. For example, on November 23, 1896, Bovril Ltd., a patent food company, started its medical dietary business with capital amounting to the huge sum of £2,000,000 and simultaneously recruited a licentiate, Dr. Robert Farquharson, to join the company as one of its directors. Farquharson had long been interested in sports' importance to enhancing and preserving public health. His association with the blatantly commercial company invited the reproach of the Censors Board of the RCP on April 9, 1897.[165] Similarly, on May 23, 1911, a licentiate of the RCP, Maurice Edmond Arnold Willis, was summoned and eventually forced to remove his name from the Medical

---

[164] See Russell Gordon Smith, *Medical Discipline: the Professional Conduct Jurisdiction of the General Medical Council, 1858–1990* (Oxford: Clarendon Press, 1994).
[165] See "The Bovril Company Ltd.," in *The Annals of the Royal College of Physicians*, April 9, 1897.

Register because of his association with "the Sandow Curative Institute, which systematically advertises for the purpose of procuring patients who are to receive, either by correspondence or by attendance at the said Institute, treatment of disease."[166] Similarly, the advertising pamphlet for Lactopeptine listed the names of seventy-three medical doctors who prescribed Lactopeptine to their patients and permitted the use of their testimonials in advertisements of the pamphlet.[167] For the sales of Coleman's Liebig's Extract of Meat and Malt Wine, M. K. Hargreaves, D. H. Cullimore, and J. Evans Jones, all members of the RCP, were charged with unprofessional conduct for providing their testimonials of the product's effectiveness.[168]

The influence of the nineteenth-century's professionalism no doubt enabled doctors to retain a strong grip on medical services. Nonetheless, even the medical profession's elite members faced the emerging expectation that science, too, was becoming an object of market activities and thereby was becoming commercialized. In contrast with older quack mongers, the problem for professionals in this period occurred in the very shady border between regular and irregular practitioners. The commodification of health services, as a matter of fact, rendered the demarcation between doctors and others involved with medicine rather blurred, with many medical commodities on the market echoing the language of the medical profession's health culture.

Before the ongoing commodification of health services, doctors' attitudes toward patent medicines seemed to be marked by ambivalence. When Andrew Wilson attributed the prevailing "little health" syndrome to the "expenditure of nervous energy which is inseparable from modern life," he fiercely denounced the patent-medicine business as preying upon on people's rash quest for tonic remedies. "Witness the fortunes which are still being made by the vendors of patent medicines," he wrote. "This is how the British public are still willing to be deceived by the Government approval of the medicine."[169] At the same time, however, he was a keen

---

[166] See *The Annals of the Royal College of Physicians*, May 25, 46 (1911): 47–49. Also, MSS 2412/285, dated July 24, 1911, in the Royal College of Physicians, London.
[167] "Medical Reprint," MSS in RCP, 2412/1.
[168] MSS in RCP, 2412/49–50.
[169] Andrew Wilson, *Brain and Body*, 14.

recommender of certain medical commodities. He advocated the "Fellow's Syrup of Hypophosphites," a frequently advertised pick-me-up, as a "medicine for ordinary cases of brain-fag and nervous depression."[170] His journal, *Health*, often carried favorable reports of patent pills and foods in its columns: Hovis biscuits were described as "thoroughly palatable," Scott's Emulsion as "the quickest builder," Cadbury's Cocoa Essence as "true nutrition of the body," and Van Houten cocoa as full of "force-producing constituents."[171] He examined, among others, Bertelli's Catramin Pills made from a "Special Tar Oil," and concluded that "they are calculated to be of great service in treating lung ailments and cases of internal catarrh at large."[172] In time, Wilson became known as a missionary of health and, to make their products look more genuine, manufacturers often printed the words "Dr. Wilson recommended" in their advertisements. That personal cleanliness was often alleged to be the basis of all health led many doctors to promote the use of sanitary soaps. Here again many doctors' alliance with commercial ventures was obvious. Wilson's pamphlet, *Disease and How to Prevent It*, discussed the medical merit of soap and provided complete commercial support to a soap company, Lever Brothers Ltd., and its product, YZ soap.[173]

In many ways, the nascent professionalism of medicine during the late nineteenth century was rooted in the period's expanding commercialism and capitalism. While professionalism was being established in the public sphere of government regulation, hospital care, and medical education, commercialism was permeating every quarter of the private sphere of drug manufacture and private practice. Understanding that medical personnel were full participants in a highly commercialized society reveals that uniformity was not, in fact, the sole or even the principal characteristic of the nineteenth-century medical profession. The interwoven mesh of a cash nexus and market mechanisms, and their irresistible magnetic

---

[170] Ibid., 136.

[171] Hovis Biscuits, *Health*, December 9, 1892; Scott's Emulsion, *Health*, October 6, 1893; Messrs. Cadbury's Manufacturers, *Health*, January 14, 1887; Van Houten Pure Soble Cocoa, *Health*, March 11, 1887.

[172] *Health*, October 23, 1891.

[173] Andrew Wilson, *Disease and How to Prevent It: A Treatise on Soap, as Related to the Prevention of Disease and the Preservation of Health* (London: Lever Brothers, Ltd., n.d.).

draw for both professionals and the public, were beginning to form the foundation of a fully professionalized society.

## *Conclusion*

The proliferation of the patent medicine business heralded a new cultural phenomenon. In the late nineteenth century, the public—both working-class and middle-class consumers—began to see being healthy as a modern manifestation of their individual desires, hopes, and aspirations. As illusions created by the advertising world began to inject market capitalism into health culture through the media related to these commodities, the public enjoyed consuming to excess a cultural imagination of "health" to be purchased, stored, exchanged, and even achieved. As a result, late Victorian society witnessed a booming medical market grounded in the consumer's highly advanced therapeutic ethos. This chapter has examined the cultural and sociopsychological environment that led the Victorians to therapeutic fantasies directed and created by modern consumers' hedonistic desire to acquire a vigorous, healthy, and ideal body.

What the investigations of this chapter reveal is that much advertising language was far from being the merely fraudulent boasts of rag-tag-and-bobtail quacks, dutifully vilified from a purely medical point of view by the British Medical Association and elite doctors. Rather, such affluent advertising clearly signified, even as it in turn helped shape, a unique socio-cultural context in which consumers' strong expectations of obtaining health through therapeutic commodities necessitated the development of complex market mechanisms to address those consumer expectations.

CHAPTER 3

# Victorian Quacks, the Body Electric, and the Commercialization of Medicine

### Victorian Quacks and the Commercialization of Medicine

In October 1851, shortly after returning from the Galapagos Islands, Charles Darwin earned himself a place in the history of electro-medicine. Seeking relief from a chronic gastrointestinal disorder, he began to wear an "electric chain" around his neck and waist.[1] The apparatus Darwin wore was known as Pulvermacher's Hydro-Electric Chain, which was invented by a German immigrant to Britain, Isaac Louis Pulvermacher. The chain was a unit composed of zinc and brass wires, and upon immersion into a vinegar solution, it was supposed to give out shocks of electric current, variable according to the ratio of water to vinegar through which the current passed.

Employing flamboyant advertisements and supported by electrical engineers eager to enter the new field of electro-medicine, Pulvermacher's electric chain business was a market success. Proclaiming "ELECTRICITY IS LIFE!" the tagline advertisements inserted in many

---

[1] See R. Colp Jr., *To Be an Invalid: The Illness of Charles Darwin* (Chicago, IL: University of Chicago Press, 1977), 45–46. Health Diary, Down House, April, August, and November 1852. F. Burkhart and S. Smith, eds., *Correspondence of Charles Darwin, 1812–1882* (Cambridge: Cambridge University Press, 1985–1991), 5: 96, 98, 100, and 194.

newspapers and magazines promised that Pulvermacher's chain would cure a variety of nervous disorders and ailments such as rheumatism, neuralgia, sciatica, and paralysis.[2] Not only Darwin but hundreds of his contemporaries purchased the electric chain in hopes of revitalizing their nervous systems (Fig. 3-1).

Pulvermacher's electric chain was hardly the only odd electrical device for which attempts were being made to carve out a niche in the Victorian medical market. A more scandalous electro-medical business was the Medical Battery Company (MBC), which was established by the aptly named Cornelius Bennett Harness, who in the 1880s and 1890s extensively advertised and sold his "Electropathic Belt" (Fig. 3-2). Basically, Harness' belt was a flannel bandage that was long enough to wrap around the user's body and was fastened with buckles and straps.[3] In addition to the glazed calico on the outside of the bandage and the flannel inside were fixed discs of zinc and copper. These discs were connected to one another with wires and were arranged in an alternating series (zinc-copper-zinc-copper). Both ends of the belt were designed to be connected to any galvanic battery or portable Leclanché battery. The belt was sold with the assumption that when it was worn the metal discs would be placed directly on the skin. This configuration would then allow the perspiration of the user's body to provide what the company termed "exciting fluid" to generate electricity by its chemical effect on the zinc discs. While highlighting its advanced technology, advertisements for the Electropathic Belts employed catchphrases such as "All in Search of Health, Strength & Vitality Should Wear Harness' Electropathic Belt," or "It Imparts New Life and Vigour."

The advertising campaigns for these quackish medical electrical apparatuses were undertaken on an unprecedented scale and widely used throughout Victorian London. The time-honored association of electricity and nervous energy in Roy Porter's elegant study of James Graham, a sex-therapist who employed "magneto-electricity" for nervous ailments

---

[2] "Pulvermacher's Patent Portable Hydro-Electric Chain for Personal Use," JJC, Patent Medicine Box 11, October 1851.

[3] The belt is described in the following pamphlet: Herbert Tibbits and Arthur Harries, *The Report on Harness' Electropathic Belts* (n.p.), The Royal College of Physicians, MS, 2411, 94–95.

and sold "electrical medicaments," serves to remind us of a lineal descent from the electro-mediccal quacks of the eighteenth century.[4] In the minds of urban Londoners, however, Victorian quacks bore no resemblance to the earlier itinerant mongers of electro-medicine. In addition to the continuing refinement and improvement of late-nineteenth-century products, the business strategies employed by the Victorian quacks also initiated a new mode of medical commercialization. These new quacks wantonly capitalized on scientific developments, using them to advertise the medical and therapeutic benefits of various products and treatments. No longer petty itinerants, the late-Victorian quacks were entrepreneurs working within a maturing capitalistic society. The clients they targeted were not uncultivated and gullible dupes; rather they were canny customers in a modern consumer society populated with health aficionados living in Britain's developing cities.

It is certainly surprising to discover the extent to which junk medical appliances were marketed to exploit the burgeoning late-nineteenth-century demand for healthy bodies and physical well-being. The plethora of advertisements and other commercial ephemera for medical commodities show that the Medical Battery Company was but the tip of the iceberg. Beneath the surface were numerous other magneto-electrical charlatans (most of them more quackish than Harness), eagerly aiming to make a fortune out of their pseudo-scientific, patented electrical technologies.

There were many electro-magnetic devices sold for the purpose of self-medication. In the 1870s, for example, Ely & Company sold "Magnetic Curative Appliances."[5] From their store at 443 West Strand, Darlow

---

[4] Roy Porter, *Health for Sale: Quackery in England, 1660–1850* (Manchester: Manchester University Press, 1989). Nicholas D. Jewson, "Medical Knowledge and the Patronage System in Eighteenth-Century England," *Sociology,* 8 (1974): 369–85. Michael Neve, "Orthodoxy and Fringe: Medicine in Late Georgian Bristol" in W. F. Bynum and R. Porter, eds., *Medical Fringe & Medical Orthodoxy 1750–1850* (London: Croom Helm, 1987). Porter explains that his underlying view of medicine and health care is that of the patient's perspective, which partly influenced by Nicholas Jewson's discussion of patient-doctor relations in the eighteenth century, led him to explore the consumer side of medical practices.
[5] "Health Giving!! Life Sustaining!!, Eley & Co.'s Magnetic Curative Appliances," JJC, Patent Medicine Box 9.

& Company began to advertise and sell not only "Magnatine," a flexible magnetic appliance designed "for the relief and cure of spinal and nervous affections," but also the dubious "Magnetic Tonic Pill" and "Magnetic Antibilious Pills" as applications of magnetism for internal medical conditions (Fig. 3-3).[6] The 1880s saw fashionable Oxford Street being crowded by a number of electro-medical stores. At 57–59 Oxford Street, the Progressive Medical Alliances opened its Men's Department, where specialists promised to restore "health and Robust Manhood" through an assortment of electrical devices. Meanwhile, the Mag-neto-Electric Battery Company, at 139 and 143 Oxford Street, imitated Harness's business strategy of printing doctors' testimonials and pub-lishing pamphlets to sell its "Feather Weight Electric Body Belt."[7] This company also sold other novelty electric goods such as electro-magnetic socks and promised to provide a "soothing, constant flow of Electricity, without shock or inconvenience," throughout the entire body.

The so-called "Vibrator," a machine invented by C. H. Liedbeck of Stockholm and introduced to England in the 1890s, was another such example. The machine was designed to deliver vibrating massage, pro-duced by a winch-handle in a driving box and moving through a flexible shaft to various kinds of contact attachments. Its makers claimed that the device provided curative "percussion- or chopping-movements" in such a way that, when applied to the desired part of the body such as the head, neck, and eyes, it would stimulate blood circulation (Fig. 3-4). The most scandalous quack of medical vibration, however, was G. J. Macaura, the recipient of a doctoral degree in medicine from a "Quiz" College in Chicago, which delivered its degrees on any subject after the successful completion, and very likely payment for, postal exams of requisite essays.[8] He established the Macaura Institute at Hanover Square, where he not

---

[6] "Darlows & Co.'s Patent Flexible Magnetic Appliances," JJC, Patent Medicine Box 9.

[7] "The Progressive Medical Alliance, for Men and Women," 57 & 59, Oxford Street, and 7, Soho Street, JJC Patent Medicine Box 9; "Dr. Lowder's Mag-neto-Electric Battery, by the Magneto-Electric Battery Company," JJC, Patent Medicine Box 10.

[8] *Report from the Select Committee on Patent Medicines, together with Proceedings of the Committee, Minutes of Evidence, and Appendices,* Ordered by the House of Commons, 1914 (London: Wyman and Sons, Ltd.), 63 and 337.

only accepted patients, but also invented and marketed a hand-operating vibrator, Macaura's Blood Circulator, a shabby pinching machine which was advertised to improve imperfect nutrition by restoring the blood circulation to nervous fibers in the affected part of the body. "All you have to do," he wrote in his pamphlet, "is to turn the handle, and you have a little piston darting forwards and backwards with lightning rapidity—a piston that will strike you hard enough to make you feel as though every fibre in your body were doing a war dance, or you can apply it so lightly that it actually puts you to sleep—a delightful sensation."[9] From this invention and his other medical enterprises, he was said to have made a fortune of £60,000 (Fig. 3-5).[10]

The late nineteenth century witnessed a proliferation of company-style quacks and electro-medical traders who far outnumbered the nostrum mongers of the Georgian period. These Victorian quacks sold just about anything in the free-for-all medical market: oxygenators, oxydonors, artificial ear-drums, pimple-squeezers, gas pine therapy, ozonized cabinets, and an assortment of other health-enhancing gadgets and devices. Truly, the late Victorian era must be called the great age of quackery. Why could these cheap and bogus medico-electrical appliances capture consumers' imaginations and gain such a considerable share of the medical market? What kinds of popular beliefs or assumptions made it possible for these charlatans to persuade the public? In what ways did electrical metaphors shift the way in which Victorians understood themselves and the invisible workings of their bodies? Certainly there were a few key popular preoccupations with electricity and magnetism in relation to the human body: the body as a storage location for electricity, nerves as paths for electricity, and blood circulation as a carrier of nutrition. What developments in electrical technology and popular understanding made it possible to apply electricity in new ways to the human body for medical purposes? How was knowledge about electricity popularized and transmitted to a broad consumers public?

To explore these questions, this chapter will focus on the activities of these new quacks in the field of medical electricity and electrotherapeutics

---

[9] G. J. Macaura, *The Cure of Disease by Vibration and Hygiene: The Book of Health; A Book for the People* (Leeds: The British Applications MFG Co.), 17.
[10] "G. J. Macaura, F.R.S.A.," JJC, Patent Medicine Box 4, 729.

and the socio-cultural background from which they emerged. In the Victorian age, many quackish entrepreneurs and profit-seeking capitalists kept a vigilant eye on the areas in which new developments and transitions in the medico-social environment began to create a source of profit. Victorian charlatans, a long-forgotten subject of historical inquiry, clearly exemplify the encroachment of capitalism and market-forces into the medical domain. And it was electricity-related treatments and commodities that appeared to be most rewarding for these ever-watchful quackish businessmen.

In order for these entrepreneurs to make their capitalistic businesses successful, it was necessary to take three conditional steps. First, this new treatment technique, electrotherapeutics, had to be legitimated by authorities—eminent doctors or scientific authors—as having a role in medical treatment. Second, after such acknowledgment of this treatment's legitimacy, popularizers had to emerge to bring the treatment to the attention of the broader public. Non-elite doctors and popular scientific writers thus had to publish articles and reports on a given treatment's effectiveness in a broad range of media, such as newspapers and semi-professional journals, to ensure that its medical potential and use were widely recognized. Third, even though these popularizers' language and rosy images created ever-increasing expectations, it had to be shown that public hospitals and other traditional institutions had failed to fully provide such treatments themselves. Hence, limited availability would further spur broad demand and desire for this new treatment. In fact, it was due to this difference between people's growing demand for these new treatments and their limited supply that capitalist forces were able to intrude into the medical domain.

The following sections examine the development of medical electricity and explore the intellectual atmosphere in which scientists and doctors associated electricity with the body's nervous forces and opened the way to considering electro-medicine as a viable and therapeutic field; many doctors and electrical engineers endorsed the new practice of electrotherapeutics and popularized its medical virtues. Accompanying a presentation of these endorsements are some scrutiny and analysis of the language and activities of popular promoters of electro-medicine and the electrotherapeutic instruments and commodities they recommended. Finally explored are the strategies of Victorian quacks capitalizing on the growing popularity of, and demand for, electro-medical healing and treatments. Using patents as their most useful tool for promoting their dubious goods, these quacks began to encroach on the established field of medicine and medical care.

## The Body Electric, Nervous Force, and Electrotherapeutics

Today's medicine is an arena where people encounter highly advanced technology amidst their daily activities. In hospitals and clinics, patients come in contact with a number of advanced scientific innovations and newly devised machines and technologies. The X-ray and the electro-cardiograph, once regarded as sophisticated hospital-based technologies, are now simply a part of routine medical care. Even computed axial tomography (CAT) scanners and magnetic resonance imaging (MRI) scanners have become indispensable tools for medical diagnosis. With these technologies, a patient's body is displayed before a doctor's eyes as a complex mechanism composed of motor and sensory nerves, glands, blood vessels, and bones that collectively respond to electric stimulation. Such infiltration of the body by electricity is not, of course, limited to the medical sphere alone. Certainly as our society becomes more and more networked by electronic media, this image of the "body electric," the view of the human body as a system of electric webs, is also being recognized as more than a metaphor.

Marshall McLuhan's *Understanding Media: The Extension of Man* argues that these technologies, working as media between the outer world and ourselves, are nothing less than an extension of our physical body, just as, for example, railways act as an extension of our legs, and telephones of our ears. For McLuhan, technological devices of the modern age such as printing tools, railways, and motor cars are all agents that have influentially and powerfully altered how humans understand their bodies and perceive their physical selves. And electricity is no doubt one of the strongest metaphors. In juxtaposing the body electric with an electric network, he writes, "physiologically, the central nervous system, that electric network that coordinates the various media of our senses, plays the central role. . . . The function of the body, as a group of sustaining and protective organs for the central nervous system, is to act as a buffer against sudden variations of stimulus in the physical and social environment. With the arrival of electric technology, man extended, or set outside himself, a live model of the central nervous system itself."[11]

But the metaphor of the body electric is not limited to the twentieth century. The nineteenth century offers other interesting examples, such as the esoteric experiments carried out by G. B. Duchenne de Boulogne, a French neuro-physiologist. Born in 1806, Duchenne trained as a professional doctor in Paris and devoted his entire life not to the hospital ward but to scientific experiments on the faradic stimulation of human muscles. Duchenne spent his life as a neuroscientist at the Salpêtrière General Hospital for the Poor, made famous at the time by Jean-Martin Charcot, the father of French neurology and a close friend of Duchenne.[12] Treating social rejects such as those with mental illness, epilepsy, cerebral palsy, or paralysis, Duchenne became interested in cataloging all sorts of neurological disorders through scientific methods. Electricity and photography were two of the fields of technological advance. First he applied an alternating faradic current and a pair of moist electrodes to particular points of muscles and nerves on the face to identify which muscle contraction mimicked representations of human emotions. Fear, joy, anger, surprise, anxiety—all of these expressions of the human mind, Duchenne insisted, can be reproduced by electrophysiological experiments on the facial nerves and muscles. For him, such electrified contractions were not simply muscle movements; they also expressed the semiotic meaning of emotional psyches. He then attempted to represent these induced expressions in photographs. The result was his *Mécanisme de la Physionomie Humaine*, which contained more than a hundred photographs of patient models displaying pseudo-emotions on their faces, all induced through electrical stimulation (Fig. 3-6).[13]

Duchenne's dramatic photographs mapping human emotions elicited much interest from Victorian intellectuals. One of them was Charles Darwin, who sought to explain the common physiological principles of

---

[11] Marshall McLuhan, *Understanding Media: The Extension of Man*, introduction by Lewis H. Lapham (Cambridge, MA: The MIT Press, 1994), 43.

[12] For the relationship between Duchenne and Charcot, see L. C. McHenry, *Garrison's History of Neurology* (Springfield, IL: Charles C. Thomas, 1969), 282.

[13] G. B. Duchenne, *The Mechanism of Human Facial Expression*, edited and translated by A. Andrew Cuthbertson (Cambridge: Cambridge University Press, 1990).

emotional expression shared by humans and lower animals. In his *Expression of the Emotions of Man and Animal and Descent of Man*, published in 1871, Darwin quoted Duchenne's theories and included photographs borrowed from Duchenne.[14] Darwin, however, was less impressed by Duchenne's use of electricity on the body; the famed naturalist's sole reference to electricity was in fact only to mention that there were experiments being carried out to create a map of artificial physiological movements of facial expression by electrifying particular facial muscles.[15] For many others, though, the notion of "the body electric" created by Victorian scientists and doctors such as Duchenne commanded a powerful place in their imagination: intellectuals and popular writers of the era often viewed the human body as an electrical organism. Neurologists tended to regard the brain as an electric dynamo conveying its current throughout the body. Physiologists attempted to measure the electricity passing through the nerves with a galvanometer. Doctors wanted to cure nervous ailments by applying electric stimulation. And even ordinary members of the public weighed in by buying medico-electrical devices for self-medication.

Many historians have shown that the application of electricity to the human body and the notion of the body producing its own vital energy—sometimes called "animal electricity"—have a history which began long before Duchenne.[16] On the Continent, Alessandro Volta disputed

---

[14] Duchenne was widely known among Victorian intellectuals as a champion of scientifically revived physiognomy. Charles Darwin relied heavily upon Duchenne's theory for his argument for the evolution of behavior. Duchenne's physiological investigation of emotional expressions gave an important clue to Darwin, who asked Duchenne for permission to use his photographs, a request that Duchenne readily agreed to. See Janet Browne, "Darwin and the Face of Madness," in W. F. Bynum, Roy Porter, and Michael Shepherd, eds., *The Anatomy of Madness: Essays in the History of Psychiatry* (London: Tavistock, 1985), 151-165. See also Sander L. Gilman, *Seeing the Insane* (New York, NY: J. Wiley, 1982).
[15] Charles Darwin, *The Expression of the Emotions in Man and Animals* (Chicago, IL: The University of Chicago Press, 1965), 132, 148, 149, 180, and 200.
[16] For medical electricity in this period, see Margaret Rowbottom and Charles Susskind, *Electricity and Medicine: History of Their Interaction* (San Francisco, CA: San Francisco Press, 1984); for the practice of electro-therapy in England, see John Senior, "Rationalizing Electrotherapy in Neurology, 1860–1920," Ph.D. thesis, Oxford University, 1994. Also the most important book on this topic is Iwan

Luigi Galvani's assertion that the stored animal electricity in the lumbar nerves of a killed frog was released when the muscle of its leg was connected to a metallic coupling of zinc and copper. Volta insisted that the electricity was simply the result of an electro-chemical reaction between two heterogeneous metals in a moist environment. Subsequent writers, however, such as Aldini, the nephew of Galvani, as well as Leopoldo Nobili, Carlo Matteucci, and Emil du Bois Reymond advanced Galvani's experiments to show that all animals were endowed with inherent electricity. Matteucci, for example, connected one electrode of a galvanometer with the external surface of a frog's large thigh muscle and the other electrode with the divided surface, measuring thereby the presence of a current from the cut surface to the exterior of the muscle. Since the intensity of the current varied with the degree of nutrition of the muscle and was strongest in those muscles gorged with inflamed blood, he argued that the electrical force depended upon the vitality of the animal and was more energetic in warmer-blooded animals. Beginning in 1841 when du Bois Reymond started to expound theories of vitalism, electricity was increasingly identified with nerve tissue. Later, though, du Bois Reymond abandoned his notion that the current-like reaction in nerves was equivalent to the transmission of electricity through a wire.[17]

Influenced by these Continental researchers, mid-Victorian British doctors began to investigate the ways in which the body, nerves, and blood conveyed electricity on their own. Despite scientific developments concerning the real nature of nerves, the analogy of electricity and nervous force remained current in British medical vocabulary. Alfred Smee, a surgeon and inventor of the popular Smee's battery, deployed in his 1848 *Elements of Electrobiology or the Voltaic Mechanism of Man* voltaic analogies of man's intellectual functions: he argued that in the human central nervous system, the brain was the main battery, and that it was closely connected with a peripheral voltaic apparatus in the muscles via the network of nerves throughout the body.[18] Thomas Savill, a doctor

Ryth Morus, *Frankenstein's Children: Electricity, Exhibition, and Experiment in Early-Nineteenth-Century London* (Princeton, NJ: Princeton University Press, 1998).

[17] Edwin Clarke and L. S. Jacyna, *Nineteenth-Century Origins of Neuroscientific Concepts* (Berkeley: University of California Press, 1987), in particular Chapter 5.

[18] Alfred Smee, *Elements of Electro-Biology or the Voltaic Mechanism of Man: Of*

who worked with nervous diseases in the West London Hospital, noted, for instance, that even as "the faradic battery, after continuous use, gradually becomes weaker—we can hear the note emitted by the interrupter become more and more feeble—and then after a rest, becomes restored again, so does nerve force require periods of intermission for recuperation." Like others at the time, Savill compared the body's brain cells and nervous centers to a "galvanic battery in constant action, whose duty it is to provide, a certain and continuous supply, of its special fluid."[19] And an American doctor, George Beard, construed the human body as a complex of electric circuits to which a central dynamo was connected in order to power a multitude of lamps throughout the body.[20]

Analogies of the reticular nerves to electric webs of batteries and induction loops were made by many Victorian doctors, including physicians such as Henry Baxter, Richard Shettle, and Charles Radcliffe.[21] When Shettle experimented to find the cause of coagulation of blood in the air, for example, he concluded that this process took place because the blood lost the electrical current it had while flowing through the body. He argued, "We cannot do less than regard the blood as the means of supplying electricity, or in other words vital energy and nervous power to that great electric organ the brain, and the whole nervous system, which may not inaptly be compared to the system of Electro Telegraphy of the present day."[22]

---

*Electropathology, Especially of the Nervous System and of Electrotherapeutics* (London: Bell and Daldy, 1848).

[19] Thomas D. Savill, *Clinical Lectures on Neurasthenia*, 2nd ed. (London: Henry J. Glaisher, 1902), 61–62.

[20] George M. Beard, *American Nervousness: Its Causes and Consequences, a Supplement to Nervous Exhaustion (Neurasthenia)* (New York: G. P. Putman & Son., 1880), 10, 12, and 42.

[21] Influenced by William Grove's fashionable conservation of energy hypothesis—that all forces, including electricity, heat, magnetism, and light were different manifestations or transformations of the one underlying force—Baxter, for example, investigated the theory that the electric force of nervous tissue could be converted into nerve force. See H. F. Baxter, "On Nerve Force—Relation of Nerve Force to Electric Force—Origin of Nerve Force," *The Electrician*, 2 (1862): 114–117.

[22] Richard Shettle, "On Electricity, as the Principle Which Causes the Vitality and Coagulation Property of the Blood," *The Electrician*, 4 (1863): 198–199.

More importantly, these scientists and doctors regarded electricity and nervous forces not as independent phenomena, but more as a manifestation or transformation of a single underlying force that also manifested itself as in such forms as heat, magnetism, or light. This is clearly reflected in Charles Darwin's argument on nervous forces. In explaining the expression of the emotions, Darwin relied heavily upon the concept of nerve force and theories of energy prevailing at the time. He argued that certain expressions such as fear resulted from an excess of nervous force or energy spilling over into other pathways, in causing particular muscles to tremble. Darwin explained that he borrowed this idea from Herbert Spencer [author's italics]:

> As Mr. Herbert Spencer remarks, it may be received as an "unquestionable truth that, at any moment, the existing quantity of *liberated* nerve-force which in an inscrutable way produces in us the state we call feeling, must *expend* itself in some direction—must *generate* an equivalent manifestation of force somewhere"; so that, when the cerebro-spinal system is highly excited and nerve-force is *liberated* in excess, it may be *expended* in intense sensations, active thought, violent movements, or increased activity of the glands.[23]

Similarly, explaining "the well known case of a bright light causing some persons to sneeze," Darwin argued that "nerve-force here *radiates* from certain nerve-cells in connection with the retina, to the sensory nerve-cells of the nose, causing it to tickle."[24] Here the nervous force in Darwin's explanation was thus an entity which could be transformed into other forms such as sensations, thoughts, or movements. By "liberating," "eradicating," or "expending" its energy, light—for example—creates a sort of "force" in the cells which in turn is transformed into a physical trembling of the membranes of the nostril.[25] In other words, here the nerve-force was understood in terms of a loose interpretation of the law of conservation of energy. In fact, many doctors in Victorian Britain applied a sort of "conservation of energy" model to explain the exhaus-

---

[23] Charles Darwin, *The Expression of the Emotions in Man and Animals*, 71; italics added.
[24] Ibid., 225–226; italics added.
[25] Ibid., 66, 71, 126, 173, 253, and 460.

tion of nervous energy. From this analogy to physics stemmed the idea held by scientists such as Darwin and Spencer that man has a fixed amount of nervous energy consumed by and mediated through the physical movements of various parts of the body. For instance, this fashionable physics-derived metaphor of force or energy—incorrectly used by today's standards—was propounded by a doctor to scientifically legitimate the conventional claim that attributed "the soundness of man's constitution" to his power of resistance or to his ability to reserve vital energy, which would combat the body's natural tendency to grow weaker and eventually die.[26]

The 1830s and 1840s saw a turning from electrophysiology to electrotherapeutics, in which the application of electricity to time-honored, popular therapeutic practices began to be considered "viable medicine."[27] This acceptance, in turn, resulted largely from the "rhetorical and practical strategies" adopted by medical electricians such as Golding Bird and his associate Thomas Addison (and later Sir William Gull), who opened an "electrifying room" at Guy's Hospital in October 1836 and carried out the first institutional application of electrotherapy in Britain.[28] To establish their experimental treatment of nervous diseases as a valid medical practice, as well as to prevent its association with mere quackery, Bird, Addison, and Gull treated patients on a daily basis, took regular notes to estimate the therapeutic power of electricity, published experimental results in hospital reports, and used diverse electrical apparatuses, all in their quest to gain professional respectability for this emerging field.[29] In this endeavor they were at least partially successful: thirty years later the *British Medical Journal* admitted that "the substantial value of electricity as a remedy has now become an acknowledged fact; and the doubts which

---

[26] Thomas Stretch Dowse, *On Brain and Nerve Exhaustion (Neurasthenia): Its Nature and Curative Treatment, a Paper Read before the Medical Society of London* (London: Baillière, Tindal, and Cox, 1880), 8.

[27] Iwan Rhys Morus, "Marketing the Machine: The Construction of Electrotherapeutics as Viable Medicine in Early Victorian England," *Medical History*, 36 (1994): 34–52.

[28] Hector A. Colwell, *An Essay on the History of Electrotherapy and Diagnosis* (London: Heinemann, 1922).

[29] Golding Bird, "Report on the Value of Electricity as a Remedial Agent in the Treatment of Diseases," *Guy's Hospital Reports*, 6 (1841): 81–120.

were formerly expressed as to its real usefulness have been dispelled by the advance of science."[30]

The rudimentary electrotherapy in which this trio engaged relied upon two types of electricity: static or frictional electricity, which was later called *Franklinism*; and galvanic electricity, which derived from the electromagnetic battery and later was known as *Voltanism*. In the former, a patient sat on an insulated stool and received an electrical charge by grasping a chain connected to a kind of early capacitor known as a Leyden jar: electric currents flowed through the limbs and spine to stimulate a lethargic organ. *Voltanism*, on the other hand, entailed the submission of the patient's body to constant or continuous electric shocks: immersing hands or feet for a set amount of time in salt water with which the conducting wires of the battery were in contact.[31]

In this milieu, the electrotherapy treatments carried out at Guy's Hospital were confined to a practice of "General Electrization" which, using electricity as a powerful nerve-tonic, aimed to have a current penetrate the whole body and stir up atrophied nerves in a haphazard way. The Guy's Hospital practitioners, however, went no further than using these experimental therapies as a final resort after other medical interventions failed to activate a patient's vital force.

By the 1860s, however, new developments in medical electricity on the Continent were gaining gradual acknowledgement in Britain through successive translations of eminent French and German authors: *L'électrisation localisée*, G. B. Duchenne de Boulogne's pioneering work on localized electrotherapy (1855), was translated by Herbert Tibbits in 1871; Wilhelm Erb's 1882 *Handbuch der Electrotherapie* was translated by L. Putzel in 1883; and his *Electrotherapie* also was translated by Armand de Watte-

---

[30] "Report on Modern Medical Electric and Galvanic Instruments, and Recent Improvements in Their Application: With Special Regard to the Requirements of the Medical Practitioner," *British Medical Journal*, 1 (1873): 44–46, 144–146, 344–345, 740–742 and 2: 493–497, 614–615, 704–705. See also *Report on Modern Medical Electric and Galvanic Instruments*, reprint from *The British Medical Journal* (London: BMA, 1874), 1–61.

[31] Samuel Wilks, "Abstract of a Lecture on the Therapeutic Uses of Electricity Delivered at Guy's Hospital," *British Medical Journal*, 1 (1873): 28–30. G. Vivian Poore, "Abstract of Lectures on Electro-Therapeutics, Delivered at Charring-Cross Hospital," *Lancet*, 1 (1874): 471–472, 539–541, 648–649, and 827–828.

ville in 1887.[32] British writers followed, and further developed the Continental researchers' technological advances in medical electricity. Julius Althaus' *A Treatise on Medical Electricity*, which appeared in 1859, was expanded into several editions by 1880.[33] Russell Reynolds, Herbert Tibbits, and de Watteville also published their own popular handbooks on electrotherapeutics in 1871, 1873, and 1878 respectively.[34]

Unlike their predecessors who regarded electricity as vitality and utilized it merely as a method of exciting nerves, this second generation of medical electricians pursued more scientific efforts to assess the particular therapeutic, physiological, chemical, and physical effects of electrical current upon specific regions of muscles, tissues, nerves, and blood. Duchenne, for example, insisting that the spark discharge from frictional currents would soon diffuse on the surface of the skin without producing substantial excitement of the subcutaneous muscles, instead found the most feasible and efficacious technique to be limiting or *localizing* electric stimulation to a single muscle or muscle group. To contract a particular muscle without resorting to strong electricity and to gain the same effect on the denuded muscle, he devised a new technique to replace the dry conductors with well-moistened sponges placed in the metallic cylinders of specially designed electrodes. In doing so, he explored and recommended a third form of electrization called *Faradism*, which denoted the therapeutic use of induced currents. These induced currents were analogous to the interrupted electricity which Faraday discovered could be generated when a current of voltaic electricity was sent to one of two

---

[32] G. B. Duchenne, *A Treatise on Localized Electrization and its Applications to Pathology and Therapeutics*, trans. Herbert Tibbits (London: Robert Hardwick, 1871); Wilhelm Erb, *A Handbook of Electro-Therapeutics*, trans. L. Putzel (London, Sampson Low & Co., 1883); *Electrotherapeutics*, trans. A. de Watteville (New York: William Wood & Company, 1887).

[33] Julius Althaus, *A Treatise on Medical Electricity, Theoretical and Practical; and its Use in the Treatment of Paralysis, Neuralgia and Other Diseases*, 1st ed. (London: Trüber & Co., 1856). A second edition was published in 1870 and a third edition by Longmans, Green & Co. in 1873.

[34] Russell Reynolds, *Lectures on The Clinical Uses of Electricity* (London: J. & A. Churchill, 1871); Herbert Tibbits, *A Handbook of Medical Electricity* (London: J. & A. Churchill, 1873); A de Watteville, *A Practical Introduction to Medical Electricity* (London: H. K. Lewis, 1878).

coils of wires parallel with, and in close proximity to, each other. Duchenne believed that the advantages of this electricity lay in the fact that interrupted currents could be applied more safely and with less damage to the patient's skin than when continuous galvanic currents were used.

As a result of Continental influence, important refinements of technique and knowledge were attempted in Britain. Julius Althaus, for example, investigated the chemical changes that galvanic current produced in animal structures and blood serum.[35] He attempted to explore electric current's capacity to split water into oxygen and hydrogen by applying a constant electric current to the human body, and—using Michael Faraday's term—labeled it *Electrolysis*. In his experiments, Althaus observed that the most powerful electrolytic effect on animal tissues was at the negative pole of the current where chemical elements such as alkalis, soda, potash, and lime were generated together with the emergence of hydrogen bubbles. Electrotherapists recommended using the electrolytic technique to remove malignant tumors.

The excitability of muscles and nerves by electricity, of course, remained one of the main interests of electrotherapy. In time, however, more accurate explanations of muscle contraction became widely recognized. Hugo von Ziemssen's mapping of motor points, the entry points at which the excited nerves stimulate the muscles, soon became common knowledge for British writers (Fig. 3-7).[36] Edward Pflügers scientifically confirmed the phenomena of electrotonus, demonstrating that during the passage of current the irritability of a nerve decreases near the anode (anelectrotonus) and increases near the cathode (catelectrotonus).[37]

---

[35] Julius Althaus, *A Treatise on Medical Electricity*, 3rd ed., 37–45 and 350–362; idem, *The Value of Electrical Treatment*, 3rd ed. (London: Longmans, Green & Co., 1899), 28–33.

[36] Hughes Bennett based his electro-therapeutics on Ziemssen's theory of motor points in his work *A Practical Treatise on Electro-Diagnosis in Diseases of the Nervous System* (London: H. K. Lewis, 1882). For enhanced practical usage, Bennett published separately his map of motor points. Tibbits also published an illustrated map of motor points: *A Map of Ziemssen's Motor Points of the Human Body: A Guide to Localized Electrization* (London: J. & A. Churchill, 1887).

[37] Rowbottom and Susskind, *Electricity and Medicine*, 99–101. The concept of electrotonus was soon accepted by those British writers who valued the application of continuous electricity rather than alternating faradic current. See Althaus,

Other technological advances were instrumental in transforming electrotherapy into more practicable medical techniques. More portable and
more easily operated electrical batteries, such as Stöher's, Forveaux's, and
Mayer's and Metzler's batteries (all named after their inventors), began to
be marketed in the second half of the nineteenth century.[38] Electrical
practitioners became more and more indebted to technology, precisely
measuring and adjusting in milliampères the exact strength of currents
and constantly testing out new apparatuses. Auxiliary instruments were
invented for the new electrotherapeutics as well. For example, various
electrodes were touted as effective terminals or conductors of electrization. Electrodes consisted of well-moistened sponges contained in metallic cups covered with comfortably-shaped insulating handles of wood,
connected to the conducting wires. These electrodes were placed on
points of the skin corresponding to the muscles that the medical electrician desired to stimulate.

Writers on medical electricity naturally could not be indifferent to
these technological advances. Many of the books on electrotherapy in this
period contained considerable technological information, concerning, for
example, the cheapness, portability, and ease of operation of the various
therapeutic apparatuses. Good electrotherapists were expected to be familiar with newly devised, portable and precise machines or instruments,
and some even invented their own; Duchenne himself designed a modified faradic battery and also marketed a small volta-faradic apparatus.[39]

By the late 1870s, the theory and practice of electrotherapeutics had
become a viable medical technique, but elite doctors still regarded electrotherapists with suspicion and disdain. Although considerable controversy existed among these doctors concerning the use of a galvanometer
for prescribing electric dosage to patients, their usual technique was
simply to put an electrode in a place where the nerves were to be stimu-

---

*A Treatise on Medical Electricity*, 3rd ed., 24–16; W. E. Steavenson and H. Lewis,
*Medical Electricity: A Practical Handbook for Students and Practitioners* (London: H. K.
Lewis, 1892), 203–231.

[38] To make their practice more effective, electrotherapists were eager to develop
an accurate galvanometer and to set up the unit quantities in absolute terms.
Wateville began to use the term "milliweber," which was later replaced by the new
term "milliampère." See Watteville, *A Practical Introduction to Medical Electricity*, 6.

[39] Duchenne, *A Treatise on Localized Electrization*, 266–269.

lated. In that sense, electrotherapeutics was less a theory-oriented practice than a mechanically applicable outcomes-oriented technology. Thus, while doctors became more dependent on the knowledge of engineering and mechanics, improved electric apparatuses inspired non-medically-trained consumers to self-medicate. It was in such a milieu that the cultures of medicine, engineering, and commerce mingled and struggled with each other, as monetary gain was sought in the gradually maturing field of medical electricity.

### *Electro-Medicine and Electrical Engineers*

By the mid-Victorian period, electrical technologies were fast becoming a part of people's daily lives. In 1858, the first submarine transatlantic electric cable was laid, and by 1860 the telegraph system, which had only been introduced during the early Victorian period, extended all over Britain. Moreover, the "electric candle" (whose novelty surprised Campbell Swinton, a British electrical engineer later famous in the early twentieth century) was quickly replaced by Thomas Edison's new electric lightbulb. By the turn of the century, the first telephone switch—established by the Telephone Company Ltd. in 1879 and using new microphone technology—began to be widely used in Britain.[40]

As the everyday usage of electricity increased throughout society, electrical engineers, a newly emerging professional group, extended their interests by seeking applications for their technology in a myriad of fields. Although they had not yet organized into a tightly structured association, a few electrical engineers had formed a professional group and by 1862 were publishing *The Electrician* for electrical engineers and manufacturers. Among the journal's many essays, editor Desmond G. Fitzgerald published a number of articles and reviews on the applications of electricity to the medical field. In 1871, British electricians founded the Society of Telegraph Engineers and Electricians (henceforth STEE), with some of the members of the former London Electrical Society (LES), an organization that since its founding in 1837 had promoted the study and

---

[40] Percy Dunsheath, *A History of Electrical Engineering* (London: Faber and Faber, 1962), 232; Carolyn Marvin, *When Old Technologies Were New: Thinking About Communications in the Late Nineteenth Century* (Oxford: Oxford University Press, 1988).

application of electricity. With its other members, the LES eventually evolved into the present-day Institution of Electrical Engineers (henceforth IEE). The LES also had close contact with a number of early medical electricians such as Golding Bird.[41]

The editorial address in one volume of *The Electrician* proclaimed: "Medical electricity, which, as an application of science, has latterly been greatly extended, will, in future, occupy its due share of attention. In this branch, we propose to obtain the assistance of competent therapeutists and physiologists, that our reader may have opportunity, when desirable, of scientifically applying the wondrous agency of electricity to cure disease."[42] One year later, this same editor expressed his satisfaction with the advancing state of knowledge regarding electricity's application to medicine:

> It is with great satisfaction we observe that the number of those who are turning their attention to various applications of electricity is constantly on the increase; and that this science, which but a few years back was comparatively speaking recondite and impracticable, now promises to become one of the most popular.[43]

In this context of rapidly proliferating electrical technologies and conscious aggrandizement on the part of electrical engineers, it is not surprising that doctors and other scientists began to see the human body no longer as simply an interlocking network of nerves, but as an interactive system of electrical impulses. Many ailments, some physicians believed, were essentially maladies of the body's telegraphic system. As one doctor wrote in 1864, "It is *electricity—Nature's life*—which constitutes nervous or *life-force* in man and animals, and whether it be a fluid or not, it undoubtedly circulates in all natural life as long as that life continues. It is electricity which gives the impulse of life to the seed and to the plant, and is the life-action constantly going on in the growth and development of life, not only in man and animals, but throughout the vegetable kingdom."[44]

---

[41] Iwan Rhys Morus, "Currents from the Underworld: Electricity and the Technology of Display in Early Victorian England," *Isis*, 84 (1993): 50–69.

[42] "To Our Reader," *The Electrician*, 3 (1863).

[43] "Electrical Manipulation," *The Electrician*, 4 (1864): 212–213.

[44] John Hitchman, "Medical Electrician: Electricity, the Life Force of Nature," *The Electrician*, 6 (1864): 56–57.

It should also be emphasized that in Britain electro-medicine and doctors inspired by it were closely connected to this emerging engineering culture. Although many historians of medicine have been reluctant to discuss the involvement of doctors with such technologies during the Victorian period, elite as well as humble local physicians in fact had a strong interest in electricity's mechanization of medical practice. An example of this was a new microphone invented by David Edward Hughes, an eminent engineer and past president of the IEE. In 1879 Hughes presented to the Royal Society his new induction-currents balance, which consisted of a pair of primary coils, one connected with a battery and microphone, plus another pair of secondary coils in another circuit with a telephone. When two circuits were placed near each other, the primary coils induced a current in the secondary coils, but as the coils in one circuit neutralized the induction of the other primary coil, no sound was heard in the telephone. When, however, the balance of induction was upset by bringing a piece of metal (such as a coin) near one or other of the coils, a sound occurred in the telephone. This electrical device, which Hughes called a "sonometer," proved to have an immediate practical application in medicine.[45]

During his experiments with this induction balance, Hughes communicated with Dr. Benjamin Richardson, a fellow of the Royal College, as to whether his device could be used as a medical instrument to obtain a quantitative measurement of the auditory range of humans. Based on numerous experiments, Richardson concluded that the instrument was very useful in determining degrees of deafness as well as in examining persons for occupations that required exceptional hearing, such as soldiers, sentries, and railway officials. Another article described how the microphone, added to a sphygmograph, could amplify the sound of a person's pulse.[46] And, in 1881, Graham Bell used the sonometer to try to

---

[45] David Edward Hughes, "On an Induction-Currents Balance, and Experimental Resources, Made Therewith," *Proceedings of the Royal Society*, 29 (1879): 56–65. See also John Munro, *The Story of Electricity* (London: George Newnes, Ltd., 1898): 159–61; G. B. Bonney, *Electrical Experiments: A Manual of Instructive Amusement* (London: George Newnes, 1894): 572–574.

[46] Benjamin Ward Richardson, "Some Researches with Professor Hughes' new Instrument of Hearing: the Audiometer," *Proceedings of the Royal Society*, 29 (1879): 65–70; "Note on the Invention of a Method for Making the Movements of the

determine the exact place of the assassin's bullet in the body of President James Garfield.[47]

Similarly, in 1899, Dr. Hughlings Jackson, an eminent neurologist at the National Hospital for Paralysis and Epilepsy, was looking for a method of standardization in diagnosis and collaborated with Dr. W. H. R. Rivers in the application of Edison's Phonogram, a new electrical device that which was believed to reveal a patient's inner disorders. He exhibited his experimental recording and its reproduction of the body's "abnormal talking" to the Hunterian Society.[48] Many medical doctors began to regard newly invented electrical devices as useful tools for deciphering disruptions to the body's inner workings.

Many of those who supported medical doctors' enthusiasm about electricity's applicability to the diagnosis and treatment of patients were primarily trained in engineering and wished to extend their scientific knowledge to other fields. In 1882, C. E. Webber, the IEE's president at the time, expressed his delight at the membership of doctors like Burdon Saunderson and David Ferrier in the Society:

> Our Society is eager for knowledge on the subject of electro-physiology, and we are now ripe to receive papers which would even place us on a level with the principles and natural law, as yet discovered, of the action of electricity as a vital agent in physiology, as well as of the application of the same agent externally, as a means of arrestation of decay, or of restoration of deficient vitality.[49]

Webber went on to celebrate as one of the examples of collaboration between medicine and engineering, the appearance of an article by Dr. W. H. Stone and Dr. W. J. Kilner on the use of continuous current in treating diabetes.

---

Pulse Audible by the Telephone: The Sphygmophone," *Proceedings of the Royal Society*, 29 (1879): 70.

[47] *The Times*, August 5, 1881, 5.

[48] Hughlings Jackson, *Abstract of the Transactions of the Hunterian Society, Session 1891–92, with the Report of the Council, and a List of Offices and Fellows, Also the Annual Oration for 1891* (London: Society Instituted February, 1819; Ash & Company, 1892), held at the Wellcome Library, Western MS: 5547, Box 19–20; "Phonographic Illustration of Disease," *Lancet*, 1 (1891): 644–645.

[49] Lt. Col. C. E. Webber, "Inaugural Address," *JSTE*, 11 (1882): 12.

William Stone and Walter J. Kilner indeed exemplify this union between medicine and engineering. In late-nineteenth-century Britain, Stone was undoubtedly one of the foremost writers on medical electricity. While affiliated with St. Thomas' Hospital as an assistant physician, a lecturer on *materia medica*, and later as a full physician from 1870 to 1890, he published numerous articles on electro-physiology and contributed a series of medical columns to *The English Mechanic and the World of Science*, a popular engineering magazine.[50] For his part, Kilner was a graduate of Cambridge, and he met Stone while working as a full-time electrical engineer at St. Thomas. He then trained to become a medical doctor and eventually rose to become a member of the Royal College of Physicians in London.

In a lecture before the STEE, Stone and Kilner expressed their shared belief that medicine should be reanimated by the adoption of the ethos and methods of electrical engineering and physics. They insisted on the importance of gaining precise measurements by applying electricity to the human body.[51] Prior to this lecture, Stone had delivered three other lectures at the Royal College of Physicians, in which he had attempted to explain physiological and pathological processes through the laws of physics. By doing this, he explained that he wished to show how physics could be applied to medicine so as to make the latter more scientific.[52] Therefore, "we wish[ed] not so much [to address] the physiologist or the physician as the physicist," Stone and Kilner declared in their article: "We beg respectfully to put the matter to this young, active, and vigorous Society. You can be of very great service to us physicians and physiologists, by giving us suggestions, especially in the department with which you are no doubt most conversant, viz., the department of measurement."[53] For young ambitious electrical engineers, medicine was becoming a field for the cultivation of professional and pecuniary opportunities.

---

[50] See his obituary, "William Henry Stone, M.A., M.B. Oxon., F.R.C.P.," *British Medical Journal*, 1 (1891): 105–106.

[51] W. H. Stone and Walter J. Kilner, "On Measurement in the Medical Application of Electricity," *JIEE*, 11 (1882): 128.

[52] W. H. Stone, "Some Application of Physics to Medicine," *Lancet*, 1 (1879): 470–71, 799–800; *Lancet*, 2 (1887): 39–41, 189–191, 305–306, 415–418, 754–756, 787–788, and 864–865.

[53] Stone and Kilner, "On Measurement in the Medical Application of Electricity," *JIEE*, 11 (1882): 109.

Stone soon became a spokesman on behalf of engineers working in the field of medicine. At the International Health Exhibition held in London in 1884, the STEE asked Stone to present a paper explaining how engineering could contribute to improving health care.[54] The paper itself summarized what Stone had long explored—the "measurement of electrical resistance of the human body."[55] Stone's paper also clearly signified that medicine was not an isolated field distinct from other pursuits of science and knowledge, but rather could be open to collaboration with engineers and their particularly technical mentality.

*Popular Medical Electricians and Electro-Therapeutic Commodities*

In the early 1860s, Harry Lobb became one of the most eloquent popular writers on electrotherapeutics as well as an enthusiastic contributor to *The Electrician*, a member of the Royal College of Surgeons, and (in July 1861) the founder of the London Galvanic Hospital in Cavendish Square, for treatment "with the aid of galvanism" of nervous disorders such as rheumatism, paralysis, nervous deafness, and the like. According to the hospital's prospectus, Lobb wished it to be not only an institution where the newly emerging therapeutic practices of galvanism were provided to outpatients, but also to be an independent medical organization. He accepted students in the hospital, offering "an opportunity of observing, studying, and testing the treatment of disease with the aid of galvanism," with the intention to train nurses in the practical use of galvanic apparatuses.[56] During this transitional period of legiti-

---

[54] W. H. Stone, "The Physiological Bearing of Electricity on Health," in *Health Exhibition Literature of International Health Exhibition*, vol. XI (London: William Clowes and Sons, 1884).

[55] See, for instance, Stone's articles, "A Note on the Influence of High Temperature on the Electrical Resistance of the Human Body," *Nature*, 28 (1883): 151–152; "The Physiological Bearing of Electricity on Health," *JSTE*, 13 (1884): 415–436; "A Third Note on the Electrical Resistance of the Human Body," *Nature*, 29 (1884): 528–529; "Mance's Method of Eliminating Polarisation: Its Relation for Testing the Resistance of the Human Body," *The Electrician*, 15–16 (1885–1886): 353–356.

[56] Harry Lobb, "The London Galvanic Hospital," *The Electrician*, 3 (1863): 270–271; "To Correspondents," *The Electrician*, 4 (1863): 32.

mating and rationalizing electrical treatment, the London Galvanic Hospital became an indispensable place for eminent young doctors to do experimental research into electro-medicine; they included C. B. Radcliffe, M. Sieveking, and R. Shettle.[57]

Around 1857, Lobb had begun his research into medical electricity, while his publication, *On Some of the More Obscure Forms of Nervous Affections*, a work on which he had spent years, garnered him some renown in the medical world.[58] By 1859, he had gained sufficient expertise in the galvanic treatment of nervous diseases to be invited to the Harveian Society to read three papers: in March and June of that year he spoke on "The Treatment of Paralysis" and in December on "The Pathology and Treatment of Idiopathic Peripheral Neuralgia."[59] Lobb's credentials and professional activities as a medical doctor clearly placed him assuredly within the ranks of the established medical profession.

Nonetheless, Lobb promoted himself first and foremost as a medical columnist on electro-therapeutics in *The Electrician*. The editorial board of this trade journal had long wished to promote electricity's applicability to other practical fields, and by invitation Lobb published many reviews, articles, reports of experiments, and correspondence on medical electricity between 1863 and 1864. His seventeen-part series, "Lectures on Electro-Therapeutics," began with the fashionably bold statement "Electricity is the Soul of Matter—the indestructible energy bound up in all that is tangible to our senses" and reviewed at length the nature of electricity and the history of medicine's endeavor to use electricity as a positive remedy.[60] Another series of his in *The Electrician*, "A Review of

---

[57] "The Medical Electrician: The Present State of the Science of Medical Electricity," *The Electrician*, 5 (1863): 6.

[58] Harry Lobb, *One Some of the More Obscure Forms of Nervous Affections: their Pathology and Treatment; with an Introduction on the Physiology of Digestion and Assimilation, and the Generation and Distribution of Nerve Force* (London: J. & A. Churchill, 1858).

[59] Harry Lobb, "On the Treatment of Paralysis by the Combined Aid of the Continuous Galvanic Current and Localized Galvanism," *Medical Times and Gazette*, 39 (1859): 327–328; *The Lancet*, 1 (June 18, 1859): 613–614; "The Pathology and Treatment of Idiopathic Peripheral Neuralgia," *Medical Times and Gazette*, 60 (1859): 591.

[60] Harry Lobb, "Lectures on Electro-Therapeutics, No. I – No. XVIII," *The Electrician*, (November 6, 1863): 18. See also other numbers, 4 (November 20,

Charles Bland Radcliffe's Course of Lectures," attempted to show that the
British school of medical electricity advanced the work of, rather than
being totally dependent on, Continental theorists.[61] In all of these reviews
and writings Lobb fully intended to demonstrate his innovative expertise
in both the fields of electrical engineering and medicine.

Although Lobb often expressed his humanitarian ideals and his wish
to maintain his hospital as a philanthropic institution, he was no doubt an
early example of a medical entrepreneur, promoting himself in the non-
professional medical marketplace. He invented his own galvanic machine
and marketed it in frequent advertisements in the *Illustrated London News.*
He appealed to the public through a steady flow of advertising in a variety
of publications and even in his own *Nervous Exhaustion: Dyspepsia and
Diabetes* and *Hypogastria of the Male.*[62] His advertisements in *The Times*
described his lifelong labor in the study of nervous diseases and their
treatment.[63] In the changing professional climate of the early 1870s,
however, his self-publicizing activities incurred the censorship of elite
doctors in the Council of the Royal College of Physicians.[64]

Of most interest for our discussion, however, is the fact that it was
Harry Lobb who promoted to the medical world a notorious chain in-

1863): 42; 4 (December 4, 1863): 66; 4 (December 18, 1863): 90–91; 4 (January 1,
1864): 114; 4 (January 8, 1864): 126; 4 (January 154, 1864): 154–155; 4 (February
5, 1864): 178; 4 (February 12, 1864): 190; 4 (February 19, 1864): 202–203; 4
(February 26, 1864): 216–217; 4 (March 4, 1864): 228; 4 (March 11, 1864): 240; 4
(March 18, 1864): 254; 4 (March 25, 1864): 266–267; 4 (April 1, 1864): 280; 4
(April 8, 1864): 294–295; 4 (April 15, 1864): 308.
[61] Harry Lobb, "Medical Electrician: A Review of Dr. Charles Bland Radcliffe's
Course of Lectures," *The Electrician*, 4 (1863): 115–116, 138–139, 150–151, 174,
186, 210, 258, and 270. See also these other articles by Lobb: "On a Case of
Complete General Paralysis Cured with the Aid of the Continuous Galvanic
Current," *The Electrician*, 4 (1863): 162; "Infantile Paralysis: General Progressive
Muscular Atrophy," *The Electrician*, 4 (1863): 210–211; "Chronic Rheumatic Paralysis, Cured by Electricity," *The Electrician*, 4 (December 11, 1863): 78.
[62] Harry Lobb, *Nervous Exhaustion: Dyspepsia and Diabetes* (London: unknown
publisher, 1872); *Hypogastria of the Male* (London: unknown publisher, 1873).
[63] See, for example, "Galvanism—Nature's Chief Restorer of Impaired Vital
Energy," *The Times*, November 1, 1867, 12.
[64] M. Jeanne Peterson, *The Medical Profession in Mid-Victorian London* (Berkeley:
University of California Press, 1978), 247–253.

vented and marketed by Isaac Louis Pulvermacher (a Breslau-born German electrical engineer and immigrant into Britain in 1859), whose aim was to build a lucrative business out of his patented medico-electrical devices. Educated in engineering in Prague and Vienna 1843–1847 (under the patronage of a Professor Hessler), Pulvermacher became an independent inventor of electro-magnetic engines and telegraphy in Germany. To meet the growing demand of electricians and physicists for a portable, adjustable, and fairly powerful battery, in 1849 he invented a Voltaic battery in the form of chain-bands called a "Goldberger." Having successfully patented his battery in France, he established a factory and a store to market it in Paris in 1850.[65]

After his business success in Paris, it was inevitable that Pulvermacher's next target would be the world's most commercially and industrially advanced city—London. His display of his medico-electric chains at the Great Exhibition in 1851 enabled him to sell them through Meining, a London merchant.[66] Thanks to brisk sales in Britain, by 1857 Pulvermacher was able to establish his own company—Pulvermacher & Company, Ltd.—at two locations in London from which he began to extensively advertise his chain batteries to the broader public.[67] The chain was usually sold with 120 elements per one set of links, and the apparatus was "mounted in two separate chains" that were advertised as being always "bright and brilliant in appearance, and as neatly and carefully finished as a piece of jewelry." According to the accompanying health manual, the general principle in determining where to place the chain was to position it in such a way that the current would pass directly over the afflicted part of the body or the nerves corresponding to that body-part. To cure a headache, for example, a chain was fitted to the patient's head so that current could pass through silver-colored wires that were strung from an ear to a nostril. A patient was supposed to adjust the strength of the current by changing the number of elements according to the extent of

---

[65] Isaac L. Pulvermacher, *Galvanic Electricity: Its Pre-Eminent Power and Effects in Preserving and Restoring Health Made Plain and Useful* (London: Galvanic Establishment, 1875).

[66] See Pulvermacher's advertisement flyers held in JJC, Patent Medicine Box 11.

[67] "To the Profession: On the Application of Electricity as a Therapeutic," in *The Medical List or English Medical Directory for 1857* (London: Lane and Laura, 1857), 488–489.

his or her disease. With toothaches, for example, a chain of sixteen elements was recommended to be placed on "the cheek farthest from the ailing side" and "a brush conductor on the hollow part of the tooth." For hoarseness or aphonia, 24 elements were said to be beneficial; 60 elements were recommended to "eliminate mineral poisons from the system;" and a chain of 70 elements was said to be strong enough to cure epilepsy. A strength that could explode gunpowder—300 elements—was considered suitable for the Galvanic Bath remedy that was very popular at many professional hospitals in London (Fig. 3-8).[68]

The widely circulated pamphlet published by Pulvermacher's Electric Chain Bands often provided advertising such as the following:

PULVERMACHER'S
Improved
MEDICO-GALVANIC SYSTEM
OF SELF-APPLICATION
of the patient
Galvanic Anti-Rheumatic Chain Bands
approved by Academie de Medicine, Paris; the Royal College of Physicians, London; the Imperial Faculty of Vienna; Rewarded at the Great Exhibition.
Demonstrating the Unequalled Success obtained by their aid:
An Authentically
ACKNOWLEDGED DESIDERATUM
for
Practitioners and Sufferers
for the easy and effectual treatment of
Rheumatism, Gout, Neuralgia, Deafness, Head and Tooth-ache, Paralysis, Nervous Debility, and other nervous,
Muscular, and Functional Maladies, &c.

---

[68] "Pulvermacher's Improved Medico-Galvanic System of Self-Application of the Patient," JJC, Patent Medicine Box 11; Pulvermacher, *A Practical Guide for the Electro-Medical Treatment of Rheumatic and Nervous Diseases, Gout, etc., by Means of Pulvermacher's HydroElectric Chains* (London: Pulvermacher's General Depot, 1856), 2–14.

In addition, the advertising pamphlet highlighted testimonials on the effective use of Pulvermacher's Electric Chain from a number of Britain's most eminent doctors: Sir C. Locock, Bart, Physician to H.M. the Queen; Sir H. Holland, Bart, F.R.S., Physician to H.M. the Queen; Sir Wm. Fergusson, Bart, F.R.S., Physician to H. M. the Queen; Sir J. R. Martin, Bart, C.B., D.R.C.S., F.R.S.; Dr. E. Sieveking, F.R.C.P., Physician to H.R.H. the Prince of Wales, and Physician to St. Mary's Hospital; Dr. R. Quain, F.R.C.P., Physician to the Hospital for Consumption, Brompton.[69]

The description of the electro-chain in Pulvermacher's pamphlet contained a long statement about how electricity could develop the balance necessary for a healthy body and, in particular, how the external application of electricity to the body would cure ailments. For example, one of these pamphlets claimed, "The all-pervading character of electricity, which gives life and movement to the physical world, makes it a remedy without a rival. In turns it replaces the *derivative* and *sedative* virtue of one remedy, the *caloric* and exciting action of another; and it will decompose and combine those bodies which no other chemical agent can assail." It went on to explain:

> What, in fact, are the results we see everywhere produced by the intervention of electricity, the basis of all the natural powers—*heat, light, chemical attraction*, etc.? The blood is regenerated: the health of the body is restored, as apparent in the return of colour, appetite, sleep, firmness of the flesh—in short, the whole system is brought back to its normal state, whence it is evident that the same power which cures us is also a preservative from disease. Many complaints originate in the blood, whence they pass to different organs.

As this pamphlet suggests, Pulvermacher included the remedy of blood disorders as one of the healing effect of his chains.

As early as 1851, Pulvermacher obtained a favorable reputation among doctors. For example, Golding Bird and T. J. Vallance welcomed "the ingenious modification of Volta's pile, contrived by Dr. Pulvermacher," whom they lauded as "a scientific man, and well acquainted with physical science generally."[70] In 1851, Bird also wrote in *The Lancet*, "The ingen-

---

[69] Pulvermacher's pamphlet, in JJC, Patent Medicine Box 11.

[70] Golding Bird, "Remarks on the Hydro-Electric Chain of Dr. Pulvermacher,"

ious galvanic chain of Dr. Pulvermacher has attracted so much attention, that an account of its value may prove interesting. . . . I cannot indeed too strongly impress upon those who have to treat a case of old Paralysis, the great importance of allowing a voltaic current to traverse the palsied limb: nutrition is certainly thus increased—its waste and emaciation prevented, and the probabilities of a permanent cure are very great. The action of the chain can be diminished or increased at will."[71]

Interestingly, in the 1850s, many well-known medical journals carried columns recommending Pulvermacher's chain. For example, in 1856, *The Lancet* wrote, "This ingenious apparatus of Mr. Pulvermacher has now stood the test for some years. Its simplicity and efficacy are so easily determined, that it commends itself at once to every one who will take the trouble to make a single experiment with it." In May of the same year, *The Medical Times and Gazette* explained that "The hydro-electric Chains of Mr. Pulvermacher are so constructed as to perform the office of a galvanic battery, the power of which may be increased or diminished at will. Each link of the Chain is in itself a battery, composed of alternate brass and zinc wires; and the apparatus is put into action by moistening it with vinegar. We have seen the Chains in action, and have felt their effect upon the body; and we have no doubt that, in all cases where a continuous stream of electricity is required, these Chains will produce the desired effect." Another example of such an endorsement comes from *The Association Medical Journal*:

> Pulvermacher's Patent Hydro-electric Chains and Accessories. —On the first apparatus of these singular Chains, we confess we had not a very high opinion of their powers, and feared that they formed one of the many methods by which simple people were imposed upon in the name of electricity. Moreover, medico-galvanisers have so quacked the use of this agent, that any new form of it which boasted salutary powers in the treatment of disease naturally fell under suspicion. An examination of this instrument, however, has completely removed all doubt as to its power, and has

---

*The Lancet*, 2 (October 25, 1851): 388–389; T. J. Vallance, "Cases of Rheumatic and Local Paralysis Treated by Pulvermacher's Chain Battery," *Medical Times*, 24 (1851): 509–510.

[71] Golding Bird, "Medical Column," *The Lancet*, 2 (1851): xvii.

satisfied us that, when the use of electricity is indicated, these Chain must in the majority of cases take the place of the more cumbrous batteries generally employed. The case with which they are applied, and the perfect control the patient has over them, is an additional advantage in their favour.[72]

But what gave Pulvermacher's chain the broad publicity that led to its substantial market success were Lobb's repeated recommendations in his own publications. Lobb, extolling the chain's "extreme portability and cleanliness," used four lectures in *The Electrician* to make detailed reports describing the chain's mechanism and its therapeutic effects in creating an intermittent electrical current. He wrote in his treatise, *On Nervous Affections*, "The method of administering Galvanism to the jaded nervous system is as follows: I am accustomed to commence with a Pulvermacher's chain of the highest power, from its ready portability enabling it to be carried to the patient, if required, without trouble. This is excited with a little vinegar, and the positive pole is applied to the cervical vertebræ, while the negative pole is placed to the pit of the stomach. Upon the first administration the Chain may be kept applied from five to ten minutes, and then the poles changed."[73] Lobb went so far as to collaborate with Pulvermacher in manufacturing a new "Bath-Chain" which was used to extract poisonous minerals such as mercury, lead, and copper from bath-water.[74]

Thanks to Lobb's trumpet-blowing, Pulvermacher's chain attracted the attention of medical doctors. On February 23, 1858, in reply to F. W. Mackenzie's talk at the Royal Medical and Chirurgical Society on the remedial power of galvanism in obstetric practice, Sir Charles Locock, a physician to Queen Victoria and president of the Society, inquired if Mackenzie had tried Pulvermacher's chains and highly recommended

---

[72] *The Lancet*, 68 (July 5, 1856): 19; *Medical Times and Gazette*, 2 (May 10, 1856): 464; *Association Medical Journal*, "On Paralysis, Neuralgia, and Other Affections of the Nervous System Cured by Galvanism," JJC, Patent Medicine Box 11.

[73] Harry Lobb, *On Some of the More Obscure Forms of Nervous Affections, With an Introduction on the Physiology of Digestion and Assimilation, and the Generation and Distribution of Nerve Force* (London: n.p., 1858), 300.

[74] Harry Lobb, *On the Curative Treatment of Paralysis, Neuralgia & C. with the Aid of Galvanism* (London: Baillère, 1856), 12–15.

them for medical purposes.[75] Russell Reynolds, a fellow of the Royal College of Physicians, reported in *The Lancet* about the successful treatment of paralysis by Pulvermacher's Chain Battery of 120 links.[76]

Benjamin Ward Richardson was another enthusiast of Pulvermacher's chain. In the 1850s, looking for an anesthetic technique, Richardson became interested in electricity's power to "remove the idea or consciousness of pain caused by operation, by a diversion of sensation." After several experiments with animals, he found that intermittent electric shocks derived from Pulvermacher's strong battery of 120 links were most effective in producing insensitivity of a local muscle. Richardson named this technique "Voltaic Narcotics."[77] Later on a fellow of the Royal College of Physicians and the Royal Society, Richardson was one of the most prolific medical writers and researchers in the latter half of the century, and wrote a report in the *Medical Times and Gazette*: "I have found by using a Pulvermacher Chain (of double size surface) in conjunction with aconite, that complete anæsthesia is produced. My first experiment was upon the ears of a rabbit: In a quarter of an hour after the Chain (with sponges moistened in aconite) had been applied, the ears could be pinched, and even punctured, without the animal shewing[sic] any signs of uneasiness; afterwards, I operated upon a child having a nævus on the shoulder, with the same remarkable results; as also extracted teeth from several persons without causing them the slightest pain; and punctured a bursa on the wrist of a girl, with similar success."[78]

With his finger on the pulse of high culture, Richardson was a main contributor to the popular scientific journal *Asclepiad* that also included articles on literature and art and was widely read by late-Victorian intellectuals. Nevertheless, his inclination toward medical technology and instrumentation prevented him from joining the privileged group of elite

---

[75] F. W. Mackenzie, "On the Action of Galvanism upon the Contractile Structure of the Gravid Uterus, and its Remedial Powers in Obstetric Practice," *The Lancet*, 1 (1858): 248–249.

[76] Russell Reynolds, "Paralysis Cured by Pulvermacher's Galvanic Chain," *The Lancet*, 2 (1858): 558.

[77] Benjamin Ward Richardson, "On Voltaic Narcotism: For the Production of Local Anaesthesia for Surgical Operation," *Medical Times and Gazette*, 39 (1859): 156–158 and 647–649.

[78] *Medical Times and Gazette*, 2 (May 10, 1856): 464.

consultants at the country's eminent hospitals; instead, he was an ambitious doctor who continued to carve out his own niche by pursuing a new specialist practice. Championing sanitary science and the hygienic movement, he edited *The Journal of Public Health: A Sanitary Science*, the official organ of Britain's Epidemiological Society. The motto included in his works, "National Health is National Wealth," is indicative of his seriousness in popularizing public health.

Here it should be emphasized that Pulvermacher's chains were used mainly because electrical engineering was highly regarded by the public. Further technical specialization within the field of medicine was abhorred by those establishment-minded medical professionals who viewed medicine as an art, but Lobb and Richardson instead were attracted to the culture of mechanization and instrumentation introduced by engineers during the second half of the nineteenth century. The next chapter addresses this "incommunicable divergence" between the dominant gentlemanly culture of the medical profession and the new entrepreneurial approaches to medical treatment that were based on science and technology, but it is worth noting here that engineers such as Pulvermacher who wished to extend the application of their technological advances found it a good strategy to seek the more socially privileged and lucrative areas of medicine.[79] This desire for greater wealth and fame alone may explain why in the 1860s there were so many articles advertising Pulvermacher's device in *The Electrician*.[80]

Pulvermacher's medical-chain business exemplifies how commercial medical entrepreneurs traded on the public's quest for a healthier and more vigorous life. Indeed, the chain was portable and easy for non-medical people to apply, and patients could even administer self-treatment to the entire body by hooking several chains together.[81] In attempting to reach

---

[79] Christopher Lawrence, "Incommunicable Knowledge: Science, Technology, and the Clinical Art in Britain 1850–1914," *Journal of Contemporary History*, 20 (1985): 503–520.

[80] See, for example, "Pulvermacher's Calvano-Piline," *The Electrician*, 3 (1862): 21; "Pulvermacher's Nitric Acid Batteries," *The Electrician*, 4 (1863): 85–86.

[81] Pulvermacher published a handbook, *A Practical Guide for the Electro-Medical Treatment of Rheumatic and Nervous Diseases, Gout, etc., by Means of Pulvermacher's HydroElectric Chains* (London: Pulvermacher's General Depot, 1856). The book contained illustrations, a historical sketch of electrotherapy, a general description

health-minded consumers directly, Pulvermacher was a forerunner of the charlatan manufacturers of electric machines and apparatuses that proliferated in the 1880s and 1890s. He based his commercial strategies on flamboyant advertisements that utilized attention-seeking catchphrases and testimonials from eminent doctors. In 1869, he even bought a whole page of *The Illustrated London News* to describe and enumerate the experiences of his customer-patients.[82]

Although the efficacy of Pulvermacher's electric chain was denied by at least one highly-regarded contemporary expert on medical electricity, the chain continued to be used by members of the public until the late nineteenth century.[83] Contributing to its longevity, of course, was effective advertising.[84] The medical establishment, however, largely ignored

---

of the chains, and authentic reports and testimonials by the authorities.

[82] "Electricity is Life: Pulvermacher's Patent Galvanic Chain—Bands, Belts, and Pocket Batteries," *Illustrated London News*, December 18, 1869, 644; "Pulvermacher's Patent Portable Hydro-Electric Chain for Personal Use," JJC, Patent Medicine Box 11, Oct. 1851.

[83] Julius Althaus, one of the eminent medical electricians in the late Victorian period, commented negatively about the electro-chain: "The chains are portable, handy, and easily put in action; but they have the drawback inherent to all modifications of the original pile, viz., that the current generated by them is liable to great and sudden variations within a short time. Moreover, in consequence of their small surface and high tension, they are not suitable for being applied to the nervous centres. A prolonged use of these chains, which is generally recommended, is not only opposed to all principles of physiology and therapeutics, but also condemned by daily experience, as, when thus employed, they cause sloughs, the cicatrices of which remain throughout life, and may aggravate the disorder for the relief of which they were brought into play." See his *Treatise on Medical Electricity: Theoretical and Practical, and its Use in the Treatment of Paralysis, Neuralgia and Other Diseases*, 3rd. ed. (London: Longmans, Green & Co., 1873), 34.

[84] For the advertisements of Pulvermacher's chains, see, for example, "To the Profession on the Application of Electricity as a Therapeutic," *The English Medical Directory for 1857* (London: Lane and Laura, 1857), 488–489; *Illustrated London News*, December 18, 1869, 644. As a trader recommended by leading Continental scholars such as Duchenne, Pouillet, and Wunderlich, Pulvermacher came to England in 1851 more for the purpose of obtaining patents on electromagnetic machines, telegraphs, and a hydroelectric chain. He opened two houses—one in Leadenhall Street and the other in Oxford Street—welcoming medical men to try out the electro-chains.

these advertisements until the 1870s, when Pulvermacher began to use names of fellows and members of the Royal College of Physicians of London in newspaper advertisements to sell "newly patented galvanic bands and belts." Sir Andrew Clark, later President of the RCP and an ardent defender of a professional medical moral code, responded heatedly to these claims and forced Pulvermacher to remove his name from the advertisements.[85]

What distinguished the arch-entrepreneur Pulvermacher from the eighteenth-century nostrum quacks Roy Porter has portrayed was that he was a professionally trained and experienced engineer. From 1857 to 1874, he procured no fewer than ten patents on medico-electrical appliances whose documentation demonstrate their innovations (Fig. 3-9).[86] In addition, during the 1850s and 1860s, when the theory of electro-physiology matured into viable medical practice, his portable electric chains and batteries served to develop doctors' interest in electrotherapy. Many eminent doctors who sought to apply new technologies to the medical domain recommended and used his chains in their hospitals. Pulvermacher's inclination to turn his scientific knowledge into profit, however, did not go over well with everyone in the gentlemanly culture of the British medical establishment.

In 1869 Pulvermacher faced a serious obstacle to his business in the form of Charles Hammond and Henry James, two entrepreneurial quacks who had carried out fraudulent medical practices in Middlesex. According to the affidavits, Hammond and James, having seen that "inventions and improvements in respect there of were deservedly bringing him [Pulvermacher] in large profits," collaborated in undercutting his patent monopoly by advertising similar apparatuses—such as "The Patent Self-adjustable Curative and Electric Belt" under the recommendation of

---

[85] See Royal College of Physicians of London (hereafter RCP), MSS. 2412/176, for the letter concerning Pulvermacher's advertisement.

[86] The following are some examples of Pulvermacher's patents: "Apparatus for Creating Electric Currents," Patent no. 2411, 1857; "Producing Galvanic Currents," Patent no. 582, 1866; "Producing and Applying Electric Currents," Patent no. 773, 1868; "Producing and Applying Electric Currents," Patent no. 2740, 1868; "Medico-Electric Apparatus," Patent no. 2771, 1872; "Electric Bands and Brushes, &c," Patent no. 3519; "Generating and Applying Electricity," Patent no. 3937, 1874.

"Dr. Hammond" and "H. James, Esq." Pulvermacher soon sued them on May 27, claiming that they had abused his trade motto by asserting in their ads that "Electricity is Life," and by promoting devices that promised "Health and Manhood Restored (without Medicine)." In court, Sir Charles Locock, an eminent doctor, and Sir Ronald Martin, a fellow of the Royal Society, approving of the medical benefits of Pulvermacher's apparatuses, insisted that Pulvermacher's products had nothing to do with Hammond and James.[87]

Although in this case the court sided with Pulvermacher, Hammond and James were not the last to cast avaricious eyes on the pecuniary benefits that medico-electrical appliances brought to their inventors. In an allegation published in 1871, *A Sincere Voice of Warning against Quacks and their Nefarious Practices*, Pulvermacher warned against "the most striking characteristics of the Englishman," which he identified as the "overweening jealousy for his liberties." This covetousness had prompted a proliferation of "the Quack Doctor, who carries on his never-ceasing endeavours to entrap the foolish."[88] One of these, "Darlow's so-called Magnetic Skeuasma," was regularly advertised in *The Christian World* and triggered a debate between its manufacturer and Pulvermacher in the 1870s.[89]

Although electric belts and other medical gadgets later produced a hotbed of professional debate and controversy, Pulvermacher's chain was an early example of electricity's offering pecuniary rewards to electrical engineers, manufacturers, and greedy quacks alike, and of commodity culture's intimate affiliation with professional medicine in mid-Victorian society.

### The Strategies of Victorian Quacks

Even compared with the extensive strategies of other Victorian quacks, Cornelius Bennett Harness and his Medical Battery Company Ltd.

---

[87] "Bill of Complaint, between Isaac Louis Pulvermacher and Charles Daniel Hammond and Henry James," published on April 29, 1869. This pamphlet is held in Oxford University, "Pulvermacher v. Hammond," May 27, 1869.
[88] Isaac Louis Pulvermacher, *A Sincere Voice of Warning against Quacks and their Nefarious Practices, on an Unerring Guide to the Nervous and Debilitated* (London: McGowan and Company, Ltd., 1872), 1–2.
[89] Ibid., 94–104.

(henceforth MBC) clamored most for attention. The company, professedly capitalized at £100,000 and founded at 52 Oxford Street around
1882, was the most scandalous purveyor of "Electropathic Belts" in
late-nineteenth-century Britain (Fig. 3-10 and Fig. 3-11).[90] Harness' and
the MBC's strategy for selling medical goods was highly innovative in
comparison with that of the older generation of electrical goods merchants. Their use of bombastic advertising, establishment of institutional
facilities, creation of strategies for patent monopolies, and employment
of company-style quacks all exemplify the extent of these medical entrepreneurs' market-oriented activities. Taking advantage of the burgeoning advertising culture of the time, Harness used his substantial
capital to extensively promote his products on a scale that far exceeded
the old-style nostrum-vendors' range of operations—their advertising
was limited to a few lines within the narrow columns of that period's
newspapers.[91] Harness, in contrast, bought whole pages in newspapers to
display the opinions and testimonials of specialists, patients, and noteworthy persons. The columns of these pages often included many repetitions of the product's name and sales messages: "HARNESS' ELECTRO
PATHIC BELTS," "A BOON TO DELICATE WOMEN," "A BLESSING TO WEAK
MEN," and so on.[92] Harness marketed his electropathic belts as a panacea
for all diseases related to nervous disorders, such as rheumatism, sleeplessness, and corpulence. The MBC's strategies and the specific socioeconomic milieu that enabled the company's meteoric rise—and fall—
merit further discussion here.

Harness was a typical Victorian entrepreneur with great ambition and
commercial talent. He started his merchant life at the age of sixteen as a
salesman at Silber and Fleming Company, one of the largest of the new
department stores at the time. On leaving the department store in 1872 at
the age of twenty-three, he started his own wholesale business, Harness
and Company, which chiefly dealt with gold and silver goods and general

[90] The amount of his capital is suggested in his pamphlet, "Massage and electrical treatment," RCP, MSS., 2412/125.
[91] The advertising culture of patent medicine is discussed by Thomas Richards.
See Chapter 4 of *The Commodity Culture of Victorian England: Advertising and Spectacle,
1851–1914* (London: Verso, 1990).
[92] See *The Daily Telegraph*, January 9, 1889; *Standard*, November 14, 1892.

merchandise.[93] Shortly after his firm went bankrupt, Harness joined the Xylonite Company where he met a Dr. Scott, an American doctor who had headed a medical electrical business in New York. Finding mutual benefit in Scott's electrical knowledge and Harness' commercial skills, together they established a medical company, the Pall Mall Electrical Association Ltd. (henceforth PMEA) in London. In 1881, Harness met a Professor Baker of Birmingham, who had patented an electric belt appliance for medical purposes. Harness quickly noticed the electric device's great business potential and purchased Baker's whole business and patents. He then employed Baker as head of the PMEA's department of medical electricity.[94]

Thanks to Baker's knowledge of electricity, the PMEA shortly became a notorious provider of many electrified medical technologies, most of which turned out to be bogus. It sold "The Electric Patent Socks," which when inserted inside shoes or boots were supposed to provide "the best means for keeping the feet warm, for creating bodily comfort, and preventing illness," on the grounds that "continual and most beneficial warmth penetrate[s] the body."[95] Another of Harness' medical gadgets was the "Electropathic Lung Invigorator," a breastplate-shaped magnetic protector covering the chest and abdomen, and supposed to prevent "asthma bronchitis, phitisis, pulmatory neuralgia, spasmodic cough and all chest affections."[96] Proclaiming on the stamp gracing all his medical goods that "The Germ of All Life is Electricity," Harness capitalized on the public's infatuation with electricity, and especially with electricity's enigmatic association with nerves, life, and energy.

In 1884 Harness' advertisements began to proclaim the merits of his merchandise, and their audacious commercialism that later made him famous was already fully evident—they claimed that his first electropathic belt promised everything short of a miracle cure: the device would cure dyspepsia, rheumatism, and sciatica; it was guaranteed "to promote the circulation; to assist digestion, to stimulate the organic action, and to

---

[93] *The Times*, July 5, 1894.

[94] *The Times*, July 4, 1894.

[95] "The Electropathic Socks," *Graphic*, November 8, 1884, 487.

[96] "The Electropathic Lung Invigorator," *Illustrated London News*, November 15, 1884, 487.

renew vital energy." The adverts even claimed that there was "no acid required" to ensure that the device would "last for years," and that it was the "only genuine galvanic belt extant."[97] They carried pictures illustrating that the belt could be adapted for use by both "ladies" and "gentlemen," they offered free daily consultations by the company's electrician, and they promised to provide—free of postage—both an 80-page illustrated pamphlet entitled "Electropacy" and the 100-page booklet, "Dr. Scott's Guide to Health."[98]

"Harness' Electric Comb" and "Dr. Scott's Electric Hair Brush," both manufactured by the PMEA, were each advertised as a "valuable adjunct to the electro-pathic belt."[99] The advertisement for "Harness' flesh brush for the generation of magneto-electric power" showed an image of the goddess of electricity scattering the charm of magnetism over her patients—despite the fact that the brush was made not of conductive wires but of "pure bristles." Furthermore, the brush was guaranteed to cure the "nervous headache, bilious headache, and neuralgia in 5 MINUTES," and also to "prevent falling hair and baldness; cure dandruff and diseases of the scalp; promptly arrest premature grayness; make the hair grow long and glossy; [and] immediately soothe the weary brain."[100] In addition, until 1885 the company sold "Harness' electric eye battery," which was claimed to be the "wonder of the 19th century," simply made of a conical cup, that an electrical engineer sneered "was impossible by any stretch of imagination to call a battery."[101]

During the first years of his business, Harness appears to have been primarily interested in simply selling an assortment of shoddy medical appliances on a small scale—much as the older generation of electrical quacks had. However, in 1883, just after opening a branch of the PMEA, Harness met with Professor Jean Martin Charcot, Dr. Vigouroux and Mr. Loreau in Paris. This meeting appears to have given Harness the confidence to penetrate the hermetic world of medical professionalism.

---

[97] "All in Search of Health: Electrotherapeutic Belt," *Illustrated London News*, February 2, 1884, 119.

[98] "The Future of Electropathy," n.d., held in JJC, Patent Medicine, Box 10.

[99] "The Charges Against C. B. Harness," *The Times*, November 23, 1893, 11.

[100] "Dr. Scott's Electric Hair Brush: A Magnificent Christmas Present," *Graphic*, December 13, 1884, 631.

[101] "The Harness Case," *The Times*, November 30, 1893.

Charcot was a world-renowned physiologist who, with Vigouroux, the government-appointed chief to the famous Salpêtrière Hospital, had already established France's first school for electrotherapy. A few years after this initial meeting, Harness invited Charcot and Vigouroux, along with Loreau (a municipal officer working in Paris) to London, in order to introduce electro-medical appliances to his new company, the Medical Battery Company, established in 1885 in London's West End.[102] During this trip to London, Loreau also visited the electrical departments of St. Bartholomew's, St. Mary's, and other hospitals, and found that none of these medical institutions had as complete an electrical facility as the one at Harness' Medical Battery Company.[103]

A more personal situation also proved to be very beneficial to Harness. Immediately before the French guests arrived, Harness' wife had suffered a cerebral hemorrhage that S. Gee and Hughling Jackson at the National Hospital attempted to heal but concluded was beyond treatment. Not to be discouraged by his British peers, however, Vigouroux employed his electrical treatment and successfully cured the woman. This was vindication indeed of electro-medicine—personal and immediate in nature—and Harness was sufficiently encouraged to bypass the country's established hospitals and other institutions, and to provide medical treatment directly on the company premises by employing his own medical doctors. Accordingly, Vigouroux became a consulting medical adviser, treated patients at the Medical Battery Company for several years, and published a small pamphlet on Harness' electric belt.[104] With the collaboration of these French doctors, Harness began his unabashed encroachment into the arena of medical professionals.

Harness' advertising strategy was both impudent and seductive. Using new advertising technology, resplendent flyers depicted memorable scenes that highlighted the appeal of the Medical Battery Company's products. For example, in one flyer inserted under the front doors of middle-class London residences, two angels are seen offering "scientifi-

---

[102] "HEALTH BELT, Harness' Electric Battery Belt," *Illustrated London News*, March 15, 1885, 264.
[103] "Brasyer v. Harness and Another Law Court Report," *The Times*, July 5, 1894, 12.
[104] Ibid., 3.

cally constructed" electropathic belts to a wealthy "gentleman" and "gentlewoman," who appear captivated by the belts, shown as being held by a nurse consultant. Another flyer depicted the Goddess of Hygeia standing on the North Pole, pointing to a shining "Harness' Electropathic Belt; for Health, Strength & Vitality."[105] In one of the company's most intriguing advertisements, "Modern Perseus and Andromeda" (Fig. 3-12), Andromeda is freed by a modern Perseus from "prejudice," "ignorance," and "incredulity" with that epitome of science and medicine, the electropathic belt:

> The above beautiful allegory aptly illustrates the position of a large portion of afflicted humanity at the present age. The Andromeda of to-day, or it may be her husband, or a sister, a cousin, or an aunt of that interesting damsel, is assailed by the pestiferous breath of the remorseless demon, Disease; she faints and droops under its baneful influence, but, being chained to the rocks of Prejudice, Ignorance and Incredulity, she is unable to resist or impede the advance of the monster, who threatens each moment to enfold her in his deadly grasp. From the summit of the rocks the modern Æsculapius has exhausted the puny armoury of his profession; one by one he has hurled phial and globule at the approaching monster, but without succeeding in checking his onward approach, and alas! many of the missiles have fallen short of their aim, and have sadly maimed and distressed the already grievously afflicted victim. In vain she implores her would-be delivery to employ more potent and more certain weapons; Æsculapius knows them not, and the unhappy damsel is on the point of resigning herself to her apparently inevitable fate, when lo! there approaches from the distance a figure of commanding presence, who bears aloft a weapon of the highest finish and most unerring precision, fresh from the prolific armoury of science. The Perseus of the Allegory, at whose approach the demon has hurriedly retreated, hands Andromeda the charm (bearing the mystic inscription "Electropathic Belt"), bids her wear it, and promises that it will act as a charm against the advance of all such insidious enemies. Andromeda, who has already revived under the magic influence of the stranger's presence, disengages herself

---

[105] "Harness' Electropathic Belt," JJC, Patent Medicine Box 10.

from the fetters which had entangled her, and from which, indeed, she might easily have released herself long since had she possessed sufficient courage to nerve her to the effort; gratefully accepts the proffered amulet; pours out her gratitude and thanks to her deliverer; bids Æsculapius with his phials and globules be gone, and resolves that henceforth she will reply for protection on the priceless treasure she has become the possessor of it.[106]

It is important to point out that many of the Victorian quacks promoted their goods via the patents that they cited in their advertisements. These medical entrepreneurs were enthusiastic about getting patents, for they viewed them as a desirable method to legitimatize their medical commodities and to expand their access to a growing consumer market. As Harold Dutton has shown, in the first half of the century, "a considerable number of inventors were indeed economic men operating in what might be termed an invention industry."[107] Unlike earlier historians, who saw early-nineteenth-century innovations as independent of pecuniary motivation, Dutton argues that patentees during this earlier period were primarily concerned with making a profit on their inventions, and he divides them into four categories: "the bulk of inventors" who took pains to invest to monopolize their pecuniary profits; "a considerable proportion of patented inventors [who were] quasi-professional inventors holding several or numerous patents;" "quasi-professional inventors [who] should diversify their inventive portfolio by inventing in a number of different areas or industries;" and "vigorous trade[rs] in (patented) inventions."[108] The pecuniary interests of "quasi-professional inventors"

---

[106] "The Modern Perseus and Andromeda," *Illustrated London News*, February 14, 1885, 181.

[107] Many economic historians agree that patent activities increased remarkably throughout the nineteenth century. See J. Jewks, D. Sawers, and R. Stillerman, *The Sources of Invention*, 2nd ed. (London: Macmillan, 1969).

[108] Harold Irvin Dutton, *The Patent System and Inventive Activity During the Industrial Revolution 1750–1852* (Manchester: Manchester University Press, 1984), 104–113. For a different account of patented innovations, see K. Boehm and A. Silverston, *The British Patent System: Administration* (Cambridge: Cambridge University Press, 1967). For the earlier history of patents in Britain, see Christine MacLeod's excellent book, *Inventing the Industrial Revolution: The English Patent System, 1660–1800* (Cambridge: Cambridge University Press, 1988).

and entrepreneurs who sought a high return by investing in high-risk inventions, Dutton argues, produced the bulk of the inventions patented during the last decades of the nineteenth century.

The great number of medico-electrical appliances that were patented between 1884 and the early years of the twentieth century shows that these quasi-professionals had recognized that there had been an upsurge in people's concerns about health and especially about their supposed nervous debilities and ailments. In response to these rising concerns, these entrepreneurs began targeting the medical market, producing everything from a magnetic hat to a well-structured exercising-machine. These new patents joined a flood of similar products that had been increasing since mid-century, such as electric baths, bandages, dumb-bells, brushes, and knee-cushions. From 1884, the number of electric-belt patents began to increase, culminating in ten patents in the single year of 1891. By 1900, there were 45 patented belts. Moreover, between 1890 and 1900, 41 machines for electric massage and gymnastics were patented. In sum, there were 141 patented electric machines and devices by century's end.[109]

Following are some examples of inventions to be found in the archives of the Patent Office: Joseph Harris' "Electric or Magnet Hat," which was patented in 1891, interlaced a narrow sheet of zinc into the inside leather of a hat and connected it with an attached electric battery.[110] Athough the growing demand for voltaic batteries designed for therapeutic purposes encouraged eminent medical electricians such as Duchenne de Boulogne, Herbert Tibbits, and Julius Althaus to market their own batteries, electrical engineers such as Willis Romer Warren and Henry Harrington Leigh also entered the fray by patenting new types of voltaic batteries.[111] From today's perspective, many of these patented batteries—such as the "Electric Urethral, Vaginal, Rectal Vitalization" invented by Boyd's Med-

---

[109] These number based on the description of "Electric and Magnetic Appliances, Medical and Surgical," in the *Patent Journal Class 81 Medicine et al.*, held in the Patent Office Archives.

[110] "An Improved Electric or Magnetic Hat Leather or Lining for Hats, Caps, and other Similar Head Coverings," Patent no. 5,382, 1891.

[111] Willis Romar Warren, "Medical Battery," Patent no. 343, dated July 20, 1882; Henry Harington Leigh, "Improvements in Therapeutic Magneto Electric Machines," Patent no. 20,190, dated January 20, 1891.

ico-Electrical Vitalizer Company[112]—were nothing more than fraudulent devices. An equally horrific device was the "improved" Electric Uterine Battery designed by the American physician Charles Hebard. This "battery" was designed to be inserted into the vagina to the point that it touched the mouth of the uterus, so that, its inventor insisted, "the secretions of the parts coming in contact with the zinc and copper form an electric current of sufficient power to act beneficially upon the parts."[113]

These engineer-inventors emphasized the role of nerves and nervous forces in causing nervous ailments among city-dwellers. Henry Gothwicke Whiting, for instance, designed a machine "for measuring the odic force or nerve force in the brain of man and beast and . . . diagnos[ing] the entire system for the different diseases afflicting man and the lower animals, through the loss or excess of nerve force."[114] The most conspicuous patents of the time, however, were undoubtedly for electric devices, none more popular than galvanic belts and bandages. Apart from Harness' devices, many other electrical engineers and associated companies—Arthur Byng, Alva Owen, William Johnson's Medico Electric Belt, the Truss and Battery Company, Charles Andrew, Noah Mitchell, and the like—obtained patents for curative electric belts. Most of these belts were composed of zinc and copper batteries arranged along a leather belt, and some even came with a portable series of batteries woven into them.[115]

---

[112] H. H. Lake, "Electric, Urethral, Vaginal, and Rectal Vitalization," Patent no. 6,566, 1893.

[113] Charles Everett Hebard, "An Improved Electric Uterine Battery," Patent no. 22,637, dated November 22, 1894.

[114] "An Instrument for Measuring Odic or Nerve Force," Patent no. 11,982, dated July 29, 1889.

[115] The following were some of the electric belts and bandages patented between 1884 and 1900: Arthur Hervey Byng, "An Improved Appliance or Band for Generating Electricity for Therapeutic Purposes," Patent no. 4,548, 1884; Alva Owen, "Improvements in Electric Belts," no. 16,351, 1887; William George Johnson, "Battery for General Electro Medical Use or as Electrical Dumb Bells Clubs, and the Like for Muscular Exercise, with Electrical Current of any Desired Strength During such Exercise," no. 4,819, 1888; Charles Andrews, "An Improved Galvanic Belt," no. 1,350, 1891; James Chadwick, "Improvements in Electric Belts for Body Wear," no. 18,272, 1891; Noah Mitchell, "Improvements Connected with Electric Belts and Bands for Curative Purposes," no. 222, 1893; Frank Dowling, "Methods of and Means for Applying Electricity to the Human

Reflecting the public's growing enthusiasm for gymnastics, muscle building, and massage exercises as new health-promoting disciplines, patent applications for both electro-massage and electro-exercising apparatuses increased in the decade before 1900.[116] Composed of positive and negative roller-electrodes connected with a battery contained in the handle and using Indian-rubber as a cushion mat between rollers, most patented electro-massage machines were designed "to produce mechanically a rolling massage action and a tapping or vibratory effect [and] to act as electrodes and produce an electrical action on the skin."[117] By promising a scientific and electrical massage, these inventions often alleged "to improv[e] the circulation of the blood and oxidate the fatty matter in the cells of the skins with a view to the reduction of weight."[118] One such device, marketed by the Portable Electric Light Company, promoted "Science and Beauty" in its advertisements, while promising to "eradicate wrinkles, crowsfeet, and all blemishes," and to act specifically "against Neuralgia, Rheumatism and other nervous attacks."[119]

Harness no doubt exemplified what Dutton calls a "quasi-professional" patentee. In 1882, when *The Electrical Review* began its campaign against the MBC, Harness decided to seek patents in order to boost the com-

---

Body," no. 10,147, 1893; Louis Cunow, "A Medicinal Light-Curative Apparatus for the Production of Complete or Partial Baths of Chemical and Electrical Rays of Light," no. 22,857, 1899; Alexander McLaughlin, "Improvements in Electric belts for the Electric Treatment of the Human Body," no. 7,200, 1900.

[116] For a further discussion of this point, see Chapter 5.

[117] Louis Casper, "Improvements in Electric Massage Instruments," Patent no. 21,807, 1899.

[118] Oscar Schneider, "An Electro-Therapeutical and Massage Apparatus," Patent no. 24,550, 1898. Other massage patents included: Henry Charles Risborough Sharman, "An Improved Electro-Massage Appliance," no. 14,340, 1894; Heinrich Simons, "Improvements in or Connected with Apparatus for the Simultaneous Shampooing or Massage of, and the Administration of Electricity to, the Human Body," no. 10,408, 1895; Theodor Bernt, "Improvements in Electric Massage Apparatus," no. 17,474, 1899.

[119] The Electrolibration Company, "Improvements in the Method of Treating Nervous and other Disorders of the Human System, and Apparatus therefor," Patent no. 1,903, 1890. See "Science and Beauty," quoted in *Practical Advertising: A Handy Guide by Practical Men, 1901–15* (London: Mather & Crower Limited, 1917), 110.

pany's claims to being bona fide. Between 1882 and 1893, Harness patented and marketed more than 30 electro-medical appliances, including an electric comb, an eye battery, a lung invigorator, many improved versions of electric belts, and even electric lamps and batteries.[120] One of them, for example, was an electrical chair that was designed to be used during surgical and dental operations "for the purpose of deadening the pain or rendering the patients insensible to the pain caused by such operations."[121] Once a patient sat in this chair and grasped conductors of the attached magneto-electrical machine under the chair, Harness explained, a mild current passing through the patient's body would produce an anesthetic effect.

Harness operated in every milieu to do with health issues. In 1890 and 1891, he patented another invention described as a home-use inhaler that was supposed to provide refreshing air charged by electricity. This apparatus featured a tube made of ebonite, India-rubber, or any other non-conductive material and a graded metal rod inside a tube that connected with an outer battery to transmit the electricity and "ozonize" the air within the tube.[122] In the late nineteenth century, the therapeutic value of "ozone" attracted much public notice, and the middle-class made popular recuperation at seaside or high-altitude health resorts—places claimed to have more ozone. Not surprisingly, "Ozone Paper" was frequently advertised—a bogus health device exploiting the public's health fantasies by

---

[120] The Patent Office holds all documentation of Harness' patents. For example, his first Electric Belt was patented on October 13, 1982, no. 4,881; the Surgical Belt and Surgery, April 24, 1883, no. 2,083; Electrical Suspensors or Suspensory Bandages, March 27, 1883, no. 5,573; the Apparatus for Facilitating the Inhalation of Medicated Vapour, July 23, 1884, no. 10,500; the Medical Eye Battery, September 17, 1886, no. 11,844; Surgical Trusses, June 13, 1887, no. 8,503; Electro-Magnetic Induction Apparatus, June 22, 1889, no. 15,689; Electrical Machines for Interrupting Use, December 24, 1891, no. 20, 215; the Electric Corset, October 17, 1891, no. 15,733; Apparatus for Restoring or Augmenting the Hearing, December 12, 1891, no. 19,472.

[121] "Improvements relating to the Treatment of Patients Preparatory to and During Surgical and Dental Operations, and to Apparatus therefore," Patent no. 20,190, dated December 10, 1890.

[122] See Harness' Inhaler, Patent no. 10,500, July 23, 1884; Improved Electro-medical Apparatus, Patent no. 16,816, February 22, 1890 and no. 17,611, 1889.

purporting to provide ozone-rich air when burned.[123]

A great deal of medical literature was written on the anti-bacterial properties of ozone as well as on its value as a protection against respiratory infections.[124] For example, Richardson—earlier discussed for his promotion of sanitation, and for his scientific approaches to medicine—emphasized the purifying and deodorizing power of ozone in his *Health and Life*, where he argued that ozone

> Is the great purifier of the dead earth, so perchance it is the physical purifier of the living animal. The light shines doubtfully here, but the direction of it is to show that when oxygen gas is brought into contact with the blood in the living lungs, it is in part transformed into ozone, and that the subtle active agent is doing its work more secretly, but as certainly, within the tissues of the organism.[125]

Richardson's discussion claiming that the best artificial method to produce ozone was "to discharge electrical sparks through the chamber while the current of air is making its way" reflected a widely held belief that ozone would appear at an electrode when electricity flashed in the air or deconstructed water.[126] Like the MBC, which employed Dr. Brabant to prescribe ozone inhalants to patients, many "ozone companies" sold deodorizing and disinfecting services, capitalizing on popularized notions about ozone's therapeutic value.

Harness soon extended his inhaler business into patenting another medical gadget—the so-called Ammoniaphone, which Dr. Carter Moffat invented for the purpose of strengthening and enriching the voice. In an 1862 paper entitled "Phosphorescence in Connection with Storms and Disease" that he delivered before the British Association for the Advancement of Science, Moffat claimed that he was one of the first medical doctors able to chemically produce ozone in the laboratory as a result of phosphorous oxidation.[127] Following his "scientific" observa-

---

[123] "Ozone Paper," *Illustrated London News*, November 3, 1894.
[124] "Ozone" *The Lancet*, 1 (1901): 609. See F. C. Trig, "The Influence of Victorian 'Patent Medicines' on the Development of Early Twentieth-Century Medical Practice," University of Sheffield, PhD dissertation, 1982.
[125] Benjamin Ward Richardson, *Health and Life* (London: Daldy, 1878), 90.
[126] Ibid., 86.
[127] Ibid., 97. See Carter Moffat, "On the Luminosity of Phosphorus," *The Elec-*

tion that the chemical properties of gases like "peroxide of hydrogen, free ammonia, and others" that occur naturally in the Italian atmosphere made that country "The Land of Song," Moffat reproduced and packed a mixture of these constituents in an instrument which was sold "for the relief of bronchitis, asthma, consumption, aphonia, loss of voice, sleeplessness, and even deafness."[128] The Ammoniaphone was a twenty-five-inch long metallic tube with handles equipped with spring valves, and it was extensively advertised by the MBC as "charged with a chemical compound, combined so as to resemble in effect that which is produced by the soft balmy air of the Italian Peninsula when inhaled into the lungs" (Fig. 3-13).[129]

It was essential for these medico-electrical inventors that the public looked upon their inventions as authentic and valuable. In addition to including testimonials from doctors and letters of thanks from customers, most of these commodities' advertisements included the term "Patented," in typically large, flamboyant fonts. Harness even listed all of his patented batteries, machines, and other electric devices in his pamphlets. Like other Victorian inventors who—as Dutton indicates—were frequently profit-driven manufacturers, these entrepreneurs intended to both monopolize pecuniary rewards and to exploit the professional-sounding potential of the term "patented."[130]

### Electricity and Victorians' Senses of the Body

As discussed in Chapter Two, the late nineteenth century was an era in which people began to seek self-realization in the fantasy of a vigorous, energetic, and satisfying life offered by therapeutic commodities widespread by that time. The proliferation of patent medicine and medical commodities reflected society's obsession with producing or tapping

---

*trician,* October 24, 1862, 296.

[128] Carter Moffat, "A Visit to the Establishment of the Medical Battery Company, Ltd., 52 Oxford Street, London, W.," *Health,* May 6, 1887, x-xi; *The Electrician,* 23 (September 20, 1888): 490-492.

[129] See, for example, *Illustrated London News,* January 10, 1885, 4; June 11, 1887, 668; and *Health,* September 5, 1887, 351.

[130] Dutton, *The Patent System and Inventive Activity During the Industrial Revolution 1750–1852,* 122–142.

abundant somatic energy and affluent health. Harness clearly capitalized on this health culture's demands, by simultaneously reinforcing the fantasy of gaining bodily health and vigor, and exploiting the perceived need for devices that were supposed to help achieve that result. The advertisements for his belts were replete with catchwords such as "All in Search of Health, Strength & Vitality Should Wear Harness' Electropathic Belt," "It Imparts New Life and Vigour," and "It exhilarates and It Restores Impaired Vitality."[131] One advertisement, promising that the belt would provide "Perfect Health" declared, "This genuine appliance is comfortable in wear, and may be relied upon to speedily and permanently invigorate the debilitated constitution, assist digestion, give strength to every nerve and muscle of the body."[132]

Why were electro-medical businesses like Harness' Medical Battery Company so successful? Why were people demanding newly devised medical instruments and technologies such as those used in electrotherapy? Chapter Two has discussed the consumer-psychology that helped the patent medicine business and broader health culture prosper in London's highly industrialized and commodity-focused environment. But what metaphorical connotations of electricity or the body electric impacted the mentality of urban inhabitants in Victorian Britain? In other words, what influence did the body electric have on Victorian sensibilities and self-sense?

Amidst broader developments in advertising and commerce, what clearly fueled the public's demand for these medico-electrical gadgets was the widely marketed image of the body electric and the association between electricity and nervous vitality. New electrical technologies, such as the telegraph and submarine cable as well as the widespread replacement of gas lights with electric ones, suggested the possibility of living a life that was similarly full of potential and seemingly boundless energy. Fully recognizing the desire for symbolic pick-me-ups and playing up the

---

[131] There are innumerable advertisements for the Medical Battery Company's products in *The Illustrated London News*, *The Graphic*, *Health*, and the like. In addition, a number of that company's advertising ephemera are held in the John Johnson Collection. Many of these advertisements used catchphrases of the kind indicated here.

[132] "In Perfect Health, Since Wearing Harness' Electropathic Belt," *Health*, January 8, 1892, iv.

businessmen's association of electricity with stamina, nervous force, and
muscle movement, Harness often advertised his belts' curative powers
over "Nervous Exhaustion," "Brain Fag," and "Weak and Languid Feelings."[133] Another example of this kind of advertised association was
Arthur E. Baines' odd but popular argument that bodily "nerve force"
and "neuro-electricity" were generated by the body's heat and movement,
and by the chemical action in brain cells. Baines was a submarine cable
engineer, working as a superintendent for the Eastern Telegraph Company, and he also was an editor of *The Electrical Engineer* and *The Electrician*.
Moreover, he was involved in Harness' electric business. At Harness'
request, Baines published a testimonial pamphlet in which he guaranteed
that Harness' belt was "capable of developing currents, whose strength
could approximate with the normal tensions of the vital organs of the
body, and which should have a large covering surface."[134]

To explain the phenomenon of a slight change on his static galvanometer when he drew close to the electric circuit of a telegraph, Baines
began to consider the possibility that the human body has an electrical
potential of its own.[135] He believed that the human body, and every living
animal's body—insofar as it consisted of a generator of electricity, a
network of conductors, and a series of condenser-like storage cells such
as ganglia—possessed a certain normal electrical potential.[136] By using
Kelvin's static galvanometer, he went on to insist that this electric potential could be measured according to an electro-diagnosis using Ohm's law:

$$C = E/R$$

---

[133] See, for example, the advertisements in *The St. James Gazette*, June 10, 1892,
and February 19, 1892.

[134] Arthur E. Baines, *A Study of Mr. Harness' "Electropathic Belt," Considered As a
Natural and Valuable Remedy for the Treatment of Disease* (London: Medical Battery
Company, 1880), 21.

[135] A. E. Baines and F. H. Bowman, *Electropathology and Therapeutics, Together with a
Prefaratory Treatise on the Nervous System and Its Relation to Neuroelectricity by F. H.
Bowman* (London: Ewart, Seymour & Company, 1913); "The Electrician as
Physiologist," *British Medical Journal*, 2 (August, 17, 1918): 160–106; A. E. Baines,
"The Electrical Condition of the Human Body," *The Electrician*, XV–XVI (1886–
1887): 376.

[136] Ibid., 45–49.

Here C represents the current of nervous energy in the body; R, the resistance of the conductor; and E, the electromotive force.

According to Baines, the amount of electricity "varies as much with individuals as physical force differs, as stature differs, as complexion and other characteristics differ."[137] Thus he argued that although electricity was not entirely identical with "nervous force" or "vitality," there was a certain connection between them:

> The currents are distributed by the conductors over the whole body. They flow as the blood flows, but by a nerve or a muscle instead of by a vein, and instead of returning to the heart, or to any other organ, they escape into air, and by the contact of the body with material objects, to the earth. There is in fact, a constant stream of Electricity flowing from every part of the body to earth. When one is weak physically, one is also weak Electrically. When vitality is at a low ebb, the Electrical system is correspondingly low. Where the body is in full vigor the tensions attain their highest normal standard, and so on through all the gradations between health and disease.[138]

Thus, Baines insisted, when the body's neuro-electrical level became very low because of disease or shock—that is, when its battery was weakened or drawn down—the body rapidly began to lose its electrical power. An artificial and continuous current from an electric battery, the engineer explained, could make up for the deficiency.[139] The most important issue, according to Baines, was to keep a good balance of electricity in the body. "If we can keep the Electrical system right," he wrote, "we can, in the ordinary course of things, dispense with the doctor."[140]

In late-Victorian society, electrotherapeutic notions about disease were widely accepted—many people believed that disease was mainly caused, or else accompanied, by disturbances in the electrical equilibrium of one's body. The fact that money could be made from exploiting this public preoccupation demonstrates that in having an obsessive-compulsive de-

---

[137] Baines, *A Study of Mr. Harness' "Electropathic Belt"*, 11.
[138] Ibid., 12.
[139] Baines, *Electropathy* (London: Ewart, Seymour & Co., 1913), 53–60.
[140] Baines, *A Study of Mr. Harness' "Electropathic Belt"*, 18.

sire to gain or maintain "perfect health," people wanted to take in or eject electricity in order to fine-tune one's bodily balance of electric energy. Beginning in 1890, for example, the Electrolibration Company patented and marketed a dubious apparatus, "The Electropoise," which was designed to leak excess electricity out of the body or else to recover it by wiring a patient to the earth. A clasp at one end of this device was connected with the patient's ankle, and the shell-shaped opposite electrode was immersed into cold water or placed in the outside atmosphere to achieve a "complete circuit" between the body and nature.[141] An advertisement for the device claimed that it was "Simple!—Safe!—Not A Battery—No Shock!" and trumpeted that "The Electropoise achieves its remarkable results by its action of the blood current . . . giv[ing] life and vitality through the blood, causing the system to absorb an extra amount of nature's own great vitality" (Fig. 3-14).[142]

Many theorists of medical electricity and engineers working on electric stimulation sought to produce more than nervous energy for patients; they also stressed that electro-therapeutic remedies could additionally produce nutritious blood circulation throughout the body. Wilhelm Erb, a German physiologist, indicated that although animal tissue was the poorest conductor, blood did contain salts, so that a good therapeutic result "depends in greater part upon the blood circulating through them [body tissues] and upon the parenchymatous fluids."[143] Similarly, in discussing the local faradization of paralyzed parts of the body, Armand de Watteville insisted that currents passed through sensitive nerves to produce a "more active flow of blood" and that "as neuralgias are usually accompanied by modifications in the capillary circulation, it follows that the argumentation and acceleration of the flow of blood may lead to the removal of the painful symptoms."[144] Hugh Campbell, on the other hand,

---

[141] "Improvements in the Method of Treating Nervous and Other Disorders of the Human System, and Apparatus therefor," Patent no. 1,903, September 8, 1880.

[142] "A Home Remedy! The Electropoise," JJC, Patent Medicine Box 10.

[143] Wilhelm Erb, *A Handbook of Electro-Therapeutics*, trans. by L. Putzel (New York: William Wood & Company, 1883), 21.

[144] Armand de Watteville, *A Practical Introduction to Medical Electricity with a Compendium of Electrical Treatment Translated from the French of Dr. Onimus* (London: H. K. Lewis, 1878), 113.

defined under-nourished blood as a main cause of nervous exhaustion, and maintained that "an impoverished state of the blood, as in anæmia, deprives the great nervous centres of the nutrition necessary for their maintenance in the health and vigour, the due performance of their functions."[145]

Given how popular these notions were, there is no doubt that many quacks marketing magnetic gadgets and mechanical devices also profited from strategies similar to those employed by entrepreneurs such as Harness and his Medical Battery Company. Ambrecht, Nelson & Company, for example, sold magneto-electrode appliances for almost every part of the body: head-pieces, spine-bands, anklets, knee-bandages, armlets, throat bandages, and corset-and-belt combinations. Its pamphlet extolled the great medical effects of the company's magnetic body suit: "The Blood with its iron and oxygen, highly charged with electro-magnetic force, reaches all parts of the system, discharging its vital principal along its course, and invigorating all parts, particularly those affected by weakness."[146] It is indicative of the late-Victorian psyche that almost all the advertisements of these electro-therapeutic treatments and appliances contain vocabulary emphasizing the importance of energetic health— "vigour," "vitality," "strong body," and so on.

Who, though, actually purchased these medical commodities—what kinds of people did these charlatans target? Undoubtedly, electro-medical devices were in greatest demand in cities, with their bourgeois residents targeted by marketers more intensely than were other sectors of society. Further, judging from the advertisements' catchphrases and pictorial information about these electric gadgets, potential buyers (whether male or female), suffered from some kind of bodily debility or run-down condition that remained inexplicable even to themselves: indigestion, biliousness, nervous disorders, neuralgia, insomnia, paralysis, and rheumatism, *inter alia*. As the advertisements explained, these people wished to be cured of their mental and physical disorders likely stemming from the

---

[145] Hugh Campbell, *The Anatomy of Nervousness and Nervous Exhaustion (Neurasthenia)*, 4th edn. (London: Henry Renshaw, 1890), 15.

[146] "Ambrecht's Patent Permanent Magneto-Electrode Appliances: A New and Improved Method of Magnetism as a Curative Agent," JJC, Patent Medicine Box 10. John Hugh Martin & Company was a similar magnetic-device business (at 272 Regent Street); see its pamphlet of the late 1880s, "Curative Magnetism, or Nature's Aids to Health," JJC, Patent Medicine Box 9.

competitive work-environments and daily stresses of city life. In 1895, Thomas Clifford Allbutt, the Regius Professor of Physics at Cambridge University, wrote the following about the apparent increase in the number of people with nervous disorders:

> Affections of the nervous system are on the increase! Not only do we hear, but daily we see neurotics, neurasthenia, hysteria, and the like: is not every large city filled with nerve-specialists, and their chambers with patients; are not hospitals, baths, electric-machines, and massages multiplying daily for their use; nerve-tonics sold behind every counter, and health-resorts advertised for their solace and restoration?[147]

Indeed, the electro-magnetic devices proliferating in the marketplace were to be demanded and consumed by those urban sufferers from nervous ailments, as the sense of nervous degeneration grew more widespread.

In the vocabulary of the day, many urban middle-class residents described themselves as suffering from "nervous prostration" and "neurasthenia"—immobilizing depression—triggered by high-stress work-environments and anxieties rife in modern urban life. In fact, residents of British cities considered health less as a physical reality than as an idealized mental image of potential being, that could be realized only momentarily or conjured up as an alternate reality. Because they often identified the human body with a complex system of networked nerves, they also viewed electricity as a natural means to achieve the chimerical combination of "sound body" and "sound mind." On a broader front, too, there was anxiety in the later nineteenth century: Britain's industrial and military hegemony were being challenged by both Germany and the United States, and along with fears of a reduced British Empire, there was widespread fear of declining national health standards.

Given this situation, it is not surprising that white-collar workers living

---

[147] Thomas Clifford Allbutt, "Nervous Diseases and Modern Life," *The Contemporary Review*, 67 (1895): 210–231. On the atmosphere of the late-Victorian nervous society, see Janet Oppenheim, *"Shattered Nerves": Doctors, Patients, and Depression in Victorian England* (Oxford: Oxford University Press, 1991). For nineteenth-century psychiatry, see Andrew Scull, *The Most Solitary of Afflictions: Madness and Society in Britain, 1700–1900* (New Haven: Yale University Press, 1993).

in cities became eager buyers of these electric devices. But how about female purchasers—did the proliferation of these health-associated commodities reflect the gendered patterns of consumption that many historians have discerned as an important feature of modern consumer society? Although the interpretation of Victorian consumerism *per se* is not the main focus of this book, it is appropriate to end this chapter by briefly considering gender and consumption as far as the commodification of the body electric is concerned. Many advertising pictures of medico-electric devices suggest that women were viewed as potential customers of their products: for instance, in the advertisement of the Electropoise, a middle-class woman rests on a couch in a languid pose, leaking her excess of electricity into a water bottle so as to adjust her body's electricity balance. However, the most popular electro-medical goods advertised for women were electric belts and electrical or magnetic corsets, and, indeed, many electrical charlatans sold very similar products. For example, Darlow and Company sold the "Patent Flexible Magnetine" for women, Ely & Company established an office that sold the "Lady's Magnetic Curative," and, in the advertisement for Dr. Richardson's Magneto Galvanic Battery, a woman warrior was replenished by donning a medico-electric battery (Fig. 3-15). Among all the manufacturers of these electric gadgets, the most notorious was—again—C. B. Harness' Medical Battery Company. In the 1880s the MBC launched an extensive campaign to sell the updated version of its electric belt for women. But the enumerated ailments it was said to treat were almost the same as those described for the belt marketed to men: a torpid liver, nervous exhaustion, sleeplessness, debility, and all muscular or organic weaknesses. Beyond a pictorial appeal to femininity, the only expression of gender difference was the adding of diseases such as hysteria and melancholic depression to its list of treatable ailments. Harness also invented an "Electric Magnetic Corset," whose colorful advertising flyers sought to woo women by boasting that it was "The Very Thing for Ladies for an Elegant Figure and Good Health," and that "By wearing this Perfectly designed Corset, the internal organs are speedily strengthened" (Fig. 3-16).

In the MBC's advertisements, the women are depicted wearing Harness' tightly laced corsets, and they mare made to look like typical Victorian middle-class ladies, with an emphasis on the traditional view of the woman as a good wife and domestic, leisured creature of the home.

Nonetheless, it is very difficult to argue that the same belt served specific functions that differed by gender of the person wearing it. In fact, nearly all of the advertising language used to market medico-electric devices expressed the common opinion of the 1880s and 1890s that both men and women (whether feminists or anti-feminists) needed to develop their body's energetic capacity. These advertisements repeatedly used expressions intoning how their products "stimulate," "strengthen," "invigorate," and "exhilarate" nervous energies. Here we see a kind of unisex commonality of viewing health as physical perfection and stamina. Although there were still heated antifeminist arguments against women partaking in prolonged physical activities, by the 1890s physical education and outdoor exercises such as gymnastics, constitutional walk, and horseback riding came to be recommended even for middle-class women living in the city. Recognizing the importance of fostering physical strength for women, the historian and essayist W. E. H. Lecky wrote about this change in 1896, "The beauty of perfect health and of high spirits has been steadily replacing, as an ideal type, the beauty of a sickly delicacy and of weak and tremulous nerves which in the eighteenth century was so much admired, or at least extolled."[148]

But it is not that these advertisements did not construct any gendered images of bodily health. As Janet Oppenheim has thoroughly demonstrated, medical doctors, evolutionary biologists, and psychiatrists contributed to an intellectual discourse in the Victorian age about women's nervousness by writing and speaking at length about the woman's tendency to suffer neurotic diseases and how female sexuality related to a woman's susceptibility to nervous illnesses. As these intellectuals' views were widely circulated, medical capitalists selling quackish commodities began quoting scientific explanations from eminent medical doctors, some of whom went so far as to write certificates for the appliances sold by these businessmen. When the MBC began to sell its Ladies' Abdominal Electropathic Belt and Electropathic Spine Bands, the company also published the 80-page booklet *A Treatise of the Special Diseases of Women and*

---

[148] From William Edward Hartpole Lecky, *Democracy and Liberty*, quoted in Barbara Harisson, "Women's Health and Women's Movement," in Charles Webster, ed., *Biology, Medicine and Society 1840–1940* (Cambridge: Cambridge University Press, 1981), 41. See also Janet Oppenheim, *"Shattered Nerves"*, 198–199.

*Their Electropathic Treatment*, which was full of information on physiological functions peculiar to the female sex. Most of these arguments in
this booklet were based on the research and writings of medical professionals. Providing a popular account of menstruation, which was singled
out as that "particular function" of women, the booklet explains how,
"amongst women in all grades of society and in various stages of life, a
large number suffers—and some even die—because of their almost total
ignorance of a particular function identified with their distinctive sex."[149]
This promotional publication then recounted many related female disorders, such as amenorrhœa, dysmenorrhœa, menorrhagia, menstrual
cessation, leucorrhœa, chlorosis, and hysteria.[150] The booklet explained to
readers that the medical information about each dysfunction was to educate
them on how women's organs were constitutionally and biologically different from men's—a fact that caused women's peculiar mental derangements, so the booklet claimed. Electricity, it emphasized, was the most
appropriate method to deal with women's particular susceptibility to
nerve-related ailments. The booklet argued that, unlike men, whose
nervous dynamo tended to be the brain, women had another dynamo—
the nerve-dominating center in their reproductive organs such as the
uterus and ovaries: "The seat of actual disease is often to be found in
some affection of the womb, which anatomically is in intimate sympathetic connection with every internal organ of the female economy."[151]

Thus Harness even invented and patented what he named "Harness'
Natural Uterine Supporter," insisting that "displacements of the uterus
are accountable for very many ailments with which women are afflicted."
The uterine supporter was composed of a cup and highly polished stem
made of Xylonite, which "is quite impervious to the acid or alkaline
reactions of the utero-vaginal excretions," and was attached to a morocco
belt, with elastic straps to buckle around the hips. With women's uteruses
fixed in the proper location, Harness argued that nervous derangements
peculiar to their gender could be avoided. "Displacements of the uterus
are accountable for very many ailments with which women are afflicted."

---

[149] *A Treatise on the Special Diseases of Women and Their Electropathic Treatment*
(London: the Medical Battery Company Limited, 1891).
[150] Ibid., 6.
[151] Ibid., 29.

Women's "well-being of the economy," the accompanying pamphlet said, depends upon the proper functions of this organ, which "abundantly supplied with nerve and blood-vessels, possessing such mysterious and remarkable sympathetic relations with the most distant organs of the body" and its "departures from its natural position, without setting in operation that long train of symptoms which eventually makes the lives of its unhappy victims wretched and burdensome."[152]

As is often the case with discourses on female sexuality, these advertisements and informational publications present a typical gendered view of bodily configuration. Men's illnesses originated from a definite cause and manifested themselves openly and externally, while on the other hand, women's ill health was often expressed as a kind of "internal weakness," frequently construed as an introverted state of mental and physical condition. It was often claimed that only women complained of "lassitude and indisposition for exertion, sinking feelings at the pit of the stomach, and distressing nervous sensations." In sickness, it was said that women tended to lose luster in their eyes and healthful bloom in their complexion, and that their hands and feet became cold. And women often complained they were below par. Harness' pamphlet quoted Sir James Paget, a famous medical pathologist: "The close and multifarious relations of the (female) sexual organs with the minds, and with all parts of the nervous system, are enough to make the disorders of these organs dominant in a disorderly nervous constitution."[153] As this internality of women's disease came from the body's deepest interior, the sexual organs, Harness' and others' electric belts and corsets were constructed to fold over women's hips to provide a mild electric current that constantly emitted tonic, stimulating, and invigorating boosts to women's sexual organs.

### Conclusion

This chapter has examined the Victorians' obsession with the body electric and its association with the field of medicine, and it has contextualized these issues amidst theories of electricity and their applications to medical treatment in the nineteenth century. The 1880s and 1890s wit-

---

[152] Ibid., 75.
[153] Ibid., 31.

nessed an unprecedented proliferation of health-related commodities, patent medicine, and the capitalistic activities of medical entrepreneurs. In such a milieu, electricity, with its time-honored relation to nervous force, became regarded as a valid technology for various nervous maladies, mental depressions, and loss of vigor. Consumers began demanding such medical devices as electric belts and massage machines as well as visiting privately owned institutions that provided electrical treatments and stimulations. Some medico-electrical professionals were also associated with these businesses, a circumstance that ignited controversies over professionalism in the medical world.

Finally, this chapter has highlighted the skills and broader context of many charlatan entrepreneurs of electrical medicine. In exploring their advertising strategies, investigating their economic activities as participants in a highly commercialized society, and attending to the implications of patents, which they often used to persuade their clients, this chapter has demonstrated that the medico-social context that allowed these quacks to flourish was not entirely separate from the established professional domains of engineering and medicine. These charlatans' profit-driven enterprises represent a deepening of capitalism's incursion into the medical marketplace, which went hand in hand with the popularization of electrotherapeutics and the endeavors of its supporters. However, as these quacks' operations became more obviously fraudulent, tensions increased with elite professionals who realized that the power of market-forces was threatening the traditional ethos of the professional medical establishment. The next chapter examines the historical drama within which these tensions emerged and grew, as well as affiliations and conflicts between elite doctors, popularizers of electro-medicine, engineers, and the capitalistic charlatans who sought to exploit the newly blurred division between electro-medicine and therapeutics.

CHAPTER 4

*Electro-Therapeutic Institutes and the Royal College of Physicians: Medical Technology and Professional Norms*

That it is undesirable that any Fellow or Member of the College should be officially connected with any Company having for its object the treatment of disease for profit.

—Resolution of the Royal College of Physicians of London, October 25, 1888[1]

That subject to the general provisions of Bye-law 190 the College desires so to interpret its Bye-laws, Regulations, and Resolutions, as no longer to prohibit the official connection of Fellows and Members with medical institutes, though financed by a company, provided there be no other financial relation than the acceptance of a fixed salary or of fees for medical attendance on a fixed scale, irrespective of the total amount of the profits of the Company.

—Resolution of the Royal College of Physicians of London, 1922, replacing the Resolution of 1888.

No Fellow *or Member* of the College shall be engaged in trade, or dispense medicines, or make any engagement with a Chemist [pharmacist] or any other person for the supply of medicines, or

---

[1] *The Charter, Bye-Laws, and Regulations of the Royal College of Physicians of London and the Acts of Parliament Especially Relating Thereto* (London: Harridan and Sons, 1908), 94–95.

practise Medicine or Surgery in partnership, by deed or otherwise, or be a party to the transfer of patients or of the goodwill of a practice to or from himself for any pecuniary consideration.

—Bye-law 178 of the Royal College of Physicians of London [italics added to show alterations made in 1922][2]

### Medical Commerce and Professional Ideals

As was discussed in the previous chapter, the techniques and practices of electro-therapeutics were gradually and steadily popularized during the late nineteenth century. The instruments, commodities, and services related to medical electricity became commonplace in the market, and for consumers in London, seeing the advertisements for these medical appliances became an everyday event. At the same time, quackish entrepreneurs and electrical engineers were scrambling to enter the promising medical market. It is small wonder, then, that emergent medical capitalism led to the development of an ideological tension between techno-medical entrepreneurs and elite medical professionals, who felt threatened by such market incursions and sought to protect their professional autonomy. This chapter examines the ideological conflict that developed between medical entrepreneurs and elite doctors.

Of special focus are the implications of a revealing drama in which the activities of two electro-therapeutic medical institutes caused heated debates at the Censors' Board of the Royal College of Physicians in the late 1880s and 1890s. In 1888, the Institute of Medical Electricity Limited (henceforth IME), which British electrical engineers had founded to explore new electrical business in the field of medicine, began to encroach upon the professional ideology of the Royal College of Physicians (henceforth RCP). Four years later, the even more commercially oriented Medical Battery Company—attached to the Zander Institute—started selling its notorious electric belts, leading to irksome disciplinary problems for the Censors' Board of the RCP. Supporting the IME were

---

[2] "Second Report from the Censors' Board on the Proposed Alteration of a Resolution of the College and of Bye-law CLXXVIII," held by the Royal College of Physicians of London (henceforth RCP), MSS., 835/51. For the resolution and bye-law, see the *Annals of Royal College of Physicians of London* (henceforth *Annals*), 51 (October 19, 1922): 159–162.

medical electricians and the Institution of Electrical Engineers. Meanwhile, Dr. Herbert Tibbits, a licentiate of the RCP, supported the Medical Battery Company (henceforth MBC) and its founder C. B. Harness by issuing a certificate for the MBC's electric belt. Opposing both of these groups were, on the one hand, traditionalist physicians of the RCP, and on the other hand, mainstream medical electricians within the IME who, seeking to advance the managerial possibilities of their institute as well as electricity's practical applications to medicine, attempted to quash the MBC and Tibbits in court battles. In exploring this struggle, this chapter shows how the interaction between capital, technology, and medicine created in the late nineteenth century a new entrepreneurial environment for the medical profession.

Facing the challenges posed by the upstart IME and MBC, the RCP was determined to thwart the commercial ventures of these entities' corporate-style medicine. However, the conflict between these three groups—the RCP, the mainstream electricians, and the IME and MBC—reveals a new medico-social context in which, just before the turn of the century, the medical profession was experiencing pressure to remodel its ideology in the face of the increased commercialization of medical practice and public demand for specialized and technology-based treatments. The RCP's enactment and amendment of its regulations in 1888 and 1922 were influenced by the two professional ideals of the physician, as gentleman and as a person dedicated to public service, with the latter ideal gradually gaining on the former in the early twentieth century.[3]

The reevaluation of medicine's relation to commerce and the marketplace, initiated largely by Roy Porter, has created an understanding of eighteenth-century medicine as client-dominated and wantonly market-oriented. In the free-for-all, regular practitioners had to compete with quack itinerants, nostrum-vendors, and empirics such as James Graham.[4] Moreover as Margaret Pelling emphasizes, "early modern practitioners

---

[3] Harold Perkin, *The Rise of Professional Society* (London: Routledge, 1989). For the increased importance of the public service ideal within the medical profession, see Andrew Morrice, "'The Medical Pundits': Doctors and Indirect Advertising in the Lay Press 1922–1927," *Medical History*, 38 (1994): 255–280.

[4] Roy Porter, *Health for Sale: Quackery in England, 1660–1850* (Manchester: Manchester University Press, 1989).

were involved in the drink trades at various levels."[5] For these reasons, it is difficult to split eighteenth-century medical practitioners into professionals versus traders solely on the basis of their behavior.

By contrast, traditional historiography asserts that in the Victorian era the rise of professionalism via bureaucratic and state control gradually replaced commercialism in medicine, and thus the professionalization of medicine served to rescue the profession from the undignified scramble for profits in the medical marketplace.[6] Traditional historiography has argued that state regulations, such as the Apothecaries Act of 1815 and the Medical Act of 1858, were effectively introduced to reinforce the boundaries between quackery and the medical profession.[7] On the doctor's side, an ethical or moral code of behavior provided powerful professional solidarity. According to Jeanne Peterson, elite London consultants used their patronage and posts in voluntary hospitals to acquire wealthy patients for their own lucrative private practices, but at the same time they protected the *esprit de corps* of the medical profession by insisting on gentlemanly professional standards for practitioners. This created an ethos according to which advertising or pecuniary ventures by doctors were seen as unprofessional and unseemly.[8]

---

[5] Margaret Pelling, "Medical Practice in Early Modern England: Trade or Profession?" in Wilfred Prest, ed., *The Professions in Early Modern England* (London: Croom Helm, 1987), 104. For the occupational diversity in early modern England, see Margaret Pelling, "Occupational Diversity: Barbersurgeons and the Trades of Norwich, 1550–1640," *Bulletin for the History of Medicine*, 56 (1982): 484–511. See also her book, *The Common Lot: Sickness, Medical Occupations, and the Urban Poor in Early Modern England* (London: Longman, 1998).

[6] The story of the transition from eighteenth-century fringe medicine to professionalism belongs to the general historical development of English society. J. H. Plumb, Porter's mentor, together with N. McKendrick and J. Brewer, found that consumers' desires for marketable goods dramatically accelerated in the eighteenth century, and that both *laissez-faire* doctrine and a "self-help" ideology sustained this rapidly emerging consumer society. N. McKendrick, J. Brewer, and J. H. Plumb, *The Birth of a Consumer Society: The Commercialisation of Eighteenth-Century England* (London: Hutchinson, 1982).

[7] William Reader, *Professional Men: The Rise of the Professional Classes in Nineteenth-Century England* (London: Weidenfeld & Nicolson, 1966).

[8] M. Jeanne Peterson, *The Medical Profession in Mid-Victorian London* (Berkeley: University of California Press, 1978).

More recent historiography, however, has judged the effectiveness of state regulation to have been rather limited.[9] The Medical Act of 1858, for example, was less restrictive than it seemed on the surface, allowing doctors freedom to espouse any doctrines (quackish or not) that they wished.[10] Even the professionalization perspective, which Peterson articulates, brings into relief the intra-professional struggles in which non-elite doctors found a way to break the monopoly of the elite by seeking other methods of financial gain.[11] At the same time, many medical men, including such practitioners as Robert Abercrombie and Harry Lobb, began to engage in self-promoting strategies of medical entrepreneurship.[12] Recent studies of the medical market show that harsh competition among a growing number of rank-and-file practitioners in the nineteenth century created "a significant downward pressure on medical incomes," which compelled practitioners to pursue a more commercial approach—with some even going so far as to endorse medical advertisements and join laymen's medical businesses.[13]

From the perspective of those physicians intent on establishing medicine as a privileged professional domain, such collaboration between commercial interests and medical professionals did not go unchallenged for long. During the last quarter of the nineteenth century, extraordinary meetings of the Censors' Board (the disciplinary body of the Royal College of Physicians) frequently convened to summon fellows, members,

---

[9] The 1815 Apothecaries Act failed to guard the status of general practitioners. See Irvine Loudon, *Medical Care and the General Practitioner, 1750–1850* (Oxford: Clarendon Press, 1987), 297–301.

[10] David L. Cowen, "Liberty, Laissez-Faire, and Licensure in Nineteenth-Century Britain," *Bulletin of the History of Medicine*, 43 (1969): 30–40. See A. M. Cooke, *A History of the Royal College of Physicians of London* (Oxford: Clarendon Press, 1972), 3: 908.

[11] Ivan Waddington, "General Practitioners and Consultants in Early Nineteenth-Century England: The Sociology of an Intra-Professional Conflict," in J. Woodward and D. Richards, eds., *Health Care and Popular Medicine in the Social History of Medicine* (New York: Holmes & Meier, 1977); Ivan Waddington, *The Medical Profession in the Industrial Revolution* (Dublin: Gull and Macmillan, 1984).

[12] Peterson, *The Medical Profession in Mid-Victorian London*, 252-253, 256.

[13] Irvine Loudon, *Medical Care and the General Practitioner*; Anne Digby, *Making a Medical Living: Doctors and Patients in the English Market for Medicine, 1720–1911* (Cambridge: Cambridge University Press, 1994).

and licentiates whose names had appeared in public advertisements.[14] Various patent foods and accessories such as Van Houten Cocoa, Coleman's Liebig's Extract of Meat and Malt Wine, and The Ladies' New Sanitary Towel were advertised as having doctors' recommendations and thus also medical virtues. As a result, all of these companies incurred the RCP's censorship. But most controversial were the testimonials or certificates that doctors actually provided for such medical goods.[15] The endorsing doctors were held censurable insofar as they voluntarily involved themselves with companies and their commercial activities. In all of these cases, the College's rationale was simple: it was "unprofessional" conduct to be officially connected with trade or market activities for the purpose of a making profit.

How did medical professionalism come to terms with the burgeoning

---

[14] A. M. Cooke explains the RCP's preoccupation with professionalism and disciplinary action as follows: "In the last quarter of the nineteenth century the College, and in particular the Censors' Board, devoted much time and trouble to disciplinary matters. . . . At almost every meeting of the Censors' Board there were several disciplinary items on the agenda, some time as many as nine at a time. Members were sometimes guilty of being associated with trade or of advertising." See A. M. Cooke, "The Close of the Nineteenth Century, 1876–99," in *A History of the Royal College of Physicians of London,* 902. The advertising files containing a number of the controversial cases of advertisements collected by the Censors' Board are held in the RCP, MSS., 2412/1–176.

[15] The following are examples of actions the RCP pursued against companies and doctors: Coleman & Company, Ltd., "Unsolicited testimonials from medical men, Coleman's Liebig's Extract of Meat and Malt Wine"; Sir William Broadbent censored in relation to "Grundy's Heating and Ventilating Apparatus," MSS., 2412/19a; John Attefield, "Correspondence re circular letter by John Attefield soliciting expert scientific evidence in defense of Van Houten's cocoa in an action of law," 1893, MSS., 2412/280–284; "Baby Magazine: Correspondence re names of fellows of RCP appearing in advertisement for *Baby,*" MSS., 2412/33–44; "William Chapman Grigg: Correspondence re testimonial by Dr Grigg for Liq. Euonymin et Pepsin Co. published by Oppenheimer Bros. & Co. 1884–85," MSS., 2412/100–105; "Archibald Keightley: Correspondence relating to Archibald Keightley's name being used in advertisements for Miss Ellen Jewson's Home for the Dietetic and other treatment of Chronic Disease, 1894," MSS., 2412/150–153; "Charles Henry Leet: Testimonials in favour of Charles Henry Leet, used in advertisements. With advertisement for Dr. Leet's Pills, 1886–94," MSS., 2412/154–56.

market capitalism of late Victorian England? In an era in which professionalization was on the rise, why was medical practice so often tainted
with commercial endeavor? Explaining doctors' market activities and the
proliferation of medical commodities only from the point of view of
medical suppliers neglects another important element: demand. Why did
commercialized medical practices flourish? What sustained them? In
improving their well-being, what kinds of medical practices or commodities did nineteenth-century consumers of medicine first begin to
seek, and how were these choices affected by the competing commercial
and professional ideologies of the day?

Irrespective of the consultants' concerns for professional ideology and
cohesion, consumers of medicine began to demand different kinds of
medical practices. Their concerns manifested themselves at various levels
from at least the late nineteenth century, when the weight of medical
authority was passing from the omni-competent physician single-handed-
ly performing diagnoses and treatments to more specialized care-giving and
institutional treatments.

In other words, specialization was an additional element amidst the
market pressures that troubled the RCP. Although technical specialists in
Britain throughout the nineteenth century were likely to be regarded as
quacks by medical professionals, younger aspiring specialists founded
their own *specialist* hospitals with the support of philanthropic laymen. In
so doing, they attempted to break the barrier created by the inner circle
who monopolized positions at general hospitals.[16] In 1859, for example,
the National Hospital for the Paralysed and Epileptic was founded to
provide electro-therapy for nervous ailments. In 1866, Julius Althaus, an
eminent writer about medical electricity, founded a Hospital for Epilepsy
and Paralysis, later renamed the Maida Vale Hospital.[17] Such specialist
hospitals multiplied so rapidly and flourished so widely that they could no
longer be ignored by the consultants at the general hospitals.[18]

---

[16] Rosemary Stevens, *Medical Practice in Modern England: The Impact of Specialization
and State Medicine* (New Haven and London: Yale University Press, 1966).

[17] Peterson, *The Medical Profession in Mid-Victorian London*, 264–266; Richard
Kershaw, *Special Hospitals* (London: Pullman, 1909).

[18] Lindsay Granshaw, "Fame and Fortune by Means of Bricks and Mortar: The
Medical Profession and Specialist Hospitals in Britain, 1800–1948," in Lindsay
Granshaw and Roy Porter, eds., *The Hospital in History* (London: Routledge, 1989);

The high demand for specialist hospitals, it has been argued, "underlay the overall success of the specialist hospital movement," and hospitals in turn easily adapted their outpatient facilities to attract and accommodate more patients.[19] The pay-hospital movement, led by Henry Burdett, was sustained by the middle classes who "could afford to make some payment" for care that was more refined than that found in voluntary charitable hospitals.[20] Para-medical activities, which were beginning to acquire a recognized place in the medical division of labor in the late nineteenth century, were similarly linked to this new domain of institutional treatment. Massage, newly legitimated as an auxiliary treatment in hospitals, was developed into a more professional physiotherapy.[21] Consequently, massage departments began to be established in both general and specialist hospitals. Many business-oriented institutions such as nursing homes advertised treatment by massage and by Swedish medical gymnastics under the aegis of resident physicians.[22] The recognized usefulness of X-rays for diagnosis nurtured the alliance within hospitals between physicians and surgeons with their technical counterparts, the radiologists and radiographers.[23] Collaboration between physicians and these skilled

Stevens, *Medical Practice in Modern England*, 27–28.

[19] Granshaw, ibid., 206.

[20] Brian Able-Smith, *The Hospitals, 1800–1948: A Study in Social Administration in England and Wales* (London: Heinemann, 1964), 102-104.

[21] In 1894, the trained nurses had founded the Society of Trained Massage, which developed into the modern Chartered Society of Physiotherapy in 1944. See Jean Barclay, *In Good Hands: The History of the Chartered Society of Physiotherapy 1894–1994* (London: Butterworth-Heinemann, 1994). Massage, an old popular means of healing, was revived in the 1880s. Julius Althaus referred to it as "The Cinderella of Therapeutics." Althaus, "The Risk of 'Massage'," *British Medical Journal*, 2 (1883): 1223–1224.

[22] *Matthews' Manual of Nursing Homes & Hydros of the British Isles and Guide to Spas and Health Resorts* (London: Alex. Matthews, 1915).

[23] The development of the paramedical profession is examined by Gerald Larkin, "The Emergence of the Para-Medical Profession," in W. F. Bynum and Roy Porter, eds., *Companion Encyclopedia of the History of Medicine* (London: Routledge, 1993), 2: 1329–1349; Bynum and Porter, eds., *Occupational Monopoly and Modern Medicine* (London: Tavistock, 1983). For medicine's internal structure and division of labor, see Harry M. Marks, "Notes from the Underground: The Social Organization of Therapeutic Research," and Rosemary Stevens, "The Curious

specialists, though maintaining a somewhat hierarchical structure, was supposed to produce more service-oriented treatment for patients.[24] As a result of this partnership, management and administration also grew in importance in order to ensure that the consumer's needs were met.[25] In this environment, capital ventures appeared parasitic on medicine.

Recent studies of American medicine have stressed the role of market forces, "managerial medicine," and "medical efficiency,"[26] in increasing occupational competition and bringing new technologies and specialty services into medicine in order to attract patients.[27] In his investigation of

---

Career of Internal Medicine: Functional Ambivalence, Social Success," both in Russell C. Maulitz and Diana E. Long, eds., *Grand Rounds: One Hundred Years of Internal Medicine* (Philadelphia: University of Pennsylvania Press, 1988).

[24] For this line of argument with emphasis on the hierarchical structure of medicine, see Roger Cooter, *Surgery and Society in Peace and War: Orthopaedics and the Organization of Modern Medicine, 1880–1948* (London: Macmillan, 1994).

[25] For a detailed elaboration of this change in twentieth-century medicine, see Steve Sturdy, "The Political Economy of Scientific Medicine: Science, Education, and the Transformation of Medical Practice in Sheffield, 1890–1922," *Medical History*, 36 (1992): 125–159. Sturdy shows that physician-scientists with strong managerial and administrative interests redirected laboratory-based techniques like bacteriology and chemical physiology to various service-oriented purposes in public health, industrial management, and civic administration. With the lay support promoted by such a scheme, they successfully reorganized the Medical School into a center of administrative machinery for the medical profession.

[26] Stephen J. Knitz, "Efficiency and Reform in the Financing and Organization of American Medicine in the Progressive Era," *Historical Medicine*, 55 (1981): 497–515; Susan Reverby, "Stealing the Golden Eggs: Ernest Amory Codman and the Science and Management of Medicine," *Bulletin History of Medicine*, 55 (1981): 156–171.

[27] Joel Howell, *Technology in the Hospital: Transforming Patient Care in the Early Twentieth Century* (Baltimore: The Johns Hopkins University Press, 1995). Glenn Gritzer and Arnold Arluke, *The Making of Rehabilitation: A Political Economy of Medical Specialization, 1890–1980* (Berkeley: University of California Press, 1985); Paul Starr, *The Social Transformation of American Medicine* (New York: Basic Books, 1982); Charles Rosenberg, *The Care of Strangers: The Rise of America's Hospital System* (New York: Basic Books, 1987); Morris Vogel, "Managing Medicine: Creating a Profession of Hospital Administration in the United States," in Lindsay Granshaw and Roy Porter, eds., *The Hospital in History* (London: Routledge, 1989), 234–260.

hospitals in Manchester, John Pickstone has highlighted medicine's growing cooperation with capital interests through its dependence on corporate funding (such as that of the Rockefeller and Carnegie Foundations, which supported expensive hospital-based research and the new technical teaching hospitals).[28] Many historians, however, have been reluctant to see a similar pattern throughout British medicine as a whole. Whatever was technological, mechanical, or practical is said to have been incompatible with the deep-seated ideological narratives legitimating the traditional rhetoric about gentlemanly ideals.[29] However, this oft-articulated "Britishness" arguably underrepresents the ongoing, somewhat overlooked historical reality of the commercialization and specialization of medicine, and the impact of these changes on the professionalism of the medical elite.

In fact, there was substantial resistance to any dispersal of centralized professional control, and acknowledgment of medicine's responsibility to serve the public need only emerged in slow though steady steps. In his 1905 treatise *Medicine and the Public*, for example, Squire Sprigge, the editor of *The Lancet*, responded to rising public demand for medicine's rehabilitation. Both the public's increasing belief in specialization and its unwillingness to accept high consultation fees, he lamented, promoted "the abuse of specialist hospital[s]." Moreover, he complained, through market forces generated by medical-aid associations or corporate-styled institutions, "the public has attempted . . . to obtain mastery over medical service."[30] Enumerating these "difficulties which medical men undergo in

---

[28] See Richard E. Brown, *Rockefeller Medicine Men: Medicine and Capitalism in America* (Berkeley: University of California Press, 1979); John Pickstone, *Medicine and Industrial Society: A History of Hospital Development in Manchester and Its Region, 1752–1964* (Manchester: Manchester University Press, 1985), especially Chapter 9, "Sciences, Specialists, and Capital."

[29] Christopher Lawrence, "Incommunicable Knowledge: Science, Technology, and the Clinical Art in Britain 1850–1914," *Journal of Contemporary History*, 20 (1985): 503–520; C. Lawrence, "Moderns and Ancients: The 'New Cardiology' in Britain, 1880–1930," in W. F. Bynum, C. Lawrence, and V. Nutton, eds., *Medical History Supplement No. 5* (London: The Wellcome Institute for the History of Medicine, 1985), 1–33. See also C. Lawrence's unpublished discussion paper, "Still Incommunicable: Clinical Knowledge between the Wars."

[30] S. Squire Sprigge, *Medicine and the Public* (London: Heinemann, 1905), 51.

their professional duties," Sprigge wished to evoke "a more widespread sympathy" for the profession and to seek "proper co-operation between the medical men and the public."[31] Certain aspects of Sprigge's views eventually carried the day: the elite medical profession gradually became more attuned to what the public wanted and to public service. Gentlemanly "medical etiquette," though still emphasized, was in the early years of the twentieth century extended beyond partisan prerogative to embrace an ethos of "serving the public."[32]

In the late nineteenth century, however, such ideas about serving the public were still regarded as undermining professional ideals. Nevertheless, the two electro-therapeutic organizations investigated in this chapter did combine corporatist medical services with new, specialized technology to respond to changes in public demand. In so doing, they permitted entrepreneurship to enter a hitherto-unoccupied niche in the medical world. Unlike the narrow-minded merchants and quacks of the eighteenth century, the entrepreneurs of medical electricity in the 1880s and 1890s transformed or appeared to transform themselves into more modern professional "institutes," financed and organized by private companies. The organizers of these institutes and other organizations, it is important to note, professed to share their profits from selling medical services and appliances with the professional medical men affiliated with these companies. In other words, this was an emergent form of collaboration between capital and the medical profession, which could be—and often was—seen as a serious threat to the integrity of the medical profession. The different code of behavior inaugurated by these business-affiliated institutes risked jeopardizing the traditional autonomy of medical professionalism. Faced with the strategies adopted by medical electricians, the gentlemanly ethos of the elite physicians of the RCP turned out to be far from unshakable. Indeed, the question that most requires answering is what was the real threat and what was the medico-social context concealed behind the fault-finding chorus yelling about "unprofessional and ungentlemanly standards" in the 1880s and 1890s? Doctors associated with many medical commercial institutions during this period as well as the IME and MBC brought to light what Andrew Abbott

---

[31] Ibid., 45.
[32] Ibid., 246.

has called intra-professional competition over professional jurisdiction. Abbot states that a "mature profession is constantly subdividing under the various pressures of market demands, specialization, and interprofessional competition. Some competitive conditions favor the less, some [the] more organized."[33] Some of these doctors wielded the new medical technologies while others trumpeted the benefits of corporate-style medical treatment. Indeed, this emergent field's potential in practical therapeutics appeared sufficiently promising to lure professional electrical engineers into the very different (for them) field of medicine. By the late nineteenth century, medical electricity was no fly-by-night, accidental business. It was a promising niche for a new profit-driven, large-scale capitalization of medicine.

### *The Institute of Medical Electricity and the RCP*

By the early 1880s, many members of the Society of Telegraph Engineers and Electricians (henceforth STEE) had become associated with new commercial medical institutions. In particular, the Institute of Medical Electricity Limited—established in 1888 by Henry Newman Lawrence, a member of the Institution of Electrical Engineers (henceforth the IEE), successor organization of the STEE—provided an important demonstration of how private enterprise could encroach on the territory of a profession.

The IME was formed in 1887 as a joint stock company capitalized at £20,000 in £1 shares, with subscribers recruited from both the electrical and the medical professions.[34] With William Lant Carpenter, a member of the STEE, as the director, and Henry Lawrence as the managing director, the Institute commenced its medical services at 24A, Regent Street in September 1888.[35] To emphasize its genuine medical purpose, the Institute successfully obtained support from "several of the best medical men," including a past president of the Royal College of Surgeons (1882), Sir T. Spencer Wells, and the then-vice-president of the Royal College of

---

[33] Andrew Abbott, *The System of Professions: An Essay on the Division of Expert Labor* (Chicago: University of Chicago Press, 1988), 86.
[34] "Institution of Medical Electricity Limited," *Telegraphic Journal and Electrical Review*, 22 (February 17, 1888): 168.
[35] *The Electrician*, 21 (July 13, 1888): 295.

Physicians, C. Handfield Jones.[36]

The Institute, however, was not led by medical men, but mainly by electrical engineers. The engineers associated with it, "trustworthy members of the Society of Telegraph Engineers and Electricians," were important electrical engineers of the time, such as Silvanus Thompson, D. E. Hughes, J. Hopkinson, W. S. Ayrton, W. H. Preece, E. Graves, C. E. Spagnoletti, Latimer Clark, and Gisbert Kapp. Most of them had been founders of the STEE, past, current, or future presidents of the STEE or the IEE, and fellows of the Royal Society.[37] On opening his electro-therapeutic business, Henry Lawrence became an associate member of the IEE in 1888 and was promoted to member-status in 1890 with the support of Silvanus Thompson, under whom he had studied electrical mechanics at Finsbury Technical College.[38] Through personal connections in the IEE, Lawrence successfully recruited the associates of his Institute from the ranks of eminent engineers. Engineers' enthusiastic commitment to, and commercial entry into, the domain of medicine heralded the advent of a new social context within which a different profession began to cast its enterprising eye on electro-medical technology.

Business opportunities in the field of medicine certainly aroused much interest among electrical engineers. *The Electrician*, a journal devoted to exchanging ideas from a wide range of electrical engineers as well as industrial managers, noted the opening of the IME several times in its columns and published an introductory article on the Institute from which one can learn about the faculty and the actual electro-therapeutic work undertaken by the Institute.[39] In addition to the considerable amount of capital invested in the "high-class instruments" and the involvement of highly esteemed professionals, the extensively organized nature of managerial medicine differentiated the Institute from old ventures in commercial medicine. The medical officers employed by the

---

[36] *The Electrician*, 20 (February 17, 1888): 370–371.

[37] The letter from Lawrence to the president of the RCP includes the names of those on the Board of the IME. See *Annals*, 35 (1888): 207. See also the memorandum attached to the letter in "Enclosure A and B," *Annals*, 35 (1888).

[38] See Lawrence's membership form held in the Institution of Electrical Engineers archive department, MSS., vol. 5A, 274 and MSS., 6B, 449.

[39] *The Electrician*, 20 (1888): 370–371; 21 (1888): 295, 483; 22 (1889): 327; and 25 (1889): 3, 370.

Institute made prescriptions for patients, on the basis of which "skilled attendants" provided electrical treatments.[40] One physician for the Institute was Dr. Arthur Harries. Lawrence and Harries were colleagues of long standing: Harries had lectured jointly with Lawrence on "Electro-Therapeutics" and had co-authored with him a popular handbook, *Practical Lessons in Electro-Therapeutics*.[41]

Lawrence's Institute had all the trappings of medical professionalism. Patients were treated in different types of electrical rooms, each fitted with "switch boards arranged with suitable connections for supplying by rheostat all the forms of current," with resistance from 2,000 to 12,000 ohms. A variety of innovative machines dictated the purpose of each room. The room for "the electro-gymnastic system," for example, held Lawrence's newly patented gymnastic machines for mechanical exercise (Fig. 4-1).[42] Connected with the switchboard, the apparatus was designed to conduct the current to or from the patient's body during his or her physical exercise—via floor electrodes of fine wire gauze at the feet, handle electrodes through the hands, and bandage electrodes through the arms or legs. This sort of combination of mechanical exercise and electro-therapeutics became fashionable treatment in commercial medicine, as will be seen in the next section

In the so-called "electrified room," "the air-space between floor and ceiling [was] converted into an electric field by the use of alternating currents of high potential." Both the floor, covered with a sheet-lead platform, and the "ceiling of light brass work" were connected to the wires of a powerful induction coil. When standing, sitting, or lying in this electrical field, a patient was supposed to obtain a tonic effect by being "electrically influenced without experiencing any shock." Moreover, the form of treatment most practiced in this room was "electro-manipulation." Lawrence, who had introduced this treatment, insisted that while patients were in this "field," the effect on their limbs or body could be

---

[40] "A Visit to the Institute of Medical Electricity," *The Electrician*, 23 (September 20, 1889): 490–492.

[41] See Henry Lawrence's membership form, held in the Institute of Electrical Engineers archive department, MSS., vol. 6B, 449.

[42] See the pamphlets of the IME held in the Institution of Electrical Engineers, Thompson Pamphlet Collection, Electro-physiology I, SPT 116/5–9 and SPT 116/11.

enormous if they were massaged by the hands of a practitioner electrified by "the high potential alternating currents." The bathroom contained "a large, well insulated oak bath, having connections conveniently arranged round it, with a switch-board." In the experiment room, a newly patented "ozonized cabinet" was installed to treat "certain chest diseases by strongly (electrically) ozonized air, aided by exercise to deepen respiration."[43]

Most noteworthy, however, was the naked commercialism of the IME. Significantly, the founder of the Institute announced that profits from the Institute's medical services were exclusively intended for its contracted professionals. Henry Lawrence proposed that "Shares were [to be] offered to Medical and Electrical men only, in order that the control should be and remain in the hands of those two professions, and that the profits should belong to those legitimately interested in the work."[44] Lawrence and the Institute's associated professional engineers believed that the application of electrical technology to medicine would be a good source of income, and they did not anticipate opposition on ethical grounds from the medical authorities. The conflict that arose highlights an in-teresting contrast between the medical and engineering elites and their attitudes toward commercialism. One of the objectives listed in the Institute's prospectus was "To provide an institute where, or in con-nection with which, people of small or limited means may obtain elec-trical treatment under the direction of qualified medical men, for the cure and relief of diseases, at moderate fees."[45] In other words, the members of the Institute did not see practicing electro-therapeutics for the benefit of the public as incompatible with monopolizing the pecuniary advantage from these practices for professionals only. Unlike the medical elite, the engineers, "governed by practical men of common sense," welcomed rather than questioned technological innovations and their commercial and industrial applications.

---

[43] "A Visit to the Institute of Medical Electricity," *The Electrician*, 23 (September 20, 1889), 490–492.

[44] "The letter from Lawrence to the Registrar of the RCP," *Annals*, 35 (May 5, 1888): 207.

[45] The other objectives given in the Prospectus were "to encourage the devel-opment of the science of medical electricity, and to provide a means by which medical men can obtain the use of reliable electrical apparatus either at the in-stitute or elsewhere." *Telegraphic Journal and Electrical Review*, 22 (January 6, 1888): 2.

These engineers were well aware of the practical applicability of science and the purposefulness of technology in the commercial and industrial spheres.[46] "Every scientific discovery which is applied for practical ends," an engineer wrote, "becomes more fertile, even of purely scientific results."[47] Placing a high value on practical applicability, they tended to paint a rosy picture of a future governed by engineering technologies that could be used to improve society. To this end, engineering technologies were easily associated with industrial and commercial spheres. "One of the most important functions of the engineers," John Perry argued in his inaugural address to the STEE, is "to convince capitalists ignorant of science that if the successful laboratory experiment is tried on the large scale it must also be successful."[48] By promoting business applicability, "our Institution . . . can assist the manufacturer, the designer, the contractor, the consulting engineer, and the capitalist."[49] Similarly, the engineering profession was also concerned about the stifling effects upon "the trade and business of private enterprise" by state monopoly. When "persons high in authority, without practical knowledge, but fascinated by an invention," ran the national-level administration of engineering enterprises, C. W. Webber warned, "valuable improvements may be lost, or the profitable use of them postponed, for want of wise expenditure." He went on to say, "The history of this subject, followed through the papers read at this Society's meetings, appears to point to the best results having been obtained when decisions have been guided by true commercial principles."[50] By its own ethos, the profession of engineers did not have any opposition to industry or commercialism.

In fact, a glance at the careers of eminent engineers would show that most of them were involved with, or even founded, commercial companies to sell their technologies. For example, a number of the IEE's presidents also established their own companies: Latimer Clark, president

---

[46] Within the IME, however, there was a political tug-of-war between theorists and practical men. See Bruce J. Hunt, "'Practice vs. Theory': The British Electrical Debate, 1888–1891," *Isis*, 74 (1983): 341–355.

[47] G. Carey Foster, "Inaugural Address," *Journal of the Society of Telegraph Engineers* (henceforth *JSTE*), 10 (1881): 10.

[48] John Perry, "Inaugural Address," *JIEE*, 30 (1900): 53.

[49] Silvanus P. Thompson, "Inaugural Address," *JIEE*, 29 (1899): 15.

[50] C. W. Webber, "Inaugural Address," *JSTE*, 11 (1882): 7.

in 1875, founded Muirhead Clark, Ltd., during that same year; Robert
Kaye Gray, president in 1903, was involved with several telegraph companies; and Charles William Siemens and John Francis Cleverton Snell,
presidents in 1893 and 1894 respectively, founded the famous Siemens
Brothers, Ltd.[51] In 1902, James Swinburne, IEE president at the time,
recalled the emergence of a more commercial atmosphere amidst the
profession during the reign of his predecessor, a "change in the attitude
of the Institution towards making it more commercial, and keeping it
more in touch with the purely technical part of our large interest."[52]

Another factor distinguishing the entrepreneurial electricians from the
medical elite was the ideology of public duty that these engineers upheld.
Edwin Layton has described the "professional responsibility" of American engineers of the period as "guided by a sense of public duty," extended to include a rejection of bureaucratic authority and a wish to
reorganize society by social engineering and planning.[53] British engineers
were less assertive but nonetheless shared this ideology of public service.
They guarded the benefit of entrepreneurship against officialdom "and
hard-and-fast regulations which, formulated with the best intentions, tend
sometimes to interfere with the public convenience."[54] "We public servants," one president commented, "rely on public criticism, and our sole
object is to serve our master, with a conscientious determination to do
our duty to the best of our ability."[55] These engineers believed that
commercialism and technological advances should be applied to medical
practice and that commercialism free of state intervention would lead
through market mechanisms to the optimal economic results of "convenience" and "lower price." They could not imagine that the provision
of inexpensive but specialized services might be considered a professional problem.

---

[51] See, for example, their obituaries in *JIEE*; "Latimer Clark," *JIEE*, 28 (1899):
667–672; "William Siemens," JIEE, 13 (1884): 442–462.

[52] Rollo Appleyard, *The History of the Institution of Electrical Engineers, 1871–1931*
(London: The Institution of Electrical Engineers, 1939), 176.

[53] Edwin Layton, *The Revolt of the Engineers: Social Responsibility and the American
Engineering Profession* (Baltimore: The Johns Hopkins University Press, 1986), 5–6
and Chapter 3.

[54] "Inaugural Address by Sir Henry Mance," *JIEE*, 26 (1897): 11.

[55] "Inaugural Address by William Henry Preece," *JIEE*, 22 (1893): 40.

The IME failed, therefore, to anticipate the reaction of the RCP to the association of its members with a profit-making enterprise. Lawrence had offered the position of consulting physician to "two of the most eminent and generally respected authorities upon Medical Electricity," W. E. Steavenson and William H. Stone, member and fellow of the RCP respectively. Steavenson accordingly asked the President of the RCP to approve his acceptance of this offer:

> I have been offered the post of physician to a company that has been formed for supplying electrical appliances to the medical profession, and establishing an Institute for the treatment of patients by electricity. As far as I am able to judge, it appears to be a bona fide and respectable company. I am anxious to know if the Royal College of Physicians would view with disfavour the acceptance by a member of the College of such a post as the one now offered to me. . . . I could not accept the post if such a step was disapproved of by the Royal College of Physicians.[56]

In its reply to Steavenson's inquiry, the Censors' Board of the RCP highly disapproved of his accepting the offer "as they considered it unprofessional for a member of the College to ally himself with a commercial company for the treatment of disease."[57] Sixteen days later, on 26 April, Steavenson apprised the Censors' Board of his obedience to the RCP and both Steavenson and Stone regretfully informed the IME that they declined the posts offered to them.[58]

It would be an over-simplification to conclude from this response that the regulatory power of gentlemanly ethics in the medical profession was overwhelmingly strong. The RCP actually vacillated when faced with repeated petitions from the managing director of the IME protesting the decision. In his first protest to the RCP, on 5 May, Henry Lawrence emphasized the "genuine and bona fide" quality of the Institute, enclosing memorandums signed by both eminent electricians and medical men who were "of opinion that the objects of the proposed Institute of

---

[56] "The Letter from Steavenson to the Censors' Board" *Annals*, 35 (April 10, 1888): 175.
[57] "Censors' Reply to Steavenson," *Annals*, 35 (1888): 176.
[58] "The Letter from Steavenson to the Censors' Board," *Annals*, 35 (1888): 198.

Medical Electricity are worthy of encouragement and that the plan of management is a good one."[59] In this way, Lawrence appealed to authoritative figures among the supporters: six fellows and two past presidents of the Royal Society, two professors of physics, one professor of mathematics, and some current members of the STEE. That most of the medical men who signed were fellows of the RCP—and some of them significantly involved with the management of the Institute—was, however, exactly what irritated the College. These signers were W. H. Stone, A. D. Waller, P. H. Pye-Smith, T. Spencer Wells, J. Mitchell Bruce, A. Julius Pollock, C. Handfield Jones, and W. Guyer Hunter. To add insult to injury, Lawrence also pointed out a double standard, evidenced by the money-acquiring activities of many RCP Members:

> We should also submit that Medical men who are members of your College do hold office under joint-stock companies, as is instanced by the many insurance companies, and also under institutions worked for profit in connection with the treatment of disease as is instanced by some of the Hydropathic and similar establishments; homes and asylums for insane; and some of the Medical Schools attached to the Hospitals.[60]

Lawrence was right. Behind the officially stated principle of professional ethics, many medical men were beginning to form or infiltrate business organizations in order to make a profit. In particular, a number of physicians consulted and performed medical examinations for life insurance companies. For example, Sir Douglas Maclagan, David Ferrier, and Sir Norman Moore were employed by the Edinburgh Life Assurance Company, Russell Reynolds and W. R. Gowers by the Guardian Fire and Life Assurance Company, and Sir J. Risdon Bennett and P. H. Pye-Smith by the General Assurance Company.[61] Far from the IME's being an exception, it was part of an ongoing—albeit largely overlooked—process by which members of the medical profession accommodated themselves

---

[59] "Enclosure B," *Annals*, 35 (May 5, 1888): 208.

[60] *Annals*, 35 (May 5, 1888): 207.

[61] For the London medical elite associated with insurance companies, see their advertisements in the *Medical Directory*, such as for example the following document: "An Index to Life Assurance Offices," *Medical Directory* (London: John Churchill and Sons, 1888), 1552–1556.

to the principle of a just profit in the late nineteenth century.

In response to Lawrence's protest, the College responded in a generous fashion, promising that "it would receive a careful consideration."[62] Lawrence wasted no time in asking the RCP to receive a representative to discuss and explain "the present position and prospects of the Institute with special reference to its medical offices."[63] On 24 July, a few members representing the Institute were given the chance to urge "the strictly scientific character and necessity for some such institution as that proposed and hoped that the College would permit its Fellows and Members to be appointed with it."[64]

Though this representation seemed to have persuaded the Censors' Board of "the good faith and intention of the prompter of the Institute of Electricity,"[65] the RCP held to their view that Bye-law 178 prohibited Fellows and Members from being "engaged in trade." As a last resort, Lawrence petitioned the RCP "to appoint a representative of that body to visit this Institute, inquire into its methods of working, and to make a report thereon to the authorities of your College at his discretion."[66] Rather than respond, the RCP's registrar simply declined this proposal.

The extent to which the RCP was embarrassed and threatened by the newborn corporate-style electro-therapeutic institute is shown by the fact that on October 25, 1888 the College passed a new resolution prohibiting members and fellows from being connected with any "Company" having for its object the treatment of disease for profit.[67] This was the first and only use of the word "Company" in bye-laws and regulations of the RCP. The IME's championing of the public's welfare put the RCP's ideology on the defensive. Its initial intention apparently was to prevent commercial marketing from breaking up the solidarity of "professional" medical ranks. What Paul Starr has argued for early-twentieth-century American medicine is just as applicable to the British medical profession thirty years earlier: "The competitive market represented a threat . . . to [physicians']

---

[62] *Annals*, 35 (May 5, 1888): 210.
[63] *Annals*, 35 (July 6, 1888): 217.
[64] *Annals*, 35 (July 24, 1888): 218–219.
[65] "Reply to Deputation," *Annals*, 35 (July 24, 1888): 219.
[66] "The Letter from Lawrence to the Registrar," *Annals*, 36 (February 7, 1889): 288.
[67] *The Charter, Bye-Laws, and Regulation of the Royal College of Physicians of London*, 94.

status and autonomy because it drew no sharp boundary between the educated and uneducated [and] blurred the lines between commerce and professionalism."[68]

Confronted with the seemingly immovable object of the RCP's regulations, electricians in the 1880s and 1890s simply attempted to forgo the College's approval. The result, however, was that the movement toward a commercial practice of medicine, which electro-therapeutics itself had initiated, became essentially subterranean. Denied RCP support, the IME was able to continue medical practice under the direction of Lawrence for only two years: "The Institute, after living long enough to prove its utility, but not long enough to pay its expenses under this relentless and powerful persecution, closed its doors." In an article carried in *Truth*, entitled "Electrifying the Royal College of Physicians," an anonymous electrician, quite possibly Lawrence, directed his deep resentment towards what he regarded as a bigoted RCP, insisting that medical electricity was nipped in the bud by the very institution that should have fostered it. He compared the RCP to the Church of England:

> Between the Royal College of Physicians and the Established Church of England there seems to be a certain fellow-feeling in practice if not in theory. Both aim at respectability, both resent freedom of opinion, both dislike innovation, both are apt to snub original investigations and habitually look askance at new institutions.[69]

On the surface, it appeared that the College's repression had been successful. According to Lawrence, electricians and their commercialistic projects died out, crushed just as earlier theological rebellions had been by that equally benighted institution, the Church: "As with theologians it is not Truth which is of importance, so with the R.C.P. pillars it is not utility or genuineness which is to be consulted. No—in each case it is, as they term it, 'the customs and the traditions of this ancient and honourable Corporation.'" However, repression in fact only drove these corporate professions underground. Quietly and through unofficial channels momentum was sustained, ultimately influencing the amendment of the Resolution and Bye-law in 1922.

---

[68] Paul Starr, *The Social Transformation of American Medicine*, 22.
[69] "Electrifying the Royal College of Physicians," *Truth*, July 1891, 134.

*Electropathic Belts and the Zander Institute*

Despite the RCP's opposition, the uneasy alliance between a number of medical professionals and electricians continued. One area in which this collaboration existed is illustrated by the development and marketing of various kinds of therapeutic electric belts. The most irksome problem for the Censors' Board of the RCP during the 1880s and 1890s was undoubtedly C. B. Harness and his electropathic belt business (Fig. 4-2). As discussed above, Harness' commercialism was extremely audacious: out-and-out marketing campaigns relying on a combination of advertisements in newspapers, publication of commercial pamphlets, and the free use of the authoritative names of distinguished medical men. Indeed, he listed in his pamphlets without their consent a number of physicians and surgeons, including the president of the RCP, Sir Andrew Clark, blatantly claiming them as medical patrons "who have sent Patients to this institute, with the most satisfaction."[70] The pamphlets themselves contained excerpts from articles written by authoritative medical electricians, carefully selected to appear as if they guaranteed the therapeutic value of his electric appliances.[71] Repeated protests from the RCP to Harness and his company received only the response that "it was for the public benefit that the approval of the Zander System [provided in Harness' Institute] by members of the medical profession should be published." Harness steadfastly refused to remove the names of fellows.[72]

Harness was attacked from every quarter of the medical world precisely because he was unabashedly combining commercialism with a semblance of medical professionalism. To the medical profession, electropathic belts smacked of charlatanism, and medical electricians, afraid of reviving the stigma of quackery that had previously been cast upon electro-therapeutics, also began to campaign against businesses such as the Medical Battery Company (MBC) for marketing "Electropathic Ap-

---

[70] *Swedish Mechanical Exercise: A Means of Cure and for the Prevention of Disease* (London: The Medical Battery Company Limited, 1889), 3.

[71] The eminent doctors whose names Harness misused numbered over one hundred fifty and included such eminent people as Sir Andrew Clark, Sir James Paget, Dr. Charles B Radcliffe, and Dr. Hughes Bennett.

[72] *Annals*, 7 (February 7, 1889): 290–293. Also see A. M. Cooke, *A History of the Royal College of Physicians of London* (Oxford: Clarendon Press, 1972), 3: 904.

pliances." *The Lancet* and *The British Medical Journal* collaborated in ostracizing Harness to protect the realms of medical discourse and professional practice from his kind of commercial intrusion.

The establishment and growth of the MBC was undoubtedly a signal event in entrepreneurs' ingenious abuse medical professionalism's rules, and it represented a late-nineteenth-century amalgamation of specialist techniques and entrepreneurial endeavor. Typical of this collaboration was Harness' strategy of establishing and using a medical "Institute" both to make his business appear more professional and to turn medical techniques to financial gain. At the MBC's inception, Harness announced the opening of a "special department for the treatment of certain diseases by the employment of Massage combined with Electrization," which he called the "Electropathic and Zander Institute" (Fig. 4-3).[73] The Zander system was a newly imported gymnastic method invented by the Swedish physician Dr. J. Gustaf Wilhelm Zander. It relied upon a specially constructed mechanical apparatus to promote the exercise and strengthening of muscles.[74] Harness wasted no time in investing in these costly examples of Swedish technology and quickly contrived to sell institutionalized mechanical exercise through his Zander Institute.

Unlike the Pall Mall Electrical Association, the MBC was founded to combine diagnosis and treatment of patients with the selling of electro-medical appliances. In addition to marketing dubious goods such as electric belts and lung invigorators, the company opened several affiliated medical departments where hired physicians and assistant officers offered consultation and direction to customers attracted by bombastic advertisements. The collaboration between doctors, medical technicians, and entrepreneurs was intended to supply new institutional medical services. In order to provide hospital-like service, Harness invested £200,000—a huge amount of capital—on magnificent institutional facilities. Determined to ensure the professional reputation of the MBC, in 1887 Harness purchased the Zander Institution for £5,000, making it a department

---

[73] "The Electropathic & Zander Institute, London," RCP, MSS., 2412/131.

[74] The Zander system was introduced to the public through several publications: Alfred Levertin, *Dr. G. Zander's Medico-Mechanical Gymnastics: Its Method, Importance, and Application* (Stockholm: Nordstedt & Söner, 1893); Gustaf Zander, *The Apparatus for Medico-Mechanical Gymnastics* (Stockholm: Nordstedt & Söner, 1894).

within the MBC, absorbing its entire staff, and renaming it the "Electropathic Zander Institute."[75]

There patients were treated by having their stiff joints and muscles exercised under the supervision of medical doctors. The first floor of the MBC had a large and extensive showroom displaying the company's latest electrical appliances: in particular, its electropathic belts as well as many other cheap medical gadgets such as lung invigorators, "electropathic spine bands, knee caps, anklets, wristlets, throat and leg appliances *et hoc genus omne* even to an electropathic sock."[76] The showroom also included electrical brushes for the grooming of hair, skin, and teeth; an electric corset; and even an anti-*mal-de-mer* comb for combating sea sickness. Every day, also on the first floor, were consulting-rooms where medical electricians were stationed and ready to discuss free of charge patients' problems in person or through correspondence. An "ADVICE FORM, Strictly Private and Confidential" was frequently included in the company's advertisements in newspapers and periodicals. Once customers sent in the form describing their symptoms and the duration of their suffering, consultant medical electricians began to correspond with them about what personalized treatments would remedy their disorders.[77] As one MBC advertisement suggests with a picture of a group of nurses assisting patients with their gymnastic movements, what Harness was most proud of was that the MBC's institutional treatment was based on collaboration between doctors, qualified nurses, and "technical officers of electricity" (Fig. 4-4).[78]

The second floor of the Institute housed the so-called "Experimental Room," "a quaint little chamber" where with "a bewildering number of galvanometers and other strange electrical instruments" visitors and patients were encouraged to experiment by themselves with the operation of curative appliances.[79] The Truss Department, intended to provide a new

---

[75] Ibid.

[76] "A Visit to the Establishment of the Medical Battery Company, Limited, 52, Oxford–street, London, W," *Health*, May 6, 1887, x–xi.

[77] "All In Search of Health," *Health*, October 2, 1885, 15 (includes a full page advertisement of the ADVICE FORM).

[78] "Group of Nurses," *Graphic*, February 13, 1892, 226.

[79] "Straight Questions! Straight Answers!," *Westminster Gazette*, October 5, 1893, 7.

branch of practice, "Orthopædics," displayed Harness' new "smooth, washable, flesh-coloured surface Truss." MBC's "Electro-Dental Department" boasted of being equipped with a "patent electro-dental apparatus for painless dental operations."[80] Similar specialized departments and sections proliferated elsewhere in the building.

Given these facilities and claims, it is small wonder that the medical semblance of the MBC, together with Harness' indefatigable capitalizing on the public's growing demand for new institutional treatments, drew substantial hostility from elite medical doctors. Precisely because Harness aimed to turn every aspect of medicine—professional or philanthropic—to financial gain, his business looked incredibly audacious. Within a few years of its establishment, the MBC opened branches in Liverpool, Leeds, and many other parts of England. All of the original directors, Harness, L. Graff, and D. G. Macrae, earned high salaries—Harness, for example, earned as much as £1,000 per annum in 1885, an amount that increased to £2,000 in 1891. This salary was a truly high reward for someone who was a non-elite doctor.

In particular, what irritated medical doctors most was the MBC's unprecedented advertising activities. Harness lavished a great deal of capital on advertising; in fact, the money the MBC spent on advertisements increased tremendously year by year: £15,862 in 1889, £26,610 in 1890, £42,074 in 1891, £49,797 in 1892, and £36,535 in 1893, making for a total of £170,880 over just five years.[81] The funds Harness spent on printing advertisements in the style of reading-columns without a clear disclaimer of their being an "Advertisement," particularly offended the *British Medical Journal*.[82] Denouncing the frequent "quasi-editorial puffs" in daily papers such as the *Westminster Review, Standard, St. James's Gazette, Black and White*, and *Christian Million*, the *BMJ* wrote that "the cash and audacity of Mr. Harness have enabled him to obtain from the weakness or carelessness of newspaper managers such invaluable help in the business of entrapping fools as must have been afforded."[83]

---

[80] "The Electropathic and Zander Institute," JJC, Patent Medicine Box 10.
[81] "The Medical Battery Company (Limited)," *The Times*, December 9, 1893, 4.
[82] "Quack Advertisements and the British Press," *British Medical Journal*, 2 (July 22, 1893): 191–192.
[83] "Mr. Harness and the Newspaper Press," *British Medical Journal*, 2 (October, 28,

Zander had based his Medico-Mechanical Gymnastics on the so-called "movement cure" developed by his Swedish predecessor, Per Henrik Ling. Ling believed that "the oneness of the human organism, and the harmony between mind and body and between the various parts of the same body" could be realized by prescribed movements of muscles. He thought that to raise the arms in a haphazard fashion produced few corporeal and no mental effects. On the other hand, Ling argued that a "Gymnastic Movement" that stretched particular muscles with forces exactly determined so as to provide properly calculated resistance would inevitably make the body and mind healthier.[84] To explain his principle, Ling classified all physical movements as active or passive: the active exercises were those in which the exerciser encountered resistance through bending, stretching, or twisting joints, while the passive ones comprised all the operations performed on an inert body, such as rubbing, tickling, tapping, and kneading muscles.

Influenced by Ling's methods early in his professional career, Zander soon recognized its limitations: the difficulty in accurately adjusting the amount of force to the strength of a patient, as well as the patient having to balance the required movement with the gradual increase of force deemed necessary for muscle-development. It appeared to Zander that the best way to overcome people's limitations was with the predictability of a machine's motion. He invented various machines—one that was awarded a silver medal at the Paris Exhibition of 1878, and another that received a gold medal at the Scientific Exhibition of 1879.[85] Sketches of typical Zander machines appear in Figs. 4-5 and 4-6. The machine in Fig. 4-5, for instance, was designed for active movement, which in this case aimed to promote the flexing of the forearms. Requiring the arms to bend upwards and stretch downward as far as possible, this machine acted

---

1893): 957–958; "The Press, the Quacks, and the Public," *British Medical Journal*, 1 (January 27, 1894): 208.

[84] For details of Ling's system, which was introduced into Britain by Dr. Mathias Roth, see Roth's *Gymnastic Exercises without Apparatus, According to Ling's System for the Due Development and Strengthening of the Human Body* (London: Myers, 1884).

[85] Marian Fournier, *The Medico-Mechanical Equipment of Doctor Zander* (Leiden: Museum Boerhaave, 1989), 8; Carolyn Thomas de la Peña, *The Body Electric: How Strange Machines Built the Modern American* (New York: New York University Press, 2003), 74–75.

primarily on the flexor muscles of the forearms and the muscles of the back. The machine in Fig. 4-6, by contrast, was designed for passive movement. The patient's arms reached through the massage-straps, which were covered with a rough surface and moved upwards and downwards to compress and release the arms. Essentially, the machine was supposed to massage the arms to produce a very pleasant friction. In the late nineteenth century, the Zander apparatus and its mechanical methods were introduced in other countries, and Zander Institutes proliferated all over Europe.[86]

Zander Gymnastics achieved a toehold in Victorian society as early as 1882 with the opening in Soho Square of "The Zander Institute." The Institute displayed many gymnastic machines at this location and published the lengthy booklet *Mechanical Exercise, a Means of Cure* showing a number of woodcuts depicting Victorian gentlemen and women exercising on a variety of machines.[87] The London-based Zander Institute, however, lasted only briefly: in 1887 Harness and his MBC took over the institution. By acquiring the Zander Institute, Harness obtained the professional-looking title of Institute, access to many new machines, and a publication format to follow. Subsequently, he focused his entrepreneurial drive on having his institution and appliances certified by professional medical men.

At the turn of the century, consumer demand was encouraging specialized group medicine and institutional treatment based on collaboration between doctors and specialist technicians. Viewed in this light, Harness' company hardly appears as the product of a single greedy quack. Irrespective of its founder's real intentions, the MBC was up to the minute in uniting managerial medicine with professional medical practice. To explain fully how the innovations of the MBC's Zander Institute

---

[86] By 1906, Zander Institutes had been founded in more than one hundred cities in Europe and America, including Berlin, Bonn, Heidelberg, Amsterdam, Budapest, and Chicago. See A. Levertin, F. Heiligenthal, G. Schütz, and G. Zander, *The Leading Features of Dr. G Zander's Medico-Mechanical Gymnastic Method and its Use in Four Separate Treatises* (Wiesbaden: Rossel, Schwartz & Co., 1906), 20–22.

[87] "The Zander Medico-Mechanical Machine," *British Medical Journal*, 1 (1882): 310; *Mechanical Exercise, a Means of Cure: Being a Description of the Zander Institute, London (7 Soho Square) its History, Appliances, Scope, and Object*, edited by the medical officer to the Institute (London: J. & A. Churchill, 1883).

rendered earlier attempts at medical entrepreneurship outmoded, however, reference must be made to several factors: the existence of skilled or
trained officers, the employment of a team of medical doctors as salaried
supervisors, and investment in costly machines and facilities sufficient to
achieve economies of scale.

First, Harness was particularly proud of the Zander Institute's maintaining "a properly-qualified officer who sees each patient, prescribes the
machines and the power that shall be used and generally supervises the
application."[88] In the Ladies' Department, "a skillful and experienced
Masseuse has been engaged (who has had the highest scientific training, is
the holder of several Hospital Certificates, and also [holds] that of the
Obstetrical Society of London)."[89] "Qualified Officers, Lady Superin-
tendents, and Certificated Masseuses," consulting free of charge, attended every day to give advice on "all matters relating to Health and the
application of Electricity as a curative agent, as also Massage, Swedish
Mechanical Exercises, Chemical, &c."[90] Harness' pride in these ancillary
medical practitioners foreshadowed the emergence of divisions of labor
in medical practices.

The second factor, supervision by physicians, was no less important in
distinguishing the Zander Institute from its predecessors. In 1887, out of
"129 registered medical men applicants," Harness selected Dr. J. F.
Leeson, a licentiate of the RCP, as the consulting physician, medical superintendent, and expert in "Massage, Medical Electricity and Hy-
dro-Therapeutics." Leeson described his work environment in a letter to a
colleague at the RCP: "I have my counseling room, with a private entrance . . . patients who consult me are ordered Massage or Electric Belts
if considered beneficial, if I think localized electrisation necessary I apply
it to them, and those for whom in my judgment, medicine is required I
prescribe."[91] With a variety of technical officers, Harness attempted to
form a "teamwork" approach to medicine among physicians and a

88 *Swedish Mechanical Exercise*, 20.
89 "The Pamphlet by the Medical Battery Company," RCP, MSS., 2412/125.
90 *A Treatise on the Special Diseases of Women and their Electropathic Treatment* (London:
The Medical Battery Company Limited, 1891), inside of the front cover and
48–49.
91 Letter from Dr. J. F. Leeson to Dr. Edward Liveing, the registrar of the RCP,
dated December 10, 1887. MSS., 2412/130; *Annals*, 36 (January10, 1888): 94–97.

number of other workers. Such recruitment, however, was blocked the next year by the RCP's 1888 resolution prohibiting members and fellows from being connected with any profit-oriented company. Urged by the Medical Defence Union to denounce Leeson's "association with a notorious quack"[92] and being anxious about the legal power of the College to bind even license-holders, the RCP summoned Leeson to the Censors' Board and successfully compelled him to renounce his connection with the MBC.[93] Though Harness' ambition was thwarted in this case, the skirmish proved only a prelude to a two-year battle over Dr. Herbert Tibbits' employment by the MBC in the early 1890s.

The final factor differentiating the Zander Institute from previous nostrum vendors was Harness' investment in costly machines. The extent of his investments is indicated by the comment of his supporter Tibbits that "nowhere have I seen such perfect Static & other apparatus as is possessed by Mr. Harness' company except at the Salpêtrière Paris under Professor Jean Martin Charcot."[94] In the ample rooms of the Zander Institute, over sixty costly gymnastic machines were assembled to perform their complicated mechanical exercises on patients (Fig. 4-7).[95]

What Harness intended to create with his impressive capital investment was the large-scale capitalization of medical practice, and within this sphere, the establishment of newly commercialized organizational arrangements. Predictably, however, Harness' innovations generated fierce hostility from medical professionals who believed that both their interests and their status were at risk. Perceived as a threat to traditional medical authority, Harness posed a challenge that had to be repressed. The RCP, however, was to prove somewhat less successful in the case of Herbert Tibbits and the Medical Battery Company.

### *Herbert Tibbits and the Gentlemanly Ideal of the RCP*

Just as the eminent electrical engineer Arthur E. Baines was a high-profile advocate of Harness' Electropathic Belts, Herbert Tibbits offered

---

[92] Letter from the Medical Defence Union to the President of the RCP, dated December 8, 1888, MSS., 2412/140.
[93] *Annals*, 35 (1888): 172.
[94] "The Statement by Dr. Tibbits," RCP, MSS., 2411/128.
[95] *Swedish Mechanical Exercise*, 15.

Harness professional endorsement on the medical side. Tibbits was typical of those ambitious non-elite specialists who made their own way forward professionally despite the domination of the medical elite. Taking advantage of the rising demand for information on new electro-medical technologies, Tibbits published extensively in this field, devoting many works to descriptions of electrical appliances and to providing technical know-how.[96] Through these works, Tibbits clearly established himself as an important source of technical expertise. Like other aspiring specialists, he founded a hospital, in this case the West End Hospital for Diseases of the Nervous System (1878), of which the Princess of Wales was patroness and the Duke of Buccleugh president.[97]

Tibbits had begun his career as a resident medical officer at Government Hospital in Berbia, Guiana, having earned his doctorate in medicine from St. Andrews. He became a licentiate of the RCP in 1865, a member of the Edinburgh branch of the RCP in 1874, and a fellow in 1876. Later, he also became a fellow of the Medical Society of London.[98] In 1872, the *British Medical Journal* reported with some surprise that Tibbits had been elected as the medical officer for electrical treatment at the Hospital for Sick Children in Great Ormond Street.[99] However, what

---

[96] The following publications were all authored by Herbert Tibbits: *A Handbook of Medical Electricity* (London: J. & A. Churchill, 1873); *How to Use a Galvanic Battery in Medicine and Surgery, a Discourse upon Electrotherapeutics, delivered before the Hunterian Society upon November 8th, 1876* (London: J. & A. Churchill, 1877); *Improved Apparatus and Improved Methods for Applying Static Electricity (Franklinism) (Abstract of a Lecture at the West End Hospital)* (London: J. & A. Churchill, 1886).

[97] The historian Rosemary Stevens explains that during the nineteenth century, when specialization tended to be associated with quacks, younger physicians aspiring to be specialists in particular fields, such as nose or ear medicine, usually followed one of two paths into the elite circle of medical professionals: through the publication of books, or through the foundation of their own specialist hospitals. Tibbits seems to have been one of these aspiring specialists. See Rosemary Stevens, "The Curious Career of Internal Medicine: Functional Ambivalence, Social Success," *American Medicine and the Public Interest: A History of Specialization* (Berkeley: University of California Press, 1998), 27–28.

[98] The only available source on Tibbits and his career is the *Medical Directory* (London: J. & A. Churchill). Tibbits' name appears every year between 1866 and 1895.

[99] "Forthcoming Report on Electrotherapeutics," *British Medical Journal*, 2 (1872): 585.

enabled Tibbits to advertise his name most impressively in the medical world was his translation in 1872 of G. B. Duchenne's *L'électrisation localisée*, done while he was a medical superintendent of the National Hospital for the Paralysed and Epileptic in Queen Square. By adding notes to each section of his translation, Tibbits capitalized on Duchenne's reputation, while also establishing his own authority.[100] At that time, Tibbits' translation was positively welcomed in British medical circles. In a long review of the field of medical electricity, Thomas Clifford Allbutt, a consultant physician to the General Infirmary in Leeds and later Regius Professor of Physic at Cambridge—and a former student of Duchenne, who had applied electro-therapy to the treatment of the insane at the Wakefield Asylum—"congratulate[d] Dr. Tibbits on his successful labours thus far."[101]

The latter part of the nineteenth century witnessed the advance of electro-therapeutics into increasingly technology-oriented medical practices. Good electro-therapists were expected to have a full knowledge of the most effective machines and instruments of medico-electric treatments. By the 1870s, Tibbits was coming to be regarded as an expert, especially in electrical apparatuses and batteries, even designing his own faradic battery, following the example of Duchenne. A. De Watteville, in *A Practical Introduction to Medical Electricity*, made a special acknowledgment to Tibbits, thanking him for allowing him to use his collections of electrical apparatus.[102] In 1876, the Hunterian Society, eager for knowledge of recent electro-therapeutic technology, invited Tibbits to give a lecture in which he mainly focused on new electrical devices including "Tibbits'

---

[100] Duchenne was widely known among Victorian intellectuals as a champion of scientifically based study of physiognomy. Indeed, Charles Darwin relied heavily upon Duchenne's theory expressed in *The Mechanism of Human Facial Expression* for his argument for the evolution of behavior in *The Decent of Man* and *The Expression of the Emotions in Man and Animals*: see Janet Browne, "Darwin and the Face of Madness," in W. F. Bynum, Roy Porter, and Michael Shepherd, eds., *The Anatomy of Madness: Essays in the History of Psychiatry* (London: Tavistock, 1985), 1: 151–165. See also Sander Gilman, *Seeing the Insane* (New York: J. Wiley: 1982).

[101] Thomas Clifford Allbutt, "Electro-Therapy," *The British and Foreign Medico-Chirurgical Review*, 48 (1871): 38–57.

[102] A. de Watteville, *A Practical Introduction to Medical Electricity* (London: H. K. Lewis, 1878), vi.

Medical Portable Battery," various types of electrodes, and how to use them.[103] Previously an unknown licentiate, Tibbits thus emerged on the medical scene as an authority in the field of electro-therapeutics.

In July 1892 Harness asked Tibbits to examine and report on his Electropathic Belts and other electric appliances. Tibbits consented to the request on the understanding that his "fee (100 guineas) should be paid at once and [his] report accepted whether favourable or unfavourable." Six weeks later, he handed over the fully detailed report, which provided the results from "exhaustive experiments."[104] Co-authored for publication with another examiner, Dr. Arthur Harries, the report became a Zander Institute pamphlet, *The Treatment of Disease by the Prolonged Application of Currents of Electricity of Low Powers*.[105] Dr. Harries, at the time employed by another electro-therapeutic institute, had previously been the physician to the Institute of Medical Electricity, which the RCP had been instrumental in shuttering (Fig. 4-8).

In his four experiments on electropathic belts, Tibbits observed that a small amount of current was generated when moist flannel or moist skin came into contact with the discs, and he then estimated, using Lord Kelvin's galvanometer, the currents penetrating the patient's skin. In another experiment, the belt was placed on the back of a killed and skinned rabbit "so that the muscles, etc., should be good conductors," and the deflection in the galvanometer's needle was recorded. Dr. Harries reported on this in more detail. Finally, he made eight grouped experiments to estimate the currents through saturated flannels with tap water, human perspiration, and a solution of salt and water, and compiled elaborate tables of the milliampères of current that flowed in each case.[106]

---

[103] Tibbits, *How to Use a Galvanic Battery in Medicine and Surgery: A Discourse upon Electrotherapeutics, Delivered before the Hunterian Society upon November 8th, 1876* (London: J. & A. Churchill, 1877).

[104] "The Statement by Dr Tibbits, RCP, MSS., 2411/128. *The Times*, "Tibbits v. Morning Newspaper Publishing Company," February 6, 1892.

[105] "The treatment of disease by the prolonged application of currents of electricity of low powers, by Herbert Tibbits, MD., etc. together with a report by Arthur Harries, MD., etc. on Mr. Harness' Electropathic Belt and the Electropathic & Zander Institute," RCP, MSS.,, 2411/94.

[106] See the *British Medical Journal*, 2 (1892): 1176–1177. Tibbits' report was nine pages long, and Harries' was fifteen.

The RCP first became aware of Tibbits' activities when his testimonials appeared in full-page advertisements in *The Standard* and *Daily Telegraph*. Corresponding frequently with Tibbits, Dr. Edward Liveing, the registrar of the RCP, warned him that his "laudatory certificate" on behalf of the Zander Institute was against the resolution and bye-law enacted by the RCP in 1882, which were intended to prevent members' engagement in such "laudatory" medical advertising.[107] Liveing went on to request that Tibbits attend a disciplinary meeting of the Censors' Board. Tibbits opposed Liveing's denunciation, maintaining that the legal power of the 1882 bye-law and resolution was strictly limited.[108] In his letter to Liveing, Tibbits insisted that

> I can not consent to be bound by any Bye-law passed by the College after August 1865 when I obtained my license. I beg also to observe that the Regulation passed by the College upon July 27, 1882, was merely an expression of opinion [in] which I was not consulted, and I say also that my Report to Mr. Harness was not "laudatory" in any unworthy sense; nor was it "misleading."[109]

It is significant that at first the RCP censored Tibbits not on the grounds of the 1888 Resolution prohibiting connections with commercial companies, but on those of the 1882 prohibition against "laudatory certificates." Nor did the RCP bring up the matter of professional or gentlemanly ethics in its censorship of Tibbits at this stage. Replying to a consultation with Liveing, Henry Roscoe, solicitor for the RCP, admitted that although Tibbits' plea of not being bound by laws enacted after his joining the College could not be sustained, the Resolution might be ruled as no stronger than a mere expression of opinion, as Tibbits himself had insisted. In response to this perceived limitation, the solicitor and the

---

[107] The Resolution that had been enacted in 1882 read as follows: "That the system of extensively advertising medical works and the custom of giving, whether for publication or not, laudatory certificates is misleading to the public, derogatory to the dignity of the profession and contrary to the traditions and resolution of the Royal College of Physicians." *Annals*, 29 (July 27, 1882): 147–149.

[108] For a description of Tibbits' reply, see *Annals*, 38 (February 27, 1893): 67–69.

[109] Letter from Tibbits to the Registrar, dated February 22, 1893, RCP, MSS., 2411/104.

Censors' Board collaborated to increase the possible charges against Tibbits. Finally the solicitor recommended:

> That though the Licentiate might thus evade the charge in its present form, another might be prepared against him of Unprofessional Conduct under Bye-law CLXXXVIII; and assuming the President and Censors be thereby *constitutional judges of what is unprofessional in conduct* [my italics], they might convict and censure him under that law.[110]

The RCP's *Annals* for 1893 clearly indicate the extent to which the College was shaken by the decided uproar Tibbits caused.[111] Knowing that Tibbits was notoriously litigious—he had filed several previous lawsuits for libel, including one against the committee of his hospital for wrongful dismissal—the RCP acted with the utmost legal circumspection, relying upon a campaign to weaken his standing in the press rather than risking direct attacks.[112] Indeed, after February 27, 1892, when he lost his pivotal post at the West End Hospital and failed to publish his latest book on massage, Tibbits' reputation increasingly came under attack from a variety of media sources. *The Lancet* and *The British Medical Journal* suddenly turned antagonistic, and *The Times* dubbed him a "professional man of straw hired by Harness." After that, the Queen's Bench became familiar ground for Tibbits' frequent litigation.

It is important to note that the RCP's initial aim was not to tackle the problem of the unprofessional conduct of one errant licentiate. Disciplining someone guilty of unprofessional conduct was considered a good legal move, a viable method for restraining doctors connected with private companies. In any event, as the RCP's solicitor admitted, the Col-

---

[110] See *Annals*, 38 (February 27, 1893): 68.

[111] The first reference to the Tibbits case in the *Annals* appears on January 26, 1893. From that date until the final decision of the RCP on June 30, 1893, the Tibbits case was referred to in more than twenty meetings. The files on the Tibbits case are held in the RCP as MSS., 2411/93–139.

[112] The lawsuits were actually filed against Lord R. Montagu, Messieurs Macmillan, and the Charity Record. See *The Times*, 6 February, 1893. *The Statement by Dr. Tibbits to the Patrons, Patroness and Governors*, RCP, MSS., 2411/132. Tibbits published the pamphlet to insist that the committee's determination to fire him was invalid.

lege's definition of "what is unprofessional in conduct" was quite arbitrary. In fact, neither in the *Annals* of the RCP nor in its correspondence is there evidence that the President and Censors fully discussed the ethical dimensions of professional or unprofessional conduct, and what these designations meant. On the contrary, their censorship was almost exclusively aimed at trapping Tibbits in their legal net. In arguing for legal sanctions against a violator of professional norms, the RCP condemned Tibbits exclusively for "gross misconduct" and unprofessional or ungentlemanly actions. As it turned out, the inappropriate actions that the RCP was most concerned about had mostly to do with the College's still somewhat shaky authority.

Essentially, the accusation of ungentlemanly behavior was principally a *political* gesture on the part of elite physicians who were reacting to the new medical climate created by the rapid establishment of commercial medical institutes such as the IME and the MBC. That the situation of the MBC was far from anomalous becomes clear when one observes the extent to which late-nineteenth-century capital vigilantly maintained its connections with the field of medical electricity: its ready-for-use technology appealed to entrepreneurs as a promising business opportunity. Even before the Tibbits case met with condemnation by elite doctors, commercialized electro-therapeutics had already begun to be practiced in many quarters.

In June 1887, William Lynd founded the Electro-Dynamic Medical Institute at 21 Bloomsbury Street. Lynd started his business to promote a "scientific administration of electricity" through practical demonstrations in a lecture-room "fully equipped with a number of very costly instruments and apparatus."[113] Soon he began using electric current to engage in medical practices. At Bournemouth, a famous health resort, he attempted to "remove paralysis from the leg of a lad by applying continuous and altering currents in combination." In September of that same year, Dr. Dudley Wodsworth followed Lynd's example by opening another electrical room at 6 Oxford Street, Southampton, where "350 patients have been treated during the last eight months."[114] Meanwhile,

---

[113] "Medical Electricity," *Telegraphic Journal and Electrical Review*, 20 (June 21, 1887): 581.
[114] "Medical Electricity," *Telegraphic Journal and Electrical Review*, 21 (September 16,

another censored member of the RCP, Dr. Jagielski, opted to resign his membership with the RCP rather than accede to its request that he leave his position at an electro-therapeutic institute.[115]

Even Harness, that bullish exploiter of medical authority, found his company a target of exploitation. In July 1887, two former employees of the MBC, named St. Clair and Wood, founded the Medical Electric Belt, Truss, and Health Appliance Company Ltd., and "started a business in Bond street exactly similar to that of the [Harness'] company," intending, like Harness, to sell electric belts and batteries. However, unlike Harness—who relied on doctors' testimonials—St. Clair and Wood contrived to establish their authority by affixing the Royal Arms on the premises. But they had neglected to seek the necessary sanction from Her Majesty or any member of the Royal Family, and Harness wasted no time in bringing the case to the attention of the Marlborough Street Police Court.[116]

What was it about these institutes that the RCP found so disturbing? What sort of threat did they present to an organization like the RCP? What did the RCP really want to protect? The cases of both the IME and the MBC, as well as later controversial cases, show that as far as medico-electrical technology was concerned, the RCP was primarily intent on safeguarding its own authority, integrity, and tradition, as well as intent on obscuring, and to a certain extent impeding, the rise of new medical practices partly represented by these companies.

In fact, the MBC, its affiliate the Zander Institute, and the capital that underwrote both organizations provided one of the most disturbing challenges ever confronted by the RCP. For the very reason that the advent of popular electro-therapeutics represented commercialism's encroachment into medical practice, medical authorities opposed the emergence of medico-electrical technology. Although the RCP wanted to maintain a monopoly on competence, the commercial power of medico-electrical technology was driving a pecuniary wedge between elite authorities and general practitioners. In so doing, it was likely to fracture the iron integrity and authority of the RCP.

---

1887): 544.

[115] A. M. Cooke, *A History of the Royal College of Physicians of London*, 905.

[116] "Rival Medical Electricians," *Telegraphic Journal and Electrical Review*, 21 (July 29, 1887): 122.

It was thus no accident that the main condemnation of Herbert Tibbits by the RCP centered on his refusal to recognize the RCP's authority
rather than on the content of his testimonials on behalf of the MBC.
Whether Tibbits' testimonials were laudatory or not was not the main
issue discussed in court with the recalcitrant experts in medical electricity:
in its frequent meetings, the RCP showed no interest in the matter. Tibbits
always denied the charge of having given a "laudatory" certificate, insisting that his evaluation was neither exaggerated nor dishonest. Responding to his protest, the Censors' Board "decline[d] to admit the
Licentiate's interpretation of the word 'laudatory,' which was used *in the
ordinary sense* [my italics]."[117] This questioning of shades of meaning,
however, was less important to the RCP than what it termed Tibbits'
"unprofessional conduct": his thoughtless facilitation of capital's entry
into medical practice and his complicity in tarnishing the integrity and
authority of the medical profession. What Tibbits represented, in short,
was nothing less than a threat to the professional and institutional authority of the RCP. Hence, the arguments in the meetings of the Censors'
Board were centered on "whether he acknowledged the authority and
jurisdiction of the College."[118]

On April 7, 1893, at an extraordinary meeting of the Censors' Board,
the first such meeting that Tibbits attended (reluctantly), the president of
the RCP referred first and foremost to the RCP's authority. Tibbits,
however, did nothing other than show his disregard for the authority of
the Board. "[Tibbits] was asked what answer he had to make to the
complaint of the Board," explained a report of the meeting. "He stated in
reply that he would not then agree [to] the legal authority of the Board as
set forth by the President."[119] At the meeting of June 15, "the discussion
mainly turned on the question of procedure, the powers and desires of
the College and the Censors' Board respectively under the Bye-Law
CLXXXVIII, and whether Dr. Tibbits should be allowed to adorn the

---

[117] "Extraordinary Meeting of the Censors' Board," *Annals*, 38 (April 7, 1893):
78–81. The quotation is from page 81.
[118] "Extraordinary Meeting of the Censors' Board," *Annals*, 38 (June 15, 1893):
121–130. See the letter from Liveing to Tibbits where Liveing strongly insisted
that Tibbits obey the authority of the RCP.
[119] "Extraordinary Meeting of the Censors' Board," *Annals*, 38 (April 7, 1893):
80.

College or not."[120] Furthermore, "The College decided that it would not hear him unless he first acknowledged its authority."[121] Indeed, the president and the Censors' Board unsuccessfully spent the entire year "pressing" Tibbits to submit to the authority of the College. But Tibbits was neither to be persuaded nor intimidated into acquiescence.

Finally on 14 July 1893, an RCP committee voted sixty-two out of sixty-three to revoke Tibbits' medical license. The College appeared to have won. But the very fact that it had spent an entire year attempting to patch up one troublesome doctor's offense says much about the degree to which the RCP was already losing authority. As Hannah Arendt notes, "Authority precludes the use of external means of coercion; where force is used, authority itself has failed. Authority, on the other hand, is incompatible with persuasion, which presupposes equality and works through a process of argumentation."[122]

It was not until 1922, more than thirty years later, that such concealed connections between capital interests and medical practitioners materialized enough—or were sufficiently acknowledged as an already-existent reality—to prompt their legal regulation and an amendment of the 1888 Resolution.

### *Clashing Medical Electricians*

Medical-technical institutions such as the MBC were viewed with suspicion—not only by medical professionals invested in protecting their own shaky authority, but also by electro-technicians seeking to establish their own professional legitimacy. In fact, electro-therapeutics had been associated with (and had attempted to distance itself from) quack medicine since the days of the earliest pioneers of medical electricity. Golding Bird had "fulminated against the activities of self-styled medical galvanists," blaming them for "duping and cheating the public."[123] This asso-

---

[120] *Annals*, 38 (June 15, 1893): 124.

[121] Ibid., 126.

[122] Hannah Arendt, "What Is Authority," in *Between Past and Future* (New York: Viking, 1961), 92.

[123] Iwan Rhys Morus, "Marketing the Machine: The Construction of Electrotherapeutics as Viable Medicine in Early Modern England," *Medical History*, 36 (1992): 34–52, 49.

ciation with quackery remained even in the later part of the nineteenth century when the technology of medical electricity had reached a relative maturity. In the course of negotiating with the RCP, therefore, medical electricians, aiming to establish a new field in technological medicine, began to recognize the dangers of being looked down upon as charlatans and of causing suspicion in the minds of elite authorities. Many such electricians, particularly members of the Institution of Electrical Engineers, participated in an anti-quack campaign through such magazines as *The Telegraphic and Electrical Review*. This periodical, an organ of the Institution of Electrical Engineers, was first published in 1888, just after the establishment of the IME, and devoted a series of columns to denouncing electro-quackery. Much work remained to be done by the IME, the author of one column argued, for "charlatans cry aloud for exposure" and "make a determined fight to turn any and every attack to their own advantage."[124]

To these engineering professionals, the MBC appeared as the most flagrant and "ubiquitous pest" by reaping profits from the extra publicity.[125] Under editors Henry Alabaster and Tom Ernest Gatehouse in the 1890s, *The Telegraphic and Electrical Review*, subsequently renamed *The Electrical Review*, carried a series of exposés, one of which resulted in the downfall of Harness' electric belt business.

The beginning of *The Electrical Review*'s attack on the MBC was a detailed report of a case brought to the County Court in Bloomsbury.[126] On May 9, 1892, a man with the surname Jeffery, a Union Bank cashier who thought he was suffering from a sprain, visited the Zander Institute and was introduced by the receiving officer to Simmonds, allegedly an expert in these matters. Simmonds examined Jeffery and recommended that he "wear one of Harness' electric belts with a suspender, in order to obviate what might develop into rupture." Because Jeffery could not afford outright the belt's £5 5s. price, Simmonds agreed to receive only £2, with an IOU for the £3 5s. balance. After he had worn it for a while, "the belt

[124] *Telegraphic Journal and Electrical Review*, 22 (August 17, 1888): 166.
[125] "The Medical Press and Quackery," *Telegraphic Journal and Electrical Review*, 22 (August 24, 1888): 205.
[126] "The Medical Battery Company v. Jeffery," *Electrical Review*, 30 (July 22, 1892): 90–101.

chafed the skin and caused an eruption, and the illness was so aggravated" that about a month later Jeffery wrote to the company to demand the return of his £2 and the IOU, threatening legal proceedings otherwise. The MBC offered in reply to exchange the belt on the announced policy of "supply[ing] a good-fitting for an ill-fitting belt free of charge." Eventually in reply to Jeffery's final letter, the company's solicitors declared that proceedings had already been taken against Jeffery, who then filed his counterclaim.

In the trial, de Witt, the barrister-at-law for the plaintiff, insisted that Jeffery did not ask to see a medical man, who if required could have been provided on the premises, and that Simmonds was a qualified specialist who had dealt with no fewer than 16,000 cases of abdominal hernia. The cross-examination of Simmonds centered on his qualification for treating hernia. Simmonds responded, "I have studied it all my life; ever since nine years of age." Pursuing the issue of his experience, the counsel for the defendant next asked, "What was your 'commercial pursuit' before you were employed by the plaintiff?" Simmonds explained that he had been a "salesman in the West End of London"—to which the counsel asked, "What, in the drapery line?" "No, in Oriental furniture," the salesman-turned-receiving-officer clarified. "You do not acquire much knowledge of the treatment of hernia in selling Oriental furniture," quipped the counsel. "No," was Simmonds' terse response.[127] Highlighting this exchange, the author of the report in *The Electrical Review* concluded, "That is to say, the health, and perhaps the lives of 16,000 people have been wantonly risked, and something like £80,000 taken as payment."[128]

In court, the electricians launched a full technical assault. Called to the witness box for the defendant as a member of IEE and allegedly an "electrical and consulting engineer of 22 years' standing," T. E. Gatehouse tested the belt himself and bitterly denied its power to generate any electricity at all. The statement he made when cross-examined by the judge exemplified the common criticism of the electric belts:

Witness: The moisture of the body would be sufficient to set up a current between two dissimilar metals, but you must have a complete circuit. If I place one half of this belt on my stomach,

---

[127] Ibid., 100.
[128] "Electropathic Belts," *Electrical Review*, 30 (August 5, 1892): 101–102.

and the other half on my back, I have the elements for a galvanic battery, but there is no completion of the electrical circuit.

His Honour: The witness [Simmonds] says the circuit is completed by the action of the moisture.

Witness: That is the internal, and not the external circuit.

His Honour: Why would not a body touched back and front and all around complete a circuit?

Witness: . . . I took salt water, and moistened the two parts, and then I connected the copper and zinc with a galvanometer, and so I got a slight deflection of the needle of about 14 degrees. I then put the belt on my legs, and on my arms, and the deflection was not in the slightest degree altered. That shows that when these belts are worn by any patient no electricity passes through the body in any way whatever, but only along the webbing and over the skin surface.[129]

The electrical engineers here conclusively argued that the chemical effect of metals on perspiring skin produced at best only a small amount of electricity, which would never have been of medical use. Putting the electric belt on the skin, they argued, was a nonsensical effort to make the human body into an internal circuit or "a human battery," for the slightest amount of electricity generated would have been discharged on the surface of the skin and would not have penetrated the body. In other words, the currents produced by connecting the zinc and copper would be too weak to overcome the resistance of the skin and to pass through the whole body, as medical purposes required (Fig. 4-9).

*The Electrical Review*'s account summarizes the arguments to which most mainstream electricians adhered. The writer (probably Gatehouse) of the column "Electropathic Belts" in *The Electrical Review* reported the result of an experiment made with the assistance of Dr. de Watteville, Dr. Inglis Parsons, Dr. Lewis Jones, and Henry Lawrence. Its purpose was to estimate the amount of electromotive force necessary to penetrate the body to have a therapeutic effect: "The E.M.F. required to develop 10 milli-ampères when the average resistance of the human body is in the circuit, is about 15 volts, so it can readily be seen that the current generated by an

---

[129] "The Medical Battery Company v. Jeffery," *Electrical Review*, 30 (July 22, 1892): 101.

electropathic belt is but a mere fraction of 1 milliampère."[130] This result was applauded by Lawrence in a series of articles entitled "The Current That Cures," which ran from August 12 to September 1892, as an attempt to save the invaluable practice of medical electricity "from being starved out by the suspicious attitude of [the medical profession] or brought into ridicule and contempt" by the blatant absurdities of advertising quacks.[131] Lawrence's argument was based on the same premises as Gatehouse's criticism of the MBC's electric belts:

> The people who sell these things tell us, however, that a very small current is sufficient to cure if it be applied constantly, and that their belts excited to action by the perspiration do this, but to pass even a tenth part of one milliampère through such resistance requires 40 volts, and this is at least 10 times more than the best of such belts is capable of.[132]

With unbridled contempt, Lawrence concluded that because of skin resistance, a "'current that cures' is *not to* be obtained from *any body belts or appliances* which rely upon the *excretion of the skin for their action.*"[133] Lawrence owed much of his argument to past experts in medical electricity such as W. H. Stone and W. E. Steavenson. Steavenson had previously written in relation to the "so extensively advertised" galvanic belts that "no weak current, such as is produced by these battery-belts, could pass through the skin. . . . If the current from these appliances were strong enough to overcome the resistance of the skin, sloughs would, in a short time, be produced at the points of application of the electrodes, a sore first appearing at the point of application of the negative pole."[134]

William Stone, a physician at St. Thomas' Hospital and fellow of the

---

[130] "Electropathic Belts," *Electrical Review*, 30 (August 5, 1892): 101.

[131] "The Current that Cures," *Electrical Review*, 30 (August 12, 1892): 208–209; 30 (August 19, 1892): 239; 30 (August 26, 1892): 262–263; 30 (September 2, 1892): 282–283; 30 (September 9, 1892): 330–331; and 30 (September 16, 1892): 350–351.

[132] Ibid., 20 (August 26, 1892): 262–263.

[133] Ibid., 263.

[134] W. E. Steavenson, "The Therapeutical Applications of Electricity," read in the section of pharmacology and therapeutics at the fifty-second annual meeting of the British Medical Association: *British Medical Journal*, 2 (1884): 1008–1011.

RCP, delivered in April 1886 the College's Lumleian Lectures entitled "The Electrical Condition of the Human Body: Man as a Conductor and Electrolyte." In this lecture, he criticized Continental electricians such as Emil du Bois Reymond and T. A. L. Moncel, who had failed to consider the effect of the body's own polarization and argued that the resistance of the human body itself was "very greatly less than had formerly been supposed."[135] Stone admitted, however, that the skin, acting as an insulator, increased the estimated resistance.

In order to reduce contact-resistance by the skin to as close to zero as possible, and to obtain an absolute measurement, Stone attempted to connnect poles of electricity with a large surface of the skin. To do so, he wrapped "a flexible strip of lead around the hands or feet, previously soaked in brine."[136] In the experiments, he charged a healthy adult for ten minutes, then measured the subject's electrical discharge with a galvanometer to estimate the currents from the body. The result Stone obtained was that the galvanometer recorded "the great initial throw" to a high level of current, which then came down again—but not to zero. This showed that the human body was capable of generating high electromotive force due to the effect of self-induction. For electro-therapeutic purposes, Stone thus argued, electricity is useful; however, the resistance of the human body varied with the kind of disease.

On 23 September 1892, *The Electrical Review*, allegedly taking up cudgels on behalf of the public, launched another attack against the activities of the MBC. The *Review* wrote, "To take advantage of that helplessness to wring money from the sufferer stamps the man [Tibbits] as a being beneath contempt; yet of such a class are the men who fatten by the sale of useless electrical appliances, and who should be effaced by the strong arm of the law." In this way, Tibbits was pilloried as an example of those educated men who only too easily wrote testimonials for the benefit of charlatans. The author suggested that though "Dr. Tibbits is, we believe, supposed to be a recognized authority in the medical world," he only took responsibility "to gild the counterfeit and make it appear to be all of

---

[135] W. H. Stone, "Abstracts of the Lumleian Lectures on the Electrical Condition of the Human Body: Man as a Conductor and Electrode," *British Medical Journal*, 1 (1886): 728–730, 812–813, 863–865. The quotation is from page 812.
[136] Ibid., 813.

sterling gold."[137] In the article, the main conclusions about Tibbits' pamphlet, *The Treatment of Disease by the Prolonged Application of Currents of Electricity of Low Powers*, were quoted to demonstrate Tibbits' "most incredible ignorance of electrical laws, an ignorance which utterly unfits him to speak as an authority." Scarcely two weeks later, on 6 October, Tibbits sued the proprietors of the magazine—Henry Alabaster, Thomas Ernest Gatehouse, and Harry Robert Kemp—claiming £5,000 for libel and the damage he had suffered.[138] The subsequent court argument attracted much attention from the medical profession, and *The Lancet* and *The British Medical Journal* issued prompt, detailed reports on "Tibbits *v.* Alabaster and others."[139]

At the Queen's Bench, "having made a lengthy opening, giving a history of his professional antecedents," Tibbits criticized the conduct of the defendants in staining his reputation.[140] However, Tibbits' lawsuit was in fact financed by Harness, who was therefore the real plaintiff, because Tibbits was "an undischarged bankrupt" at the time of action.[141] The principal witness for the plaintiff was Tibbits himself, while the principal witnesses for the defendants were numerous electrical engineers and scientists, including—most eminently—Lord Kelvin, president of the

---

[137] "Electricity and the Medical Profession," *Electrical Review*, 30 (September 23, 1892).

[138] The documents related to Tibbits' trials are held in the Public Record Office: *Depositions*, J17/283, IND 1/1675; *Pleadings*, J54/765, January-March 1893; *Affidavits*, J4/4891. See especially the writ issued on October 6, 1892 and submitted to the High Court of Justice, "Statement of Claims" by Tibbits, XC 5658, J54/765. The Depositions of J17/283 hold the pamphlet of the Zander Institute; the Harness' Electropathic Belt was itself presented as evidence to the court. This belt has a tag with Lord Kelvin's memorandum in his own writing (see Fig. 4-9).

[139] "Medico-Legal and Medico-Ethical, Queen's Bench Division before Mr. Justice Mathews and a Special Jury, Tibbits *v.* Alabaster and Others," *British Medical Journal*, 1 (1893): 436; "Tibbits *v.* Alabaster and Others," *British Medical Journal*, 1 (1893): 368 and 436; "Tibbits *v.* Alabaster and Others," *The Lancet*, 1 (1893): 425, 439–440, 447, and 487; "Dr Tibbits and the Medical Battery Company," *British Medical Journal*, 2 (1893): 1182.

[140] The courtroom battle between Tibbits and *The Electrical Review* attracted much public attention. See *The Times*, February 16, February 17, and February 18, 1893.

[141] *The Times*, February 6, 1893.

Royal Society. In court, Lord Kelvin examined one of Harness' belts and testified that in the condition in which the belt was sold, the connection of the metal discs was imperfect, so that it would never be capable of generating electricity at all, though "in cross-examination, he stated that [by] putting the belt on the body with metallic connections there would be a small current."[142] Professor Silvanus Thompson, another witness who had himself worn the belt, made a sarcastic remark about the therapeutic effect of the low dosage of electricity the belt could generate.[143] Tibbits replied, "scientific men always differ (laughter)."[144]

The verdict was returned in favor of the defendants on 17 February 1893. Nevertheless, Tibbits still sought to wage another round of legal battles with the media whom he believed were unjustly besmirching his reputation. The day after the verdict, the *Morning* stated scornfully that Tibbits was "a professional man of straw" and wrote, "The jury, by giving a verdict for the defendant, have found that the plaintiff had virtually no reputation to maintain."[145] Another newspaper, *Science Siftings*, entered the arena to do battle against Tibbits on March 4, crowing over "a distinct triumph of right over wrong in its most drastic sense, so far as Dr. Tibbits is concerned, in having endeavored to give impetus to the imposition upon the suffering public of a worthless appliance."[146] Tibbits at once sued both newspapers, but in both cases his claims were rejected.

This was the final fall for Tibbits. His medical license was revoked by the Royal College of Physicians in 1893, his name was struck by the General Medical Council from the *Medical Register* in 1895, and in the

---

[142] "Medico-Legal and Medico-Ethical," *British Medical Journal*, 1 (1893): 436.
[143] Thompson "proved that a current greater than that which the belt generated could be produced by merely plunging a pin and a needle together into a small drop of ink. With a moist skin he had obtained a current equal to one-fifth of a milliampère, with a dry skin a current as small as the two-hundredth part of that quantity." "Tibbits *v.* Alabaster and Others," *The Lancet*, 1 (1893): 439–440.
[144] *The Times*, February 6, 1893.
[145] "Harness' Belt," *Morning*, February 18, 1893; "Tibbits *v.* the *Morning* Newspaper Publishing Company, Limited," *British Medical Journal*, 1 (1894): 332.
[146] "Harness' Belt, the Verdict of a British Jury," *Science Siftings*, March 4, 1893, RCP, MSS., 2411/113. Tibbits sued the proprietors of the newspaper, claiming £1,000 in damages, and published the statement of claim as *Tibbits v. Messrs. Woolf & Hymann*, on 21 April, 1893. The pamphlet is held in the RCP, MSS., 2411/113.

public press he was branded as "a creature" and a commercial quack. Thereafter, Tibbits disappeared from public view.[147] Yet though the electrical engineers won their battle with the MBC, this triumph did not help advance their original aim of getting support from the elite doctors of the RCP for their efforts in developing electro-medicine. The Royal College of Physicians adhered to its regulations against collaborating in entrepreneurial endeavors. As already noted, amendment of this policy would not occur until 1922.

*Harness and the MBC in the Courts*

The professional electricians' exposé of the MBC's electro-medical business was first brought into the court as a battle between Herbert Tibbits and the proprietors of the *Electrical Review*—Henry Alabaster, Tom Ernst Gatehouse, and Harry R. Kemp. Soon after the verdict in favor of the electricians, Harness found that the articles in the *Review* and the verdict "threatened all sorts of pains and penalties and would drive him into the workhouse." He therefore began to send to five hundred newspaper vendors in London a circular signed by the MBC's solicitor, "describing the articles in the *Review* as 'malicious libels,' and cautioning the newsagents against selling it, the result of which was that the newsagents were afraid to sell the *Review*." When Harness threatened them with legal proceedings or else the exhibition of placards at their storefronts "if these or any future publications containing defamatory articles or paragraphs were sold," newsagents such as W. H. Smith (then as now the largest in the country) thereupon declined to sell the *Review* unless indemnified. The proprietors of the *Review*, however, fought fire with fire, suing Harness for the alleged libel; the subsequent court battles were reported by *The Times* as "a novel and important action—the first of the kind." In court Harness insisted upon his "right of self-defence" and his

---

[147] Tibbits was summoned by the General Medical Council on November 18, 1893, and eliminated from the *Register*. See Russell Gordon Smith, "The Professional Conduct Jurisdiction of the General Medical Council: Its Compliance with Aspects of Substantive and Procedural Justice," Ph.D. thesis, University of London, 1990, Appendix III, 896. See also his *Medical Discipline: The Professional Conduct Jurisdiction of the General Medical Council, 1858–1990* (Oxford: Clarendon Press, 1994).

need to protect his business and reputation, while the owners of the *Review* attempted to prove that their articles were fair criticism in denouncing Harness' electric belts and pills as "a species of quackery and imposture."[148] After Chief Justice Lord Coleridge remarked that "it was undoubtedly for the public interest that such pretences, under guise of a spurious science, and fictitious remedies should be exposed and denounced," the jury concluded on March 8, 1893 the verdict in favor of the plaintiffs, in the amount of £1,000.[149]

The victory for the *Review* instigated Harness' final downfall. Five months later, he was forced to wind up the company,[150] and soon after that, criminal charges against him and the MBC began to be pursued by the Marlborough Street Police Court—investigations that continued through February 8, 1894. In the police court, the discussions centered on whether the company had induced the public to buy its "ingenious useless instruments . . . by a false and fraudulent pretence" in its advertisements.[151] A series of nineteen detailed reports in *The Times* under the title of "The Harness Case" shows the extent to which the public's attention was drawn to this case. As many as forty-nine doctors, electricians, and customers of the MBC were called as witnesses for either the MBC or the electrical engineers—who turned out to be the real prosecutors of the case—and two hundred and fourteen letters were examined.[152]

---

[148] "Alabaster v. The Medical Battery Company, Queens Bench Division (Before Lord Coleridge Justice and a Special Jury)," *The Times*, March 8, 1893.

[149] "Alabaster v. The Medical Battery Company," *The Times*, March 9, 1893; "Supreme Court of Judicature, Court of Appeal," *The Times*, March 10, 1893.

[150] "High Court of Justice, Chancery Division, Wilkinson v. The Medical Battery Company," *The Times*, October 28, October 31, November 6, November 9, and November 16, 1893.

[151] "Police," *The Times*, November 9; "The Charges Against Harness," *The Times*, November 23, 1893.

[152] "The Harness Case," *The Times*, November 30, December 1, December 14, December 21, December 22, and December 28, 1893 as well as January 4, January 11, January 18, and January 23, 1894; "The Medical Battery Company," *The Times*, December 9, 1893; January 3, 1894; "The Harness Prosecution," *The Times*, February 1 and February 8, 1894; "Action Against Harness, Defendant In the Box: He gives his Autobiography," *Pall Mall Gazette*, July 4, 1894; "The Action against Harness, Mr. Collyer in the Witness," *Pall Mall Gazette*, July 9, 1894; "Science Notes," *Pall Mall Gazette*, July 16, 1894.

As we have seen, the Royal College of Physicians had been mainly concerned with protecting its authority and had no interest in any possible medical value that electro-therapeutics may have offered. However, it was in this court struggle that medical electricians offered their differing professional opinions on why Harness' electric business should or should not be regarded as quackery. The electricians represented by Gatehouse insisted, for example, that a current generated by the belt would be so minute that it would discharge on the surface of the skin and the only possible effect would be the production of sores. "Perspiration," he said, "was largely composed of chloride or sodium, and the contact of the perspiration with the zinc disc in the presence of the air would produce oxychloride of zinc, which was a very poisonous salt." Doctors such as Henry Lewis Jones, then a medical officer at the St. Bartholomew's Hospital, supported the electricians in attempting to prove that "the belts had no value whatever as electrotherapeutic agents."[153]

Opponents of the MBC, however, did not entirely deny the belt's efficacy in court. Both Gatehouse and Jones grudgingly admitted that Dr. Arthur Harries' experiments on Harness' belt, described in his favorable report on the product, had shown that the belt produced a small amount of current.[154] An authority on electro-therapeutics, Harries was a silver medalist graduate of University College, London and had competed with Jones for a post at St. Bartholomew's Hospital. Furthermore, Jones had also opposed Gatehouse by stating that such a weak current could indeed overcome the skin's resistance to penetrate the body; he agreed that there was some therapeutic value to be gained from the Zander System provided by the MBC.[155]

What was most debated in this cross-examination was the technical question of whether or not such a mild current induced a therapeutic effect. In his testimonial pamphlet "The Treatment of Disease in the Prolonged Application of Currents of Electricity of Low Power," Herbert Tibbits saw the belt's efficacy in its ability to provide "currents of low power for lengthened periods." He wrote, "for some years I have conducted experiments, both in Hospital and private practice, with currents

---

[153] *The Times*, December 1, 1893.
[154] *The Times*, December 28, 1893.
[155] *The Times*, December 21, 1893.

of low tension for many hours, and I am satisfied that such an apparatus is a valuable addition to the medical armamentarium."[156]

This was simply a reiterated point of his electro-therapeutics. In other earlier writings, he had argued that the application of weak currents for long periods was most beneficial in combating fatigue-induced illnesses, the loss of functional power, general prostration from overwork or anxiety, and cases of sleeplessness. He wrote that "the prolonged action of a continuous current upon an exhausted muscle produced a restoration of it; that is, that the depressed excitability increased."[157] Like many other writers about medical electricity, Tibbits believed the romantic fiction that electricity generated vital energy. He wrote that "currents of electricity (generated perhaps by the friction of the stream of blood against the coats of arteries) are always present in the body. When we are awake, when we are undergoing the wear and tear of our daily life, that supply of vital energy, that supply of electricity stored up and accumulated during sleep is used up; is exhausted."[158] Thus considering the amount of electricity absorbed in the body as a sort of pick-me-up medicine to recover from the scarcity or loss of vital energy, Tibbits recommended that physicians measure exactly the dose of electricity:

> The dose of electricity is made up of two factors— (1) Its strength; (2) The *time* during which it is applied to the patients. *Can we determine its strength?* It is, as you know, a Force, and, as with other *forces*, it has its standard of measurement. You graduate *time* into hours, minutes, and seconds, and our graduated measure is a clock or watch. We graduate electricity into what are called *ampères*, and our graduated measure is a galvanometer.[159]

---

[156] "The treatment of disease by the prolonged application of currents of electricity of low powers, by Herbert Tibbits, MD., etc. together with a report by Arthur Harries, MD., etc. on Mr. Harness' Electropathic Belt and the Electropathic & Zander Institute," RCP, MSS., 2411/94.

[157] Herbert Tibbits, *A Handbook of Medical Electricity* (London: J. & A. Churchill, 1873), 85.

[158] Herbert Tibbits, *Massage and its Application: A Concluding Lecture Delivered to Nurses and Masseuses* (London: The School of Massage and Electricity, 1887), 21.

[159] Herbert Tibbits, *Electrical and Anatomical Demonstrations, Delivered at the School of*

According to Tibbits, as electro-therapeutics became better understood, a physician would be able to prescribe the amount of current to patients just as he would do "a tablespoonful of any medicine."[160]

In the cross-examination, Gatehouse and Jones centered their criticism on this point. Jones argued that "minute currents could not influence the body in any way" and that "the prolonged application of mild currents had not been studied sufficiently."[161] Against this, Horace Avory, a barrister for the MBC, argued that other authorities of electro-therapeutics such as von Ziemssen and Wilhelm Erb, a professor at Heidelberg University, held different opinions upon the effect of long-continued galvanic treatment with gentle currents. Although Avory quoted Erb's *Handbook of Electro-Therapeutics*, which insisted that "to secure the therapeutic effects desired the plates should be worn every day for several hours, or even for whole days or weeks,"[162] Jones conservatively interpreted such support, replying that "Dr. Erb did recommend them, but that he did so in a very guarded manner." Jones and Gatehouse insisted that in order to have a therapeutic value, "a current of one milliampères was the *minimum* dose of electricity to be given," while in contrast "the current to be obtained from a Harness' belt, if any, would be from one-hundredth to four-hundredth of a milliampère." Gatehouse argued that if the belt were efficacious, it should be able to ring a bell. "Human perspiration," he said, "was an electrolyte, and was as strong as a film of salt and water. The belts, he should say, were not advertised to be able to ring bells (laughter)." The *Times* reported the following exchange:

Mr. Avory—If you wanted to prove that an appliance was electrical, it would be fair test to show that it would ring a bell?
Gatehouse (the witness)—Yes.
Mr. Avory—If the belt was put on flannel and soaked in salt and water or perspiration and placed round the body would it ring a bell?
Gatehouse—No.[163]

---

*Massage and Electricity* (London: J. & A. Churchill, 1887), 75.
[160] Ibid., 77.
[161] *The Times*, December 21 and December 22, 1893.
[162] Wilhelm Erb, *Handbook of Electro-Therapeutics*, trans. by L. Pitzel (New York: William Wood & Company, 1883), 286.
[163] *The Times*, December 22, 1893.

To defend Harness, many witnesses were called on to testify, including doctors, patients, and eminent customers of the MBC such as the Rev. Edward Francis Shaw. For example, Cecil Greenwood, Member of the Royal College of Surgeons and licentiate of the Royal College of Physicians, testified that he sent a testimonial "speaking highly of the beneficial results which he had experienced from using the belt."[164] On February 7, the Magistrate, Mr. Hannay, brought in the verdict to discharge Harness, the defendant, citing *"caveat emptor."* Hannay acknowledged that "Yet there are probably thousands of persons in the country who are firmly persuaded of its efficacy, and who, up to a certain point have apparently respectable grounds for their faith," but insisted that, "It is for the buyer after all to form his own estimate."[165]

Though the criminal charge failed to get Harness jailed, civil proceedings, also supported by the electricians, were subsequently brought against the MBC on July 2, 1893.[166] One of the cases was an action by Jeremish Brasyer, an eighty-three-year-old retired colonel suffering from sexual dysfunction. Harness' ingenious advertisements had induced him to visit the MBC in June 1892. To his request to see Harness, "whoever the man was that spoke to me he said, 'We are all Harness,'" and he was introduced to Dr. James Montgomery M'Cully in his practice room on the second floor. He was asked to sit down on a chair, whereupon "M'Cully began all sorts of antics, such as I [Brasyer] had seen the Fakirs in India do."[167] Brasyer explained to M'Cully that "I was getting old" and "I wanted to get married again." When he found that he had received no therapeutic benefit, Brasyer sued one of the MBC's physicians for damages from alleged fraud. The disgruntled Brasyer claimed in the court, "I wanted to be made a different man: they promised to make a *man* of me; and they might have made a monkey of me."[168]

Brasyer's desire for rejuvenation illustrates clearly the kind of imaginary projections that nourished the period's proliferating medical treat-

---

[164] *The Times*, January 18, 1894.
[165] *The Times*, February 1 and 8, 1894.
[166] "Brasyer v Harness and Another, High Court of Justice, Queen's Bench Division," *The Times*, July 4, July 5, July 6, July 7, July 10, July 11, and July 14, 1894.
[167] *The Times*, December 6 and December 7, 1893.
[168] *The Times*, July 4, 1894.

ments and commodities. As described in Chapter Two, for *fin-de-siècle* consumers of medicine, being healthy meant having an energetic, muscular, young, and vital body and life, and a huge number of medical boosters and pick-me-ups as well as electric gadgets and appliances were trading on the public's strong aspiration for this kind of vigorous health. Small wonder, given the growth of this health culture, that over four hundred people daily crowded the Queen's Bench with a desire to see the court drama of the Harness case. The competing claims for and against Harness' electric belt not only stimulated these attendees' voyeuristic curiosity but also cultivated their illusions about the healthy body.

According to the detailed reports of *The Times*, Brasyer had actually been suffering for many years from an abdominal hernia, and M'Cully claimed to have told him "Colonel, at your time of life electricity or any medical man in London can do you very little good, but I will do my best." M'Cully made private calls on Brasyer over seventeen times and treated him in collaboration with Dr. Stanley Boyd, a surgeon at the Charing Cross Hospital. For all of these treatments Brasyer was asked to pay a total of £52 10s. But Brasyer got very little in return; indeed, he only not failed to gain ground, but even lost some, through the MBC's intervention. According to Brasyer, one evening M'Cully induced a strong electric shock to Brasyer's right shoulder, which resulted in him losing the ability to move his arm freely. As a result, Brasyer not only rejected paying £52, calling the fee "exorbitant," but also sued M'Cully for alleged negligence and fraudulent misrepresentation. Denying that he "in any way inflicted the injury to the colonel's shoulder as alleged," M'Cully counterclaimed for damages for malicious prosecution.[169]

Thanks to *The Times'* reporting on the innumerable lawsuits connected with Harness, we can see in great detail the MBC's actual business operations. Indeed, the MBC illustrates the market's rapid intrusion in the late nineteenth century into seemingly established professional domains. Like other collaborations between commercial capital and medical professionals at the turn of the century, what distinguished Harness' electro-medical business from the practices of Georgian-era nostrum quacks was that it employed a team of medical doctors as salaried supervisors. M'Cully, then fifty years old, was unmistakably an experienced—though

[169] *The Times*, July 6 and July 7, 1894.

not an elite—doctor: he was an MD of Queen's University in Ireland and a Fellow of the Royal College of Surgeons, and had worked for a total of thirty years on a military medical staff in India and as a sanitary officer in London. He first became acquainted with Harness in 1891, and was employed by the MBC at a salary of £327 a year, to be increased annually by £100. M'Cully, moreover, was not the sole physician connected with the MBC: there were at least seven medical doctors employed as its medical officers. Apart from Dr. Scott and Dr. Willis—both original founders and shareholders of the MBC—Dr. Wallace, Dr. Layard, Dr. Brabant, Dr. Stephens, and Dr. Daniels were all employed as supervisors of the different departments within Harness' company.

Although disciplinary organizations such as the General Medical Council were becoming increasingly strict in their policing of the professional conduct of errant doctors, commercial pressures and market mechanisms never stopped inducing medical professionals to join the lucrative business world of medical consumerism. Far from the MBC's employment of doctors being an exception, doctors' names were frequently used in medical advertisements as a registered trademark in the sale of electro-medical appliances. In turn, doctors, placed in the free-for-all cash nexus, tended to share pecuniary benefits alongside the capitalistic entrepreneurs who employed them. Dr. Carter Moffat, co-patentee with Harness of the Ammoniaphone, was associated with London Health Electrical Institute Limited on Oxford Street and sold "Dr. CARTER MOFFAT'S Feather Light ELECTRIC BODY BELT" for "Excessive Weakness, Nervous Debility, and Spasm." Its advertisements, using trendy catchphrases such as "The Blood is the Life, But Electricity is the Life of the Blood," promised to "Invigorate, Strengthen and Brace Up" women's bodies and to increase "Vitality, Strength, and Energy" for men (Fig. 4-10).[170] Similarly, Dr. Lowder's patented "Magneto-Electric Belts, Batteries and Socks" were sold as "The Great Health Restorer" by the Magneto-Electric Battery Company (Fig. 4-11).[171] Dr. Richardson's Battery was another example of the appliance marketed for "Renewed Life and Energy," as were Dr. Nelson's Medicated Loofah Socks, sold by the

---

[170] Many advertisements for this belt are held along with the following flyers: "Dr. Carter Moffat's Health Appliances," JJC, Patent Medicine Box 10.
[171] "Dr. Lowder's Magneto-Electric Battery," JJC, Patent Medicine Box 10.

Nottingham Hosiery Company.[172] In putting all these dubious medical products on the market, doctors and capitalists cooperated to squeeze as much money as possible from late-nineteenth-century consumers, whose health aspirations were burgeoning.

### The Amendment of the Resolution

Although to a large extent constrained and opposed by the RCP, the newly emerging realm of entrepreneurial medicine was increasingly strong and provided a sympathetic space for doctors disillusioned with the RCP's hypocrisy over its own principles of professional ethics. Indeed, long after its battles with the Institute of Medical Electricity and Medical Battery Company, the RCP continued to be troubled by the prospect of a commercialized medical profession. The polemical uproar caused by the IME, however, was recalled as the turning-point that eventually made possible the amendment, in 1922, of the RCP's earlier Bye-law and Resolution. This amendment, a clear demonstration of the tenacity of commercialism's allure, finally allowed RCP members to receive financial gain through their official affiliation with companies and institutions. In 1920, the move of a fellow of the RCP, Dr. Edmund Spriggs, to Ruthin Castle Ltd. in Wales, manifestly "an institution treating diseases for profit," elicited the objection of Sir Wilmot Herringham and initiated a debate among the Censors that moved them to reconsider the legal regulation of the RCP. Dr. Spriggs, who had been an eminent consultant at Guy's and St. Thomas's Hospitals until he fell ill, was summoned to the Censors' Board to defend himself in 1922. At the meeting of the Censors' Board, he argued that effective diagnosis and treatment required a large-scale organization with a strong financial base and the coordinated teamwork of specialists. In making these arguments, he invoked the IME's earlier though primitive attempt at a beneficial alliance between the medical profession and capital—although he admitted that it was "a far cry from the electrical emporium of Regent Street to a modern private hospital or sanatorium."[173]

---

[172] "Dr. Richardson's Magneto-Galvanic Battery" and "Dr. Nelson's Medicated Loofah Socks," JJC, Patent Medicine Box 10.

[173] "Dr Spriggs' speech planned (but not delivered) for the meeting of the RCP, 19 October, 1922," RCP, MSS., 835/47, 2.

Spriggs also made the point that in such a modern medical institution, group medicine was essential for effective diagnosis and treatment. He then enumerated the great benefits possible through "professional work in an Institution, which is owned by a Company," namely:

a. The advantages or necessity of what is called "team work."

b. The fact that few physicians can provide or organize such work out of their own resources.

c. That there is no financially safe way of combination except the legal one of a Limited Company.[174]

Following this argument, Sir Humphry Rolleston, the senior censor of the RCP, proposed on 26 January 1922 "That the Censors' Board should look into the question of how the Resolution of 25th Oct, 1888 should be interpreted in view of recent developments in medical practice."[175] He argued "that owing to the increasing complexity of medicine and the growth of specialities, it was becoming common for medical men to unite together for the purpose of attaining better diagnosis or better treatment than could be secured by an individual physician." Hence "group medicine," "diagnostic clinics," or "institutional treatment"—by which Rolleston meant the "teamwork" of many clinicians and technicians with different specialties within a single institution—was viewed as a necessity to meet society's and patients' demands for appropriate medical treatment.[176] To cover the high expenses associated with specialized auxiliary examinations, Rolleston insisted during the next meeting, on May 11, that the association with public companies would enable patients to get "a pecuniary advantage from the closer union of special investigation, whether in the form of a 'group,' 'team' or 'firm' or as brought together in an institution."[177]

---

[174] Ibid., 4.

[175] "Report from the Censors' Board dated 28th April, 1922, recommending the alteration of the College (dated October 25th, 1888), and of Bye–law CLXXVIII," RCP, MSS., 835/50.

[176] "College Meeting," *Annals* 51 (January 26, 1922): 71. The several meetings related to these revisions were held between January 26 and October 19, 1922. See the following issues of *Annals*: 51 (May 8, 1922): 77; 51 (May, 11, 1922): 108–113; 51 (July 7, 1922): 119; 51 (July 13, 1922): 125–134; 51 (July 20, 1922): 132–134; and 51 (October 19, 1922): 156–163.

[177] "College Meeting," *Annals*, 51 (May 11, 1922): 108.

The members of the RCP's governing body affirmed Rolleston's proposal and the president, Sir Norman Moore, nominated the Censors' Board, headed by Rolleston, to investigate this issue. On April 28, the Board submitted a report recommending the alteration of the Resolution. Pointing out the public's need for specialized diagnosis and treatment, as well as the need to rely on corporate medical institutions to provide such services, Rolleston emphasized the ethical obligation of the College to promote medicine's service-oriented responsibility toward the welfare of society:

> The welfare of the community must transcend the traditions of any of its component units. This College is but a unit of the body-politic, though a unit of high valency. They feel, therefore, that, if with the passage of years it has come about that conflict exists between the ordinances of the College and what they con-ceived to be the highest interest of the community, no course is open to them but to advise their amendment.[178]

Seeking to further legitimize its role in society, during the interwar years the medical profession as a whole thus began to emphasize the impor-tance of public service and public responsibility, matters that electrical engineers had raised long before in establishing the IME but that had been discounted by the elite physicians in favor of the gentlemanly ideal.

In subsequent meetings of the RCP's governing body, the amendment of the Resolution and Bye-law was furiously debated. Diehards such as Sir John Bradford and Sir Wilmot Herringham resisted any alteration of the rules, for fear of commercialization's further encroachment into the profession following the acceptance of "group medicine." At the other extreme, some radicals, represented by William Dowson and Dr. James Taylor, tried to abolish all regulations regarding doctors' professional affiliations. Finally, however, on October 19, 1922, the RCP decided to amend both the Resolution and Bye-law. The new Resolution officially allowed fellows and members to be financially associated with medical institutes; however, the alteration of the Bye-law was minimal since it was not considered a serious obstacle to "group medicine." The actual med-

---

[178] "Report from the Censors' Board dated 28th April, 1922," RCP, MSS., 835/50.

ico-social context that had manifested itself in the 1880s had finally gained regulatory recognition in 1922.

Through an analysis of the polemical upheaval caused by the IME and the MBC, this chapter has illustrated how a triangular struggle between a profession, capital, and technology created a new social climate for the development of medicine. In doing so, it shows how the mainstream model of medical history has failed to include an important aspect of this historical process: the beginning of managerial and entrepreneurial medicine in the late nineteenth century. The establishment of corporate-style electro-therapeutic institutes as early as 1888, kept at arm's length from the broader medical profession by the RCP's Resolution of that same year, expressed the challenges posed by commercialization and specialization. Moreover, at that same time, the public service ideal began to jeopardize the elite medical establishment's ethos of gentlemanly professionalism. While the RCP's forceful resistance may have impeded the momentum of commercialization, specialization, and the public service ideal, these integral aspects of modern medicine were eventually realized with the RCP's regulatory revisions of the 1920s.

Harness and his company's strategy typified the collaboration of capital and professionals in serving the demands of a highly commercialized society. Even in the age of triumphant professionalism, some young doctors responded eagerly to these demands, often with the full cooperation of capitalists such as Harness, using vigorous methods of self-promotion to become medical entrepreneurs themselves. As the history of Harness' company suggests, in the face of a rising commodity culture and medical consumerism, the medical profession revealed itself as less monolithically controlled and more fragmented in socio-economic terms than traditional historical analyses have suggested.

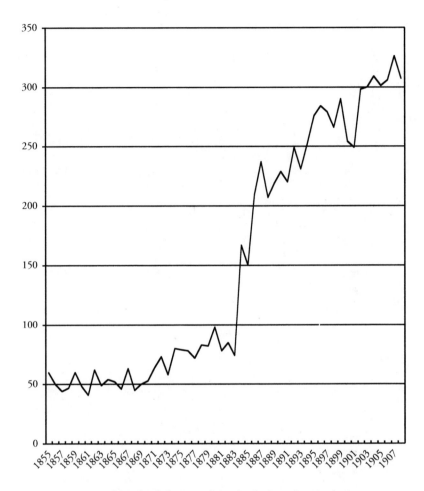

Fig. I-1. Patented Medical Commodities (including electric devices, disinfectants, emulsions, inhalers, and massage machines), 1855–1906, from Abridgments of Specifications Class 82, Medicine, Surgery, and Dentistry, UK Patent Office.

**The Historic Convention.**

To the lords of Convention the Alderman spoke,
"We here are assembled to throw off our Yoke,
And all who are bound by the Cutter to free,
Be he Welshman from Cardiff or Scot from Dundee.
  So fire off your speeches and empty your guns;
  'Tis making of history, helping your sons.
  'Tis a wonderful sight, quite a marvel to see,
  This gathering from everywhere—even Dundee."

Then the lords took to talking; their tongues were unloosed,
And the Alderman helped them when things got confused.
They resolved that the way to be happy for aye
Was to get every patent marked "P.A.T.A."
  So well they applauded, so loud they acclaimed,
  That Chiefs in the Viaduct district complained;
  For it frightened them sore to see chemists agree,
  And a lawyer was sent with a note, "Instantlee."

The Fisherman spoke, but the delegates grinned,
And welcomed the Men who confessed they had sinned.
They cheered Reuter's message, for Umney went Wylde,
And "private protection" and Grossmith reviled.
  So the Fisherman left with a flea in his ear,
  While Davenport roused them to cheer after cheer,
  And Rogers said straight, if they'd but let him be,
  He'd cheerfully pay up a seven-year fee.

The Glinn is triumphant, his banner's unfurled,
And hopefulness reigns in the pharmacist's world
But plotting, *sub rosa*, they say, has begun,
And the battle will not be so easily won.
  So come ye from Glasgow, and come ye from Leeds,
  From Oxford and Cambridge, that next year the deeds
  That to-day ye have done may bear fruit, and the tree
  That is planted may flourish from Deal to Dundee.

Fig. 1-1. The Protest by the Proprietary Articles Trade Association (P.A.T.A.), from *The Chemist and Druggist*, December 6, 1902. (Reproduced with permission from the Royal Pharmaceutical Society of Great Britain.)

Fig. 1-2. Pharmacy Bill, from *The Chemist and Druggist*, April 11, 1903.
(Reproduced with permission from the Royal Pharmaceutical Society of Great
Britain.)

Fig. 2-1. Hall's Coca Wine, from the John Johnson Collection at the Bodleian Library. (Reproduced with permission from Oxford University.)

# INTERNATIONAL HEALTH EXHIBITION,
## LONDON, 1884.

NO. 40, SOUTH GALLERY.

# PEEK, FREAN & CO.,
## BISCUIT MANUFACTURERS, LONDON.

PRIZE MEDALS AT EIGHT EXHIBITIONS.

GOLD MEDAL
Awarded by the National Academy of Agriculture, Manufactures, and Commerce, Paris. 1874.

GOLD MEDAL, PARIS, 1878.

By Appointment to H.R.H. THE PRINCE OF WALES, the COURT OF BELGIUM, and COURT OF ITALY,

FANCY BISCUITS, in about 250 varieties.

CAKES of all descriptions.

These celebrated Biscuits may be obtained from the leading Dealers in Town, Country, and on the Continent, also in various Foreign and Colonial Markets throughout the World.

Speciality for the present Season—the "HEALTH" Biscuit, a choice delicacy of extraordinary lightness. Packed in square Tins, holding about 4 lbs., and in special sized 2 lb. Tins.

Fig. 2-2. The Food Section, International Health Exhibition, London, 1884, *The Illustrated London News*, June 28, 1884. (Reproduced with permission from the British Library.)

Fig. 2-3. Guy's Tonic for Vivacity and for Strength, from the John Johnson Collection at the Bodleian Library. (Reproduced with permission from Oxford University.)

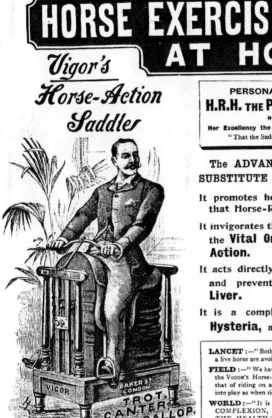

Fig. 2-4. Vigor's Horse-Action Saddle, *The Graphic*, January 11, 1896. (Reproduced with permission from the British Library.)

Fig. 2-5. Members using the parallel bars at the gymnasium of the London Polytechnic Institute. (Reproduced with permission from the University of Westminster Archives, London.)

Fig. 2-6. Bovril Gives Strength, *The Illustrated London News*, March 17, 1894. (Reproduced with permission from the British Library.)

Fig. 2-7. Hovis Bread and Biscuits Form Good Bone, Brain, Flesh, and Muscle, *The Graphic*, January 29, 1898. (Reproduced with permission from the British Library.)

# No Superfluous Fat, but Good Muscle.

Mr. ROBERT TUCK, 7, Richmond Road, Southsea, writes on Oct. 25, 1898—

"Please send a sample of 'Frame Food' Jelly, for which I enclose 3d. for postage. I am desirous of trying it for our baby, who has been brought up entirely on 'Frame Food' Diet from **six weeks old**, with results most gratifying to ourselves, and to the utmost benefit of the child. The way he has thrived on it is truly wonderful. He is now just over nine months, and we think he will walk at twelve months, he is so strong.

"I may add, that I am satisfied the food does everything that is claimed for it: not making a lot of superfluous fat, but good muscle."

*(All testimonials published by the Frame Food Co. are absolutely unsolicited and gratuitously given.)*

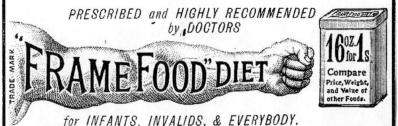

## PRESCRIBED and HIGHLY RECOMMENDED by DOCTORS

TRADE-MARK

## "FRAME FOOD" DIET

**16 OZ. for 1s.**
Compare Price, Weight, and Value of other Foods.

### for INFANTS, INVALIDS, & EVERYBODY.

**Most Nutritious. Very Digestible.**

"FRAME FOOD" DIET supplies the ORGANIC PHOSPHATES, ALBUMINOIDS, and other constituents necessary for the full development of the bones and muscles of young INFANTS and growing CHILDREN; it builds up the strength of the INVALID wasted by disease. To expectant and nursing mothers it is invaluable, as it helps to replace the loss in the maternal system, and adds largely to the value of the milk as a food; and as "FRAME FOOD" DIET is composed of all the constituents forming a perfect food, it should be taken by all who seek to preserve their health.

*Sold Everywhere in Tins, 1 lb. at 1s., 4 lb. at 3s. 9d.*

---

**Nourishing as Malt Extract; Delicious as Jam.**

### "FRAME FOOD" JELLY,

like "FRAME FOOD" DIET, contains the Organic Phosphates and Albuminoids (extracted from Wheat Bran) which are vitally necessary for Developing the Human Frame, and invigorate and strengthen at every period of life. It possesses the nutritive and digestive properties of Malt Extract, and is much cheaper and more palatable. Children eat it readily on bread and butter or in puddings, and grow stout and strong when using it. It builds up the strength of the invalid; it keeps the athlete in perfect condition; and adults find it invigorates and vitalises all the functions of the body.

Sold in Air-tight Covered Jars of about **1-lb. at 9d.**

¼-lb. Sample "FRAME FOOD" DIET, or Sample 5-oz. JAR of "FRAME FOOD" JELLY, sent FREE on receipt of 3d. to pay postage; both samples sent for 4d. for postage. **Mention this paper.**

**FRAME FOOD CO., Ltd., Dept. T., Battersea, LONDON, S.W.**

---

Fig. 2-8. "Frame Food" Diet for Infants, Invalids, & Everybody, *The Illustrated London News,* November 26, 1898. (Reproduced with permission from the British Library.)

Fig. 3-1. Pulvermacher's Chain Belt, "Electricity is Life," from the John Johnson Collection at the Bodleian Library. (Reproduced with permission from Oxford University.)

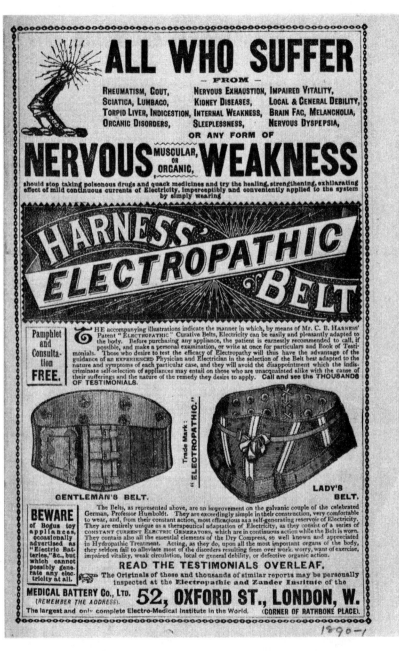

1890-1

Fig. 3-2. Harness' Electropathic Belt, from the John Johnson Collection at the Bodleian Library. (Reproduced with permission from Oxford University.)

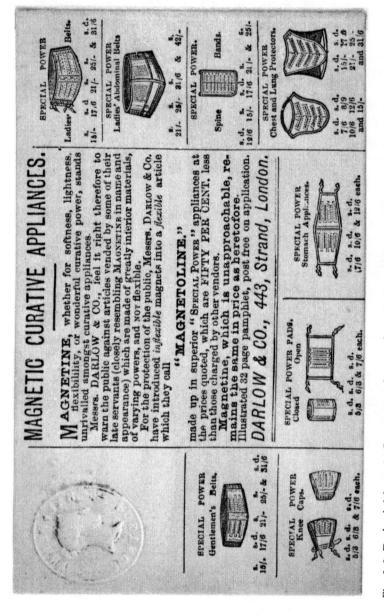

Fig. 3-3. Darlow's Magnetic Curative Appliances, from the John Johnson Collection at the Bodleian Library. (Reproduced with permission from Oxford University.)

Fig. 3-4. Macaura Vibrator, from "A Description of the Vibrator (Engl. pat. 1890. No. 4390.) and Directions for Use," 1891. (Reproduced with permission from the Wellcome Library, London.)

Fig. 3-5. G. J. Macaura, F.R.S.A., Macaura Institute, from the John Johnson Collection at the Bodleian Library. (Reproduced with permission from Oxford University.)

Fig. 3-6. C. B. Duchenne's experiment in physiology, Facial Expressions.
(Reproduced with permission from the Wellcome Library, London.)

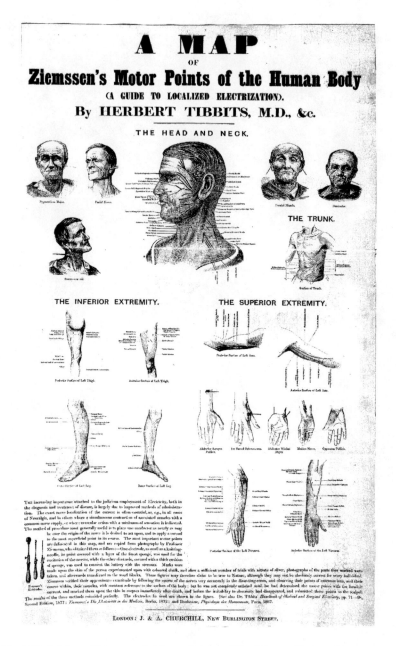

Fig. 3-7. A Map of Ziemssen's Motor Points of the Human Being, from an illustration in "A Guide to Localized Electrization," by Herbert Tibbits, M.D. (Reproduced with permission from the British Library.)

# PULVERMACHER'S
## PATENT PORTABLE
# HYDRO-ELECTRIC CHAIN,
## FOR PERSONAL USE,

(INVENTOR AND PATENTEE—J. L. PULVERMACHER,)
**FIRST BROUGHT BEFORE THE PUBLIC IN THE
GREAT EXHIBITION of ALL NATIONS for 1851, ENGLISH DEPARTMENT,
SECTION 10, NORTHERN GALLERY OF THE NAVE, No. 437,**

IS

## AN INVENTION OF THE MOST EXTRAORDINARY DESCRIPTION,
**Which will open a new Era in the History of Electricity,
and will spread the knowledge and use of this Wonderful Agent
among all Classes of Society.**

BY MEANS OF THIS APPARATUS

## ALL ACUTE NERVOUS PAINS,
SUCH AS ACUTE RHEUMATIC PAINS OF EVERY DESCRIPTION,
AND IN ALL PARTS OF THE BODY, NERVOUS HEAD ACHE, TOOTH ACHE,
EAR ACHE, &c.

## ARE REMOVED INSTANTANEOUSLY
*The moment the Chain is applied;*

While an immense number of chronic diseases of long standing, such as gout, inveterate rheumatism, sciatica, lumbago, tic-douloureux, hemorrhoides, spasms, congestion of the blood to head, chest and heart, female complaints, hysteria, liver complaints, paralytic and epileptic affections, &c.—in short, all curable diseases arising from stagnation of the blood and juices, and from depression or hypersensibility of the nervous system, are cured within a proportionately very short time by a continuous action of the chain on the body.

The astonishing—almost miraculous—effects on the human frame of this small instrument (not weighing above two ounces), originate in a *mild but continuous* electric current, which, the moment the chain is applied, circulates from one end of the same to the other, through any part of the body interposed between those two ends; on its way supplying the nerves with vital energy, sufficient to counteract the cause of the disease. When the affection is in an early stage, as is usually the case when acute nervous pains are experienced, the relief is instantaneous; whereas inveterate diseases, which may have inured themselves for years into the constitution, can, of course, only be expected to give way when the chain is worn for some time.

Although the chain acts so mildly, that no shocks or other disagreeable sensations are experienced, still every person instantly feels the effect as a slight pricking or burning at the places of application, and a flash is seen passing the eyes, whenever the current is made to traverse the nerves of sight.

[Please turn over.]

OCT - 51

Fig. 3-8. Pulvermacher's Patent Portable Hydro-Electric Chain, from the John Johnson Collection at the Bodleian Library. (Reproduced with permission from Oxford University.)

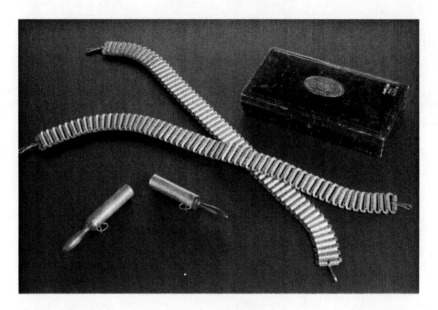

Fig. 3-9. Pulvermacher's Copper and Zinc Chains. (Reproduced with permission from the Wellcome Library, London.)

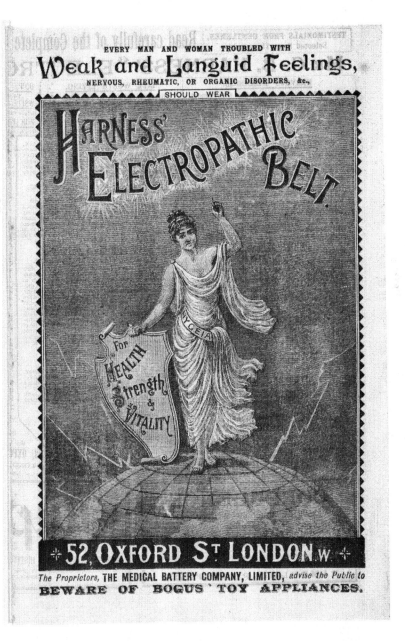

Fig. 3-10. Harness' Electropathic Belt for Health, Strength, and Vitality, from the John Johnson Collection at the Bodleian Library. (Reproduced with permission from Oxford University.)

Fig. 3-11. Harness' Electropathic Belt for Suffering Men & Women, from the John Johnson Collection at the Bodleian Library. (Reproduced with permission from Oxford University.)

Fig. 3-12. The Modern Perseus and Andromeda, *The Illustrated London News*, February. 14, 1885. (Reproduced with permission from the British Library.)

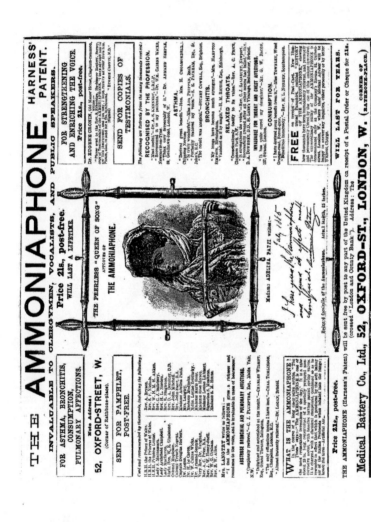

Fig. 3-13. The Ammoniaphone, *The Illustrated London News*, June 11, 1887. (Reproduced with permission from the British Library.)

# A Home Remedy!
## THE ELECTROPOISE.

 IN curing or greatly alleviating actual disease, especially chronic cases of Rheumatism, Indigestion, Nervous Disorders, Neuralgia, Insomnia, Paralysis, Liver and Kidney troubles and the like, the **Electropoise** has won its way, succeeding often where all else has failed. But it is also an invaluable and unequalled tonic and builder up of a system generally run down without being afflicted with any special malady. You should have one if only for the promotion of sleep and the assimilation of food, for the benefit of the general health. No family should be without an **Electropoise**.

ORDINARY METHOD OF USE.

## SIMPLE!—SAFE!—NOT A BATTERY!—NO SHOCK!

☞ Any Intelligent Person can apply it. ☜

The **Electropoise** achieves its remarkable results by its action on the blood current, causing an equal distribution throughout the body, relieving congestions and supplying those parts where the blood is deficient. It promotes the process of nutrition in every part of the body, gives life and vitality through the blood, causing the system to absorb an extra amount of nature's own great vitaliser—

## PURE ATMOSPHERIC OXYGEN.

*April 1896*

Fig. 3-14. A Home Remedy! The Electropoise, from the John Johnson Collection at the Bodleian Library. (Reproduced with permission from Oxford University.)

Fig. 3-15. Dr. Richardson's Magneto Galvanic Battery, from the John Johnson Collection at the Bodleian Library. (Reproduced with permission from Oxford University.)

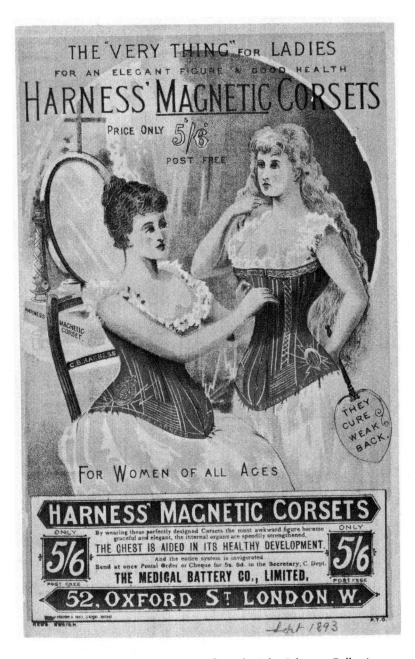

Fig. 3-16. Harness' Magnetic Corsets, from the John Johnson Collection at the Bodleian Library. (Reproduced with permission from Oxford University.)

Fig. 4-1. IME's Mechanical Exercise Machine, from *The Electrician*, 20
September 1889. (Reproduced with permission from *The Electrical Review.*)

Fig. 4-2. Harness' Electropathic Belt, from the John Johnson Collection at the Bodleian Library. (Reproduced with permission from Oxford University.)

Fig. 4-3. Harness' Electropathic Belts, from the John Johnson Collection at the Bodleian Library. (Reproduced with permission from Oxford University.)

Fig. 4.4. A group of nurses at the Medical Battery Company, *The Graphic*, February 13, 1892. (Reproduced with permission from the British Library.)

## FLEXION OF THE FOREARMS. (*Active.*)

Fig. 4-5. Flexion of the Forearms (Active), from *Mechanical Exercise: A Means of Cure* (London: J & A Churchill, 1883), p. 10. (Reproduced with permission from the Wellcome Library, London.)

SHAMPOOING MACHINE FOR THE ARMS. (Passive.)

Fig. 4-6. Shampooing Machine for the Arms (Passive), from *Mechanical Exercise: A Means of Cure* (London: J & A Churchill, 1883), p. 66. (Reproduced with permission from the Wellcome Library, London.)

VIEW SHEWING DR. ZANDER'S MACHINES.

Fig. 4-7. Harness's Zander Machines, from *Swedish Mechanical Exercise*, Medical Battery Co. Ltd., 1889. (Reproduced with permission of the British Library.)

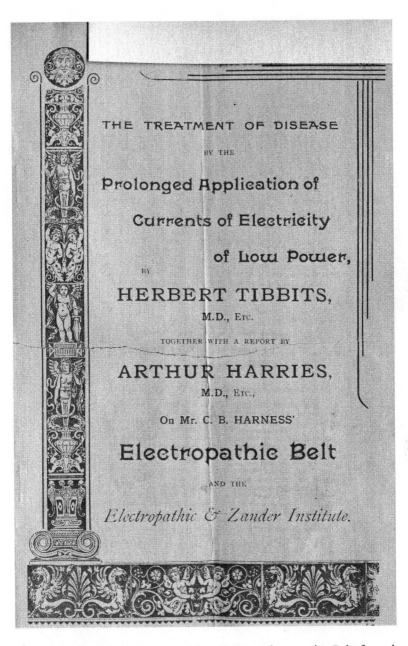

Fig. 4-8. Herbert Tibbits' testimonial to Harness' Electropathic Belt, from the Royal College of Physicians, MSS., 2411/94. (Reproduced with permission from the RCP, London.)

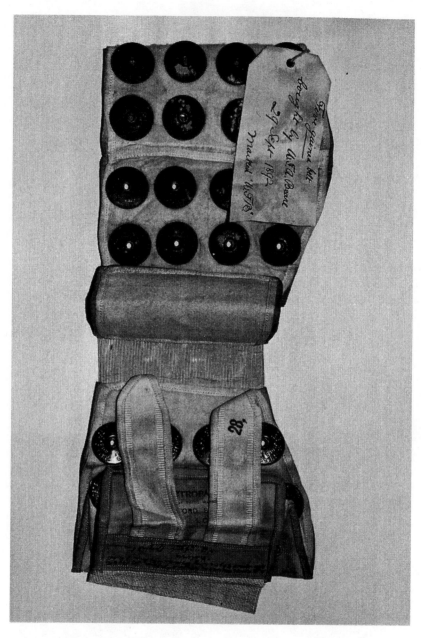

Fig. 4-9. Harness' Electropathic Belt presented to the court as evidence, from the Public Record Office, Deposition J17/283. (Photographed by the author, with permission from the P.R.O.)

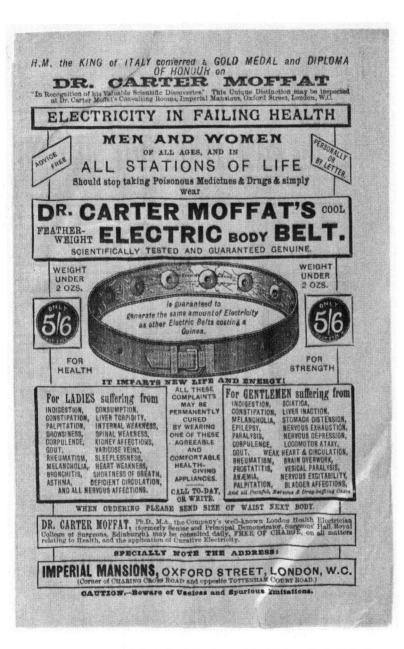

Fig. 4-10. Dr. Carter Mofatt's Cool Featherweight Electric Body Belt, from the John Johnson Collection at the Bodleian Library. (Reproduced with permission from Oxford University.)

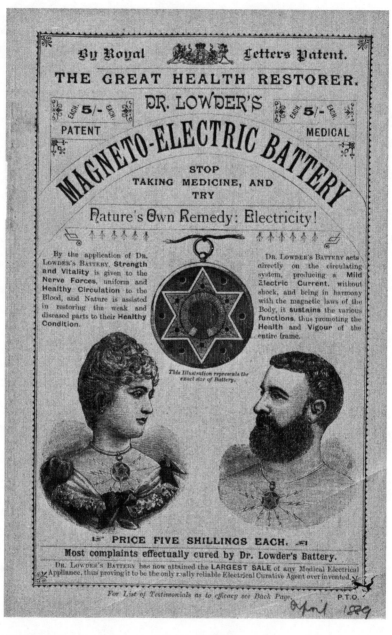

Fig. 4-11. Dr. Lowder's Magneto-Electric Battery, from the John Johnson Collection at the Bodleian Library. (Reproduced with permission from Oxford University.)

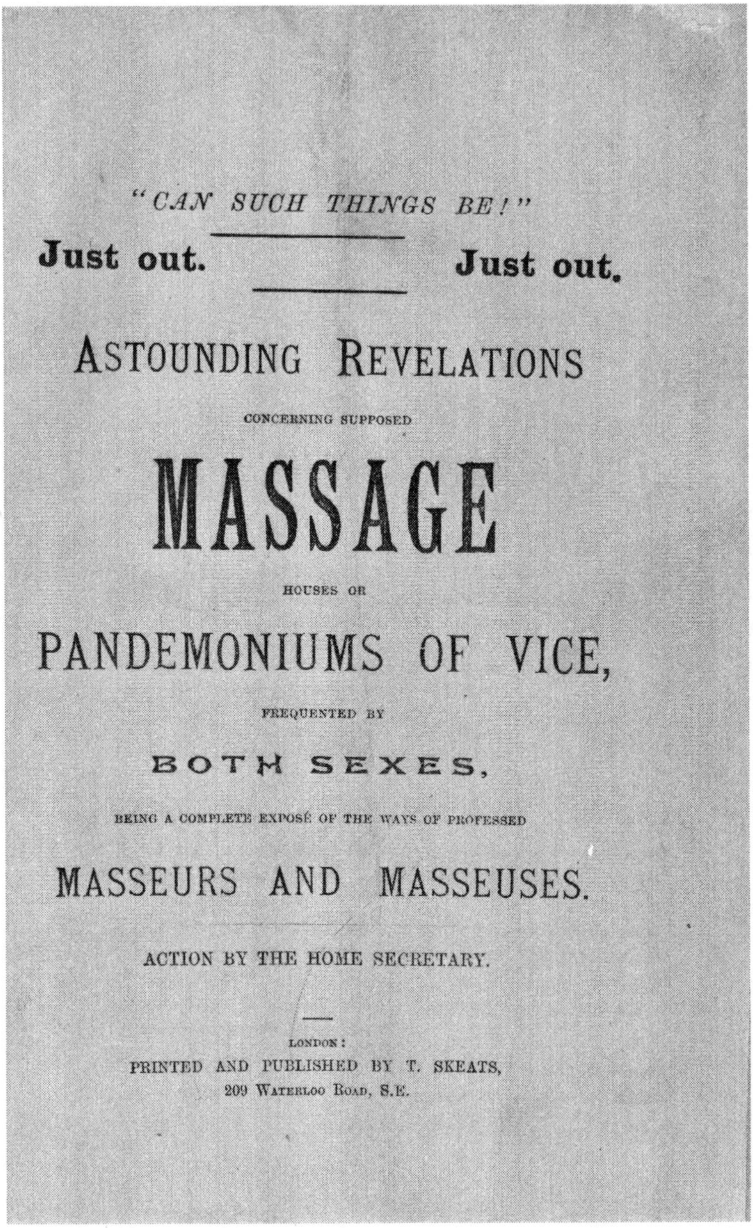

"*CAN SUCH THINGS BE!*"

Just out.     _____     Just out.

ASTOUNDING REVELATIONS

CONCERNING SUPPOSED

# MASSAGE

HOUSES OR

PANDEMONIUMS OF VICE,

FREQUENTED BY

BOTH SEXES,

BEING A COMPLETE EXPOSÉ OF THE WAYS OF PROFESSED

MASSEURS AND MASSEUSES.

ACTION BY THE HOME SECRETARY.

_____

LONDON:
PRINTED AND PUBLISHED BY T. SKEATS,
209 WATERLOO ROAD, S.E.

Fig. 5-1. "Astounding Revelations Concerning Supposed Massage Houses or Pandemoniums of Vice," from the Wellcome Institute Archives, SA/CSP/P1/2. (Reproduced with permission from the Wellcome Library, London.)

## PARLIAMENTARY BILLS COMMITTEE.

# MEMORANDUM ON THE MASSAGE QUESTION.

On November 14th the Home Secretary intimated that he considered that the steps which should be taken to check the abuses which it had been shown in the Journal had grown up in connection with certain massage establishments was a matter suitable for private conference, and added that it was possible that the law required amendment.

Shortly afterwards, Dr. Donald Macalister received a communication from Dr. R. Anderson, one of the Assistant Commissioners of the Metropolitan Police, with whom he is on terms of private friendship, suggesting a conference. In consequence, a conference took place between Dr. Anderson, Dr. Macalister and Mr. Costelloe, Barrister, who was acquainted with all the circumstances and had all the documents in his hands. In the course of this conference Mr. Costelloe pointed out that with reference to certain of the offences suspected to have been committed provision was made in the Criminal Law Amendment Act, and that in other cases an indictment might lie at the common law for conspiracy to promote immorality. Dr. Anderson, without disputing this position, pointed out that even if the difficulties of obtaining legal evidence could be overcome, a prosecution, even if successful, would only affect certain of the worst cases, and would only have the further effect of giving warning to the keepers of such irregular massage institutions of the exact lengths to which they might go. The question of dealing with such institutions as disorderly houses was also considered, but this course did not commend itself either to Dr. Anderson or Mr. Costelloe.

The general outcome of the conference was the expression of the opinion that the best course to adopt with a view of checking the abuses brought to light, and others known to exist, was, with the assistance of several Members of Parliament, including representatives of members of the profession in the House of Commons, to frame and put forward a

Fig. 5-2. "Parliamentary Bills Committee: Memorandum on the Massage Question," from the National Archives, Mepo, 2/460. (Reproduced with permission from the National Archives.)

CHAPTER 5

*Massage Therapy, Sexuality, and the Commercialization of Medicine*

On July 14, 1894, one of Britain's leading professional medical journals, the *British Medical Journal* (henceforth *BMJ*), then edited by a reform-minded propagandist, Ernest Hart, began to run a series of columns disparaging "Immoral Massage Establishments." These columns shockingly reported that massage establishments mushrooming in the West End and the City of London were hotbeds of vice, where innocent girls, dreaming of being professional masseuses, were expected to be "agreeable" to the gentleman clients.[1] According to the *BMJ*, many proprietors, opening their massage shops "with little capital," advertised in fashionable daily papers, such as the *Morning Post* and *Daily Telegraph*, "for half-a-dozen young lady assistants to do work." These proprietors, mostly women, called themselves "Madame," and their advertisements for massage customarily announced "that Madame X., assisted by Nurses Y. and Z. receive patients daily at some addresses within easy reach of clubland."[2] In some establishments "the lady assistants are

---

[1] *British Medical Journal:* "Immoral 'Massage' Establishment," 2 (July 14, 1894): 88–89; "Immoral Massage," (July 21 1894): 145–146, 148; "The Massage Scandal," 2 (July 28, 1894): 235; "Immoral Massage Establishments," 2 (August 4, 1894): 291; "Massage Establishments," 2 (August 25, 1894): 445.
[2] "The Scandal of Massage: Report of the Special Commissioners of the British Medical Journal, No. 1," *British Medical Journal*, 2 (November 3, 1894): 1003–1005.

commended to the public by the significant addition [of] 'fresh staff'" while other houses advertised the employment of "a page boy" masseuse.[3] Many massage shops used advertisements, the *BMJ* noted, to lure staff by promising to train girls who wanted to be a professional masseuses. Although these girls were recruited as professional nurses, their remuneration was nominal and they were expected "to accept presents from the customers, who pay the principal from half-a-guinea to two guineas for each visit."[4]

The massage parlors for their part proclaimed the bona-fide character of their "treatments," but such assertions made little headway once the *BMJ* published a column exposing the existence of "establishments where the name of massage is but a thin disguise for another business [that] is a matter for police."[5] Very often inside a massage room, the *BMJ*'s column reported, "general" massage applied by a woman to a man easily crossed the line into immoral conduct, but even more surprisingly, rich women's excursions to male masseurs were also prevalent. The massage scandal was soon recognized by journalists as revealing one of the seamiest sides of urban life. An influential conservative magazine, *Truth*, admonished: "This is a proceeding which we would like to taboo utterly and as regards all other forms of massage we would like to keep sex to sex."[6]

This series of massage scandals closely resembles similar public exposés about sexuality and poverty in late-Victorian society. W. T. Stead's 1885 "Maiden Tribute," Andrew Mearns's 1883 *Bitter City of Outcast London*, and James Greenwood's 1866 "A Night in a Workhouse" together revealed the shocking underbelly of Victorian London: the existence of urban poor crowded together in appalling conditions; the prevalence of vice and violence; and the metropolis's hidden sex life.[7] For example, W.

---

[3] Ibid., 1004.
[4] Ibid., 1005.
[5] "Organised System of Vice," *Truth*, July 18, 1894.
[6] "Immoral Massage," *British Medical Journal*, 2 (July 21, 1894): 146.
[7] On Mearns, see Gareth Stedman Jones, *Outcast London: A Study in the Relationship between Classes in Victorian Society* (Oxford: Clarendon Press, 1971). On Stead, see Raymond L. Shults, *Crusader in Babylon: W. T. Stead and the Pall Mall Gazette* (Lincoln: University of Nebraska Press, 1972); Deborah Gorham, "'The Maiden Tribute of Modern Babylon' Re-Visited," *Victorian Studies*, 19 (Spring 1976): 353–

T. Stead, as the editor of the *Pall Mall Gazette*, issued a series of sensational stories that documented in lurid detail how poor girls were trapped and forced to work as prostitutes in London's West End. Over a period of several weeks, Stead and the "Secret Commission" of the *Pall Mall Gazette* masqueraded as clients while visiting one of these ignominious establishments. Stead published his "findings" as a dramatic unfolding of the ongoing sexual vices of the city in a series entitled the "Maiden Tribute of Modern Babylon." Stead's stories revealed the ways in which Victorian gentleman victimized young girls, and he used his journalism to arouse public condemnation. In a similar exposé, James Greenwood, also of the *Pall Mall Gazette*, famously infiltrated the eroticized underworld of Victorian London. Having been inspired by Ernest Hart's investigations into workhouses in London, Greenwood disguised himself as a homeless man and spent a night in a men's casual ward of a workhouse. Based on his undercover reporting, he suggested the putative sexual practices of homeless men.

As the proliferation of such texts suggests, the last decades of the nineteenth century witnessed a marked upsurge of social anxiety over sexual immorality and, as a result, a proliferation of social-purity movements that attempted to suppress unscrupulous "social evils" and "social diseases." Emerging in the 1870s and the 1880s, vigorous social-purity organizations such as the National Vigilance Association tapped a deep vein of public anxiety about perceived sexuality immorality. Previously, the Society for the Suppression of Vice put pressure on the government to pass the Obscene Publications Act, which became law in 1857. Influenced by such movements, in 1885 Parliament passed a long-delayed Criminal Law Amendment Act, which, by raising the age of consensual sex for girls from thirteen to sixteen, attempted to provide a legal basis to prosecute brothel-keepers as well as suppress male homosexual behavior.[8]

---

379, and Judith R. Walkowitz, *Prostitution and Victorian Society: Women, Class, and the State*, (Cambridge: Cambridge University Press, 1980). Regarding Greenwood's "A Night," there is much literature on the topic, but the following work by Seth Koven on the homoerotic dimension of this sensational exposé is singularly informative: Seth Koven, *Slumming: Sexual and Social Politics in Victorian London* (Princeton and Oxford: Princeton University Press, 2006).

[8] For the background to Victorian anxieties about sexuality and social-purity

These manifestations of Victorian morality presupposed an ideological separation between private and public spheres in urban life: modesty in the domestic domain as opposed to libertinism in public circles; and a seemingly established gentlemanly morality on the one hand and the promiscuous masses on the other. But Stead's dramatic accounts, uncovering the hidden vices of the rich, successfully revealed the two-faced morality of the Victorian age and ultimately led to the questioning of a long-standing hypocritical demarcation between "private morality" and "public vices." Hidden inside "diabolical" dens were the private vices and profligate sexual lives of Victorian gentlemen—activities that signaled the intermingling of private and public spheres.

Although the scandals surrounding massage therapy were furiously debated by medical professionals at the time, modern social historians of crime and sexuality as well as historians of medicine have yet to explore the medico-social context that brought massage therapy into the public gaze, and the historical significance of this. One reason for this neglect is that unlike other exposés, the massage scandal emerged from a therapeutic technique long practiced in the closed world of medical professionals. Moreover, even after the scandal became national news, its documentation was scattered among a plethora of newspapers and periodicals, making it difficult for historians to grasp the overall picture.

More importantly, historians' failure to explore such a significant and tantalizing scandal arguably owes much to the common, Whiggish assumption that the medical profession was strongly united in its desire to eliminate such an immoral and deceptive use of a legitimate medical treatment. Indeed, medical historians have customarily associated the transformations in nineteenth-century medicine with the rise of professional society. For example, they have argued that the movement for professional reform in the first half of the nineteenth century made it possible to distinguish categorically between regular practitioners and

---

movements, see Lucy Bland, *Banishing the Beast: English Feminism and Sexual Morality, 1885–1914* (London: Penguin Books, 1995); Frank Mort, *Dangerous Sexuality: Medico-Moral Politics in England since 1830* (London and New York: Routledge & Kegan Paul, 1987); Jeffrey Weeks, *Sex, Politics, and Society: The Regulation of Sexuality since 1800* (London and New York: Longman, 1989); and Ian Gibson, *The English Vice: Beating, Sex, and Shame in Victorian England and After* (London: Duckworth, 1978).

fringe quacks—who were gradually marginalized and nearly extinguished from medical practice.[9] Throughout the chapters of this book, I have stressed the inadequacy of this simplifying view of the medical profession, which, I believe, loses sight of substantial divergences within the practice of medicine. Britain's late-nineteenth-century medical scene was not an orderly, established professional sphere, but in fact a capitalistic public marketplace in which qualified practitioners vigorously competed with quacks for patients and their approval, as well as for the profit that came from providing various kinds of medical services. To put it another way, in the late nineteenth century, a gray zone emerged between old-fashioned, self-promoting quacks and gentlemanly professional doctors. Intra-professional struggles—highlighted by the historian Jeanne Peterson and fully investigated by the sociologist Andrew Abbott—drove not a small number of practitioners to adopt profit-seeking strategies that were questionable enough to be called "quackish."[10]

Indeed, the difficulty of making clear demarcations between legitimate and illegitimate practices in Victorian medicine underlines the significance of the massage scandal among other public exposés. When Henry Labouchère, the editor of *Truth* and a militant prosecutor of social vices, followed the *BMJ*'s lead and called massage therapy "an organized system of vice," he clearly understood what was at stake.[11] Recognizing the depraved character of the burgeoning massage business, Labouchère had hesitated to bring it to public prosecution mainly because "from the nature of the case it is almost impossible to obtain witnesses in support of specific allegations against particular individuals or particular establishments." Labouchère's difficulty in finding witnesses was not only the result of clients' desires for privacy, but also a conse-

---

[9] Noel and José Parry, *Rise of the Medical Profession* (London: Croom Helm, 1976); Magali Larson, *The Rise of Professionalism: A Sociological Analysis* (Berkeley: University of California Press, 1977); William Reader, *Professional Men: The Rise of the Professional Classes in Nineteenth-Century England* (London: Weidenfeld & Nicolson, 1966).

[10] M. Jeanne Peterson, *The Medical Profession in Mid-Victorian London* (Berkeley: University of California Press, 1978); Andrew Abbott, *The System of Professions: An Essay on the Division of Expert Labor* (Chicago: University of Chicago Press, 1988).

[11] "Organised System of Vice," *Truth*, July 18, 1894.

quence of massage parlors having disguised their businesses as bona fide medical practices. But because the *BMJ* had condemned massage therapy as a new social evil, the journal opened the way for muckraking journalists to expose the "inward" malpractice of medicine. Labouchère wrote, "This is a real evil, and tends to whittle away the boundary line between propriety and impropriety, if not immorality. . . . Against that evil it is the duty of the medical profession to guard us. It is a good sign that the *British Medial Journal* partially recognises this duty by suggesting the registration of qualified massage practitioners, and though the writer discovers a good many difficulties in the way, they will hardly strike the unprofessional reader as insurmountable."[12]

What aspect of this new medical technique, touching upon a vulnerable area of medical practice, most troubled medical doctors? Though some decried massage treatments simply as a non-medical practice, by no means was it the case that all medical doctors rejected massage as a legitimate medical therapy. The question then arises: Was the campaign against massage a necessary step to completing the professionalization of medicine in the nineteenth century?

In response to these questions, I would like to suggest that the medical profession in the late nineteenth century cannot be viewed as a simple monolithic structure. Rather, a great diversity of economic and occupational standings can be found in the "gray zone" of practitioners between what Margaret Pelling has described as the "remote and gentlemanly investment in land or consols" and the "desperate and ungentlemanly selling [of] pills and ointments."[13] This chapter focuses on the wider economic and social circumstances that encouraged doctors to adopt a range of occupational behaviors while also protecting them from the vulgar commercial gaze of those who aimed to make money under the aegis of professional medicine.

The four sections of this chapter address the above questions. The first section explores the medical and scientific writings on massage therapy and explains why the medical profession was involved in the

---

[12] Ibid.

[13] Margaret Pelling, "Medical Practice in Early Modern England: Trade or Profession?," in Wilfred Prest, ed., *The Professions in Early Modern England* (London: Croom Helm, 1987), 118.

massage scandal. Massage techniques and their academic credibility were introduced from Continental Europe by young and ambitious non-elite doctors. This section discusses how massage therapy was first welcomed in British medical circles as a supplementary technology to electro-thera-peutics. Like electro-therapy, it was supposed to stimulate the workings of the muscles and blood circulation and produce beneficial effects in the body. Particularly because of the fashionable concept of neurasthenia, massage therapy was legitimated and received wide public recognition.

The second section introduces various narratives about the massage scandal as presented in the *BMJ*'s series of four in-depth reports and sets up the historical background of the chapter. To understand why mas-sage therapy was censored by medical professionals, the section analyzes the following two issues: first, that massage therapy suggested a possible parallel between the doctor's healing hands and the seducer's sexually arousing hands; and second, that doctors who provided "certificates" to dubious massage parlors were jeopardizing the professionalism of medi-cal practitioners. In exploring these issues, this section also provides further historical context.

The third section analyzes the process by which massage techniques were increasingly accepted among medical doctors as a viable form of treatment. In focusing on Thomas Stretch Dowse and Lauder Brunton, influential popularizers of massage therapy, this section explores how qualified doctors helped to make massage respectable and how this new-found legitimacy allowed profit-seeking doctors and entrepreneurs to enter the newly emerging domain of public therapy, in some cases by establishing massage institutions and schools.

The final section functions as an extended postscript that explores responses to the massage scandal. Massage turned out to be a profitable niche for doctors and businessmen alike, which induced an angry exposé not only by established doctors within the British Medical Association, but also by journalistic antagonists who wanted to eradicate social evils. The furious campaign of new journalism eventually opened the way for the intervention of state authorities such as Scotland Yard and Parlia-ment. This section ends with the discussion of the Criminal Law Amendment Act to regulate massage establishments and the formation of a professional British Massage Association and its successor, the Chartered Society of Physiotherapy.

The previous chapter, looking at the incursion of electro-therapeutics into medicine, shows the ways in which an arcane medical practice attracted a new entrepreneurial spirit that saw medicine as an arena for profit. Professional ethics were thus jeopardized by the commercialization of medicine earlier and more often than historians have hitherto supposed. The episodes and debates treated in the present chapter supplement this argument by focusing on another new medical technique, massage therapy, which originated from and had close connections with electro-therapeutics. What we shall see is that in reality the strong power of market forces was permeating a seemingly secure bastion of established medical orthodoxy, opening up new possibilities for financial gain by blurring the distinction between the false claims and unethical practices of erotic massage and the medical efficacy of doctors' healing hands. Once again we see the emergence of a form of vigorous medical capitalism.

### Electro-Therapeutics, Neurasthenia, and Massage

In December 1886, Lady Janetta Manners' article on "Massage" for the magazine *Nineteenth Century* popularized massage therapeutics in England. Although massage first flourished in the Orient and Rome, the recent popularity of the "Swedish Movement Cure" by Peter Ling and the rumors concerning Dr. Metzger's successful, crowd-drawing massage treatments in Amsterdam made "rubbing the spine" and "friction with pine oil" sound like a new healing art.[14] Julius Althaus, an eminent author in the field of medical electricity, called it the "Cinderella of therapeutics."[15] Massage therapy suddenly drew much attention not only from the public but also from professional doctors seeking alternative therapeutic methods for the treatment of nervous disorders, which were increasingly diagnosed in the last half of the century.

Beginning in the 1880s when massage techniques were gradually legitimated in British medical culture, a flood of publications on the theory and techniques of massage practices permeated the medical market

---

[14] Janetta Manners, "Massage," *The Nineteenth Century*, December 1886, 824–828.

[15] Julius Althaus, "The Risk of Massage," *British Medical Journal*, 2 (1883): 1223–1224.

Although requiring no mechanical devices or instruments, the techniques of massage shared with electro-therapeutics a definite technical setting, not only because it was approved of by British medical electricians, but also because its central nature was as a mechanical technique that worked externally on the human body through skilled application of the operator's hands—which in the view of electro-therapists played the same role of extended stimulant as any machine. Interestingly, similar to medical electricity, massage also caused professional problems for some doctors and created a hotbed of more serious, potentially criminal scandals. What was central in this controversy was the process of legitimation whereby massage therapists sought a foothold in British medicine, and the strategies of resistance by traditional medical practitioners who resisted this incursion.

Although Lady Manners was the popularizer of the term "massage," it was in fact William S. Playfair who introduced the practice into Britain. Both a professor of obstetric medicine at King's College and an obstetric physician at King's College Hospital, Playfair imported into the British medical world the famous "rest cure" invented by Silas Weir Mitchell, an American neurologist who focused on women's nervous diseases, and in so doing first authorized the massage practice upon which Mitchell's method heavily relied.[16] In his successful 1877 book *Fat and Blood: and How to Make Them*, Mitchell described his rest cure as requiring the total isolation of patients, thorough bed rest, and good diet. In addition, he recommended the massage and electrical stimulation of fatigued muscles and nerves.[17] Mitchell explained that the success of treatment lies in "certain methods of renewing the vitality of

---

[16] To Althaus's warning against thoughtless introductions of massage, which had "become as thoroughly fashionable as mesmerism and homeopathy have been at previous period in the history of medicine," Playfair immediately replied "as one of the first in this country to draw special attention to the use of this therapeutic agent," and wrote that "massage is a thoroughly scientific remedy based on good physiology and sound common sense." W. S. Playfair, "To the Editor of the BMJ: The Risks of 'Massage,'" *British Medical Journal*, 2 (1883): 1306–1307.

[17] Weir Mitchell, *Fat and Blood: And How to Make Them* (Philadelphia: J. B. Lippincott Company, 1877); *Fat and Blood: An Essay on the Treatment of Certain Forms of Neurasthenia and Hysteria* (Philadelphia: Lippincott Company, 1898).

feeble people by a combination of entire rest and of excessive feeding, made possible by passive exercise obtained through the steady use of massage and electricity." He is probably best known today for treating the famous American feminist Charlotte Perkins Gilman, who was psychologically torn between the still-strong "domestic role" of Victorian women and her own desire to reject these values. Mitchell recommended that Gilman have total bed rest and isolation from her entire family and all social activities—an exceedingly harsh treatment. Gilman's *The Yellow Wallpaper* was said to have been written to suggest to Mitchell that his therapy was trapped by the dominant gender assumption that women should be domestic and submissive, and Gilman hoped Mitchell might change his method by reading it. However, Mitchell's book, first published in America in 1877, soon acquired in Britain and parts of Europe medical admirers who had treated—particularly in their women patients—mental disorders with such symptoms as nervous exhaustion, hysteria, anemia, anorexia, and the like. By the 1880s, both American and British neurological writers began to identify neurotic women from their hysterical, restless, and anorexic conditions. By prescribing Mitchell's rest cure for his own patients, Playfair quickly became Mitchell's most enthusiastic and persistent promoter in Britain.

In his 1883 book *The Systematic Treatment of Nerve Prostration and Hysteria*, Playfair found this new rest-cure treatment, combined with massage and electrical stimulation, to be well adapted for treating the functional disorders of neurotic women.[18] His typical patient was "the worn and wasted, often bedridden woman, who has broken down, either from some sudden shock" or from some other cause, and who may have experienced "coincident with this . . . the total loss of appetite, the profound amæmia, and the consequent wasting of the tissues."[19]

By the mid 1880s in Britain, the practice of massage was gradually acquiring recognition as a valuable therapy, especially as treatment of nervous maladies. In particular, when the American neurologist George Beard's all-inclusive concept of neurasthenia was imported and employed in the British medical vocabulary, massage became acknowledged

---

[18] W. S. Playfair, *The Systematic Treatment of Nerve Prostration and Hysteria* (London: Smith, Elder & Co., 1883).
[19] Ibid., 72.

as one of the most feasible remedial treatments, when combined with, and used as, a complementary technique to electro-therapy. Whereas the latter's physical effect was considered to be mostly instrumental in giving a tonic effect to atrophied nerves, "charging" the weakened nervous system, in the treatment of neurasthenia the combination of massage and electro-therapy was recommended as working effectively in tandem. Together they comprised what was called in Britain the "Mitchell-Playfair method."[20] In this context, massage was regarded as a legitimate medical treatment. Mitchell himself wrote in his *Fat and Blood*, "The firm grasp of the manipulator's hand stimulates the muscle, and, if sudden, may cause it to contract sensibly, which, however, is not usually desirable or agreeable. The muscles are by these means exercised without the use of volitional exertion or the aid of the nervous centres, and at the same time the alternate grasp and relaxation of the manipulator's hands squeezes out the blood and allows it to flow back anew, thus healthfully exciting the vessels and increasing mechanically the flow of blood to the tissues which they feed."[21]

Neurasthenia was not only a new name for nervous breakdown, collapse, and prostration, but it also represented a new attempt by mid-Victorian medical doctors to standardize contemporary medical terminology. Before the 1880s, a great number of different terms, observations, and etiologies were given of widely known phenomena such as mental depression, loss of nervous energy, and other nervous disorders. Physical and mental symptoms earlier associated with melancholy, hysteria, and hypochondria had long been explained on a variety of causal grounds. From the eighteenth through the mid-nineteenth century, hypochondria (a term with origins in Greek medicine) described any kind of neurotic loss resulting from nervous disorders. Alienists such as Henry Maudsley used terms like "exhaustion" or "prostration" to argue that a person's amount of nervous energy was supplied from the central nervous system, consumed in intellectual activities, and was of "a definite and not inexhaustible quantity."[22]

---

[20] Clifford Allbutt, "Neurasthenia," in Clifford Allbutt and Humphry Davy Rolleston, eds., *A System of Medicine* (London: Macmillan, 1910), 8: 727-791, 778.

[21] Weir Mitchell, op. cit., 89.

[22] See Janet Oppenheim, *"Shattered Nerves": Doctors, Patients, and Depression in*

Given this jumble of terms and ideas about mental disorder, the new diagnostic term "neurasthenia" was welcomed by the British medical establishment as a more helpful and clinically specific term. Some authoritative die-hards such as Sir Andrew Clark lamented the adoption of this new terminology, on account of it "violat[ing] a fundamental canon in the framing of a scientific nomenclature, [which] is, in the order of science, an unpardonable sin."[23] Nonetheless, neurasthenia was to be found in the headings of most books on nervous disorders from the 1880s through the early twentieth century.

The concept of neurasthenia was most applicable to mental disorders of city dwellers. Beard's definition of it as a "deficient quantity and impaired quality of nerve force," or as "the impoverishment of nervous force resulting from imperfect metamorphosis of nerve tissue," was based on the commonly shared notion among late-nineteenth-century physicians that human nerve energy was limited and exhaustible. The mental manifestations of neurasthenia, they believed, appeared when the consumption of nerve force exceeded the supply from the central nervous system.[24] Because nervous force was consumed not by physical exercise but by activities of the brain, neurasthenia was considered a disease of civilized, rather than savage or backward, people. Attributing its extrinsic cause to modern city life dominated by stressful and restless brain work and the forced repression of the emotions, Beard and other medical writers tended to root the appearance of neurasthenia in the laws of evolution.[25]

Moreover, Beard argued, "If we know what a nation eats, we know what a nation is or may become." Thus in his view the person at the top of the social hierarchy should "diminish the quantity of cereals and fruits, which are far below him on the scale of evolution, and increase the quantity of animal food, which is nearly related to him in the scale of

---

*Victorian England* (Oxford: Oxford University Press, 1991), particularly Chapter 3.

[23] Andrew Clark, "Some Observations Concerning What Is Called Neurasthenia," *Lancet*, 2 (1882): 1–2.

[24] George M. Beard, *Sexual Neurasthenia (Nervous Exhaustion): Its Hygiene, Causes, Symptoms, and Treatment, with a Chapter on Diet for the Nervous* (New York, 1884), 36.

[25] George M. Beard, *American Nervousness: Its Causes and Consequences, a Supplement to Nervous Exhaustion (Neurasthenia)* (New York: G. P. Putman & Son., 1880).

evolution."[26] Although Beard termed neurasthenia the "American Disease," signaling his view of American society as the most technologically evolved civilization, European doctors looked less at America as an evolutionary forerunner than at the brutal competition in American manufacturing and commercial circles. The "Desire to 'get up higher,' not alone for their own sakes, but for one's descendants," and "the fear of political, financial, and commercial crises," H. V. Ziemssen, a German neurologist argued, was generating this "American Disease" nowhere "on so extensive a scale as in the United States."[27] Even in Europe the nineteenth century was seen, in Thomas Clifford Allbutt's words, as "a century of stress and of unsatisfied desires" in which "the struggle for life has revealed itself in naked and brutish forms."[28] Beard's terminology, rooted in the most stressful and nervous aspects of life in America, would soon, however, prove all too applicable to other countries.

Precisely because neurasthenia as a disease of the civilized presupposed a hierarchy among humans and the workings of evolution, hereditary and racial predispositions were seen as important elements. Some people, as Alfred Shofield put it, "are born nervous; that is, they are born with the nervous system unduly predominant, less under control, less orderly in its action than in other people."[29] Medical opinion in the Victorian and Edwardian eras subscribed heavily to theories of biological determinism, and a biological pessimism rooted in Lamarckian warnings of degenerate characteristics being passed to next generation, along with fears of nervous degeneration causing national deterioration, were widespread among the educated public. Subsequent eugenic observations raised the specter of more ominous racial prejudice and discrimination. Ziemssen, for example, emphasized that the "semitic race is especially inclined to neurasthenia. . . . Obstacles and difficulties in the ordinary course of events are overcome

[26] Ibid.

[27] H. von Ziemssen, "Clinical Lectures on Neurasthenia and Its Treatment," trans. by Edmond J. McWeeney, in *Clinical Lectures on Subjects Connected with Medicine and Surgery*, by various German authors, 3rd. ed. (London: New Sydenham Society, 1894), 57.

[28] Clifford Allbutt, "Nervous Diseases and Modern Life," *The Contemporary Review*, 67 (1895): 210–231.

[29] Alfred T. Shofield, *Nerves in Disorder: A Plea for Rational Treatment* (New York and London: Funk & Wagnalls, 1903), 135.

by the Jew with astonishing energy and good sense, but an emotional depression, an illness in the family, may utterly paralyse him."[30]

Just as the catch-all concept of neurasthenia encompassed a range of
various, if seemingly related, symptoms, so a variety of different intellectual tools were employed to make neurologists' arguments appear fashionable and to link them to the contemporary scientific discoveries.
Late-nineteenth-century medical doctors were eager to borrow concepts
or language from other established fields of the natural sciences. As we
have seen, evolutionary theories of inheritance were no doubt common
property: for example, in his writings, Beard made frequent remarks especially on the Spencerian theory of evolution and dissolution.[31] Besides
their biological language, however, those writers who attempted to explain neurasthenia from hard naturalistic and mechanical perspectives
had in their minds, even if not articulated, a metaphorical language that
connected the law of conservation of energy with the electrical nature of
nervous impulses.

In 1880, for example, in his work *On Brain and Nerve Exhaustion (Neurasthenia)*, Thomas Stretch Dowse, one of the most enthusiastic writers
on neurasthenia in Britain and an ardent promoter of massage therapy,
applied the Maxwellian concept of "conservation of energy" to account
for the exhaustion of nervous energy. He argued that "in the inorganic
world the material and energy were indissolubly associated," because
materials such as atoms and molecules were "nothing more nor less than
a material form of energy."[32] He regarded the forces or energy of affin-
ity and cohesion between atoms and molecules as constituting their
power of resistance, which made it possible for the material to sustain its
original form. In applying this argument to nervous forces or energy, he
conjectured that just as the reduced condition of inorganic resistance
produced the destruction or transformation of a form of material, so a
weakening of man's power of resistance—that is, his nervous force or

---

[30] Ziemssen, op. cit., 59–60.

[31] George Beard, "The Case of Guiteau—A Psychological Study," *Journal of
Nervous and Mental Diseases*, 9 (1882): 112.

[32] Thomas Stretch Dowse, *On Brain and Nerve Exhaustion (Neurasthenia): Its Nature and Curative Treatment, a Paper Read Before the Medical Society of London* (London: Baillière, Tindal and Cox, 1880), 4.

energy—could analogously lead to ill health. In a nutshell, Dowse argued, "whatever may be the precise nature of nervous energy, it is, I think, apparent that it governs and controls all other forces that [in] health and even life itself are preserved."[33]

The properties of electricity were also used as a metaphor to explain neurasthenia. The physical symptoms of this disease—including irritable mental weakness, sick headache, vague pains, spinal irritation, and spasmodic deficiency—were explained by an analogy between resistance in electricity and the resistance of a similar current-carrying nerve force throughout the body. Rudolf Arndt, a German contributor to Tuke's *Dictionary of Psychological Medicine*, argued that in the state of fatigued or degenerated nerves of neurasthenic patients,

[T]he nervous excitability as such is decreased, but nevertheless appears at first increased on account of the greater capacity of conduction in consequence of the decreased resistance; this exaggerated excitability still increases, at first rapidly, thereby producing painful and spasmodic symptoms.[34]

Physical pains, he insisted, appear when a decrease of resistance hindered the control of an appropriate amount of the substance's entry into the nerves; neurasthenic ailments, in short, were caused by over-excitability in the nerves. He went on to say that the power of resistance depended upon "good nutrition"—that is, not only on muscular apparatus, but on molecular composition as well.[35]

Other writers, too, focused on diet. Thomas Savill, for example, believed that since "a purely vegetarian diet lowers the nutrition of the body generally, and especially the neuro-muscular apparatus," the deficiency of nervous force seen in cases of neurasthenia was often associated with problems of nutrition and diet.[36]

When applied to neurasthenic patients, electro-therapeutic treatment mostly aimed to contribute "nutritious" effects to the blood, peripheral

[33] Ibid., 6.
[34] Rudolf Arndt, "Neurasthenia," in D. Hack Tuke, ed., *A Dictionary of Psychological Medicine, Giving the Definition, Etymology, and Synonyms of the Terms Used in Medical Psychology* (London: J. & A. Churchill, 1892), 840–850, 842.
[35] Ibid., 843.
[36] Thomas Savill, op. cit., 47n.

nerves, and central nervous system. By the 1880s, "nutrition" had become one of the central therapeutic objects of electricity's physical,
chemical, and physiological effects. For example, according to Beard
and de Watteville, the physical effect of "a weak current that causes no
muscular contraction" produces a "thermal effect" on the body that
promotes the circulation of blood and lymph. Among the physiological
effects, de Watteville explained, were "vaso-motor effects" of electric
current, which "when applied to the nervous trunks or centres containing vasomotor nerves . . . increased circulation due to their dilatation" of
the blood vessels.[37] Emphasizing the galvanic current's "electrolytic,
endosmotic, and thermal effects," Hugh Campbell pointed out that
"electric currents have a marked effect on the blood, and on its circulation, and also powerfully influence nutrition."[38]

It was mainly through this belief in a "nutritious" effect, I would like
to emphasize, that electricity and massage were seen as complementary
therapeutic techniques for the remedy of neurasthenia. As will be shown
in the third section, the technique of kneading or rubbing muscles
gradually became a viable medical practice largely because many respectable physicians devoted themselves to ascertaining scientifically its nutritious effects in broadening the blood vessels and enhancing tissue respiration. Thus the scientific gateway by which massage entered British
medicine was by way of the related elements of fashionable neurasthenia, the concept of nervous force, and electro-therapeutics.

### The Massage Scandal of 1894

#### The British Medical Journal's Exposés

A few months after publishing several warnings against the prevalence of "immoral massage parlours," the BMJ's allegations grew into a
furious exposé campaign when its editor convened an investigative team
of "special commissioners," ostensibly consisting of Dr. Donald Macali-

---

[37] A. de Watteville, *A Practical Introduction to Medical Electricity with a Compendium
of Electrical Treatment form the French of Dr. Onimus* (London: H. K. Lewis, 1878),
35.
[38] Hugh Campbell, *The Anatomy of Nervousness and Nervous Exhaustion (Neurasthenia),* 4th. ed. (London: Henry Renshaw, 1890), 103.

ster, Dr. R. Anderson, and Mr. Costelloe, the Barrister employed by the British Medical Association.[39] This team conducted a secret investigation of the inside affairs of the massage shops which subsequently led to the *BMJ*'s publishing a series of reports entitled "The Scandals of Massage: Reports of the Special Commissioners of the 'British Medical Journal'" on "immoral massage parlours." The commissioners' description of the dens' interiors was so vivid that only a direct quote can convey its documentary flavor. According to the first report, published on November 3, 1894, most of the establishments were flats of four or five rooms whose entrances were guarded according to various arrangements for privacy.

> As the visitor enters, an electric bell rings automatically and he will find himself received in a well furnished room by a lady of middle age, with a certain capable air of respectability. She will make no inquiry as to his name, and probably none as to his complaint. He will be invited, with little loss of time in preliminaries, to adjourn to a room luxuriously furnished, where he will find a bed or couch spread with blankets. He will be informed, unless it is assumed that he knows it already, that the terms are for an hour a guinea, but that he can stay as long as he pleases by the same rate. In some instances it will be suggested to him that it would be a good thing to have a bath first and the massage afterwards. It will be assumed, as a matter of course, that he intends to have "general massage," that he will want a young lady to do it, and that he will undress completely.[40]

On November 10, the second report by the commissioners appeared in the *BMJ*, which turned to spotlighting the way in which petty capitalists camouflaged massage brothels with medical trappings. In these establishments, the clients were mostly gentlemen but were described as not being "persons reduced by illness to a hospital bed; they are men for

---

[39] See the document prepared by British Medical Association's Parliamentary Bills Committee, "Memorandum of the Massage Question," held in Public Record Office, London, Mepo 2/460.

[40] "The Scandals of Massage: Report of the Special Commissioners of *The British Medical Journal*, No.1," *British Medical Journal*, 2 (November 3, 1894): 1003–1004.

most part fresh from the clubs, and very often not only full of health, but full of wine. They come upon no kind of medical prescription, and, indeed, with no pretence that their object is genuine medical treatment or that they are suffering from any complaint which requires it. They walk in and order 'general massage' in the same fashion as they might order a Turkish bath." It is perhaps no wonder that the Turkish bath parlors where all the attendants were attractive young women would incur the same suspicion of serving as venues for sexual improprieties. Surprisingly enough, the report alleged, "not only is the client treated by the so-called nurse in a condition of nudity, but the two are left deliberately alone for as long a period as the gentleman chooses to pay for."[41] In one parlor, the article went on to describe,

> [T]he gentleman is supposed to lie down on a bed or couch and cover himself with a blanket, but as often as not he does nothing of the kind. Where there is a bath, the lady attendant calmly attends upon him all the time, and he lies down and has the massages applied to him immediately afterwards.[42]

The report continued by introducing the correspondence of one of the commissioners who narrated vividly what went on inside one of the massage dens. "It was," the commissioner reported, "a more pretentious establishment, and things were conducted on a more lavish scale. I was introduced to the proprietress, who was called 'Madam' in the advertisements, but who appeared to be more familiarly known as 'Boss.'" He explained to her that he was suffering from a slight rheumatic affliction in his joints. The Madam was very sympathetic and assured him of immediate relief after adopting her system for a while. "She thought that a *Bain de Luxe* would be appropriate," the commissioner continued,

> [B]ut when I told her that I preferred massage, she assured me that it would do equally well. I was shown into a cosily-furnished room in which Madam left me, telling me that I would find it

---

[41] Ibid., 1069.

[42] "The Scandals of Massage: Report of the Special Commissioners of *The British Medical Journal*, No. 2,'" *British Medical Journal*, 2 (November 10, 1894): 1069–1070; "Report of the Special Commissioners, No. 3," *British Medical Journal*, 2 (November 17, 1894): 1140–1141.

more convenient if I would completely undress, assuring me that the correct principle, and the only one followed in the establishment, was complete general massage, with the special massage of the affected part. I followed her instructions and in a few minutes was visited by a gracefully attired young lady, who performed general massage, and made herself generally agreeable. I had some conversations with her, from which I gathered that three or four assistants, all young women, were trained by Madam, and that they had to work from 10 in the morning till 7 in the evening.

The report of the commissioner continued to describe an episode during his next visit to the same establishment. In meeting the proprietress, he asked to be served by the same woman who had previously looked after him. The proprietress suggested that he take a bath in addition to receiving a massage. "She took me upstairs to a room furnished with a bed or couch, and having a bath in an anteroom. She herself prepared the bath, and told me to undress and get in. In a few minutes she returned, and remained talking to me for some minutes whilst I was in the bath, explaining that the young lady would be with me in a few minutes." Moreover, when instructed to enter into the bath, he was astonished to discover that "no dress and no bathing costume of any kind were produced, and the patient was evidently expected to expose himself fully to the gaze of the attendant." Later, when the young attendant arrived, she "proceeded to wash my face and soap my arms and legs and thighs, and finally my back. After a few minutes of desultory conversation she helped me out of the bath, and without any attempt [to cover me] laid me on the couch and repeated the massage as before. I remained for about an hour, and at the expiration of my visit offered her a small present." He found that the young attendants were living largely on presents or tips and that their salaries were very small. The proprietress, he explained, "pays them next to nothing, and leaves them to make their own arrangements with the gentleman patients in the way of tips, while she reaps a rich harvest from the stated fee."[43] In the lively and vivid narrative based on this commissioner's actual experiences, the style of the *BMJ's* articles was much less typical of a professional journal

---

[43] Ibid., 1070.

than of sensational journalism. But by using this technique in the first
two reports, the *BMJ* was certainly successful in highlighting—not just
to its own members, but to the larger audience of respectable society—
the mushrooming problem of London brothels falsely masquerading as
legitimate massage establishments.

*The Touch of Massage: Eros and Healing*

Obtaining complete legitimacy had long been problematic for medical practitioners. For professional purposes, doctors were privy to many
of the most personal problems of their patients, an experience that rendered them especially sensitive to the boundaries between legitimate and
illegitimate behavior. Like priests' confessionals or lawyers' offices, physicians' consultation and examination rooms were regarded as private
and confidential settings. Unlike with other professions, however, the
doctor's office was a space in which the most private of spheres was—
and had to be—unveiled in a semi-public light: doctors' hands were
permitted to touch the bodies of the patients who stripped themselves
mentally and bodily before the profession's legitimate authority.

The outrage of the medical profession against massage parlors in
1894 was remarkably fierce: massage raised questions about the most
sensitive aspect of the profession, since it blurred the dividing-line between legitimate medical treatment and techniques of sensual arousal
and pleasure. The 1894 scandal was an abomination to those who
sought to further legitimate the medical profession precisely because
medical massage relied "naturally" and inevitably on the direct contact
of the therapist's hands on the patient's body within a private space.

In particular, touching, an obviously essential technique for medical
massage, was bound to evoke a sexual association. As Ashley Montagu
has interestingly shown, the sense of touch on the skin is "the mother of
the senses" and acquired in the earliest stage of the development of the
human embryo. Montagu writes that "tactual sensitivity, however, reap-
pears more strongly than ever at puberty or shortly thereafter, and becomes a major need-objective, to touch and to be touched, not merely
as an impersonal sensory stimulation, but as a symbolic fulfillment of
the search for intimacy, acceptance, reassurance, and comforting or, in

some who have been failed, a continual avoidance of such contact."[44] Indeed, scientific writings about massage and massage therapy enthusiastically referred to the technique of gentle touching. Douglas Graham, for example, wrote that in "the principal seat of the sense of touch, there is no sensation that can be felt by the skin so delightful as that arising from the contact of the hands in properly done massage."[45]

In many theories and manuals on massage, the hands of the person giving the massage were often described as important physical instruments, essential to producing the desired delicate touch. "The perfect hand for massage work," wrote Thomas Stretch Dowse in *The Treatment of Disease by Physical Methods*, "should be soft, smooth, dry and fleshy and of good normal healthy temperature."[46] According to J. K. Mitchell, "Great manual strength is not necessary, though a hand not too small is desirable; but very large and muscular hands lack the delicacy of touch which is so desirable."[47] Elsewhere, A. Symons Eccles insisted that "physical conformation and muscular development of the hands should be broad and fleshy: the skin being smooth, the muscles, both of the fingers and palm, firm and resilient."[48] Through being touched by such skilled hands, Douglas Graham concluded, "the patients will often delight in almost being lifted up by the skin, like one of the agile domestic animals."[49]

This therapeutic use of massage techniques, however, also invoked in the late Victorian imagination a suspected association of massage with sexuality. As Sander Gilman illustrates in his discussion of the social construction of touch, by the early nineteenth century touch came to be asso-

---

[44] Ashley Montagu, *Touching: The Human Significance of the Skin* (New York: Columbia University Press, 1971), 171–172.

[45] Douglas Graham, *A Treatise on Massage: Its History, Mode of Application and Effects, Indications and Contra-Indications* (Philadelphia: J. B. Lippincott Company, 1902), 78.

[46] Thomas Stretch Dowse, *The Treatment of Disease by Physical Methods* (Bristol: John Wright, 1898), 53.

[47] J. K. Mitchell, "Massage, Physiology, and Therapeutic Indications," in Allbutt and Rolleston, eds, *System of Medicine*, 2nd ed., (London: Macmillan, and Co., 1908), 1: 422–434.

[48] A. Symons Eccles, *The Practice of Massage: Its Physiological Effects and Therapeutic Uses* (London, Macmillan, 1895), 12–13.

[49] Douglas Graham, *A Treatise on Massage*, 78.

ciated with the irrational, unreflective "libido."[50] But if massage became associated with sex in the Victorian public's imagination, it cultivated a sphere of sexuality without intercourse and ejaculation, a sphere that focused on arousal through the soft, erotic touch on sensitive skin. Thomas Stretch Dowse's odd description of "moral massage," by which he meant the effect of the operator's spirit and intellect on the patient being rubbed, was thus central to the therapy: "The moral massage is both inductive and seductive . . . it works seductively, inasmuch as it leads astray by a process of delicate, and, to the sufferer, misleading manipulations, which are of courting, wooing, and coaxing character."[51]

This association between massage and Eros, and between a doctor's healing hands and a seducer's sensual touch, posed a potentially dangerous dilemma for the medical profession. The *BMJ*'s furious exposé of massage parlors reflected the inevitability of an association between even legitimate massage and sexuality. Massage shops, the *BMJ* reported, competed in advertising their number of good looking "lady assistants." "Young men about town often make a tour of these establishments," the *BMJ* went on to say, and "It has become a fashionable fad for certain ladies of position to frequent the rooms of a young and good-looking masseur."[52] As massage was gradually legitimized as a viable medical technique, medical doctors themselves noticed that this new therapy made problematic a delicate area of their practice, just as the Victorian public often regarded gynecology as dubious. "Massage of the uterus again," the *BMJ* wrote, "is a proceeding which, with all respect to those gynecologists who have advocated it as a method of treatment, we cannot help regarding with the extremest suspicion and dislike."[53] As a way to avoid all charges of impropriety against the medical profession,

---

[50] Sander L. Gilman, "Touch, Sexuality, and Disease," in W. F. Bynum and Roy Porter, eds., *Medicine and the Five Senses* (Cambridge: Cambridge University Press, 1993); idem, *Goethe's Touch, Seeing, and Sexuality* (New Orleans: The Graduate School of Tulane University, 1988).

[51] Thomas Stretch Dowse, *The Modern Treatment of Disease by the System of Massage: Three Lectures on this Subject Delivered at the West End Hospital for Nervous Disease, Paralysis, and Epilepsy* (London: Briffith, Frran, Okeden, & Welsh, 1887), 49.

[52] "Immoral 'Massage' Establishments," *British Medical Journal*, 2 (July 14, 1894): 88–89.

[53] "Immoral Massage," *British Medical Journal*, 2 (July 21, 1894): 145–146.

the *BMJ* urged a prohibition of women massaging men and vice versa:

> [T]o order a woman to apply "general massage" to a man, suffer-
> ing perhaps from nothing worse than restlessness and insomnia, is
> either to be contemptuously indifferent to the self-respect, and
> perhaps even the good conduct of the masseuse, or to neglect that
> element of sex which is present in human affairs, and which re-
> fuses to be ignored.[54]

As the *BMJ* knew altogether too well, the intermingling of genders was
precisely the point in commercial massage parlors. It therefore seemingly imagined that maintaining strict separation of the sexes would be
one way to demarcate legitimate medical massage from non-legitimate
sexual massage. It was to discover to its chagrin, however, that maintaining such lines of demarcation were far from easy, since maintaining a
professional distance from commercial massage was the last thing on
some doctors' minds.

### *The Legitimacy of Massage: Doctors' Certificates*

If the medical profession in general was most disturbed by the sham
use of a medical technique to mask illicit sexual practices, what the
commissioners found most censurable from a professional point of view
were the certificates granted by qualified physicians on behalf of the
masseurs and masseuses. The *BMJ*'s third and fourth reports, published
on November 17 and 24 respectively, focused on the doctors' certificates, which helped the massage establishments to openly continue their
businesses. In one of the establishments, a Madam's framed certificate
signed by a physician was hung on the wall as a diploma; and "nurses"
also described themselves as being "a certificated London hospital masseuse," or as having the "highest English medical certificate" obtainable
from a massage school.[55] The *BMJ*'s reason for this last concern was
chiefly professional: the journal felt that the doctors who provided certificates not only had blameworthy pecuniary interests at heart, but were

---

[54] Ibid.
[55] "Report of Special Commissioners, No. 3," *British Medical Journal*, 2 (November 17, 1894): 1140.

also guilty of fostering immorality. The *BMJ*'s position was abundantly
clear on this: it lamented that "under the cloak of a useful form of medical treatment the grossest immorality should be practised, that under the
guise of 'massage establishments' houses, not unfortunately of ill fame
but of equally evil morals, should be publicly advertised, and that under
the pretence of teaching massage girls should be introduced to an immoral life."[56] The *BMJ* turned a blind eye to the fact that Madams sometimes advertised themselves as offering certificates to resident assistants
or boasted of their own licensing at institutions of dubious quality—for
example, one Madam described herself as having qualified in massage at
the "Kensington School of Massage and Electricity." What deeply dis-
tressed the *BMJ* was the existence of a gray zone in which qualified doctors engaged in commercial ventures that could arouse public suspicion
or be viewed as dubious: this was a very serious matter, likely to jeopardize the standing of the medical profession itself.

The doctors most often pilloried by the *BMJ* were Thomas Stretch
Dowse and Herbert Tibbits.[57] The *BMJ* reported that Dowse had signed
certificates of proficiency in massage as an acknowledged expert in the
field, while Tibbits' West-End School had been issuing "hospital certificates." The advertisements for this school appeared in the *Morning Post*
as follows:

> At the WEST-END SCHOOL of MASSAGE AND ELECTRICITY, Wey-
> mouth Street, Portland, Place (established 1886), Students are
> Trained and Hospital Certificated and Masseurs, Masseuses, and
> Electricians attend private patients. PRIVATE LESSONS also are
> GIVEN, especially in Face Massage.[58]

"This establishment," the BMJ warned, "now prefers to describe itself
boldly as 'The Massage Hospital,' and . . . we believe there is no real
hospital in London where any such certificate is to be had. With this
enterprise Dr. Herbert Tibbits is intimately connected; and we have before us a reply which he wrote to a recent application from a lady who

---

[56] "Immoral Massage," *British Medical Journal*, 2 (July 21, 1894): 145.
[57] "Report of Special Commissioners, No. 3," *British Medical Journal*, 2 (November 17, 1894): 1141.
[58] Ibid.

was anxious to procure a 'certificate' with the least possible expenditure of time and money."

As the *BMJ*'s investigation showed, Tibbits' school was just the tip of the iceberg. The *BMJ* noted that there were many similar institutions attracting lots of young women who dreamed of becoming professional masseuses. Tibbits himself warned against less than reputable institutions in a remark on one of his school's advertisements: "Ladies' maids and others entirely without medical training or any medical supervision, established themselves as 'masseuses,' and advertised that they gave lessons and 'granted' certificates." Tibbits explained that his school, by contrast, offered a systematic education: students attended three or four days weekly, learning practical techniques of massage, and other subjects like physiology, pathology, and anatomy of the human body, together with electro-therapeutic technologies.

What the *BMJ* was most concerned about was the difficulty of maintaining clear lines of demarcation between legitimate and non-legitimate establishments and schools. "Massage has its proper place in medical treatment," the journal noted, "and the healing art will suffer if it falls into permanent discredit."[59] The professional medical men feared the influence of market forces, and they believed that a proliferation of bogus establishments and schools and harsh competition among them would stain the reputation of medical massage for healing. The *BMJ* described the deleterious influence of the market as follows:

> [L]arge number of such girls have, in the desperate hope of obtaining a respectable living, scraped together a fee of, say 10 guineas, and attended a course, and taken out a certificate, only to find in the end that there was no opening for them whatever, unless they were prepared to accept the repulsive conditions of such establishments as we have already described. It is, in fact, this monstrous overcrowding of the market which has made it so easy for the proprietors of undesirable establishments to carry on their trade.[60]

---

[59] "The Massage Scandal," *British Medical Journal*, 2 (July 28, 1894): 235.
[60] "Report of Special Commissioners, No. 4," *British Medical Journal*, 2 (November 24, 1894): 1199.

Both Dowse and Tibbits quickly refuted the *BMJ*'s accusations about their massage schools. Referring to his statement in *On Massage and Electrization*, Dowse defended his reputation and explained that he "had no connection with advertising Schools of Massage, Institutes of Massages, Agencies of Massage, or Home for Massage."[61] Tibbits in his letter to the editor impeached other schools run by "Ladies maids and others without medical training or any medical supervision." And in subsequent advertisements, he trumpeted the bona-fide qualifications of his school, such as having "Royal Patronage" and the support of the Dean of Lichfield. Moreover, Tibbits insisted on emphasizing the stringent standards of his school by claiming that "ten out of twelve students attend for three months and upwards, and . . . no student has ever passed [in] under one month." The *BMJ* simply replied to Tibbits' letter by saying that "It may be that some of the persons concerned have had a serious training in massage, but the public has no guarantee that in any individual instance this is to be assumed."[62]

### *The Making and Marketing of Massage Therapy*

#### *Massage as a Viable Medical Technique*

For those who were engaged in massage therapy in hospitals or marketing massage therapy to the public, Thomas Stretch Dowse's *Lectures on Massage and Electrization*, first published in 1889, was one of the most credible pieces of writing on the subject.[63] It was influential in making hitherto-discredited folk-healing more scientific and scholarly. In a number of the minor manuals on massage techniques that were published in the period, Dowse's text was frequently referred to as an accepted source on massage's physiological and anatomical effectiveness for the treatment of nervous diseases.

For medical doctors who had been excluded from the opportunities open to elite physicians with Oxbridge degrees, the new medical special-

---

[61] Thomas Stretch Dowse, *Lectures on Massage and Electrization in the Treatment of Diseases: (Masso-Electrotherapeutics)* (Bristle: John Wright, 2nd. ed., 1891, first published 1889), Preface.
[62] Ibid.
[63] Ibid.

ties such as medical electricity were frequently seen as a rewarding field. Such specialized, technical, and segmented practices, once regarded as quackish, began to attract medicine's favorable attention. Medical electricity in particular provided intellectual and financial possibilities for run-of-the-mill physicians attempting to make headway in the medical world. Dowse fell into this category. He obtained his MD from a less-elite medical school, the University of Aberdeen, and his career was in minor hospitals such as the North London Hospital for Consumption, the Hospital for Epilepsy and Paralysis, and the like. His career pattern was very similar to that of Herbert Tibbits, who, as we have seen, was ejected from the medical mainstream on the grounds that he had collaborated with Harness' company: both men concentrated their energies on fashionable diseases of nervous disorder; both preferred mechanical and technical modes of treatment (electricity and massage); and both undertook the supplementary strategy of publishing many books to enhance their reputations in the medical world. With so much in common, it is interesting but not altogether surprising to note that they became close colleagues at the West End Hospital for Diseases of the Nervous System, where they cooperated to create an affiliated school of massage to train nurses to be masseurs or masseuses.

Dowse's views on massage resonated with his interpretation of the law of conservation of energy. "Physical science," he argued, "has now ascertained that the phenomena with which it deals are only different modes of a common energy. Heat, light, electricity, magnetism, etc., are but different modes of motion produced under different constitutions, and they are all, either directly or indirectly, convertible into each other." Dowse believed that nature's potential energies, if they took the form of a material entity, would reveal themselves as substances—or if converted within the body, would be revealed as "the transformation of this potential energy into kinetic [energy] or otherwise." In other words, "life is transformed physical energy, and . . . energies of the animal frame, muscular, nervous, and so on, are resolvable into molecular force."[64] For Dowse, the medial mechanism that makes possible this transformation or exchange between material and energy was "metabolism": plants absorb and transform the kinetic energy of sunlight into potential en-

---

[64] Ibid., 3.

ergy, which animals—by eating, oxidizing, and metabolizing plants—re-transformed into the kinetic energy for their physical activities. By framing massage within this understanding of energy, Dowse highlighted its physiological value "in bringing about the oxidation and metabolism of tissues, and the conversion of potential into kinetic energy."[65] The influence of pressure, pinching, or petrissage movements (that is, putting force on living matter), therefore, was considered a technique that altered the molecular configurations and improved the metabolic activity of tissues.

Thus in Dowse's terms the insufficient nervous force in neurasthenic patients resulted from a malfunctioning of the metabolic mechanism that converted material into kinetic energy. What caused this metabolic defect, Dowse emphasized, was the lowering of nutrition that took place when blood failed to carry enough nutrient material and oxygen to nerve cells and tissues. Believing "that the value of massage depended upon its influence in promoting respiration of tissue," he argued that massage's therapeutic efficacy consisted in promoting metabolism by dilating vessels of "blood as a respiratory medium" whose red corpuscles absorbed oxygen and became oxyhaemoglobin.[66] Massage, he believed, possessed an "ability *which no other agent does possesses*, in restoring the nutrition and regenerating the growth of nerve and muscular fibre."[67]

Dowse argued that massage aimed not only to improve the nutritious environment of peripheral tissues and organs, but also, tracing a path from periphery to center, to stimulate "the dominant vaso-motor centre in the medulla oblongata [which] plays [the important part] in the great processes of nutrition, assimilation, and exertion."[68] Thus insofar as both aim to stimulate the peripheral organs or vessels, massage and electro-therapeutics originated from the same therapeutic model. Dowse argued that since

[T]he periphery of a nerve is a direct continuation of that centre. . . . [W]e are fairly and reasonably permitted to arrive at the conclusion that we can indirectly influence that centre, with regard to its

---

[65] Ibid., 7.
[66] Ibid., 21.
[67] Ibid., 84.
[68] Ibid., 16.

blood and nutritional supply, through its periphery, by those manipulation and galvanic processes.[69]

In Dowse's mind the value of massage was to convey the same peripheral effect that electricity did. Thus he combined the use of these
two tools in his effort to bring massage techniques into the scientific
domain. He advocated "electrical massage," "the method of applying
faradization by passing the current first through the body of the masseur."[70] In this procedure, the masseur put a large electrode on the ster-
num of a patient who was lying face down, and a smaller electrode was
fixed in the masseur's hand or on some other part of the patient's body.
Then the surface of the masseur's hand engaged in "effeuraging" "over
the surface of the back generally, up and down the spine," which,
Dowse argued, would provide refreshing stimulation "exceedingly useful
in all functional troubles of the spine, neurasthenia, hysteria" and so
on.[71] Through stimulation derived from the combination of electricity
and the masseur's touch, Dowse sought to achieve what was in effect a
scientifically legitimate revival of mesmerism.

The therapeutic path it established from the peripheral vessels and
organs to the central nervous system was commonly assumed as massage's remedial advantage. As Douglas Graham, the American advocate
of massage therapy, wrote, "appropriate stimuli such as massage and
electricity [exert] influence upon disturbances at their other ends in the
brain and spinal cord."[72] Following his own hypothesis that "literal wave-
like movements" transmitted the impulse for movements in the axis-
cylinder of nerve fibers, he insisted that "manipulation or deep-kneading
is to massage what the constant current is to electricity, and the ultimate
effects of each are very much alike."[73]

Massage was thus held to be very effective in improving blood nutrition and circulation, and this attracted the attention of scholars from

---

[69] Ibid., 86.
[70] Ibid., 229.
[71] Ibid., 230.
[72] Graham Douglas, *A Treatise on Massage: Its History, Mode of Application, and Effects, Indications and Contra-Indications* (Philadelphia: J. B. Lippincott Company, 1902), 78.
[73] Ibid., 116.

specialties other than neurasthenia who wanted to ascertain the scientific
utility of massage therapy. Lauder T. Brunton, a physician at St. Bartholomew's Hospital and one of the first great physician-scientists, began to perform extensive experiments on dogs and cats to estimate any
change in the amount of blood flowing through massaged muscles during and after massage. He devised special experimental equipment that
consisted of cannulas with large bulbs and short necks, which were inserted into an anesthetized animal's femoral vein; an air-pressurized
beaker filled with a solution of magnesium sulphite; and a long horizon-
tally placed tube. What he discovered was that compared with simple
bleeding, the flow of blood was increased during the massage of the
muscles, and that massage had the effect of accumulating blood, resulting in an increased post-massage yield. Brunton also estimated the effect
of massage on blood pressure by a mercurial manometer, showing an
initial rise of pressure during the massage, and then a gradual fall
throughout it.[74]

Though Lauder Brunton was mostly a laboratory-based scientist, he
was also very keen on therapeutic applications. Underpinning his *Lectures
on the Action of Medicine* was the Weir Mitchell Treatment, which had been
the subject of so many of Brunton's own experiments. He concluded
that massage had a twofold effect: it both brought fresh material and
fresh oxygen to the muscles by increasing the flow of blood, and
squeezed the waste products out of the muscle into lymph spaces.[75]
"The masseur or masseuse removes the waste-products from the muscles," he wrote, and "at the same time quickens the flow of blood
through them by kneading them so as to squeeze the lymph into the
interspace between the layers of the fascia."[76] Interestingly, Brunton understood the effect of improving nutrition by massage as identical with
"self-massage" mechanisms by the muscular movements of the heart,

---

[74] T. Lauder Brunton and F. W. Tunnicliffe, "On the Effect of Kneading Muscles upon the Circulation, Local and General," *Journal of Physiology*, 18 (1894):
364–377.

[75] T. Lauder Brunton, *Lecture on the Action of Medicine: Being the Course of Lectures
on Pharmacology and Therapeutics Delivered at St. Bartholomew's Hospital* (London:
Macmillan, 1897).

[76] T. Lauder Brunton, "On the Use of Rest in Cardiac Afflictions," *Practitioner*
51 (1893): 190–203.

which produced blood circulation by the constriction of its ventricles.[77] This mechanism also operated in "the arteries which run in the same sheath as the nerves [and] exercise a kind of massage upon them."[78] As Brunton saw it, massage was nothing less than a supplementary method of health maintenance that assisted the internal maintenance techniques performed by the autonomous nervous system.

With such therapeutic objectives, Brunton focused his attention on the physiological processes of digestion.[79] In his 1885 "Lettisomian Lectures on Disorders of Digestion," he compared man to a steam engine, and explained that in order for people to "run," they required oil, fats, and proteins "to repair the wear and tear of the tissues," and carbohydrates "like coal, supplying energy to the organism by their combustion." Brunton noted that disorders in digestion originating from improper cooking, a weak internal canal, or mental depression impeded the proper performances of three main functions necessary for health: tissue-change, removal of waste, and supply of new material.[80] For remedial treatment of indigestion, Brunton emphasized massage as "one of the most important methods and one which sometimes gives results little short of miraculous." Supplementing his lecture were two sets of engravings made from photographs of a Scottish man who had suffered from neurotic dyspepsia.[81] These photographs, which depicted the man before and after massage treatment—first as "a living skeleton," and then as a healthily recovered patient—became famous, and were widely circulated among those who wished to legitimate massage therapy.

Brunton's genuinely scientific examination of massage therapy was echoed throughout the late-nineteenth-century medical scene, which increasingly accepted the legitimacy of massage therapy. Inspired by Brunton's Lettisomian Lectures, Dr. Alexander Morison treated and

---

[77] T. Lauder Brunton, *The Therapeutics of the Circulation: Eight Lectures in the Spring of 1905 in the Physiological Laboratory of the University of London* (London: John Murray, 1908), 94–100.

[78] Ibid., 131–136.

[79] T. Lauder Brunton, "Digestion and Secretion," in Sanderson's *Handbook for the Physiological Laboratory* (London: J. & A. Churchill, 1873).

[80] T. Lauder Brunton, *On Disorders of Digestion: Their Consequences and Treatment* (London: Macmillan, 1886); from *British Medical Journal*, 1 (1885): 3–20.

[81] Ibid., 78.

cured a narcolepsy patient through massage, which ostensibly improved this patient's nutriment absorption and tissue-respiration.[82] Brunton's pupil, Arthur Symons Eccles, published a series of scientific evaluations of massage therapy. In a paper read at the Glasgow meeting of the British Medical Association in 1888, Eccles reported on his experiments showing changes in body temperature when the extremities of muscles and abdominal regions were kneaded: temperature changes were recorded in the axilla, palm, calf, sole, and rectum.[83] The result he obtained was that "as the auxiliary and surface temperature rose by massage, the internal temperature in [the] rectum falls, while the exactly opposite effect [was] produced by [massaging the] abdomen."[84]

Also well illustrated by Eccles' tracings of the pulse under massage was "the increase of amplitude of the ascending line with a more rapid fall after muscle-kneading." With these results he argued that muscle massage made blood move from the internal organs to the peripheral ones, causing blood vessels to dilate, blood flow to increase, and the rise in pulse rate to produce an increase in blood pressure. In another experiment overseen by Brunton on dogs' ingestion of salol, a white crystalline powder, Eccles demonstrated the effectiveness of massage in increasing absorption by estimating the amount of excreted salol in the urine. Supplementing a number of articles intended to make scientific claims about medical masssage, Eccles's 1885 book *The Practice of Massage* was dedicated to Brunton and included many records of experiments on the efficacy of massage in treating diseases such as rheumatism, indigestion, skin problems, and nervous system disorders. With these scientific claims and descriptions of massage therapy, the book became one of the most circulated manuals for professional masseurs and masseuses. Accepted by eminent physicians and scientists as well, massage had at last entered the respectable medical domain. What is more, with its seeming ease of application as a medical technique, its legitimation left it vulner-

---

[82] Alexander Morrison, "Somnolence with Cyanosis Cured by Massage," *Practitioner*, 42 (1889): 277–281.
[83] A. Symons Eccles, "The Internal and External Temperature of the Human Body as Modified by Muscle-Kneading: With Spygmographic and Sphygmomanometric Records," *British Medical Journal*, 2 (December 1, 1888): 1211–1214.
[84] Ibid., 1211.

able to certain forms of abuse—just as had occurred with medical electricity before it.

## Marketing Massage Therapy

Although massage had probably been practiced quietly by popular healers for some time, the efforts of many bona fide medical doctors in the early 1880s to validate this therapy scientifically effectively provided—or at least were seen as providing—a legitimate public space for massage therapy. The acceptance of massage therapy as a valid medical technique, however, opened a Pandora's box within the medical marketplace of the 1880s and 1890s. As we have seen with medical electricity and electro-therapeutics, profit-oriented pseudo-medical practices soon attempted to occupy this hitherto undeveloped niche of the medical sphere. The would-be "scientifically" trained masseurs and masseuses appeared in many quarters and set up their therapeutic businesses in so-called massage establishments, which advertised intensively in newspapers and other periodicals.

From the 1880s onward, the proliferation of schools for teaching massage techniques constituted a related gray-zone strategy of medical entrepreneurs. Although massage was a brand new discipline and no institutions or associations were officially entitled to issue massage certificates, the number of young women who wished to be credentialed in some way as masseuses dramatically increased between 1880 and 1890. In the same decade, a substantial amount of capital was unsurprisingly invested in the pedagogical domains of massage. Dr. John Fletcher, a medical electrician, opened the London School of Massage at Portland Place, and the "South Kensington School of Massage and Electricity," run by Mrs ——, was often advertised in newspapers and periodicals.[85]

Most noteworthy was the West End School of Massage and Electricity. Established in 1886 by Dr. Herbert Tibbits, the school opened at 55 Weymouth Street as an institution attached to the West End Hospital for Diseases of the Nervous System. At the new school, T. S. Dowse collaborated with Tibbits to create joint courses to teach electro-therapeutics and massage. Tibbits subsequently published the lectures he gave

---

[85] "The Scandals of Massage: Report of the Special Commissioners, No. 3," *British Medical Journal*, 2 (November 17, 1894): 1140.

at the school under the title *Electrical and Anatomical Demonstrations*, a
work that was designed as a companion textbook to Dowse's *Lectures on
Massage and Electrization*.[86] Running the school was no simple business.
In 1894 Tibbits boasted that the school's ex-students numbered 300 and
were residing in London, elsewhere in Britain, and in the British colo-
nies. At this time, student fees were £10 10s per term, which usually
lasted from three to six months. Students attended courses three or four
days a week; as one student recollected, they studied practical massage
techniques, received technical lectures on how to electrolyze local parts
of the body, and listened weekly to three ninety-minute lectures on anatomy, physiology, and the "Charcot suspension system." After passing
examinations on both massage and anatomy, students received hospital
certificates as masseuses. The school sometimes also acted as an intermediary to introduce patients to its graduates.[87]

The profit-seeking activities of these schools can hardly be identified
with those of avaricious quacks. This difference does not owe simply to
their being certified by qualified physicians; it derives also from their
capitalizing on the legitimate position of massage within the medical
world. In the gray zone where "pukka" doctors had to compete with
"ragtag-and-bobtail" quacks, what was most at stake was whether the
medical practice in question was legitimate or non-legitimate. Not surprisingly, the steady acceptance of massage therapeutics in the 1880s was
accompanied by increasing numbers of massage establishments, not all
of which were to appear legitimate or professional in the RCP's eyes.

More interestingly, as massage became acknowledged in the British
medical repertoire, massage techniques were gradually recognized as an
important component of nursing skills. In the late-Victorian and Edwardian periods, when professional opportunities for women remained
very limited, nursing was undoubtedly one of the more promising careers. Not surprisingly, nursing also became the target of business ventures. Judging from the advertisements in the *Medical Directory*, institu-

---

[86] Herbert Tibbits, *Electrical and Anatomical Demonstrations: Delivered at the School
of Massage and Electricity, in Connection with the West-End Hospital for Diseases of the
Nervous System, Paralysis and Epilepsy* (London: J. & A. Churchill, 1887).
[87] "Report of the Special Commissioners, No. 3," *British Medical Journal*, 2 (November 17, 1894): 1140.

tions established with the purpose of training resident nurses and providing them to wealthy families had become common in the early 1870s.
By 1885, Mr. D. E. Wilson's Hospital Trained Nurses had provided its
nurses to 4,000 families since its opening in 1867. Similarly, Miss Dean's
Mildmay Nursing program sent nurses for a fee of £1 11s to assist with
general diseases; and the Westminster Training School and Home for
Nurses (of which the Queen was patron and the Duke of Westminster
the Chairman) provided similar nursing services. In 1875, only three
institutions—the General Nursing Fund, Wilson's Institution, and the
Nightingale Fund—provided funding for the training of nurses; however, the number of training establishments for nurses dramatically increased, to eighteen in 1885, and then to thirty-three in 1891. The advertisements of these institutions in the Medical Directory, it is important
to observe, were gradually mixed in with those of schools for masseuses.
Many of them advertised that their nurses were trained as masseuses
expert in massage and electricity, or simply advertised themselves as the
suppliers of masseurs and masseuses as well as nurses.

The competition for profits from massage therapy soon expanded in
a more capitalistic venture. In August 1894, the American and Parisian
Massage Company, founded at 72 Guildford Street, circulated a prospectus to the newspapers soliciting public subscriptions to construct
medical centers "for the proper and scientific carrying out of the sciences and arts of massage and electricity" in the West End of London
and at Edinburgh, Brighton, Hastings, Bournmouth and other fashionable resorts. It promoted its plan to capitalize the company at £10,000 in
2,000 shares of £5 each by telling investors that they could expect to
"earn from £5,000 to £15,000 net profit yearly."[88] The directors of this
company were Dr. David A. Birrell, a licentiate of the Royal College of
Physicians and Surgeons of Edinburgh, and Mr. R. D. Jewell. The strategy they employed to give their capitalistic ardor a professional façade
appeared very similar to the strategy used by the Medical Battery Company and the Institute of Medical Electricity in their efforts to institute
group health care by employing physicians and skilled officers to super-

---

[88] "Massage (Limited)," *Medical Press*, July 25, 1894; "A 'Massage Company,'"
*British Medical Journal*, 2 (August 18, 1894): 377; "American and Parisian Massage
Company," *British Medical Journal*, 2 (September 8, 1894): 560.

vise treatments and by using unique medical techniques. The Massage Company's prospectus boasted that "an efficient staff of skilled assistants will be engaged for each branch of the business, under the superintendence of a duly qualified physician, who will be in daily attendance at the various establishments for consultation."[89] Though it is unclear whether Thomas Stretch Dowse was associated with this company, his definition of massage as "the application of sentient living matter to sentient living matter in multifarious ways" was quoted in the prospectus as if he had supported this corporate-style resort business.[90] The proprietor of this company sent a full-page advertisement for insertion in the *British Medical Journal,* which promptly—and with some suspicion— declined to publish the announcement.

With such commercial activities by both doctors and businessmen, the marketplace for massage enterprises soon became saturated. An anonymous writer to *The Family Physician*, probably Professor Playfair, stated in around 1882 that since "foolish women were induced to devote their savings to obtaining such instruction as was available, the market speedily became over-stocked, and much misery and disappointment resulted." The writer warned "young women who came up to London from the country in answer to attractively worded advertisements" to reconsider the marketability of massage.[91] The *BMJ*, reporting that the salary of "a thoroughly competent masseuse who could nurse and attend upon a young gentleman with paraplegia" was rapidly declining, wrote that in the overstocked market a masseuse would be regarded as a "person who not only has to make herself generally agreeable, but who will do anything and everything without question."[92] The appearance of this warning article coincided with the beginning of the massage sexual scandal in 1894.

---

[89] "Massage Limited," *Financial News*, August 17, 1894.

[90] Ibid.

[91] Anonymous (circa 1882), "Massage and Allied Forms of Treatment," in Marsh, ed., *The Family Physician: A Manual of Domestic Medicine,* New and Enlarged Edition (London: Cassel, Petter & Galpin, 1882), Chapter 25, 272–281.

[92] "The 'Massage Market' Overstocked," *British Medical Journal,* 2 (September 15, 1894): 628.

*Responses to the Massage Scandal*

*New Journalism*

A great irony emerged from the debate over the massage scandal of the 1890s. The *BMJ*'s reports constituted a voyeuristic and dramatic disclosure of hidden secrets and suggested a self-righteous war against social evils. This was new journalism—an approach that fueled the public appetite for more such disclosures. In discussing W. T. Stead's tactics in his "Maiden Tribute in Modern Babylon," Judith Walkowitz has elegantly described new journalism's formula for success since the 1870s: to pursue "that wealth of intimate picturesque detail, and that determination to arrest, amuse or startle."[93] Thus the massage scandal, ignited first by the *BMJ*'s professional anxieties but fueled by techniques of new journalism and the collusion of the entire British daily press, soon became national news. Massage's own problematic legitimacy, combined with its appeal to wealthy peoples' hedonistic pleasure—and associated with the prurient exposure of secret sexual seductions in bogus medical rooms—stimulated both the media's new journalistic ethos and its self-appointed mission to be the guardian of social morality.

For new journalism, the massage scandal was no ordinary news item to be publicly disrobed like other criminal cases. Several elements contained in this moral campaign, it should be emphasized, appealed to the imaginary landscape of the late-Victorian public's cultural fantasies about class behavior, the medical profession, and the sexual connotations of nurses' and doctors' consulting rooms. For this reason not only conservative media such as *The Truth* and *Whitehall Review* but also radical half-penny presses such as *Reynold's Newspaper*, *Lloyd's Weekly Newspaper*, and others joined in the emerging public debate over this social problem of the 1890s.

The first element fueling the journalistic fervor was that massage, now on the fringe of the medical world, was masquerading as legitimate therapy even as its medical operation was conducted "under semi-medical sanction." *The Morning* lamented, "The very nature of the operation is of such a strictly private character that it is highly improbable any

---

[93] Judith Walkowitz, *City of Dreadful Delight: Narratives of Sexual Danger in Late-Victorian London* (London: Virago, 1994), 84.

account of what takes place in the operating room would be made the subject of common conversation."[94] Thus the *BMJ*'s reports on this highly private subject were greatly welcomed by other journalistic media. The commentator in *The Truth*, which had called attention to the subject "now several months back," wrote that "the use and abuse of massage are professional questions which doctors are bound to face." He added that, "A medical journal having thus broached the subject, I feel bound to add my testimony to the gravity of the evil."[95] As massage therapy became more respected in the medical field, the assault on its legitimacy was the target of prodigious criticism by the new journalism.

What was needed to penetrate this medical camouflage was the disclosure of the "inside story," since, "although there was strong proof that immoral practices were carried on, there was not sufficient legal proof to bring the matter home to the proprietors."[96] For this reason papers published narratives of the goings-on in the massage parlors in the City and the West End that their representatives infiltrated.[97] One of the often-cited stories concerned a criminal trick to cajole young girls into the "most pernicious demoralisation."[98] A lady and her daughter, answering an advertisement in a daily newspaper recruiting massage pupils, made an agreement that £20 should be paid to the proprietress for the girl to receive instruction in massage treatment and board and lodging for six months. "After a few days residence in the home, the girl was told that she might, if she chose, try her skill upon one of the customers." In one of the gorgeously furnished rooms, her youthful hands were placed on an old gentleman of prominence, who in the course of the procedure suggested to her that lady assistants in massage establishments were expected to treat "friendly" customers in other ways. The only response the proprietress offered to the complaint of the enraged assistant was a cool warning to make herself agreeable, "as the others did." The local police, informed by the mother and daughter, visited the massage house without finding any positive evidence of wrong-doing,

---

[94] "Massage Secrets: Extraordinary Revelations," *The Morning*, July 17, 1894.
[95] "An Organized System of Vice," *The Truth*, July 18, 1894.
[96] "The Massage Scandals: Some Additional Facts," *The Morning*, July 14, 1894.
[97] *Today*, July 21, 1894; *The Morning*, July 15, 1894; *People*, July 15, 1894.
[98] "An Organised System of Vice," *The Birmingham Mail*, July 18, 1894.

except the proprietor's comment "that he did not know who the customer was against whom the complaint had been made."[99]

The *BMJ*'s initiative not only spotlighted dubious massage practices
but contributed to dissolving the psychological prohibition that popular
journalism had felt toward entering medicine's sacred space. For perhaps the first time, a medical practice was exposed for discussion in the
public sphere. In order to investigate whether "those engaged . . . in the
dubious branches of the business are certificated by medical men," the
*BMJ* sent a medical doctor to massage establishments, while *The Morning*
employed another representative, Thomas Maltby, who had worked as a
"massage practitioner of much ability and repute." In his interview with
*The Morning*, Maltby explained that massage "contains no fewer than 720
distinct and separate manipulations, each one having its own physiological action." Many would-be massage applicants who visited him with
"what is really a worthless certificate," he said, clearly lacked the knowledge of anatomy and physiology that bona fide masseuses possessed.[100]

Long before, Maltby had actually opened his own school of massage
and hypnotism at 1-2 Sloane Square, operating it with his wife, who
conducted massage cures through home visits and by receiving patients
there. After the interview with *The Morning*, Maltby wasted no time in
tapping the heightened journalistic interest to make his name better
known in the commercial scene.[101] He circulated his own fifteen-page
allegation against vicious massage dens, *Astounding Revelations Concerning
Supposed Massage Houses, or Pandemoniums of Vice Frequented by Both Sexes*
(Fig. 5-1). Its intent, mimicking W. T. Stead's new journalism, was ex-
plicitly "to publish facts—unsavoury though they be—and thus cause
official notice to be taken of Modern Babylon's latest development of
immorality."[102] The very strategy that Maltby learned from Stead was to

---

[99] "The Massage Scandals: Some Additional Facts," *The Morning*, July 14, 1894;
"London Massage Houses: Police Officer's Remarkable Statement," *People*, July
15, 1894; "Massage Scandals," *Today*, July 21, 1894.

[100] "Massage Secrets: Extraordinary Revelations," *The Morning*, July 17, 1894.

[101] See the other source of Maltby in "The 'Massage' Scandals," *Evening Herald
Post*, July 21, 1894.

[102] Thomas Maltby, *Astonishing Revelations Concerning Supposed Massage Houses, or
Pandemoniums of Vice Frequented by Both Sexes, Being a Complete Exposé of the Ways
of Professed Masseurs and Masseuses* (London: T. Skeats, n.d.), held in the Wellcome

position himself in the traditional political scene as a champion of work-ing-class people, and to worry aloud that "Christian England—especially the more aristocratic portion of it"—was becoming immoral. Drawing on other popular articles, he finally attributed the "moral nausea" aroused by the recent massage scandal to "aristocratic English vices." In the view of the popular press, rheumatic and other nervous ailments were diseases of the extravagant and the aristocratic, and it was in order to cure them that "above all, rich and titled people seemed to have a special craving for massage." Drawing an analogy between the Roman baths' degradation into places of "assignation for men and women" and "the deceiving massage institutions of London," Maltby thus concluded that ancient Romans "lived in ostentatious luxury and sensual indul-gence on the labours of the masses just as the 'gentleman of England' [do] to-day."[103]

Such views had ties with another belief exacerbated by the medical scandal: the old socio-political melodrama about aristocratic seducers ruining young and innocent working-class girls. In the daily press, the sensationalist landscape of the massage scandal was juxtaposed with the more political anxieties of a class-ridden society. "Something far more dreadful than the existence of these immoral massage establishments," the *Whitehall Review* scathingly noted, was that they were symbolic of Victorian double standards that celebrated private domestic virtues while accepting public profligacy.[104] Again and again crusading journal-ists likened massage parlors to the corrupt life of ancient Roman nota-bles: at fault was the desire for "sexual intercourse on the part of rich and aristocratic classes in 'Christian England,' . . . who lead in Society [but] who toil not, neither do they spin."[105] The similarity was striking, the radical *Reynold's Weekly* wrote:

> The country [ancient Rome] was owned by great landlords and deserted by the people, who flocked into big cities, just as we see to-day. Then the rich grew richer and the poor poorer, just as now. Then, as now, people paid a lip-homage to conventional

---

Institute Archives, SA/CSP/P1/2, p.1.

[103] Ibid., 13.

[104] "Immoral Massage," *Whitehall Review*, July 28, 1894.

[105] "Massage and Aristocracy," *Reynold's Weekly*, July 22, 1894.

moral and religious phrases, while disbelieving them in their hearts.[106]

Such suspicions also fed *fin-de-siècle* British fears of cultural degeneration. "The old silly superficial notion about our beautiful modern civilization" was in fact, the *Reynolds Weekly* observer noted, nothing but "that which sickens and disgusts us to-day"—hypocritical "gentlemanly" morality. Working people must resist such decadent morality: "The real aim of the working-class movement is not to make of every workman a copy of a 'gentleman' or of every workwoman a copy of the 'lady'."[107] In pursuit of this goal, aristocratic and other wealthy "ladies" were often admonished for their "shameless" patronage of bogus massage dens. Radical press commentary played upon working people's deep-seated prejudices about rich women's supposed sexual desire, caged in bourgeois domestic purity. "Ladies in fashionable society," it was confidently asserted, "actually frequent the rooms of young and good-looking masseurs."[108] Maltby in his pamphlet harshly ridiculed these leisured woman patrons "of middle age and in no way of good looking," who, pretending to be "demure," were introduced to "a well set-up and well toileted young masseur" by a so-called Madam. Knowing her customer's ailments were imaginary, the Madam would recommend "a strong hand," to which the lady would reply, "'If you please, I prefer a masseur' with hesitancy in her speech and with heart fluttering with pleasurable excitement." Thus, according to Maltby, she would become one of the Madam's best customers.[109]

The final factor sometimes highlighted in the anti-massage campaign was that professional practices by both doctors and nurses could have sexual connotations. To indicate their attractive qualities, as the *BMJ* early on reported, lady assistants in the massage shops were described by their pet names as "Nurse Dolly," or "Nurse Kitty." Thus the nurse's professional image, symbolic of the new woman acting independently of

---

[106] Ibid.
[107] Ibid.
[108] *Aspinall's Neigeline Society*, April 20, 1895, 310, in Wellcome Institute, CSP Archives, SA/CSP/P.1/2.
[109] T. Maltby, *Astonishing Revelations*, 8.

a man's economic power, became colored by sexual humiliation.[110] "Nothing is more honourable," the *BMJ* wrote with anger, "than the profession of a genuine nurse, and certainly no one would suggest in this Journal that mere questions of necessary exposure in the difficult and delicate business of nursing could be stigmatised as indecent."[111] The representative of the *Reynold's Weekly*, centering its condemnation on this abuse of the nurse's image, reported that massage shops were profiting by having assistants wear "when at work a costume of cap and apron, so as to look like a nurse."[112]

A second wave of the newspapers' crusade against massage parlors started on October 22, 1898. *Society*, a journal that had hitherto remained distant from the fray, published "How Nurses for Massage Dens Are Made," which—based on its representative's report—vividly revealed how proprietors recruited good-looking girls and obtained certification of them as nurses from doctors with "medical degrees granted by American institutions." It argued that Florence Nightingale's noble efforts to enhance the nurse's status were being jeopardized. The pureness of the nurse, "a calling in a spirit of beneficence rather than from a desire of gain," was being defiled by fraudulent practices. "'Nurse' is a word to conjure with, for it implies qualities of heart and head in every way commendable," *Society* wrote, but now "it is in the bogus massage establishments that the counterfeit flourishes in all its rank luxuriance."[113]

But the cultural fantasies of the press concerning the sexuality of massage were not confined to defending nursing's professional image. For the radical press, which sought to voice the concerns of the working class, the doctor's consulting room itself formed an authoritative, sacred, and very much private space, which was to be protected from the outsider's inspection. Intrusions on this space, the radical press insisted, were as heinous and as likely to cause serious scandal as violations of the

---

[110] "Report of Special Commissioners, No. 1," *British Medical Journal*, 2 (November 3, 1894): 1004.

[111] "Report of Special Commissioners, No. 2," *British Medical Journal*, 2 (November 10, 1894): 1069.

[112] "The Massage Scandals," *Reynold's Weekly*, August 12, 1894.

[113] "Massage Dens, Physician's Certificate: How Nurses Are Made Massage Certificates," *Society*, October 22, 1898. Newspaper cutting in the Public Record Office, Mepo 2/460.

priest's confessional. "In this best-of-all-possible worlds," the radical-conservative weekly *St. Paul* wrote, the eradication of the immorality that daily infiltrated choirs, vestries, and physicians' consulting rooms through human passions and human infirmities would require "calling upon authorities to sweep the clerical and medical professions off the face of the earth" and "every medical man keep[ing] a detective behind a screen in his consulting-room."[114]

*Authority's Action and the Formation of a Profession*

From the very beginning of its allegations, the *BMJ* had urged Scotland Yard to inspect and take action against the fraudulent massage establishments. On July 21, 1894, the *BMJ* reported that the Home Secretary, on the basis of information derived from the *BMJ*'s article, had ordered a police investigation that was expected to "lead to an early repression of some of [the] abuses at these establishments."[115] A few days later in the House of Commons, S. Smith, MP, asked H. H. Asquith, then Home Secretary, whether the *BMJ*'s statement had "attracted the attention of the police; whether some of the best known of these places have been raided and stopped; and whether Government proposed to take any steps for the registration of massage shops."[116] Denying the *BMJ*'s assertion that the police had stopped one of the false massage operations, Asquith replied that "up to the present no sufficient evidence has been forthcoming to warrant police action, or to show the necessity of an amendment of the law."[117] Though blamed by various critics for having started "an unnecessary and undesirable commotion," the *BMJ* continued to push Scotland Yard to act on the information the

---

[114] "The Massage Affair," *St. Paul*, August 4, 1894.

[115] "Immoral 'Massage' Establishments," *British Medical Journal*, 2 (July 21, 1894): 148. This news was soon picked up by many newspapers in Britain. See *The Glasgow Evening Times*, July 17; *The Star*, July 19; *Glasgow Echo*, July 20; *Yorkshire Daily Post*, July 20; *Pall Mall Gazette*, July 20; *Sheffield Daily Telegraph*, July 20; *Evening News Post*, July 20; *South Wales Times*, July 21; *Woman*, July 25; *Newcastle Daily Chronicle*, July 25; and so on.

[116] *Midland Evening News*, July 20, 1894.

[117] *Parliamentary Debates*, Hansard, July 23, 1894, c. 663; "House of Commons and Massage Establishments," *Daily Chronicle*, July 24, 1894.

*BMJ* had obtained. But the *BMJ* continued to meet with resistance. On November 24, 1894, for example, Ernest Hart, the editor of the *BMJ* and part of a deputation from the "Parliamentary Bills Committee" formed through him by the British Medical Association, brought the matter directly to the attention of the Home Secretary. But Asquith, "appear[ing] to defend the action or inaction of Scotland Yard," intimated that "the steps which should be taken to check the abuses . . . [were] a matter suitable for private conference."[118] (Fig. 5-2.)

Shortly afterward, the BMA itself took action. Dr. Donald Macalister, a member of the Parliamentary Bills Committee, in consultation with his friend Dr. R. Anderson, "one of the Assistant Commissioners of the Metropolitan Police," organized a conference with another member, Mr. Costelloe, a Barrister "who was acquainted with all the circumstances and had all the documents in his hands."[119] At this private conference, discussing the limited legal capacity of the Criminal Law Amendment Act to regulate massage shops, the participants reached the conclusion that it was necessary "with the assistance of Members of Parliament, including representatives of members of the profession in the House of Commons, to frame and put forward a Bill" to regulate the free market in massage establishments.

The Bill, drafted by Costelloe and entitled "The Massage and Hypnotism [and Electro-Therapeutics] Act, 1895," consisted of eight clauses. The four main points of the Bill were, first, that any institution or establishment intending to provide "masso-therapeutics" or "hypnotism" or electro-therapeutics "shall be registered with the Secretary of State"; second, that the establishments in which such treatments are applied "to any person of the opposite sex . . . shall be deemed to be a disorderly house" unless a registered medical practitioner had expressed the need for massage in a prescription; third, that "it shall be lawful for the Secretary of State to cause any such registered place to be inspected from time to time by any officer of police appointed by him"; and, finally, that

---

[118] "The Scandals of Massage: Report of the Special Commissioners of the British Medical Journal, No. 4," *British Medical Journal*, 2 (November 24, 1894): 1199–1200.
[119] "Parliamentary Bills Committee: Memorandum on the Massage Questions," Mepo, 2/460, National Archives.

any person receiving money to provide such treatments be required to "file the original prescription and to produce the file at any time upon demand to any such inspecting officer." Offenders against these clauses would be guilty of a misdemeanor offence and forced to acquiesce to "a fine not exceeding £100 or to imprisonment for a term not exceeding six calendar months."[120]

This private Bill was in all probability submitted to a number of MPs and the Home Office. However, because there is no record of the bill being seriously discussed in *Parliamentary Debates*, the *Journal of the House of Commons*, or the Home Office papers, it was probably abandoned on the grounds that conflicts of this sort remained semiprivate affairs between massage parlor operators and visiting patients.

Contrary to its initial intention of safeguarding a bona-fide medical treatment, the *BMJ*'s moral campaign produced the opposite result. The subsequent journalistic uproar, adding to the public's prejudice toward massage, ruined the legitimate massage industry while at the same time increasing the advertising of bogus establishments as new places of sexual amusement.[121] Within a few years of the *BMJ*'s reports, massage parlors in London had degenerated into purely criminal dens, notorious enough to be placed under secret investigation by police. Ironically, the 1885 enactment of the Criminal Law Amendment Act to suppress brothels in fact resulted in pushing prostitutes into massage parlors as shelters for their trade.

By the time the *London Figaro* sent out its own commissioner to investigate and took over the journalistic exposé of massage shops in 1897, the massage establishments had far more to reveal than just their medical disguise. In addition to advertisements in the press, the proprietors "employed sandwich men to walk about in the vicinity."[122] Moreover, the profitable sexual business was known to have attracted foreign managers and proprietors. Moreover, since the word "massage" had began to accumulate negative associations, the promoters carried on their en-

---

[120] "An Act to Regulate Establishments for Massage and other Purposes," PRO. London Mepo 2/460, National Archives.

[121] "The Massage Question," *The Hospital Nursing Mirror*, Feb. 23, 1895.

[122] "Bogus Massage and Similar Establishments," Metropolitan Police's private report, Mepo, 2/460, National Archives.

terprises under "the name . . . of manicure or chiropody," which still sounded innocent. Although the assistants were still called nurses, they discarded nurses' garb and wore the more conventional attire of prostitutes, which consisted "of a chemise-like loose-fitting dress of the most diaphanous textured silk, which permitted [a view of] every line of the figure." In response to the investigation by the *Figaro*, one proprietress, "Madame Alvarey" of Hanover Square, admitted that "many of your statements are quite correct" and sneered at the media exposé, insisting that "the article in *Figaro* has been of 'immense service' to her as 'gratuitous advertisement'"—adding, "Since it appeared, she has been 'literally besieged' with patients." The *Figaro* also reported the case of a gentleman whose threatened prosecution under the Criminal Law Amendment Act cost him £200, and warned that "the hideous debaucheries" in the establishments regularly tended to trap customers into becoming the victims of blackmailing operations: the assistants sold names of clients to expert blackmailers for £5 each.[123]

In a May 6, 1897 article, the *Figaro* strongly accused the police and vestry authorities of "neglecting an obvious public duty" and of "still hesitat[ing] to take the necessary steps to close the houses. . . . The vestry chiefly concerned has had a through investigation made into all the so-called massage houses . . . but why these bodies should require to be instructed in their plain duty by the Home Secretary, we entirely fail to conceive."[124] The public seemed to agree. Mrs. Bailhache, the Honourable Superintendent of the National British Women's Temperance Association, sent a clipping of the *Figaro* article to the Metropolitan Police to urge their inspection of massage dens.[125]

The *Figaro*'s article motivated the Vestry of St. James, Westminster, which had long faced complaints by parish inhabitants about disorderly houses, to concentrate on the massage establishments.[126] After several

---

[123] "The Massage Scandal," *London Figaro*, April 22, 1897. Newspaper cutting in the Public Record Office, Mepo/460, National Archives.

[124] "The 'Massage' Exposure," *London Figaro*, May 6, 1897; "'Massage' Once Again," *London Figaro*, May 13, 1897.

[125] The letter from Mrs. Bailhache, Superintendent of the National British Women's Temperance Association, is held in the Public Record Office, Mepo, 2/460.

[126] Parliamentary Bills and General Purposes, Parliamentary Bills Committee, Minutes, May, 25, 1897, p. 253. Westminster City Archives.

communications with Sir Matthew Ridley, then Home Secretary, the Vestry finally received a letter intimating that "if the Vestry have any practical suggestions to make on the subject, Sir Matthew will be very glad if they will lay them before him by letter."[127] On January 25, 1898, the National Vigilance Association, sending the Vestry a copy of a private Bill "dealing principally with the foreign men who live on the prostitution of women," asked the Vestry to pass a resolution in favor of the Bill.[128] Such incentives encouraged the Vestry to form on March 15, 1898, the "Parliamentary Bills and General Purposes Committee on the Subject of Massage Establishments." Here the possibility of new legislation on massage establishments "to really strike at the root of the evil" was intensively discussed among Thomas Mitchell (chairman), Dr. Edmunds (Medical Officer of Health), Alfred Barry (then rector of the parish), and others. Barry submitted to the Committee as a basis of discussion a draft of the Bill prepared in 1895 by the British Medical Association. Most of the clauses received the Committee's consent and were employed in the "Suggested Clauses for a Bill" drafted by the Committee on April 26, 1898, which included clauses calling for the registration and inspection of massage establishments, mandatory certificates of proficiency for masseuses and masseurs, and prohibition of practicing massage on any person of the opposite sex.[129]

The only substantial difference from the previous Bill was a clause that enabled the prosecution of the lessor or landlord of vicious massage parlors under "Section 13 of the Criminal Law Amendments Act, 1885." This provision, reflecting a collaborative effort between the police and the Vestry, was intended to suppress brothels by charging landlords "for knowingly permitting the premises to be used as brothels." This application of Section 13 represented the best and most viable method of suppressing immorality in the massage establishments. But once again, government intention and action were far apart.[130] From 1898 onward, some

---

[127] Correspondence: The Home Secretary to the Vestry of St. James," November 23, 1897, in Minutes, 299–300. Westminster City Archives.

[128] The Minutes of the Vestry, Jan. 25, 1897, 320–322. Westminster City Archives.

[129] The Minutes of the Vestry, March 15, 1898, 348–349. Westminster City Archives.

[130] "Report of Parliamentary Bills and General Purposes Committee on the

police divisions, such as the Vine Street Station and Tottenham Court Road
Station, began secret inspections of some massage houses and submitted
to the vestries evidence showing that these establishments were doing
business as "mere brothels [which made] the nurses prostitutes."[131] Little
action, however, was taken, and the Bill itself was abandoned once again,
although this draft too was probably submitted to the Home Secretary.

About this same time, in 1897, the *Figaro* and the *BMJ* took up the
cudgels again and reignited public indignation against the massage establishment, which it believed "is too often simply another name for a lu-
panar or a bagnio" and whose "'sisters' and 'nurses' . . . are capable of
giving lessons to the heroine of Lesbos."[132] The next month the National Vigilance Association, responding to the allegations of the *BMJ*
and the *Figaro*, urged that the most viable solution to this problem was
the formation of a massage profession. "The whole question," the association's pamphlet *The Vigilance Record* announced, "can be easily settled
by the medical profession. Why not insist upon the necessity of those
who desire to practice massage as a profession, undergoing certain examinations, and, on proof of efficiency, let them become possessors of a
duly qualified certificate?"[133]

Indeed, attempts to make massage into an institutionally recognized
profession had commenced in some quarters right after the outbreak of
the massage scandal in 1894. In January 1895, for example, Maltby announced the foundation of the British Massage Association, "a healthy
and trustworthy institution of educated, efficient, and reliable masso-
therapeutists who will prove a credit to themselves [and] to their profession."[134] The Association, with over sixty rules for regulating masseurs

---

Subject of Massage Establishments: To the Vestry of St. James, Westminster."
Public Record Office, Mepo, 2/460, A56145/17.

[131] The inspecting records on bogus massage houses are held in the Public Record Office, Mepo, 2/460: Metropolitan Police, Vine Street Station, C. Division, Oct. 24, 1898; Metropolitan Police, Executive Branch, Oct. 29, 1901; and
Metropolitan Police, Tottenham Court Road Station, Nov. 16, 1901.

[132] "Massage à la Mode," *British Medical Journal*, 1 (1897).

[133] Tottenham Court Road Station.

[134] "The Massage Question," *The Nursing Record*, January 9, 1895; "The Massage
Question," *St. James's Gazette*, January 6, 1895; "The Massage Question," *The Hospital Nursing Mirror*, February 23, 1895.

and masseuses, aimed at enhancing the position of massage as a medical therapy and regulating the issuance of certificates by examining the applicants to the Association.

This Association, however, was short-lived, probably because it failed to find lasting patronage from any leading medical men or laymen. Even before the massage scandal, some practitioners had given thought to establishing professional credentials for massage to distinguish legitimate establishments from those that offered visitors other services. Indeed, in 1895 four masseuses—Rosalind Paget, Lucy Robinson, Annie Manley, and Margaret Palmer—became anxious about the diminished status of their profession brought about by the scandal, and they formed the Society of Trained Masseuses, which after 1944 developed into the present institution, the Chartered Society of Physiotherapy.[135] On March 1, 1895, the Society's publication, *Nursing Notes*, declared the rules of the Society: "1. No Massage to be undertaken except under Medical direction; 2. No Advertising permitted in any but strictly Professional Papers; and 3. No sale of Drugs to Patients allowed.[136] Through its lectures, courses, examinations, and issuance of certificates, the Society effectively ostracized non-medical massage at least until the outbreak of the First World War in 1914.

## Conclusion

By examining the implications of the massage scandal and the medico-social context in which it arose, this chapter has illustrated how the strong forces of late-nineteenth-century commercialization exploited medicine's most vulnerable area: the public's potential association of sexuality with the professionalism of medical practice. With the abundance of medical commodities in the market, late-Victorian Britons came to regard their health increasingly as a commodity that could be purchased, and they began to seek their own methods of medication. Thus despite the seemingly well-established professionalization of medi-

---

[135] For a detailed history of the Chartered Society of Physiotherapy, see Jean Barclay, *In Good Hands: The History of the Chartered Society of Physiotherapy, 1894–1994* (published in association with the Chartered Society of Physiotherapy, Oxford: Butterworth-Heinemann, 1994).

[136] "Massage Notes," *Nursing Notes*, March 1, 1895, 37–38.

cine at the end of the nineteenth century, medical practices and treatments were far from representing a monolithic and dignified edifice.

It is well known that late-nineteenth-century society witnessed a dramatic increase in nervous disorders such as neurasthenia and nervous prostration, in both women and men. This was hardly surprising: the increasingly commercialized and industrialized society of the era placed people under greater stress. At the same time, the decline of Britain's hegemony in the world economy nurtured the fear that the British nation itself was being undermined and corrupted, as shown by its mental and nervous degeneration. It was thus perhaps inevitable that the proliferating medical literature of the period became interested in various forms of nervous debility and in the apparent depletion of people's mental and physical energies. Less well known, however, are the ways in which the social, commercial, and medical interests in nervous prostration nourished one another.

The massage scandal remains an extremely interesting episode in medical history—one that sheds new light on the complicated relationship between medical practice and market capitalism. Just as with electro-therapeutics, the endorsement of massage therapy as a legitimate medical practice encouraged its appropriation by non-medical entrepreneurs. A number of these entrepreneurs, some of whom were doctors, capitalized on a growing anxiety about nervous ailments; and by successfully mimicking the trappings of medicine, were able to attract significant numbers of clients. (Others obviously capitalized by using massage to mask blatantly illegal enterprises.) And again just as with electro-therapeutics, massage therapy confronted the British medical establishment with the specter of professional apostasy—of doctors who initiated, supported, and profited from commercial ventures—and the blurring of boundaries between the professional and commercial worlds. The waning years of the nineteenth century thus saw not only highly scandalous charlatans jostling for commercial influence, thereby calling into question the legitimacy of what had been (for however short a time) a respected medical practice—massage—but also qualified medical doctors being associated with and supporting quasi-medical businesses. The massage scandal, like the debates over medical electricity and electro-therapeutics, highlights both the fragility of the medical domain and the strength of doctors' pecuniary interests. As a result, the scandal ultimately illustrates that the late-nineteenth-century medical field found it difficult to reconcile burgeoning market capitalism and ideological professionalism. However, the maturity of medical practice was not merely achieved through its scientific advances, but also through its responses to the increasingly commercialized marketplace in which it operated. Together these factors gave rise to an embryonic collaboration between medical care and capitalistic enterprise.

# Conclusion

This book starts with the patent medicine controversy, which most fully epitomizes modern medicine's early movement toward a highly capitalistic and profit-driven endeavor. Pharmaceutical titans of the modern world, such as Boots, Beecham, and Wellcome, all started as patent-medicine manufacturers. Such companies both confronted and also helped to produce the rapid transformation of the socioeconomic structure of medicine into one that was increasingly customer-oriented, commercial, and capitalistic. Moreover, these companies sought to take advantage of these changes by expanding their influence in health care. The alliance we see in our world today between capitalism, chemistry, medicine, and research and development was just coming into being at this time.

Victorian London was no doubt one of the first modern cities to experience the onslaught of hyper-commercialized advertising, the product of rough-and-tumble business competition. At the same time, the influence of modern market-mechanisms was beginning to make its mark. In particular, medicine and therapeutics emerged as an arena in which doctors, engineers, entrepreneurs, and others collaborated within and through integrated corporate entities, seeking commercial dominance by enlarging the scale of their markets. In the 1880s and 1890s, this trend toward market capitalism was often abhorred as "Americanization"—an intrusion of a particularly American brand of commercialism into British society. Irrespective of Britons' traditional aversion to both open competition and the overt pursuit of private gain, this nineteenth-century globalization of market priorities penetrated deeply into Londoners' urban lives.

This book has articulated the ways in which the intrusion of commercialism and capitalism into the medical domain jeopardized the ideal of public health, which itself was just becoming established and accommodated within society. It is important to stress again that the professional ideology of medicine had long been tied to a public service ideal in Britain: to provide professional service to the public and pursue community welfare were the goals expected of the medical profession. Whereas governmental policy in France and Germany directly regulated market mechanisms to protect the public nature of health care, Britain preferred to rely on professional control. The regulatory power of professional bodies such as the British Medical Association, the Royal College of Physicians, and the General Medical Council (a non-governmental trust) served to constrain doctors' practices, primarily by revoking doctors' licenses whenever their conduct was deemed unprofessional or contrary to the public good. In fact, the records of the disciplinary board of the General Medical Council are full of summonses and censorships of unprofessional doctors in the latter half of the nineteenth century.

However, we *also* need to recognize that by the late nineteenth century, this ideology of professionalism was on the defensive as market capitalism advanced into the realm of health care. Certainly the nineteenth century was an age in which various kinds of professionals, including doctors, lawyers, and teachers, began to exert both tangible and intangible influence in society.[1] But as Andrew Abbott's sociological analysis shows, different social groups within the various professions struggled for control of professional jurisdiction.[2] In accordance with

---

[1] Harold Perkin, *The Origins of Modern English Society, 1780–1880* (London: Routledge & Kegan Paul, 1968) and *The Rise of Professional Society: England since 1880* (London: Routledge & Kegan Paul, 1989). Also see Magali Larson, *The Rise of Professionalism: A Sociological Analysis* (Berkeley: University of California Press, 1977).

[2] From Parsons and Willensky to Elliot and Friedson, theorists have stressed the monopolizing and dominating mechanisms of professionalism. Some of these scholars stress the functional structure of the profession as regulating power within expert-client relationships, while others, focusing on the process of the rise of professionalism, tend to associate this power with social functions like

Abbott's understanding of intra-professional tension, this study highlights the conflict among medical doctors between those favoring market-driven enterprise and those rejecting it.[3]

The relationship between professional knowledge and market power
indeed remained an intricate one. The exchange between providers and
recipients of professional services was carried out within a complex domain, full of both competing powers and resistance to those powers.
Inspired by Michael Foucault's delineation of the knowledge/power
nexus,[4] Penelope Corfield has attempted to articulate the interdepen-
dency that existed between professional knowledge and its consumers.
She writes, "Consumer responses [to professionalism] were more
complex than a mere submission to external power. There was scope
for evasion, rival interpretations, or outright refusal. That applied to patients who declined the doctor's prescription, litigants who refused to
take advice, parishioners who avoided going to church, and students

---

justice or treatment for patients. See Talcott Parsons, "Professions," in *Interna-
tional Encyclopedia of the Social Sciences*, ed. D. L. Sills (New York: Free Press,
1968), 12: 536–547; Harold L. Willensky, *Organizational Intelligence: Knowledge and
Policy in Government and Industry* (New York: Basic Books, 1967); Eliot Friedson,
*Professional Powers: A Study of the Institutionalization of Formal Knowledge* (Chicago:
U. of Chicago Press, 1986) and *Profession of Medicine: A Study of the Sociology of
Applied Knowledge* (New York: Dodd, Mead & Co., 1971); Philip R. C. Elliot, *The
Sociology of the Professions* (London: Macmillan, 1972). Haskell also stresses the
cultural authority of the profession and argues that professionalization entails
the process of cultural legitimation. See T. L. Haskell, ed., *The Authority of Experts: Studies in History and Theory* (Bloomington: Indiana Press, 1984). The conventional theories on professionalization by sociologists have emphasized this
regulatory structure as the source of professional dominance and authority.
[3] Andrew Abbott, *The System of Professions: An Essay on the Division of Expert
Labor* (Chicago: University of Chicago Press, 1988).
[4] In particular, see Michael Foucault, *Power/Knowledge: Selected Interviews and Other
Writings, 1972–1977*, ed. by C. Gordon (Harvester, Brighton, 1980). For Foucault's
theory as applicable to the professions, see J. Goldstein, "Foucault among the
Sociologists: The 'Disciplines' and the History of the Professions," *History and
Theory* 23 (1984): 170–192. *Essays in Reassessing Foucault: Power, Medicine, and the
Body*, ed. by C. Jones and R. Porter (London: Routledge, 1994) is useful for con-
sidering the relationship of Foucault's theory of knowledge to medical dis-
course.

who ignored their tutor's best precepts. Other clients, meanwhile, took professional counsel but then neglected to pay for it."[5] Foucaultian analysis of power and the professions, like Corfield's, helps us to understand the ways in which professionalism faced a difficult challenge in adapting its meritocratic power to function within a burgeoning, commercializing mass society.

The chapters of this book dealing with the rapid expansion of the patent-medicine business have attempted to illuminate the changing relationships between commercialism, medical capitalism, and the ideology of public service. The unprecedented proliferation of patent-medicine businesses in the latter half of the nineteenth century shows that consumers' therapeutic fantasies made it possible for the health market to become a source of great profit. Here market capitalism typically played a leading role in professional debates. Before the full efflorescence of commodity culture in the twentieth century, medical professionalism had already showed itself to be both fragile and susceptible to fragmentation.

Chapter Two has shown how late-nineteenth-century consumers of medicine were very different from the more easily cajoled and passive consumers of the previous century. Blending their desires, needs, fantasies, and hedonistic illusions with their lived reality, modern consumers began to extend their imaginary landscape to every aspect of consumption. The language and pictorial images of Victorian advertisements reflect consumers' materialistic visions at play in a dream of consumption.

Medicine and health were no exception to this modern transformation. With the abundance of medical commodities such as electric belts, Turkish baths, electro-massage machines, and numerous patent medicines, the public began to regard health as commercially purchasable and to seek its own means of medication. Furthermore, modern consumers' hedonism was directed not merely toward obtaining purely medicinal relief but rather toward what can be called therapeutic fantasies, to be fulfilled through various medical commodities. They wished to achieve vigorous, overflowing, and richer health, an imaginary ideal formed in a mutually reinforcing process between illusion and reality. The democra-

---

[5] Penelope J. Corfield, *Power and the Professions in Britain 1700–1850* (London and New York: Routledge, 1995), 246.

tization of consumption, permeating people's psyches, transformed the basic concept of personal health, turning what had been previously considered outside market mechanisms into another commodity for sale.

As Chapters Three and Four indicate, widely commercialized electro-medicine provided a niche particularly congenial to *fin-de-siècle* capitalism and its stimulation of marketable therapeutic practices. The confluence of capital and medicine represented by the Institute of Medical Electricity and the Medical Battery Company, as distinguished from mid-Victorian medical entrepreneurship, spared no pains to integrate medicine and technology into a new, profitable enterprise. However, in the ensuing triangular battle between quasi-professional entrepreneurs, professional electrical engineers, and elite medical doctors, it is important to note that the Royal College of Physicians, despite its regulatory power, was put on the defensive, faced with the challenges of a rival profession's competing professional ideals and open attempts to commercialize medical activities. In the 1880s, more than a few medical doctors were quietly engaged in profitable activities. Whatever the College said to the contrary, its official morality of gentlemanly professionalism was already on flimsy ground and in jeopardy. Maintaining at least on the surface its own authority and integrity seems to have been about as far as the Royal College of Physicians could go in the face of the business strategies of companies already successfully infiltrating the medical profession.

Behind this uproar about professional medicine was a growing health culture and burgeoning popular demand for healthy bodies and minds. Late-Victorian society witnessed a dramatic increase in nervous complaints such as neurasthenia and nervous prostration, in both men and women. The commercialization and industrialization of society threw people into stressful workplaces, while at the same time the decline of Britain's hegemony in the world economy cultivated a fear that the British nation itself was becoming corrupt and manifesting mental and nervous degeneration. For that reason, the proliferating medical literature of the time became interested in various forms of nervous debility and in neurotic loss of mental and physical energy. In addition, new types of labor—white collar and desk work—left people feeling exposed to competition, stress, and other forms of urban emotional anguish that led them to demand quasi-medical release.

Like electro-therapeutics, massage therapy provides another good example of the competing interests at stake as people—professionals, skilled technicians, and entrepreneurs alike—capitalized on a growing public and consumer anxiety about nervous ailments. Many doctors and theorists began to explain this new therapy by borrowing fashionable scientific concepts such as the conservation of energy, which resulted in massage becoming seen as a viable medical technique by 1890. Even as scandalous charlatans jostled each other and raised suspicions about the legitimate benefits of massage, qualified medical doctors became associated with massage-related medical businesses. The massage scandal described in Chapter Five was thus not simply about prostitution practised under the guise of a medical therapy, but rather a symbolic manifestation of medicine's exploitation by a ubiquitous form of commercialism. It demonstrates the power of the market to permeate the medical arena in search of profits, and the extent to which medical doctors had to struggle with this commercial penetration.

Indeed, in some respects the medical marketplace of the nineteenth century was similar to the commercial free-for-all of the eighteenth century. Modern medical practice, however, had to deal with naked capitalism, which demonstrated itself as a new and more challenging threat to professionalism. The mid-Victorian years witnessed a flood of doctors becoming involved in self-promotion and medical entrepreneurship, as well as a flood of disciplinary problems that greatly disturbed the more elite circles of the profession. There were, without a doubt, more quacks in the nineteenth century than in the eighteenth. However, facing harsh occupational competition in medicine, many legitimate doctors decided to collaborate with "quackish" capitalists who wished to make a fortune from lucrative medical enterprises. The large-scale capitalization of patent medicine, for example, unquestionably offered attractive pecuniary opportunities to doctors—in the nineteenth century no less than today.

Thus with respect to late-Victorian London, the history of medicine and technology requires us to consider the extent to which the cash nexus united medical men with a range of commercial entrepreneurs, all of whom shared a growing commitment to market strategies. To see what actually happened to medicine in the most industrially and commercially developed country of the time, it is essential to view medicine within the context of a burgeoning commodity culture, which led to an increased commercialization of medicine, a transformation of professional attitudes, the emergence of quackish medical services, the development of early pharmaceutical industries, and the proliferation of health-food businesses. In examining these changes, I have attempted to articulate the ways in which market capitalism permeated the seemingly well-established professional purity of medical practice in the Victorian era.

This book has explored the various historical boundaries between regular and irregular medical practices, professionalism and unprofessional conduct, public-benefit ideology and the power of market forces, bedside medical care and technology-oriented treatment, doctors' professional aspirations to heal diseases and the public's ballooning desires to acquire healthy bodies, and the voluntarism of traditional medicine and proprietary medical organizations. It has also traced the emergence of the patent-medicine business and the socio-medical environment in which early pharmaceutical manufacturers struggled with the medical profession over questions involving pecuniary interest. Today we are still witnessing the vigorous co-evolution of medicine and capitalism. What this book has attempted to show by investigating these historical episodes is the strength of capitalism's power to penetrate new boundary zones and thereby find new sources of profit.

This power has both merits and demerits. According to an ideal theory of capitalism, independent, self-interested entrepreneurs—whether they be doctors, medical engineers, or patent-medicine manufacturers—would benefit society more than they benefit themselves from their economic activities. Moreover, this view holds that capitalism most efficiently drives forward innovation and progress. By contrast, critics of capitalism argue that the elevation of self-interest undermines ethical values and that markets require proper state oversight to guard against their exploitative tendencies. In order to make capitalism appropriately benefit society, this book urges that we need to carry on fine-tuning the very mechanisms through which capitalism works, the way people exchange things and make their decisions about market forces and for-profit activities. To promote our own watchfulness, we need to have a better understanding of the history and workings of medical capitalism, which would help all of us make better sense of its influence and capacities. Hence this book has stressed that capitalistic forces began to exert their power in the medical sphere from the initial encounter of medicine with modern market mechanisms. I would like to conclude by observing that the power and logic of capital have consistently affected medicine and health care, areas often thought to be free of these market mechanisms and manipulations.

*Reference Matter*

# *Archival Sources*

*Note: the items without dates means that they are undated.*

BRITISH MEDICAL ASSOCIATION, LONDON

British Medical Association, MSS., MCSC, XVII, Minutes of Council. Jan. 27, 1909, pp. 70-71. *Secret Remedies: What They Cost and What They Contain.* London: British Medical Association, 1909.

GUILDHALL LIBRARY ARCHIVES, LONDON

London Chamber of Commerce, Owners of Proprietary Articles Section, Special Committee, Council Minutes, MSS 16,456, vol. 5, 1911-14, pp. 42, 51, 94, 106, 131, 222, 287, 348.

London Chamber of Commerce, Owners of Proprietary Articles Section, Special Committee, vol. 1, pp. 15, 18, attachment to pp. 39, 119, 120, MSS. 16,718.

"Patent Medicines," in *The Chamber of Commerce Journal,* Mar. 1911, p. 77; "Sale of Patent Medicines," Dec. 1911, p. 375; "Sale of Patent Medicines," June 1912, p. 167; "Select Committee on Patent Medicines," June 1912, p. 177; and "Report of Select Committee on Patent Medicine," Oct. 1914, pp. 349-350.

*The Agitation Against Patent and Proprietary Medicines and Food, the 'Owners of Proprietary Articles Section' of The London Chamber of Commerce,* published in Oxford Court, Cannon Street, London, 1912, MSS. 16,688, p. 8, no. 14.

INSTITUTION OF ELECTRICAL ENGINEERS, LONDON

Lawrence's membership form. MSS., vol. 5A, p. 274 and MSS., 6B., p.449.

Pamphlet, "The Institute of Medical Electricity," pp. 1-7.

Thompson Pamphlet Collection, "Electro-Physiology I." MSS., SPT 116/5-9 and SPT 116/11.

LONDON HOSPITAL, LONDON

*Minutes of Meetings of the House Committee.*
"Letter from Medical Council,' April 25, 1904.
"Letter from Mr. Openshaw," Nov. 7, 1904, p. 359.
Meatron's Report.
"Re Massage Department." Feb. 26, 1906, p. 108.
"Re Massage treatment." Feb. 15, 1905, p. 420.
"Re: Douche Massage." July 18, 1899, p. 393.
"Re: Letter from the Medical Council," May 7, 1906, pp. 149-150.
"Re: Recommendations by Medical Council. Notes on the Massage De-partment," Feb. 18, 1907, p. 334.
"Re: The employment of a teacher of Swedish Massage." Feb. 11, 1907, p. 330.
"Re: The question of Wet Massage to the Medical Council." 15 May, 1899, p. 360.


OXFORD UNIVERSITY

*SJS/03.95, John Johnson Collection of Printed Ephemera, Patent Medicines Boxes.*
"Allen & Hanbury's "Bynin' and "Tonga."" Patent Medicine Box 1.
"Boyd's Celebrated Blood Purifier." Patent Medicine Box 1.
"Bromo-Phosph or Brain Food." Patent Medicine Box 1.
"Dr. Birley's Syrup of Free Phosphorus, the Great Brain and Nerve Food." Patent Medicine Box 1.
"Figuroid, Scientific Obesity Cure." Patent Medicine Box 2.
"Guy's Tonic Treatment." Patent Medicine Box 2.
"Hall's Coca Wine." Patent Medicine Box 2.
"Marza Wine." Patent Medicine Box 3.
"Dr. William's Pink Pills for Pale People." Patent Medicine Box 4.
"Bile Beans and Beecham's Pills." Well Known Patent Medicines Box 5.
"Bile Beans for Biliousness." Patent Medicine Box 5.
"Fraser's Supphur Tablets." Patent Medicine Box 5.
"Dr. de Jongh's Light-Brown Cod Liver Oil." Well Known Patent Medicines Box 6.
"Hood's Sarsaparilla (blood purifier)." Patent Medicine Box, 6.
"Norton's Camomile Pills." Well Known Patent Medicines Box 6.
"The Morisonian Monument Erected in front of the British College of Health, New Road, London, the 31st of March, 1856." Patent Medicine Box 6.
"Vaccine Poison." Patent Medicine Box 6.
"Curative Magnetism, or Nature's Aids to Health, by John Hugh Martin & Co." Patent Medicine Box 9.
"Darlows & Co.'s Patent Flexible Magnetic Appliances." Patent Medicine Box 9.

"The Progressive Medical Alliance, for Men and Women,." 57 & 59, Oxford Street and 7, Soho Street. Patent Medicine Box 9.

"Health Giving! Life Sustaining!, Eley & Co.'s Magnetic Curative Appli-ances." Patent Medicine Box 9.

"A Home Remedy! The Electropoise." Patent Medicine Box 10.

"Ambrecht's Patent Permanent Magneto-Electrode Appliances: A New and Improved Method of Magnetism as a Curative Agent." Patent Medicine Box 10.

"Dr. Carter Moffat's Health Appliances." Patent Medicine Box 10.

"Dr. Lowder's Magneto-Electric Battery, by the Magneto-Electric Battery Company." Patent Medicine Box 10.

"Dr. Lowder's Magneto-Electric Battery." Patent Medicine Box 10.

"Dr. Nelson's Medicated Loofah Socks." Patent Medicine Box 10.

"Dr. Richardson's Magneto-Galvanic Battery." Patent Medicine Box 10.

"The Electropathic and Zander Institute." Patent Medicine Box 10.

"The Future of Electropathy." Patent Medicine, Box 10.

"Harness's Electropathic Belt." Patent Medicine Box 10.

"Pulvermacher's Improved Medico-Galvanic System of Self-Application of the Patient." Patent Medicine Box 11.

"Pulvermacher's Patent Portable Hydro-Electric Chain for Personal Use," Oct. 1851. Patent Medicine Box 11.

"Sandow Curative Physical Culture," Special Supplement to *The Daily Mail*, April 26, 1909. Outsized material Box.

"Hood's Sarsaparilla." Well Known Patent Medicines, Outsized Material.

*Others*

"Bill of Complaint, between Isaac Louis Pulvermacher and Charles Daniel Hammond and Henry James," published on April 29, 1869 held in Oxford University; "Pulvermacher v. Hammond," on May 27, 1869.

PATENT OFFICE, LONDON

"Electric and Magnetic Appliances, Medical and Surgical." in *the Patent Journal Class 81 Medicine et al.*

*Pulvermacher's Patents*

"Apparatus for Creating Electric Currents." Patent no. 2411, 1857; "Producing Galvanic Currents." Patent no. 582, 1866; "Producing and Applying Electric Currents." Patent no. 773, 1868; "Producing and Applying Electric Currents." Patent no. 2740, 1868; "Medico-electric Apparatus." Patent no. 2771, 1872; "Electric Bands and Brushes, &c." Patent no. 3519; "Generating and Applying Electricity." Patent no. 3937, 1874.

*Harness's Patents*

For example, his first Electric Belt was patented on Oct. 13, 1982, no. 4881; Surgical Belt and Surgery, April 24, 1883, no. 2083; Electrical Suspensors or Suspensory Bandages, Mar. 27, 1883, no. 5573; Apparatus for Facilitating the Inhalation of Medicated Vapour, July 23, 1884, no. 10,500; Medical Eye Battery, Sept. 17, 1886, no. 11,844; Surgical Trusses, June 13, 1887, no. 8503; Electro-magnetic Induction Apparatus, June 22, 1889, no. 15,689; Electrical Machines for Interrupting Use, Dec. 24, 1891, no. 20, 215; Electric Corset, Oct. 17, 1891, no. 15,733; Apparatus for Restoring or Argumenting the Hearing, Dec. 12, 1891, no. 19,472.

*Others*

Alexander Mclaughlin, "Improvements in Electric belts for the Electric Treatment of the Human Body." 1900. Patent no. 7200.

Alva Owen, "Improvements in Electric Belts." 1887. Patent no. 16,351.

"An Improved Electric or Magnetic Hat Leather or Lining for Hats, Caps, and other Similar Head Coverings." 1891. Patent no. 5382.

"An Instrument for Measuring Odic or Nerve Force." 1889. Patent no. 11,982.

Arthur Harvey Byng, "An Improved Appliance or Band for Generating Electricity for Therapeutic Purposes." 1884. Patent no. 4548.

Charles Andrews, "An Improved Galvanic Belt." Patent no. 1350, 1891.

Charles Everett Hebard, "An Improved Electric Uterine Battery." 1894. Patent no. 22,637.

Frank Dowling, "Methods of and Means for Applying Electricity to the Human Body." 1893. Patent no. 10,147.

"Improvements in the Method of Treating Nervous and Other Disorders of the Human System, and Apparatus therefore," dated Sept. 8, 1890. Patent no. 1,903.

H. H. Lake, "Electri Ureteral, Vaginal, and Rectal Vitalization." 1893. Patent no. 6,566.

Heinrich Simons, "Improvements in or connected with Apparatus for the Simultaneous Shampooing or Massage of, and the Administration of Electricity to, the Human Body." 1895. Patent no. 10,408.

Henry Charles Risborough Sharman, "An Improved Electro-Massage Ap-pliance." 1894. Patent no. 14,340.

Henry Harington Leigh, "Improvements in Therapeutic Magneto Electric Machines." 1891. Patent no. 965.

"Improvements relating to the Treatment of Patients Preparatory to and During Surgical and Dental Operations, and to Apparatus therefor." 1891. Patent no. 20,190.

James Chadwick, "Improvements in Electric Belts for Body Wear." 1891. Patent no. 18,272.

Louis Casper, "Improvements in Electric Massage Instruments." 1899. Patent no. 21,807.

Louis Cunow, "A Medicinal Light-Curative Apparatus for the Production of Complete or Partial Baths of Chemical and Electrical Rays of Light." 1899. Patent no. 22,857.

Noah Mitchell, "Improvements connected with Electric Belts and Bands for Curative Purposes." 1893. Patent no. 222.

Oscar Schneider, "An Electro-Therapeutical and Massage Apparatus." 1898. Patent no. 24,550.

The Electrolibration Company, "Improvements in the Method of Treating Nervous and other Disorders of the Human System, and Apparatus therefor." 1890. Patent no. 1903.

Theodor Bernt, "Improvements in Electric Massage Apparatus." 1899. Patent no. 17,474.

William George Johnson, "Battery for General Electro Medical Use or as Electrical Dumb Bells Clubs, and the Like for Muscular Exercise, with Electrical Current of any Desired Strength During such Exercise." 1888. Patent no. 4819.

Willis Romar Warren, "Medical Battery." 1882. Patent no. 343.


PHARMACEUTICAL SOCIETY, LONDON

"Letter from Ernest Hart, "The Sale of Poisonous Proprietary Preparations." The Pharmaceutical Society *Minutes of Council*, vol. 10, pp. 194-195 and reply from the President.

"The correspondence between Ernest Hart and M. Carteighe, President of the Pharmaceutical Society." The Pharmaceutical Society *Minutes of Council*, vol. 10, pp. 194-196.


NATIONAL ARCHIVES, LONDON

"An Act to Regulate Establishments for Massage and other Purposes." Mepo 2/460.

"Bogus Massage and Similar Establishments." Metropolitan Police's private report, Mepo, 2/460, Public Record Office.

""Massage Dens, Physician's Certificate: How Nurses are Made Massage Certificates." Newspaper cutting, *Society*, Oct. 22, 1898, Mepo 2/460.

"Memorandum of the Massage Question." Prepared by British Medical Association's Parliamentary Bills Committee, Mepo 2/460.

"Parliamentary Bills Committee: Memorandum on the Massage Questions." Mepo, 2/460.

"Report of Parliamentary Bills and General Purposes Committee on the Subject of Massage Establishments: To the Vestry of St. James, Westminster." Mepo,

2/460, A56145/17.

"Statement of Claims" by Tibbits, XC 5658, J54/765.

The inspecting records on bogus massage houses are held in the Public Record Office, Mepo, 2/460: Metropolitan Police, Vine Street Station, C. Division, Oct. 24, 1898; Metropolitan Police, Executive Branch, Oct. 29, 1901; and Metropolitan Police, Tottenham Court Road Station, Nov. 16, 1901.

"The Letter from Mrs. Bailhache, the Superintendent of the National British Women's Temperance Association." Mepo, 2/460.

"The Massage Scandal." Newspaper cutting from *The London Figaro*, April 22, 1897, Mepo/460.

"The Records of Tibbits Trials": *Depositions*, J17/283, IND 1/1675; *Pleadings*, J54/765, Jan.-Mar.,1893; *Affidavits*, J4/4891.

ROYAL COLLEGE OF PHYSICIANS, LONDON

*Manuscripts*

"Archibald Keightley: correspondence relating to Archibald Keightley's name being used in advertisements for Miss Ellen Jewson's Home for the Dietetic and other treatment of Chronic Disease, 1894." MSS., 2412/150-153.

"Baby Magazine: correspondence re names of fellows of appearing in ad-vertisement for *Baby*." MSS., 2412/33-44.

"Charles Henry Leet: testimonials in favour of Charles Henry Leet, used in advertisements. With advertisement for Dr. Leet's Pills, 1886-94." MSS., 2412/154-56.

"Correspondence re circular letter by John Attefield soliciting expert scientific evidence in defence of Van Houten's coca in an action of law." 1893. MSS., 2412/280-284.

"Dr M. E. A. Wallis's association with the Sandow Curative Institute." MSS., 2412/285.

"Dr Spriggs' speech planned (but not delivered) 19 Oct., 1922." MSS., 835/47.

"Electropathic & Zander Institute, London." MSS., 2412/131.

"Grundy's Heating and Ventilating Apparatus." MSS., 2412/19a.

"Harness's belt, the verdict of a British jury." *Science Siftings*, Mar. 4, 1893. MSS., 2411/113.

"Letter from Dr Leeson to Dr Edward Liveing, the Registrar of the RCP, dated Dec. 10th, 1887." *Annals*, Jan. 10, 36 (1888): 94-97. MSS., 2412/130.

"Letter from the Medical Defence Union to the President of the RCP, dated Dec. 8th, 1888." MSS., 2412/140.

"Letter from Tibbits to the Registrar, dated Feb. 22, 1893." MSS., 2411/104.

"Massage and electrical treatment." MSS., 2412/125.

"Medical Reprint." MSS., 2412/1.

"Report from the Censors' Board dated 28th April, 1922, recommending the alteration of the College (dated October 25th, 1888), and of Bye-law CLXXVIII." MSS., 835/50.

"Second report from the Censors' Board on the proposed alteration of a Resolution of the College and of Bye-law CLXXVIII." MSS., 835/51.

*The Charter, Bye-laws, and Regulations of the Royal College of Physicians of London and the Acts of Parliament Especially Relating Thereto.* London: Harridan and Sons, 1908.

"The letter concerning Pulvermacher's advertisement." MSS., 2412/176.

"The Medical Botanical Institute re: Herb Healing." MSS., 2412/95.

"The pamphlet by the Medical Battery Company." MSS., 2412/125.

*The Report on Harness' Electropathic Belts* by Dr Herbert Tibbits and Dr Arthur Harries. MSS., 2411/94-95.

*The Statement by Dr. Tibbits to the Patrons, Patroness and Governors.* MSS., 2411/132.

"The statement by Dr Tibbits." MSS., 2411/128.

"The treatment of disease by the prolonged application of currents of electricity of low powers, by Herbert Tibbits, MD., etc. together with a report by Arthur Harries, MD., etc. on Mr. Harness' Electropathic Belt and the Electropathic & Zander Institute." MSS., 2411/94.

"The treatment of disease by the prolonged application of currents of electricity of low powers, by Herbert Tibbits, MD., etc. together with a report by Arthur Harries, MD., etc. on Mr. Harness' Electropathic Belt and the Electropathic & Zander Institute." MSS., 2411/94.

*Tibbits v. Messrs. Wolf & Hymann,* 21 April, 1893. MSS., 2411/113.

"Unsolicited testimonials from medical men, Coleman's Liebig's Extract of Meat and Malt Wine." MSS., 2412/19a.

"William Chapman Grigg: correspondence re testimonial by Dr Grigg for Liq. Euonymin et Pepsin Co. published by Oppenheimer Bros. & Co. 1884-85." MSS., 2412/100-105.


*The Annals of the Royal College of Physicians*

"The Letter from Lawrence to the President of the RCP." *Annals,* 35 (1888): 207.

"Enclosure A and B." Attached to the letter from Lawrence. *Annals,* 35 (1888): 209.

"The Letter from Steavenson to the Censor's Board." *Annals,* 35 (April 10, 1888): 175.

"Censor's Reply to Steavenson." *Annals,* 35 (1888): 176.

"The letter from Steavenson to the Censor's Board." *Annals,* 35 (1888): 198.

"The alteration of the Resolution and Bye-law." *Annals,* 51 (Oct. 19, 1922): 159-162.

"Reply to Deputation." *Annals,* 35 (July 24, 1888): 219.

"The letter from Lawrence to the Registrar." *Annals,* 36 (Feb. 7, 1889): 288.

"Tibbits' reply to the Censor's Board." *Annals,* 38 (Feb. 27, 1893): 67-69.

"Extraordinary Meeting of the Censor's Board." *Annals*, 38 (April 7, 1893): 78-81.

"Extraordinary Meeting of the Censor's Board." *Annals*, 38 (June 15, 1893): 121-130.

"A Case of a Fellow's Partnership with a Company at Brighton." *Annals*, 38 (1894): 247.

"A Licentiate's Consultation to a Nursing Home." *Annals*, 38 (1894): 248.

"Dr. Robert Farquharson's Connection with Bovril Company Ltd." *Annals*, 40 (1897): 95.

"Dr M E A Wallis's association with the Sandow Curative Institute." *Annals*, 46 (1903): 47-49.

"College Meeting." *Annals*, 51 (Jan. 26, 1922): 71.

"College Meeting." *Annals*, 51 (May 8, 1922): 77.

"College Meeting." *Annals*, 51 (May 11, 1922): 108-113.

"College Meeting." *Annals*, 51 (July 7, 1922): 119.

"College Meeting." *Annals*, 51 (July 13, 1922): 125-134.

"College Meeting." *Annals*, 51( July 20, 1922): 132-134.

"College Meeting." *Annals*, 51 (Oct. 19, 1922): 156-163.

"The Bovril Company Ltd." *Annals*, 40 (April 9, 1897): 95.

ST. BARTHOLOMEW'S HOSPITAL, LONDON

*Medical Council Minutes*, MC1/2, vol. 2, 1878-1903.

*Medical Council Reports*, MC4/1, 1867, p. 161.

UNIVERSITY OF WESTMINSTER ARCHIVES, LONDON

*The Polytechnic: (The Pioneer Institute for Technical Education), Its Genesis and Present Status*. London: The Polytechnic, 309 Regent Street, 1892. Gerard Van de Linde, "Mr. Quintin Hogg and the London Polytechnic." *The Clerks' Journal*, Oct. 1, 1888.

Sarah A. Tooley, "The Polytechnic Movement: An Interview with Mr. Quintin Hogg." *The Young Man: A Monthly Journal and Review*, No. 101 (May 1895): 145-150.

WELLCOME INSTITUTE FOR THE HISTORY OF MEDICINE, LONDON

*Aspinall's Neigeline Society*, April 20, 1895, p. 10, CSP Archives, SA/CSP/ P.1/2.

"Extracts of articles related to the London Chamber of Commerce's agitation against doctors." May 4, 1912 article in *The Newspaper Owners*, SA/BMA/C.429/9; April 27, 1912 article in the *Daily Press*, SA/BMA/ C.429/10; May 18, 1912 article in *John Bull*, SA/BMA/C.429/11; and May 7, 1912 article in *Daily Dispatch*, SA/BMA/C.429/14.

Maltby, Thomas, *Astounding Revelations Concerning Supposed Massage Houses of Pandemonium of Vice Frequented by Both Sexes, Being a Complete Exposé of the Ways of Professed Masseurs and Masseuses* (London: T. Skeats, n.d.). Wellcome Institute Archives, SA/CSP/P1/2.

"Massage and Aristocracy." *Reynold's Weekly*, July 22, 1894.

"Private and Confidential," Mar. 18, 1911, was circulated by the London Chamber of Commerce to the owners of many newspapers. This docu-ment, signed by Thomas J. Barratt, Chairman of the London Chamber of Commerce, is held in the Wellcome Institute Archives, SA/BMA/ C.429.

WESTMINSTER CITY ARCHIVES, LONDON

"Parliamentary Bills and General Purposes, Parliamentary Bills Committee." Minutes of the Vestry of St. James, May, 25, 1897, p. 253.

"The Letter from the Home Secretary to the Vestry of St. James." Minutes of the Vestry of St., James, Nov. 23, 1897, pp. 299-330.

The Minutes of the Vestry, Jan. 25, 1897, pp. 320-322.

The Minutes of the Vestry, March 15, 1898, pp. 348-349.

# Secondary Sources Not Cited in the Footnotes

Ackerknecht, Erwin H. *A Short History of Medicine*, paperback edition. Baltimore: Johns Hopkins University Press, 1982.

Ackerknecht, Erwin, H. "Aspect of the History of Therapeutics." *Bulletin of the History of Medicine*, 36 (1982): 389-419.

Adas, Michael, *Machines as the Measures of Men: Science: Technology and Ideologies of Western Dominance*. Ithaca: Cornell University Press, 1989.

Altlick, Richard D. *Victorian People and Ideas: A Companion for the Modern Reader of Victorian Literature*. New York: W. W. Norton, 1973.

Baker, Robert, ed. *The Codification of Medical Morality: Historical and Philosophical Studies of the Formalization of Western Medical Morality in the Eighteenth and Nineteenth Centuries*, Volume Two. Anglo-American Medical Ethics and Medical Jurisprudence in the Nineteenth Century. Netherlands: Kluwer Academic Publishers, 1995.

Barns, Barry, and David Bloor. "Relativism, Rationalism, and the Sociology of Knowledge." In Martin Hollis and Steven Lukes, eds., *Rationality and Relativism*. Oxford: Blackwell, 1982.

Barry, Jonathan, and Colin Jones. *Medicine and Charity before the Welfare State*. London: Routledge, 1991.

Becker, Robert O., and Gary Selden. *The Body Electric: Electromagnetism and the Foundation of Life*. New York: Quill, 1985.

Benson, John. *The Rise of Consumer Society in Britain: 1880-1980*. London: Longman, 1994.

Berrios, G. E. "Obsessional Disorders during the Nineteenth Century: Terminological and Classificatory Issues." In W. F. Bynum, Roy Porter, and Michael Shepherd, eds., *The Anatomy of Madness: Essays in the History of Psychiatry*. London: Tavistock, 1985.

Berrios, German, and Hugh Freeman. *150 Years of British Psychiatry: 1841-1991*. Gaskell: Royal College of Psychiatrists, 1991.

Bijker, Wiebe E., Thomas P. Hughes, and Trevor Pinch, eds. *The Social Construction of Technological Systems.* Cambridge, Massachusetts: MIT Press, 1990.

Bland, Lucy. *Banishing the Beast: English Feminism and Sexual Morality, 1885-1914.* London: Penguin Books, 1995.

Briggs, Asa. *The Age of Improvement, 1783-1867.* London, Longman Paperback, 1979.

Brown, P. S. "Herbalism and Medical Botanists in Mid-Nineteenth-Century Britain." *Medical History,* 26 (1982): 398-420.

———. "Social Context and Medical Theory in the Demarcation of Nineteenth-Century Boundaries." In W. F. Bynum and R. Porter, eds., *Medical Fringe and Medical Orthodoxy, 1750-1850.* London: Croom Helm, 1987.

———. "The Vicissitudes of Herbalism in Late Nineteenth- and Early Twentieth-Century Britain." *Medical History,* 29 (1985): 71-92.

Butler, Stella V. F. "Centres and Peripheries: The Development of British Physiology. 1870-1914." *Journal of the History of Biology,* 21 (1988): 473-500.

Bynum, W. F. "Medical Values in a Commercial Age." In T. C. Smout, ed., *Victorian Values: A Joint Symposium of the Royal Society of Edinburgh and the British Academy.* Oxford: Oxford University Press, 1990.

———. *Science and the Practice of Medicine in the Nineteenth Century.* Cambridge: Cambridge University Press, 1994.

———, C. Lawrence, and V. Nutton. *The Emergence of Modern Cardiography.* London: Wellcome Institute for the History of Medicine, 1985.

Carlson, Eric T. "Medicine and Degeneration: Theory and Praxis." In J. Edward Chamberline and Sander Gilman, eds., *Degeneration: The Dark Side of Progress.* New York: Columbia University Press, 1985.

Chamberline, J. Edward, and Sander Gilman, eds. *Degeneration: The Dark Side of Progress.* New York: Columbia University Press, 1985.

Chen, Wai. "The Laboratory as Business: Sir Almroth Wright's Vaccine Program and the Construction of Penicillin." In Andrew Cunningham and Perry Williams, eds., *The Laboratory Revolution in Medicine.* Cambridge: Cambridge University Press, 1992.

Collini, Stefan, Donald Winch, and John Burrow. *That Noble Science of Politics: A Study in Nineteenth-Century Intellectual History.* Cambridge: Cambridge University Press, 1983.

Conrad, Lawrence, Michael Never, Vivian Nutton, Roy Porter, and Andrew Wear. *The Western Medical Tradition, 800 BC to AD 1800.* Cambridge: Cambridge University Press, 1995.

Cooter, Roger, ed. *Studies in the History of Alternative Medicine.* London, Macmillan Press, 1988.

Cunningham, Andrew, and Perry Williams, eds. *The Laboratory Revolution in Medicine.* Cambridge: Cambridge University Press, 1992.

Danziger, Kurt. *Constructing the Subject: Historical Origins of Psychological Research.*

Cambridge: Cambridge University Press, 1990.

Dingwall, Robert, Anne Marie Rafferty, and Charles Webster, eds. *An Introduction to the Social History of Nursing*. London: Routledge, 1988.

Dowbiggin, Ian. "Degeneration and Hereditarianism in French Mental Medicine, 1840-90." In W. F. Bynum, Roy Porter, and Michael Shepherd, eds., *The Anatomy of Madness: Essays in the History of Psychiatry*. London: Tavistock, 1985.

Durey, Michael. "Medical Elites, the General Practitioner, and Patient Power in Britain during the Cholera Epidemic of 1831-32." In Ian Inkster and Jack Morrell, *Metropolis and Province: Science in British Culture, 1780-1850*. London: Hutchinson, 1983.

Emsley, Clive. *Crime and Society in England, 1750-1900*. London: Longman, 1987.

Evans, Hughes. "Losing Touch: The Controversy over the Introduction of Blood Pressure Instruments into Medicine." *Technology and Culture*, 19 (1993): 784-807.

Figlio, Karl. "Chlorosis and Chronic Disease in Nineteenth-Century Britain: The Social Constitution of Somatic Illness in a Capitalist Society." *Social History*, 3 (1978): 170-199.

Gay, Peter. *The Bourgeois Experiences: Education of Senses*. Oxford: Oxford University Press, 1984.

Geison, Gerald L. "Divided We Stand: Physiologists and Clinicians in the American Context." In Morris J. Vogel and Charles Rosenberg, eds., *The Therapeutic Revolution: Essays in the Social History of American Medicine*. Philadelphia: University of Philadelphia Press, 1979.

Gilman, Sander L. "Touch, Sexuality and Disease." In W. F. Bynum and Roy Porter, eds., *Medicine and the Five Senses*. Cambridge: Cambridge University Press, 1993.

Gooding, David, Trevor Pinch, and Simon Shaffer. *The Uses of Experiment: Studies in the Natural Sciences*. Cambridge: Cambridge University Press, 1989.

Hall, Thomas S. *History of General Physiology, Vol. II: From the Enlightenment to the End of the Nineteenth Century*. Chicago: University of Chicago Press, 1969.

Harding, Sandra. "Knowledge, Technology, and Social Relations." *Journal of Medicine and Philosophy*, 3 (1978): 346-359.

Herzlinger, Regina. *Market Driven Health Care: Who Wins, Who Loses, in the Transformation of America's Largest Service Industry*. Massachusetts: Perseus Books, 1997.

Himmelfarb, Gertrude. *Poverty and Compassion: The Moral Imagination of the Late Victorians*. New York: Vintage Books, 1991.

Home, Roderick, W. "Electricity and the Nervous Fluid." *Journal of the History of Biology*, 3, no. 2 (1970): 235-251.

Houghton, Walter E. *The Victorian Frame of Mind, 1830-1870*. New Haven: Yale University Press, 1957.

Inkster, Ian, and Jack Morrel. *Metropolis and Province: Science in British Culture,*

*1780-1850*. London: Hutchinson, 1983.

―――. "Marginal Men: Aspects of the Social Role of the Medical Community in Sheffield 1790-1850." In John Woodward and David Richards, eds., *Health Care and Popular Medicine in Nineteenth Century England: Essays in the Social History of Medicine*. New York: Holmes and Meier, 1977.

Jackson, Stanley W. "Force and Kindred Notions in Eighteenth-Century Neurophysiology and Medical Psychology." *Bulletin of the History of Medicine*, 44 (1978): 397-410, 539-581.

Jacob, Margaret C. *Scientific Culture and the Making of the Industrial West*. Oxford: Oxford University Press, 1997.

Jacyna, L. S. "Somatic Theories of Mind and the Interests of Medicine in Britain, 1850-1879." *Medical History*, 26 (1982): 223-258.

―――. "The Laboratory and the Clinic: the Impact of Pathology on Surgical Diagnosis in the Glasgow Western Infirmary, 1875-1910." *Bulletin of the History of Medicine*, 62 (1988): 384-406.

―――. "The Physiology of Mind, the Unity of Nature, and the Moral Order in Victorian Thought." *British Journal of the History of Science*, 14 (1981): 114-115.

Jameson, Eric. *The Natural History of Quackery*. London: Springfield, 1961.

Kittler, Friedlich A. *Discourse Networks 1800/1900*, trans. Michael Metteer. Stanford: Stanford University Press, 1990.

Kutschmann, Werner. "Scientific Instruments and the Senses: Toward an Anthropological Historiography of the Natural Science." *International Studies in the Philosophy of Science*, The Dubrovnik Papers, From Galileo to Newton, 1 (1986): 106-123.

Larkin, Gerald. "The Emergence of Para-medical Profession." In W. F. Bynum and Roy Porter, eds., *Companion Encyclopedia of the History of Medicine*. London: Routledge, 1993.

Latour, Bruno. *Aramis or the Love of Technology*, trans. Catherine Porter. Cambridge, Massachusetts: Harvard University Press, 1996.

―――. *Science in Action: How to Follow Scientists and Engineers Through Society*. Cambridge, Massachusetts: Harvard University Press, 1987.

―――. "The Costly Ghastly Kitchen." In Andrew Cunningham and Perry Williams eds., *The Laboratory Revolution in Medicine*. Cambridge: Cambridge University Press, 1992.

――― and Steve Woolgar. *Laboratory Life: The Construction of Scientific Facts*. Princeton: Princeton University Press, 1986.

Lawrence, Christopher. *Medicine in the Making of Modern Britain, 1700-1920*. London: Routledge, 1994.

Leach, William R. "Transformation in a Culture of Consumption: Women and Department Stores, 1890-1925." *Journal of American History*, 71 (1984): 319-342.

Lee, Martyn J. *Consumer Culture Reborn: The Cultural Politics of Consumption*. London:

Routledge, 1993.

Lenoir, Timothy. *Instituting Science: The Cultural Production of Scientific Disciplines.* Stanford: Stanford University Press, 1997.

———. "Laboratories, Medicine, and Public Life in Germany, 1830-1849: Ideological Roots of the Institutional Revolution." In Andrew Cunningham and Perry Williams, eds., *The Laboratory Revolution in Medicine.* Cambridge: Cambridge University Press, 1992.

Lightman, Bernard. *Victorian Science in Context.* Chicago: University of Chicago Press, 1997.

Loeb, Lori Anne. *Consuming Angels: Advertising and Victorian Women.* Oxford: Oxford University Press, 1994.

Longo, Lawrence D. "Electrotherapy in Gynecology: The American Experience." *Bulletin of the History of Medicine,* 60 (1989): 343-366.

Loudon, Irvine S. L. "The Origins and Growth of the Dispensary Movement in England." *Bulletin of the History of Medicine,* 55 (1981): 322-342.

Martin, Steven C. "Chiropractic and the Social Context of Medical Technology, 1895-1925." *Technology and Culture,* 34 (1993): 808-834.

Mason, Michael. *The Making of Victorian Sexuality.* Oxford: Oxford University Press, 1995.

Matthews, Leslie, G. *History of Pharmacy in Britain.* Edinburgh: E. and S. Livingstone, 1962.

Maulitz, Russell C. "Physicians versus Bacteriologist: The Ideology of Science in Clinical Medicine." In Morris J. Vogel and Charles Rosenberg, eds., *The Therapeutic Revolution: Essays in the Social History of American Medicine.* Philadelphia: University of Philadelphia Press, 1979.

McLaren, Angus. *A Prescription for Murder: The Victorian Serial Killings of Dr. Thomas Neil Cream.* Chicago: University of Chicago Press, 1993.

Merrill, Lynn L. *The Romance of Victorian Natural History.* Oxford: Oxford University Press, 1989.

Peter Morton. *The Vital Science: Biology and the Literary Imagination, 1860-1900.* London: George Allen and Unwin, 1984.

Morus, Iwan Rhys. "Correlation and Control: William Robert Grove and the Construction of a New Philosophy of Scientific Reform." *Studies in History and Philosophy of Science,* 22 (1991): 589-621.

———. "The Politics of Power: Reform and Regulation in the Work of W. R. Grove." Ph.D. thesis, Cambridge University, 1988.

———. "Manufacturing Nature: Science, Technology and Victorian Consumer Culture." *British Journal for the History of Science,* 29 (1996): 403-434.

Murphy, Terence D. "Medical Knowledge and Statistical Methods in Early Nineteenth-Century France. *Medical History,* 25 (1981): 301-319.

Nevett, T. R. *Advertising in Britain.* London: Heineman, 1982.

Nugent, Angela. "Fit for Work: The Introduction of Physical Examinations in

Industry." *Bulletin of the History of Medicine*, 57 (1983): 578-595.

Oliver, Hermia. *The International Anarchist Movement in Late Victorian London*. London: Croom Helm, 1983.

Owens, Larry. "Pure and Sound Government: Laboratories, Playing Fields, and Gymnasia in the Nineteenth-Century Search for Order." *Isis*, 76 (1985): 182-194.

Perrin, Michael W. "The Influence of the Pharmaceutical Industry on the Evolution of British Medical Practice." In F. N. L. Poynter, ed., *The Evolution of Medical Practice in Britain*. London: Pitman Medical Publishing Co., 1961.

Pick, Daniel. *Faces of Degeneration: A European Disorder, c. 1848-c.1918*. Cambridge: Cambridge University Press, 1989.

Pickstone, John V. "Musecological Science?: The Place of the Analytical/ Comparative in Nineteenth-Century Science, Technology, and Medicine." *History of Science*, 32 (1994): 11-38.

———. "The Professionalization of Medicine in England and Europe: The State, the Market, and Industrial Society." *Nihon Ishigaku Zasshi, Journal of the Japan Society of Medical History*, 25 (1979): 520-550.

———. "Ways of Knowing: Towards a Historical Sociology of Science, Technology, and Medicine." *British Journal for the History of Science*, 26 (1993): 433-458.

———. "Establishment and Dissent in Nineteenth-Century Medicine: An Exploration of Some Correspondences and Connections between Religious and Medical Belief-Systems in Early Industrial England." In W. J. Sheils, ed., *The Church and Healing*. Oxford: Blackwell, 1982.

Poovey, Mary. *Making a Social Body: British Cultural Formation 1830-1864*. Chicago: University of Chicago Press, 1995.

Porter, Dorothy. "Medicine and Industrial Society: Reform, Improvement, and Professionalization." *Victorian Studies*, 37 (1993): 129-139.

——— and Roy Porter. *Patient's Progress: Doctors and Doctoring in Eighteenth-Century England*. Stanford: Stanford University Press, 1989.

Porter, Roy. "Medicine and the Decline of Magic." *Bulletin of the Society for the History of Medicine*, 41 (1987): 24-27.

———. *The Popularization of Medicine, 1650-1850*. London: Routledge, 1992.

——— and Andrew Wear, eds. *Problems and Methods in the History of Medicine*. London: Croom Helm, 1987.

Poynter, F. N. L., ed. *The Evolution of Medical Practice in Britain*. London: Pitman Medical Publishing, 1961.

———, ed. *The Evolution of Pharmacy in Britain*. London: Pitman Medical Publishing, 1965.

Qualter, Terence H. *Advertising and Democracy in the Mass Age*. New York: St. Martin's Press, 1991.

Ramsey, Matthew. "Property Right and the Right to Health: The Regulation of

Secret Remedies in France, 1789-1815." In W F Bynum and Roy Porter, eds., *Medical Fringe and Medical Orthodoxy, 1750-1850.* London: Croom Helm, 1987.

Rosenberg, Charles, ed. *Right Living: An Anglo-American Tradition of Self-Help Medicine and Hygiene.* Baltimore: The Johns Hopkins University Press, 2003.

———. "Body and Mind in Nineteenth-Century Medicine: Some Clinical Origins of the Neurosis Construct." *Bulletin of the History of Medicine,* 63 (1989): 185-197.

———. "Inward Vision and Outward Glance: The Shaping of the American Hospital, 1880-1914." *Bulletin of the History of Medicine,* 53 (1979): 346-391.

———. "The Therapeutic Revolution: Medicine, Meaning, and Social Change in Nineteenth-Century America." *Perspectives in Biology and Medicine,* 20 (1977): 485-506.

———. *No Other Gods: On Science and American Social Thought,* revised and enlarged edition. Baltimore: The Johns Hopkins University Press, 1997.

——— and Janet Golden, eds. *Framing Diseases: Studies in Cultural History.* New Jersey: Rutgers University Press, 1992.

Sadler, Judy. "Ideologies of 'Art' and 'Science' in Medicine: The Transition from Medical Care to the Application of Technique in the British Medical Profession." In Wolfgang Krohn and Edwin T. Layton, eds., *The Dynamics of Science and Technology: Social Values, Technical Norms, and Scientific Criteria in the Development of Knowledge.* Dordrecht, Holland: D. Reidel Publishing Company, 1978.

Schiller, Francis. "Neurology: The Electrical Root." In Clifford Rose and W. F. Bynum, eds., *Historical Aspects of the Neuroscience.* London: The Mitre Press, 1946.

Schivelbusch, Wolfgang. *Railway Journey: The Industrialization of Time and Space in the Nineteenth Century.* Berkeley: University of California Press, 1986.

Scull, Andrew, ed. *Madhouses, Mad-Doctors, and Madmen: The Social History of Psychiatry in the Victorian Era.* Philadelphia: University of Pennsylvania Press, 1981.

Shapin, Steven. *A Social History of Truth: Civility and Science in Seventeenth-Century England.* Chicago: University of Chicago Press, 1994.

——— and Simon Shaffer. *The Leviathan and Air Pump: Hobbes, Boyle, and the Experimental Life.* Princeton: Princeton University Press, 1985.

Sheehan, James, and Morton Sosna, eds. *The Boundaries of Humanity: Humans, Animals, and Machines.* Berkeley: University of California Press, 1991.

Short, S. E. D. "Physicians, Science, and Status: Issues in the Professionalization of Anglo-American Medicine in the Nineteenth-Century." *Medical History,* 27 (1983): 1-68.

Showalter, Elaine. *The Female Malady: Women, Madness, and English Culture, 1830-1980.* New York: Pantheon, 1985.

Sibum, Heinz Otto. "Reworking the Mechanical Value of Heat: Instruments of Precision and Gestures of Accuracy in Early Victorian England." *Studies in*

*History and Philosophy of Science*, 26 (1995): 73-106.

Sicherman, Barbara. "The Use of a Diagnosis: Doctors, Patients, and Neurasthenia." In Judith Waler Leavitt and Ronald L. Numbers, eds., *Sickness and Health in America: Readings in the History of Medicine and Public Health*. Madison: University of Wisconsin Press, 1978.

Singer, Charles, and E. Ashworth Underwood. *A Short History of Medicine*, 2nd ed. Oxford: Clarendon Press, 1962.

Smith, Crosbie, and M. Norton Wise. *Energy and Empire: A Biographical Study of Lord Kelvin*. Cambridge: Cambridge University Press, 1989.

Smith, F. B. *The People's Health, 1830-1910*. London: Weidenfeld and Nicolson, 1990.

Smith, Roger. "The Background of Physiological Psychology in Natural Philosophy." *History of Science*, 11 (1983): 75-123.

———. *Trial by Medicine: Insanity and Responsibility in Victorian Trials*. Edinburgh: Edinburgh University Press, 1981.

Smith, Russell Gordon. "The Development of Ethical Guidance for Medical Practitioners by the General Medical Council." *Medical History*, 37 (1993): 56-67.

Soloway, Richard A. *Demography and Degeneration: Eugenics and the Declining Birthrate in Twentieth-Century Britain*. Chapel Hill: University of North Carolina Press, 1990.

———. "Counting the Degenerates: The Statistics of Race Deterioration in Edwardian England." *Journal of Contemporary History*, 17 (1982): 142-151.

Süsskind, Charles. "The Invention of Computed Tomography." *History of Technology*, 6 (1981): 39-80.

Tattersall, Robert. "Pancreatic Organotherapy for Diabetes, 1889-1921." *Medical History*, 39 (1995): 288-316.

Temkin, Owsei. "The Dependence of Medicine upon Basic Scientific Thought." In idem, ed., *The Historical Development of Physiological Thought*. New York: C. McC. Brooks and P. Cranefield Hafner, 1959.

Thompson, C. J. S. *The Quacks of Old London*. New York: Barnes and Noble, 1928.

Vigarello, George. *Concepts of Cleanliness: Changing Attitudes in France from the Middle Ages*. Cambridge: Cambridge University Press, 1988.

Vogel, Morris J., and Charles Rosenberg, eds. *The Therapeutic Revolution: Essays in the Social History of American Medicine*. Philadelphia: University of Philadelphia Press, 1979.

Walkowitz, Judith R. *Prostitution and Victorian Society: Women, Class, and the State*. Cambridge: Cambridge University Press, 1980.

Wear, Andrew. *Medicine in Society:* Cambridge: Cambridge University Press, 1992.

Wiener, Martin J. *English Culture and the Decline of the Industrial Spirit, 1850-1980*. Cambridge: Cambridge University Press, 1981.

Willensky, H. L. *Organizational Intelligence*. New York: Basic Books, 1967.

Williams, Raymond. *Culture and Society, 1780-1950.* New York: Columbia University Press, 1983.

Young, G. M. *Portrait of an Age: Victorian England.* Oxford: Oxford University Press, 1936.

Youngson, A. J. *The Scientific Revolution in Victorian Medicine.* New York: Homes and Meier, 1979.

# Index

Abercrombie, Robert, 174
Addison, Thomas: electrifying room, 124-25
Advertising, advertisements, 2, 4, 62, 65, 262, 278-79, 281; agencies, 70-71; electro-medicine, 112-14, 136, 138-39, 143, 144-45, 150-51, 222-23; feminine images in, 66-67; Harness' 147, 148-49, 150-52, 157, 158, 159, 160, 165-66, 191-94, 196-98; health care, 11-12; individual health, 96-97; massage shops, 227-28; medical information in, 80-81; medical professionals and, 109, 110, 175; for muscular vitality, 106-7; for nurses and masseuses, 260, 261; for patent medicines, 25-26, 50, 54-55, 75-76; in print media, 29-30; professionalism of, 72-73; protection from, 60-61; pseudo-science in, 81-84; skepticism about, 73-74; for various conditions, 77-80
"Agitation against Patent and Proprietary Medicines and Foods, The," 47
Alabaster, Henry, 213, 215
Allbutt, Thomas Clifford, 164, 200, 239
Allen, William, 2
Allen & Hanburys Ltd., 1, 2, 3, 92
Allinson, Dr., 99-100
Althaus, Julius, 126, 127, 144n83, 176, 234

Ambrecht, Nelson & Company, 163
American and Parisian Massage Company, 261
Ammoniaphone, 157
Anderson, R., 243, 270
Anesthetics: electrical devices used in, 142, 156
Animal electricity, 120, 121
*Anti-Cutting Record,* 34
Anti-semitism: neurasthenia and, 239-40
Apothecaries Act (1815), 17, 173, 174n9
Armbrecht Coca Wine, 80
Arndt, Rudolf: on neurasthenia, 241
*Art of Advertising, The* (Stead), 71-73
Asquith, H. H., 269, 270
*Astounding Revelations Concerning Supposed Massage Houses, . . .* (Maltby), 265-66
Avory, Horace, 219
Ayer, N. W., 70

Baines, Arthur E., 160-61
Barry, Alfred, 273
Batteries, 122, 128, 137, 153-54, 200-201. *See also* Medical Battery Company
Beard, George, 122, 236, 238-39, 240, 242
Beecham, Joseph, 2, 26, 28, 43, 44n63
Beecham, Thomas, 2, 26
Beecham Company/Group, 1, 2, 43
Beecham's Pills, 47

Newspapers: advertising in, 70-71; ad-
vertising revenues, 29-30; on massage,
263-65, 268-69
"Night in a Workhouse, A" (Green-
wood), 228, 229
Nightingale Fund, 261
Norton's Camomile Pills, 85
Nottingham, 4; Jesse Boot's chemist
shop in, 33-34
Nottingham Hosiery Company, 222-23
Nurses: massage therapy and, 267-68;
training, 260-61
Nutrition: and neurasthenia, 241-42

Obesity: patent cures for, 81
Obscene Publications Act, 229
Obstetrics, 141
Owners of Proprietary Articles Section,
44
Ozone: as health property, 156-57

Paget, James, 168
Paget, Rosalind, 275
Pall Mall Electrical Association, Ltd.
(PMEA), 148-49
Palmer, Margaret, 275
Paralysis: electrotherapeutic treatment
of, 142
Parks, chain of pharmaceutical stores, 33
Parliament, 32; massage legislation, 270-
71
Parliamentary Bills Committee (BMA):
opposition to patent medicine, 27-28
Parry, Ernest: testimony of, 48-49
Parsons, Inglis, 210
PATA. *See* Proprietary Articles Trade
Association
Patent Flexible Magnetine, 165
Patent medicine, 2, 3-4, 45, 54; British
Medical Association opposition to, 31-
32; chemists and, 33-34; commerciali-
zation of, 36-38; conditions treated
with, 77-84; consumption of, 76-77;
doctors' use of, 48-52; free market
and, 56-57; ingredients in, 47-48;

mass-production of, 55-56; opposition
to, 60-61, 109-10; preventive, 85-86;
prices, 34-36
Patent medicine business, 2, 3-4, 278;
advertising, 25-26, 29-30, 66-75, 83-
84; capitalization of, 24-25; health care
market, 54-55; market forces and, 56-
57; medical profession and, 26-29, 46-
47, 50-53; and Pharmaceutical Society,
31, 36-38; and Proprietary Articles
Section, 43-44
Patents, 13; Harness', 157-58; medico-
electrical, 152-56, 162
Patronage: medical, 173
Pepsalia, 78
Perkin, Harold, 17
Perry, John, 185
Pflügers, Edward, 127
Pharmaceutical companies, 3, 4; influence of, 33-34; origins of, 1-2; research funded by, 10-11. *See also* Drug
companies
Pharmaceutical Society, 29, 30, 31, 44;
and market capitalism, 40-41; on pro-
fessionalization vs. commercialization
in, 36-40
Pharmacists/chemists, 33; competition,
53-54; vs. doctors, 41-42; and proprie-
tary medicines, 52-53. *See also* Chem-
ists
Pharmacy Act (1868), 29-30
Philadelphia, 1, 70
Phillips, Frederick: *A Sequel to "Secret
Remedies,"* 44-46
Phonogram, Edison's, 132
Photography: of human emotions, 119-
20
Physical culture, 98-99; body-building,
101-3; education, 100-101, 105; gym-
nasiums and, 100-101; Sandow on,
103-6. *See also* Health; Muscles
Physical education, 98, 103, 104
Physicians. *See* Doctors; Medical profes-
sionals
Pickering, E., 44

Playfair, William S., 235, 236, 262
PMEA. *See* Pall Mall Electrical Association
Poisons, 29-30, 48; Pharmacy Act and, 48
Police: and massage shops/parlors, 273-74
Pollock, A. Julius, 188
Portable Electric Light Co., The, 155
Porter, Roy, 172
Poverty: sexuality and, 228-29
*Power of Evidence, The* (Sandow), 105
*Practical Introduction to Medical Electricity, A* (de Watteville), 200
*Practical Lessons in Electro-Therapeutics* (Harries and Lawrence), 183
*Practice of Massage, The* (Eccles), 258-59
Prescriptions, 43, 48
Prices: maintaining retail, 34-36, 40
Professionalism, professionalization, 173, 176, 186; of advertising, 72-73; of doctors, 41-42, 175n14; and drug store employment, 40-41; and market, 279-81; massage therapy, 267-68, 274-75, 276-77; of medicine, 4, 17; medical, 109, 110-11, 175n14, 230-31; medical electricians, 207-215; Pharmaceutical Society on, 30, 36-38; of pharmacists and chemists, 39-40; and profit-seeking, 25-26
Profits, 3, 12, 108, 233; for medical treatment, 51-52
Profit seeking: massage therapy schools, 260, 261-62; professionalism and, 25-26
Proprietary Articles Section (PAS) London Chamber of Commerce, 28, 43-44; opposition to doctors, 46-48; *A Sequel to "Secret Remedies,"* 44-46
Proprietary Articles Trade Association (PATA), 37; retail price maintenance, 34-36
Proprietary medicine. *See* Patent medicine
Protectionism: chemists and pharmacists, 38-39

Pseudo-science, 84; Morison's, 81-83. *See also* Electro-Medicine; Quackery
Public health, 7, 56; capitalist, 9-10; corporate, 223-26; in Great Britain, 17-18; and medical commodities, 8-9; and medical professionals, 179-80
Pulvermacher, Isaac Louis, 112; electric chains, 137-46
Pulvermacher's Hydro-Electric Chain, 112-13; advertising for, 138-39
Putzel, L., 125
Pye-Smith, P. H., 188

Quacks, quackery, 5, 25, 75-76, 95, 231; electrical, 114-17; electro-medical, 145-58, 207-8; massage and, 265-66; pseudo-science and, 81-84

Racism: neurasthenia and, 239-40
Radcliffe, Charles B., 122, 135
Ratcliffe, C., of W.J. White Ltd., 44
RCP. *See* Royal College of Physicians
Recession, 33
Regulations, 17-18, 173, 174, 279
*Report from the Select Committee on Patent Medicine*, 32, 41, 44, 49, 60, 61, 76, 84, 115
Reproductive organs: electro-medical devices, 167-68
"Resale price maintenance," 34-35
Research: pharmaceutical company funding, 10-11
Rest cure, 79, 235-36
"Review of Charles Bland Radcliffe's Course of Lectures, A" (Lobb), 135-36
Reymond, Emil H. du Bois, 121, 212
Reynolds, Russell, 126, 142, 188
Richardson, Benjamin Ward, 86, 157, 222; on electro-medical devices, 142-43, 165; on sonometers, 131-32
Ridley, Matthew, 273
Rivers, W.H.R., 132
Robinson, Lucy, 275